## THE IMPERIAL WAR MUSEUM BOOK OF

# 1914

Conceived as the last of his Imperial War Museum books about the 1914–18 war, Malcolm Brown sees this as, in effect, a flagship work, to take its place at the head of a series which has come to be regarded as an important contribution to the world of military history. His previous titles include *The Imperial War Museum Book of the First World War, The Imperial War Museum Book of the Western Front, The Imperial War Museum Book of the Somme* and *The Imperial War Museum Book of 1918.*

After Oxford and National Service in the Royal Navy, Malcolm Brown was for many years a BBC TV documentary producer, specializing in historical and military subjects. He became a full-time author in 1986 and has been a freelance historian at the Imperial War Museum since 1989. Previous books include *Tommy Goes to War, Verdun 1916, Christmas Truce* (co-written) and, also co-written, *A Touch of Genius,* a biography of T. E. Lawrence which was shortlisted for the NCR Award for Non-Fiction. In 2002 he became an Honorary Research Fellow of the Centre for First World War Studies at the University of Birmingham.

**The Duke of Westminster's Medal for Military Literature**

In 2005 this series of Imperial War Museum books in association with Pan Macmillan was awarded the Duke of Westminster's Medal for Military Literature in recognition of its achievement in consistently producing quality works in this field.

**By Malcolm Brown**

The Imperial War Museum Book of the First World War

The Imperial War Museum Book of the Western Front

The Imperial War Museum Book of the Somme

The Imperial War Museum Book of 1918: Year of Victory

The Imperial War Museum Book of 1914: The Men Who Went to War

**By Major General Julian Thompson**

The Imperial War Museum Book of Victory in Europe

The Imperial War Museum Book of the War at Sea, 1939–1945

The Imperial War Museum Book of War Behind Enemy Lines

The Imperial War Museum Book of the War in Burma, 1942–1945

The Imperial War Museum Book of the War at Sea, 1914–1918

The Imperial War Museum Book of Modern Warfare *(editor)*

**By Field Marshal Lord Carver**

The Imperial War Museum Book of the War in Italy

**By Adrian Gilbert**
*Editor-in-Chief: Field Marshal Lord Bramall KG GCB*

The Imperial War Museum Book of the Desert War

# MALCOLM BROWN

## THE IMPERIAL WAR MUSEUM BOOK OF

# 1914

## THE MEN WHO WENT TO WAR

**PAN BOOKS**

*in association with*
*The Imperial War Museum*

First published 2004 by Sidgwick & Jackson

This edition published 2014 by Pan Books
an imprint of Pan Macmillan, a division of Macmillan Publishers Limited
Pan Macmillan, 20 New Wharf Road, London N1 9RR
Basingstoke and Oxford
Associated companies throughout the world
www.panmacmillan.com

ISBN 978-1-4472-7033-1

1 3 5 7 9 8 6 4 2

A CIP catalogue record for this book is available from
the British Library.

Typeset by SetSystems Ltd, Saffron Walden, Essex
Printed and bound by
CPI Group (UK) Ltd, Croydon, CR0 4YY

# Contents

# Acknowledgements

In all my books written under the banner of the Imperial War Museum about the First World War it has been my practice to express my greatest gratitude to those people without whose vivid accounts of their wartime experiences, consigned either by themselves or their relatives and friends to the Museum's scrupulous and caring custody, none of them would have been written. Since I see this as the final volume in my IWM series, it seems appropriate to give so important an acknowledgement pride of place and I therefore begin this far from routine part of the book by sincerely thanking all those – servicemen, servicewomen, war-workers of various kinds, civilians, children, not to mention those engaged on the Allied or the enemy side – whose words I have quoted in what has developed since I began my work at the Museum into an oeuvre of some 1,500 pages. Estimating precisely how many participants I have enlisted as contributors is not easy, but the number must be in the region of at least 600. It has been a great privilege to be able to put into public print previously unpublished evidence of the kind the Museum has been accumulating for many decades, and is still acquiring today, and I take this opportunity to salute all those whose collections I have researched over the years, including those of many whom I did not quote but who added in their own way to my knowledge and awareness of an ever fascinating if arguably unfathomable subject.

In so far as it has become accessible to me it is primarily through the first-hand accounts which had provided the basic seed corn of my books, so that while being aware that I was dealing with a major cataclysm I have also found much that was positive, enriching, even at times humorous, about it. Thus I have come away from my extensive revisiting of the Great War with a feeling of humility at one extreme and uplift at the other, and with the sense of having made not a few friends on the way. It is astonishing how often, when looking through some ancient crumpled diary or reading a clutch of letters still in their original envelopes, you get a feeling of closeness to the person who held the pen, or more likely the stubby indelible pencil, that wrote them. But there is, of course, a reverse side to this experience. When you find yourself reading a last letter, or the final entry in a diary which suddenly stops, it can almost seem as if you have suffered a kind of bereavement. Arguably historians should not be sentimentalists, but especially in this field of study they should surely take into account that the documents from which they work were not produced as elements for an argument or to support a particular trend but were in very many cases the utterances of men and women in a situation of extreme personal stress and danger. Being human they wished to survive, but being engaged in the lethal game of war they also knew that they might not. That is one reason why, as explained in the Prologue, in the case of a book which deals with the first five months of a four-and-a-half-year war, it seemed necessary that it should have its own dedicated Roll of Honour, in memory of those who did not live to tell the tale and come safe home.

All such evidence can only be used with the full agreement of those who hold the copyright of the collections quoted. Every effort has been made to seek the approval of such copyright holders, who, when known (contact can all too frequently be lost even in the case of recently acquired collections), are named along with the people quoted in the Index of Contributors at the end of the book.

As always I am grateful for the support of the Museum's Director-General, Robert Crawford, and with his name I couple that of Dr Christopher Dowling, who has encouraged the devising and creating of Imperial War Museum Books since the idea was conceived back in the late 1980s. I wish also to express my thanks to Elizabeth Bowers, who is now responsible for the Museum's publishing programme, and the ever helpful ladies of the publishing office.

First among the departments which have provided the seed corn for this and my other books is the Department of Documents, where I have been based since 1989. I would like therefore to express my great gratitude to its Keeper, Roderick Suddaby, and to the always friendly members of its staff, especially Anthony Richards, who has been particularly helpful in the matter of devising the Roll of Honour and providing the Index of Contributors. My very special thanks also go to Messrs Suddaby and Richards for keeping me plied with well-chosen documents during the difficult months in 2003 when I was waiting for and then recuperating from a hip operation, thus enabling me to continue working, if at times all too slowly, on a book which might otherwise have totally stalled.

Among other Museum staff to whom I wish to express my gratitude is

Sarah Paterson of the Department of Printed Books, to whom I now submit my Bibliography for expert scrutiny as a matter of routine and who is always ready to answer questions of a literary or historical nature. Her colleagues in that department are equally supportive and welcoming. I am also grateful to the staff of the Photograph Archive for their professional assistance in the selection of suitable illustrations.

No one can hope to navigate so complex and dramatic a year as 1914 without help from knowledgeable advisers. In this respect I have been fortunate in having been able to call on the services of a number of kindly though, correctly, sharply critical readers: Roderick Suddaby, already named, who has been my chief mentor at the Museum over many years and with whom I have twice made extensive visits to the 1914–1918 battlefields; Terry Charman, a veritable polymath in the Museum's Research and Information Department; Sonia Batten, a post-graduate student at the Centre for First World War Studies at the University of Birmingham, to which I am myself attached as an Honorary Research Fellow; and Gavin Roynon, former history master at Eton, whose book covering this period, *The Massacre of the Innocents: The Crofton Diaries, Ypres 1914–1915*, is being published simultaneously with this one. I am pleased to acknowledge their key contribution, and also that of my wife Betty; her careful checking of the text and critical comments on the contents have as ever been vital to the process of writing, while her proofreading skills are crucial to any book I write in the final stages before the book goes to the printers.

I have been very fortunate in having my customary help and support from my publishers, Sidgwick & Jackson. I am also supremely grateful to them for their patience at the unavoidably delayed delivery of the manuscript. Ingrid Connell could not have been kinder or more encouraging, and I am glad also to express my thanks to Jacqui Butler as project editor, who has improved the text considerably by her wise comments and suggestions, to Nicholas Blake for his editorial assistance in the final stages before the book went to print, and to Lisa Footitt for compiling the index. Additionally I should like to thank Wilf Dickie as the book's designer, Martin Lubikowski for his cartography, Anna Mitchelmore, my production controller and Bob Eames for the creation of its striking dust jacket.

I could not complete these acknowledgements without mentioning the name of William Armstrong, founding father of the concept of producing Imperial War Museum Books about the two world wars and to whom I shall always be aware of owing a very special debt. In effect he has kept the wolf from my door for fifteen years and, following my first career as a BBC documentary film producer, has been crucial in helping me to build a second career as a military historian. I offer my warmest thanks to a most distinguished, sagacious and benevolent publisher.

The book has offered me one other satisfaction. Rupert Brooke is too often seen just as a poet of 1914 and a casualty of 1915, dying on his way to the grim battleground he never reached, Gallipoli. Yet he was close to the sharp end of war in 1914 during the dramatic but failed attempt to save Antwerp and wrote powerfully about his experiences there and about other aspects of the year in his letters. He is quoted at some length in this book. The publishing house that made him famous was Sidgwick & Jackson, and it is good to be able to republish some of his finest prose writings under his original imprint.

## Permissions Acknowledgements

The author and publishers gratefully acknowledge the following for permission to reproduce copyright material: the map on page 59 by kind permission of the *Telegraph & Argus*, Bradford; the two cartoons from *Punch*, on pages 119 and 202, with the permissions of Punch Ltd; the material from football programmes published by Leyton Orient (in 1914 Clapton Orient) and Tottenham Hotspur by courtesy of the respective clubs; and the advertisement for the 'thresher' trench coat on page 262 courtesy of Messrs Thresher & Glenny of Greasham Street, London. Quotations from *John Scott Lidgett: Archbishop of Methodism?* by Alan Turberfield are reproduced courtesy of the author and the publishers; excerpts from *The First World War*: Volume I, *To Arms* by Hew Strachan are reproduced courtesy of David Higham Associates; and the quotation from Osbert Sitwell's *Great Morning* is included with the permission of his literary executors. All other sources consulted or quoted are acknowledged either in the Notes and References or the Bibliography or both. All photographs unless otherwise stated are reproduced courtesy of the Trustees of The Imperial War Museum.

# *Historical Note*

## The British Army in 1914

The British Expeditionary Force (BEF) of regular troops and reservists which left for France in mid August 1914 consisted of four infantry divisions and five brigades of cavalry. Three more divisions arrived between August and November, plus substantial reinforcements from the Indian Army, so that by December, of 9,610 British officers in France 20 per cent were from the Indian Army, while of 76,450 other ranks 16 per cent were from the Indian Army. Additionally before the end of the year the first units of the Territorial Force to be deployed overseas (they had originally been raised for British home defence only) were also coming into action.

Troops moved and fought in divisions but lived and thought in smaller units, such as battalions (infantry) or batteries (artillery) or squadrons (cavalry). Normally there were four (later three) battalions in a brigade, and three brigades in a division. An infantry battalion at full complement consisted of up to a thousand men, of whom thirty were officers. Battalions were subdivided into companies, platoons and sections. The lowest rank in infantry units was that of private, the equivalent in artillery units was gunner, in cavalry units, trooper, and in units of the Royal Engineers, sapper.

With regard to the naming of regiments and their battalions, there were several conventions in use at the time. To take the example of a regular army battalion, the 2nd Battalion, the King's Own Yorkshire Light Infantry, which is the first such unit mentioned in this book (see Prologue, page xxiii), its title is given in full at the first reference and thereafter shortened to 2nd/King's Own Yorkshire Light Infantry (in this particular case it proved impossible not to echo the usage of the time and at some points I call it the 2nd KOYLIs). This is in contrast to the practice of the British Official History (see Bibliography) which uses the shortened formula, '2/King's Own Yorkshire Light Infantry'. Complications arise in the matter of battalions of the Territorial Force and the Yeomanry, where so-called fractional numbers were used to distinguish them from units of the regular army; thus, for example, the official name of the first Territorial battalion to take part in active fighting, the 'London Scottish', was 'The 1/14th (County of London) Battalion (London Scottish)': the formula 1/14th being pronounced 'First Fourteenth'. Similarly the 'Queen's Westminster Rifles' was formally the 1/16th: i.e. the 'First Sixteenth'. These were both 1st line battalions; subsequently the regiment raised a substantial number of 2nd, 3rd and 4th line battalions (the last in this category being the 4/4th ('Fourth Fourth'), producing a total of eighty-two territorial battalions. The London Regiment was part of the Infantry Territorial Force, in which a total of 87 field and 37 reserve battalions served. The Territorial battalions of the regular infantry regiments were also increased in this way, and eventually formed a total of 399 field and 169 reserve battalions. Guards regiments did not have territorial battalions. A further term liable to cause confusion, the word (Service) inserted in a battalion's official name, does not apply to the 1914 campaign, as this was widely used for the battalions of Kitchener's New Army: these new battalions were raised as additional battalions of existing infantry regiments and numbered accordingly.

Those in active contact with the enemy were supported by a vast range of ancillary services, provided by, among others, members of the medical corps (not forgetting nurses), farriers, veterinary experts, drivers of lorries or ambulances, chaplains, military policemen, postal units, transport personnel, the Army Service Corps and the vital if often much criticized members of the army's staff, the vast organization necessary for carrying out the administration and conduct of the campaign.

The BEF's first Commander-in-Chief was Field Marshal Sir John French. The BEF was constituted into two Armies on 26 December 1914, with General Sir Douglas Haig appointed to command First Army, and General Sir Horace Smith-Dorrien to command Second

Army. Both Smith-Dorrien and French lost their commands during the course of 1915, Haig succeeding the latter as Commander-in-Chief in December that year. He would retain that position until the end of the war, reaching the rank of Field Marshal in early 1917.

While hostilities intensified in France and Belgium, in Britain the first divisions of Kitchener's citizen army of volunteers, who had enlisted in their thousands following the outbreak of war, were undergoing their training. These would play an increasingly important role as the war continued, as would the forces of the Empire from Canada, Australia, New Zealand and South Africa, while Newfoundland, the British West Indies and Bermuda also offered their forces to the cause. However, the brunt of the fighting in 1914 was fought by the British Regular Army, which by the end of the year was reduced to a shadow of its former self. This book is very largely concerned with what has come to be seen as the demise of that proud and legendary force.

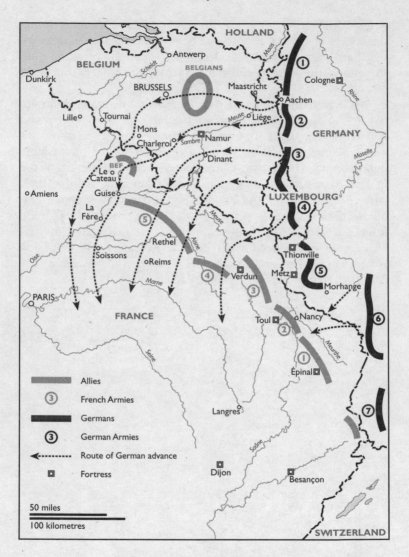

## I. THE GERMAN OFFENSIVE, 1914

Germany's original war plans envisaged the encirclement of Paris; therefore the advance of her invading forces, though rapid and dramatic, represented a strategic failure. Note the position of the BEF at the opening of the campaign.

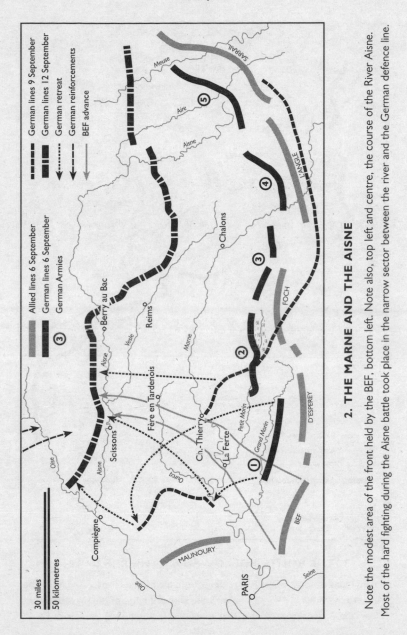

**2. THE MARNE AND THE AISNE**

Note the modest area of the front held by the BEF, bottom left. Note also, top left and centre, the course of the River Aisne.

Most of the hard fighting during the Aisne battle took place in the narrow sector between the river and the German defence line.

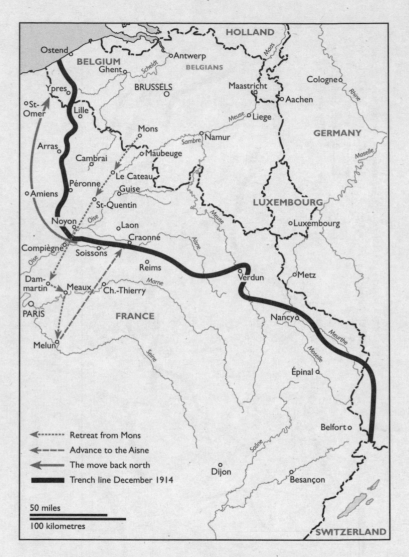

**3. THE ROUTE FOLLOWED BY THE BEF IN 1914**

From Mons to south of the River Marne; from the Marne to the Aisne; from the
Aisne to the vicinity of Ypres. The map also shows the line of the Western Front,
from the Channel coast to the Swiss fontier, as established by the end of 1914.

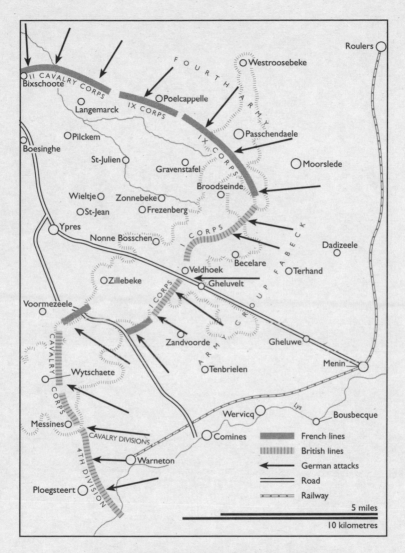

## 4. THE FIRST BATTLE OF YPRES

The map show the crucial situation at the end of October 1914:
if the Germans broke through the war would be lost; if they failed to do so
the war would be won.

# Prologue: Voices from a Distant War

If anyone were to draw up a shortlist of the most significant years of modern times, 1914 would surely be a strong candidate for a leading place. This was, after all, the year when the earthquake struck; the seismic fault that made the last century what it was runs through it. It began with a world at peace, it ended with a world at war. The difference between those two worlds was total. Looking back from the standpoint of the 1920s, the writer and artist Wyndham Lewis, himself a former soldier, wrote: 'The War is such a tremendous landmark, that ... it imposes itself upon our computations of time like the birth of Christ. We say "pre-war" and "post-war", rather as we say BC or AD.'

In this lies the appeal of this dramatic, tragic year. Its first half, falsely or otherwise, seems to have about it the air of a long summer afternoon, the second the atmosphere of a cold, bitter winter. In a matter of weeks the scene changes from what can seem like Eden before the serpent to a landscape of bewilderment and desolation, in which the fruit of the Tree of the Knowledge of Good and Evil is being eaten to the full. What was more, the old world had gone for ever. This book, as its title indicates, is about the men who went to war. There would be something very different about the men who came back – those, that is, who survived to do so.

How this sea change came about is one of the central themes of this book – and how quickly. It is often assumed that 'innocence' somehow survived the first campaigns of 1914, that the regular divisions which took the brunt of the fighting in the spectacular war of movement that preceded the long months of trench warfare which have permanently scarred the image of the Great War did so almost as uncomplainingly as the troopers of the Light Brigade at Balaclava: 'Theirs not to reason why. Theirs but to do and die.' The first few months – before the *thinking* soldier got to the front – are somehow condensed into a rather breezy, exhilarating affair fought with few

qualms by regiments of plucky, well-trained regulars who failed to
see what their successors would see when they encountered the
rigours of the Somme or Passchendaele: the horrors of modern war.
As the editor of a recent anthology of wartime letters put it:

> Initially, the war was like a scouts' picnic adventure for young officers
> typical of the generation of eager, well-conditioned public schoolboys
> with a rural background. They found manhood in the exhilarating
> excitement of the fighting and the affection they felt for their fellow
> soldiers grew out of the common pursuit of killing the enemy whom
> they despised; yet they could feel ashamed when actually faced with a
> prisoner. For most of the subalterns there was no time to get worn
> down by trench warfare: they fell in a ratio of 6:1 to the soldiers.
> Julian Grenfell (Eton-Balliol-Regular Army) who was a zestful poet
> ('Into Battle' is perhaps one of the best war poems) confessed: 'I
> *adore* war . . . Nobody grumbles at one for being dirty.'

The anthology quotes a letter sent by Grenfell to his parents giving
his first impression of Flanders, writing on 3 November 1914:

> . . . I have not washed for a week, or had my boots off for a fortnight.
> It is all the *best* fun. I have never felt so well, or so happy, or enjoyed
> anything so much. It just suits my stolid health, and stolid nerves, and
> barbaric disposition. The fighting excitement vitalizes everything, every
> sight and word and action. One loves one's fellow man so much the
> more when one is bent on killing him. And picknicking in the open
> day and night (we never see a roof now) is the real method of
> existence.

And so forth. The problem is that Grenfell's attitude has seized the
agenda, he himself having arrived some weeks after the shock of such
earlier actions as the Retreat from Mons and the Battles of the Marne
and the Aisne (though it is fair to say that experience did not change
his views, and that his most famous and most heroic poem, 'Into
Battle', was written in April 1915).

The following pages include much first-hand evidence suggesting
that there were numerous officers who took, not so much an opposite
as a *realistic* view of what was happening around them and were
shocked and dismayed at what they saw. What is more, this reaction
was almost immediate. On 2 September Major Herbert Trevor, serving

in the 2nd Battalion, King's Own Light Infantry, following the second action in which the British were engaged, at Le Cateau, wrote in a letter to his sister: 'War is a rotten game and none of us would be sorry if it was over ... where the fun comes I don't know.' Admittedly, as a senior officer in his forties Trevor was not of Grenfell's generation, but there were certainly some in that category who in their varying ways soon came to share his perception. I refer, for example, to the letters or diaries of Second Lieutenant Geoffrey Loyd, Lieutenant Angus Macnaghten, Lieutenant Rowland Owen, Captain C. J. Paterson, and Lieutenant Lionel Tennyson, all quoted at length in this book, of whom only one, the last-named, survived the war, while among the fallen, only Lieutenant Owen lived beyond the end of 1914. If a more famous Lieutenant Owen could state in 1918 that the best thing he could do was 'warn', this Owen and the others named 'warned' in their way in 1914.

As for the so-called 'other ranks', there were certainly those who, while initially looking forward to the prospect of battle, saw before long that going to war entailed a great deal more than having a bracing combat with the enemy. Thus Gunner B. C. Myatt of the Royal Field Artillery, having commented in his diary in mid-September that he was 'eager for the front', was writing by mid-October: 'Roll on peace. You never saw such sights, all the houses and shops turned inside out, furniture thrown all over the streets and everything smashed in the houses and cosy little homes ruined. It makes you weep to think what a terrible thing is war.'

Yet none of this should be taken as suggesting that the regulars of 1914 were anything other than determined to do what was asked of them. One of their number, General Sir Tom Bridges, is credited with the famous statement: 'Our motto was, "We'll do it. What is it?"' Similarly, when E. J. Cummings, a non-commissioned officer in the Royal Horse Artillery, wrote up his almost day-by-day diary at the end of the year, he broke off his narrative at one point to refer to one of the best-known comments made about the British Army of 1914, doing so with an obvious glow of pride:

Before proceeding further I should like to quote what I consider to be a passage of praise for the British troops. I only had it read to me once, but if the words are not correct, the gist is. The Kaiser's

command to his troops August 19th. 'It is my Royal and Imperial
Command that you concentrate for the immediate present all your
energies and all the valour of my soldiers against the treacherous
English: that you do not rest until General French's contemptible little
army is completely exterminated.'

The key word in this quotation, *verächtlich*, has been much discussed;
did the German Emperor really mean 'contemptible' or was he actually intending to describe the British Expeditionary Force as militarily
insignificant? Whatever the fact, the outcome is beyond question: the
Kaiser's unfortunate choice of word, or at any rate its swift translation,
offered the British regulars a challenge that they took up with a
mixture of anger, wry humour and determination. Every soldier who
came through the crucible of 1914 would be proud to call himself for
the rest of his life one of the 'Old Contemptibles'.

(It is perhaps necessary to add that there are serious doubts as
to whether the Kaiser ever made the comment ascribed to him; he
certainly denied it himself, claiming that he was always a great
admirer of the British soldier. It was very possibly 'spun' in Whitehall,
as a way of motivating the British fighting soldier in the field.
Whatever its origin it was undoubtedly a potent factor of 1914.)

It will be evident to the reader that the comments by soldiers used
so far in this Prologue were made at the time, not in retrospect. This
is true of the whole book. Except in a handful of clearly indicated
cases, all the extracts from the writings of participants included were
written in 1914 or very soon afterwards. Books built around the
memoirs of or interviews with survivors undoubtedly have their place
and there have been numerous successful examples in recent years.
But survivors should not have the stage to themselves. What about
those who did not survive? Should they not also have their voice?
Since this book is about the war's first year, in fact its first five
months, it is hardly surprising that many quoted in it did not survive;
indeed, as already indicated, some did not even see out 1914.

Whether they came through the war or not, all those whose
accounts have been quoted were writing, not with hindsight, but with
the immediacy of people attempting to record or interpret what was
happening to them as it happened. This means that this is not a book
of emotion recollected in tranquillity. It would not be far wrong to

claim that much of it was, in fact, written under fire. There is a great difference between writing about a war when you are still involved in it and might not survive, and writing about it when the war is over and you know that you have. Not only the tense changes, so also can the tension. There is nothing like the prospect of the next shell for concentrating the mind.

Here I must inject a personal observation. In one way or another I have been involved in conveying to the public the experience of soldiers of the Great War for a quarter of a century. My first effort in this area, *Tommy Goes to War*, to be republished in a new edition early next year, was written in 1978. I have no idea how many letters, diaries and other accounts I have studied – not continuously but with substantial surges as a new volume was commissioned – over this period. What I do know is that I have found again and again a deep urge on the part of countless people in the front line of war, whatever their rank, or indeed their sex, to get across to anyone who might read their writings what it was they were going through. Nor was it just the disenchanted ones who were eager to speak their minds, it was the cheerful and optimistic ones too. They wanted to bear witness; they wanted to be heard.

In some cases I found that they seemed to be addressing a larger audience than the relatives and friends who would be their immediate readers. A notable example is that of a reservist in a Yorkshire battalion, Private Charles Rainbird, who was called back to the colours as soon as the war began. His account was written in a German prison camp after having been captured during the Battle of the Aisne in September. In an early paragraph, having described what he called 'a tearful and heartbreaking farewell' as the time came for him to leave, he wrote this:

> You readers who have never felt the loving arms of your little children round your neck, or the loving embrace of your wife, cannot under-stand the feeling. You readers, who have felt them, understand.

Clearly he was writing not just for his family, or for his own satisfaction, but for posterity. There is no doubt that he was one who wanted his voice to be heard. His account, not transcribed or printed, but in its author's original, not always very legible handwriting, came to the Imperial War Museum in the year 2001. Apart from his immediate family it would seem that readers of this book, published ninety years later, are Rainbird's first readers. He is quoted briefly in Chapter 4 and at some length in Chapter 8. His is a valued and memorable contribution to the history of 1914 from which it is a privilege to quote, though sadly there is so much more in his account than could be included here.

Reading this and many other such accounts written in 1914 inevitably prompts the question: what happened to these men in that distant war who were so anxious for their voices to be heard? In particular the question that dominates is: did they survive? To answer this question a special Roll of Honour has been included in the book, listing those quoted or referred to in its pages who lost their lives in the course of the war, together with their date and cause of death and place of burial or commemoration. They are also named in the normal way in the Index of Contributors or in the General Index, as appropriate.

The book must speak for itself, but it is perhaps worthwhile at this point emphasizing the often forgotten but important fact that all the countries involved went to war supremely confident in the righteousness of their cause. Most wars begin with the belief that God is on everybody's side, this one arguably more than most. It should not be assumed that because the Germans began the war by marching into France and Belgium, they saw themselves as wicked invaders. On the contrary, they believed that they were launching a legitimate pre-emptive strike against countries which it was assumed would be bound to attack them sooner or later anyway. This sense of patriotic justification could be expressed in many ways. To offer two widely contrasting examples: Kaiser Wilhelm II (not always felicitous in his public pronouncements) was widely derided in Britain for a speech he made in October when he claimed: 'The Holy Spirit has descended on me because I am Emperor of the Germans. I am the instrument of the Most High. I am his sword, his representative.' At the opposite end of the scale, when Private W. R. Bird, in the 2nd Battalion, Dorsetshire Regiment, a member of the Indian Army Expeditionary Force despatched to invade Turkish-held Mesopotamia in November, wrote up his immaculately kept war diary, he quoted a fragment of unattributed verse ending with the line: 'Who dies for England, *sleeps with God.*' When such certainties meet head to head, the possibilities of a cataclysmic result occurring are high. It duly occurred.

\* \* \*

This is the fifth book I have written for the Imperial War Museum about the 1914–18 war. It might seem curious, however, that, having produced books about the First World War as a whole, about the Western Front, about the Somme, and about the year 1918, I should now go back to the beginning.

One thing that persuaded me to do this was the fact that, since I had 'visited' 1914, a remarkable amount of newly discovered first-hand material relating to the war's first year had been reaching the Imperial War Museum's archives, much of it of high quality. Indeed, some quite excellent collections arrived while the book was being written, such as those of Lieutenant Ralph Blewitt DSO, Gunner S. W. Crowsley, the already mentioned E. J. Cummings of the Royal Horse Artillery and Private Rainbird, while the deeply moving letter written after the Battle of Mons by Captain W. G. Morritt reached the Museum as the text was undergoing its final revision. In the same way I can claim that the chapter which deals with the Christmas Truce, about which, with Shirley Seaton, I wrote a book in 1984, has been compiled using exclusively evidence that has come to light since the latest edition of that book was published, some of that material too having been very recently discovered.

However, another factor led me to wish to write this book. I felt the need to conclude the series with, as it were, a kind of 'flagship' work, which, while focusing on the year in which the war began, would also try in some way to assess how this vital touch-and-go first phase of the conflict affected not only the subsequent course of the war but also the subsequent history of the last century and beyond. Indeed, the ripples from it can still be detected today. Whether I have achieved that must be left for readers to judge, but I am glad to have had the opportunity to make the attempt.

This consideration also led to the adoption of the book's subtitle, 'The Men Who Went to War', in that it could be seen as standing for all the books in my Imperial War Museum series. All five books are about men – though there has always been space for a number of gallant women – who left their homes and civilian backgrounds to offer their best for what they saw as a worthy cause in one of the greatest crises of modern times. One of the keynote poems of 1914 was written by the veteran novelist and poet Thomas Hardy in the war's second month. He called it 'Men Who March Away' (Song of the Soldiers; September 5, 1914). Hardy was clearly struck, as were count-less others, by one of the predominant images of the time: of young men marching, cheerfully, thoughtfully, ardently, fearfully, hopefully, bravely, towards who knew what uncertain future. In essence it was Hardy's title that inspired the subtitle for this book – with the variant that whereas from his viewpoint the men were marching away into the unknown, we with the benefit of hindsight know what they were marching to. Seeing where they went and how they fared is the basic purpose of this book as it was of its predecessors. I hope this book's subtitle can stand for all of them.

On another level, the book has given me a uniquely important personal opportunity. I have long wished to write about the Antwerp Expedition, a brave but failed attempt by a force of mainly Royal Navy regulars and reservists, transformed overnight into infantrymen and shipped across to the Continent while barely knowing one end of a rifle from the other, to prevent Belgium's most important port from falling into German hands. The vast majority of those involved came safe home, but some ended up interned in neutral Holland, where they could do nothing but watch impotently as the war went on, while just under a thousand were captured by the Germans. Becoming a prisoner of war in the third month of hostilities that lasted almost four and a half years guaranteed a very long ordeal, an ordeal which many did not survive. One who did survive, a twenty-year-old in 1914 who returned deeply affected by experiences he never disclosed, but which he managed to overcome to become a valued citizen of his community and a fine and much-loved family man, was my father-in-law. (Readers might be interested to know that his experience was very close to that of Ordinary Seaman Ernest Myatt, as quoted at length in Chapter 9.) He was one of the many for whom the year 1914 provided the beginning and the end of their fighting war. It is to his memory that I have requested that this book should be dedicated.

**Malcolm Brown**
*April 2004*

# CHAPTER ONE

# BEFORE THE FALL

MONDAY, 22 JUNE 1914, was the official birthday of His Majesty King George, more formally titled 'George the Fifth by the Grace of God, King of the United Kingdom of Great Britain and Ireland and the British Dominions beyond the Seas, Defender of the Faith, Emperor of India'. Now just into his fiftieth year – his actual birthday was 3 June – he had been on the throne since the death in 1910 of his father, Edward VII, and would occupy it until his own death in 1936, by which time he would have been King for over twenty-five years.

The occasion was marked in London by the hugely popular ceremony of 'Trooping the Colour', which drew vast crowds to Horse Guards Parade and the environs of Whitehall and the royal parks. The colour trooped was that of the 1st Battalion, the Grenadier Guards, and the event was watched by Queen Mary, Queen Alexandra the King's mother, Dowager Empress Marie Feodorovna of Russia and four Princesses. On the conclusion of the ceremony, His Majesty rode back to Buckingham Palace at the head of the King's Guard, preceded by the Household Cavalry and the combined bands of the Brigade of Guards. This was a departure from previous practice, the result of which, according to an approving report in *The Times*, 'was that a large number of the King's subjects, for whom there was no room on the Horse Guards' Parade, had a close view of their Sovereign and the brilliant staff by which he was accompanied, as well as the glitter and pomp of the Massed Bands of the Foot Guards'.

The King's eldest son and heir, the Prince of Wales – as it happened one day short of his own twentieth birthday – was not present. He was making a more modest appearance at Aldershot as a corporal of the Oxford Battalion of the Officers' Training Corps, which he had joined in his capacity as an undergraduate of Oxford's most elegant college, Magdalen. In what was effectively the British Army's 'capital', the Aldershot Command was to stage its own grand event that day, a Birthday Parade in honour of the King on its noted parade ground, Laffan's Plain. The young Prince (the future Edward VIII), there not to participate but to observe together with his OTC comrades, was dazzled with the rest of the watching crowd by the magnificent sight of Britain's finest soldiery streaming past in full-dress review order. Looking back from the standpoint of over three decades later, in his post-abdication status as the Duke of Windsor, he would comment in his memoir, *A King's Story*: 'Little did we suspect that within a few months their ranks would be decimated in war. In June 1914, the atmosphere was deceptively tranquil.'

Also present that day was a seventeen-year-old schoolboy, Charles Carrington, who would serve in and write about the war to come. He had been motored across with members of his family from the nearby town of Fleet to join the sightseers. What most impressed him about the occasion was that after the infantry had marched past, the artillery had trotted past, and the cavalry had galloped past, the sky was suddenly filled with the stunning sight and engine roar of no fewer than twelve aircraft of the Royal Flying Corps passing over the parade ground. Rarely had he seen a single aeroplane before that, let alone a whole squadron airborne. It was, though he could not be aware of it, a symbol of things to come.

At ground level the scene was a blaze of colour: the line regiments in scarlet, the riflemen in green, the 11th Hussars in their cherry-coloured breeches. The horse-gunners were in busbies and sling-jackets, the Highlanders in kilts and feathered bonnets. 'Each regiment marched with its band playing the quick-step,' wrote Carrington, recalling the event fifty years and two wars later, 'and among the old familiar tunes I particularly enjoyed that of the Army Service Corps, who trundled along at a round trot to the favourite "nigger minstrel" air of *Wait for the Wagon*. But what we did not foresee,' he continued, 'was that within two months the Coldstream Guards would win new honours in the night alarm at Landrecies, that the Worcesters before the year was out would have tipped the scale of destiny by the decisive counter-attack at Gheluvelt, that the Oxfordshires, the old 52nd Light Infantry, would have broken the Prussian Guard, as their forerunners had broken Napoleon's Old Guard at Waterloo, and that within six months half of these hearty, healthy young men would be maimed or dead.'

There was a further portent that day. Carrington was much impressed by the distinguished figure of the general in the cocked hat who took the salute, and inquired as to who he was. 'I was told he was Sir Douglas Haig, a name I had never heard before.'

The day also saw the publication of the King's Birthday Honours List. A prominent name towards the head of the list was that of Britain's most admired soldier, Lord Kitchener of Khartoum, who was made an Earl. The famous proconsul of Empire, who had spent most of his long years of service in Africa and the Middle East, was on one of his rare visits to Britain. He was due to return to Egypt on 3 August, intending to leave Britain by the Dover ferry. By that time the march of events would ensure that the ferry sailed without him and that two days later he would become the Secretary of State for War, effectively Britain's military supremo.

Notwithstanding the military splendour on display at Aldershot and in London, Britain's virtual superpower status at this time was based not on her reputation as a land power but as a naval one. Her Home Fleet was, if not the envy of the world, certainly the envy of its nearest rival, the High Seas Fleet of Imperial Germany, whose ruler was the volatile, unpredictable, loose cannon of Europe, Kaiser Wilhelm II. Curiously, during the summer of 1914 that rivalry was very much on hold. The last days of June witnessed a remarkable display of comradeship between Europe's two greatest navies, with a special visit by two British squadrons to Kiel for the Yachting Week. The scenes at this venue were particularly notable, and, in retrospect, poignantly memorable. 'For the first time for several years,' wrote the then First Lord of the Admiralty, Winston Churchill, in the eloquent description he included in his book *The World Crisis*, 'some of the finest ships of the British and German Navies lay at their moorings side by side surrounded by liners, yachts and pleasure craft of every kind. Undue curiosity in technical matters was banned by mutual agreement. There were races, there were banquets, there were speeches. There was sunshine, there was the Emperor. Officers and men fraternized and entertained each other afloat and ashore. Together they strolled arm in arm through the hospitable town, or dined with all goodwill in mess and wardroom. Together they stood bareheaded at the funeral of a German officer killed in flying an English seaplane.'

If there were any war clouds over Britain at this time, they related more to Ireland than to Europe. The attempt by the Liberal Government under Prime Minister Herbert Henry Asquith to pass an Irish Home Rule Bill through parliament had produced a furious backlash from Ulster, and, since the British Army was rich in Ulstermen, from that institution too. The word 'mutiny' was heard in the land, most notably in relation to the barracks near Dublin known as 'The Curragh', while gun-running by both Irish nationalists and Ulster 'volunteers' raised the atmosphere to fever pitch. Meanwhile the contentious Ulster leader, Sir Edward Carson, addressing rally after rally, threatened a resort to armed force if the need arose. Even as late as 26 July nationalist anger in Dublin would erupt in a brief rising in which lives were lost, the subsequent funerals bringing out massive crowds. The situation was partly, though not entirely, retrieved by the shelving of the Home Rule Bill on 30 July. The Ulstermen might switch overnight from near rebels to ardent loyalists, but the nationalist fires would keep burning underground to emerge in later years.

If there was any actual violence in England, it came from what might seem at first a somewhat unlikely source: the campaign for women to win the right to vote. On 10 March a suffragette slashed Velázquez's nude masterpiece, the *Rokeby Venus*. On 17 April a suffragette bomb destroyed Great Yarmouth's Britannia Pier. On 6 May an attempt to staunch this wound by legalizing a Women's Enfranchisement Bill was thwarted by the House of Lords. The campaign continued. On 22 May a band of more than fifty suffragettes stormed Buckingham Palace in an unsuccessful attempt to deliver a petition to the King. On 11 June a bomb exploded in the Chapel of Edward the Confessor in Westminster Abbey.

Meanwhile, the standard events of national life proceeded as normal. On 28 March, on the River Thames in the heart of London, Cambridge defeated Oxford in the University Boat Race. On 5 April the small northern mill town of Burnley beat Liverpool 2–1 in the annual Football Association Cup Final. The venue was the Crystal Palace, South London, with the King present. The event would not be held there again; by the following year the ground would have been assigned to military training and the Cup Final moved to Manchester. On 27 May at Epsom the greatest race of the flat-racing season, the

Derby, was won by Mr H. B. Buryea's horse 'Durbar', itself a name not without imperial connotations.

Other events of the early part of the year included a strike in late March by 100,000 miners, and the drowning of a pilot, Gustav Hamel, when attempting to fly across the English Channel on 23 May. Meanwhile beyond that Channel the consequences of a high-profile *crime passionnel* occupied the fascinated attention of the French nation. On 3 January the influential Paris newspaper *Le Figaro* accused the Government's Finance Minister of corruption. On 16 March the Finance Minister's wife shot the editor of *Le Figaro* dead in his office. The trial of the aggrieved if revengeful Madame Caillaux would remain headline stuff almost to the outbreak of war.

\* \* \*

There are various views as to what life was like in the period which we now see as the calm before the cataclysm of 1914. Doubtless to many on the bottom rungs of society conditions were hard and restrictive and prospects were poor. That industrial peace was far from guaranteed is evident from the reference above to the miners' strike. That political peace was not secure was demonstrated by the activities of the suffragettes; while the Derby of 1914 passed off peacefully, that of the previous year had been marred by the death of a suffragette who had thrown herself under the King's horse. But the concept of – for some at least – a doomed paradise, of, almost, an Eden before the Fall, is not easy to dismiss as merely myth or make-believe. There could be no more eloquent advocate of that interpretation than Osbert Sitwell, writing in his book *Great Morning*, the third volume of his autobiographical trilogy, *Left Hand, Right Hand*:

> How is it possible to capture the sweet and carefree atmosphere of 1913, and 1914 until the outbreak of the First World War? Never had Europe been so prosperous and gay. Never had the world gone so well for all classes of the community: especially in England, where an ambitious programme of Social Reform had just been carried through, and Old Age Pensions and Insurance schemes had removed from the poor the most bitter of the spectres that haunted them. . . . In Western Europe there had been no war of any sort for nearly two generations, and for a thousand years, if an outbreak had occurred,

standards of chivalry prevailed. And I remember from my own childhood, what must have been a common experience with members of my generation, reading the Bible, and books of Greek, Roman, and English history, and reflecting how wonderful it was to think that, with the growth of commerce and civilization, mass captivities and executions were things of the rabid past, and that never again would man be liable to persecution for his political or religious opinions. This belief, inculcated in the majority, led to an infinite sweetness in the air we breathed. Even if war came one day ... it would be played according to the rules: the loss of life would be on the Boer War scale ...

There was, as yet, no hint to be detected of the sorrows and terrors that lay in front of the most highly cultured races of the world.

It is certainly a partial view, conditioned by sadness at the long tragedy that was to follow and nostalgia for the apparent innocence that preceded it. It can also be seen as a questionable view in the light of, for example, Barbara Tuchman's assertion that the pre-war period 'was not a Golden Age or *Belle Epoque* except to a thin crust of the privileged class', and that to most people 'it did not seem so golden when they were in the midst of it'. 'A phenomenon of such extended malignance as the Great War,' she stated as a further caution, 'does not come out of a Golden Age.'

It also fails to take account of a long-running subculture of suspicion about German intentions that had festered in Britain in popular 'tabloid' newspapers such as Lord Northcliffe's *Daily Mail*, or more disturbingly in such highly successful novels as Erskine Childers' *The Riddle of the Sands*, or mockingly in P. G. Wodehouse's farcical fable entitled *The Swoop: or How Clarence Saved England*. All these publications portrayed Germany as a potential aggressor, with a German invasion of Britain as a real, not a fanciful, option. Perhaps the most influential of this curious genre was William Le Queux's *The Invasion of 1910*, originally published in 1906, which sold a million copies and was translated into twenty-seven languages. It was instantly popular in Germany, where the Kaiser ordered the staff of the Army and Admiralty to analyse the work for useful information. Meanwhile spymania became so rife that foreign agents were thought to be at work everywhere and any foreign tourist with a camera was immediately suspect. Churchill, not averse to war when necessary but deeply suspicious of phoney warmongering, is on record as having stated: 'We live in a period of superficial alarms, when it is thought patriotic and statesmanlike, far-seeing, clever and Bismarckian to predict hideous and direful wars as imminent.' Yet it appears that as First Lord of the Admiralty from 1911, he reacted sufficiently strongly to *The Riddle of the Sands* – with its hints of possibly nefarious German naval activity in the region of the River Elbe and the North Sea – to make it required reading for his staff since it highlighted his own fears of German intentions towards Britain.

Others who believed conflict was only just across the horizon were Field Marshal Lord Roberts and his circle, which campaigned ceaselessly for conscription, arguing that Britain's reliance on the volunteer principle would seriously disadvantage the country in what they saw as the inevitable crisis to come. Certain more strident voices, such as that of J. L. Garvin of the *Observer*, were so outspokenly anti-German that the Kaiser himself was driven to protest at what he called 'this continuing and systematic poisoning of the wells'.

Germany was not without its own would-be disturbers of the peace, whose self-appointed aim was nothing less than to prepare their country for a conflict they saw as inevitable. Prominent among them was General Friedrich von Bernhardi, who had served in the Franco-Prussian War as a cavalry officer and had subsequently risen to the post of chief of the Military History section of the General Staff. In 1911 he published a book whose keynote chapter titles carried their own explicit message: 'The Right to Make War', 'The Duty to Make War' and, most ominous of all, 'World Power or Downfall': in German *Weltmacht oder Niedergang*, a phrase that would have a terrible echo in the last days of the Third Reich in 1945. The book appeared in English in 1914, under the title *Germany and the Next War*. For someone like Osbert Sitwell there would be small interest either in the trashing of a potential enemy by the popular press or the bizarre utterances of an obscure retired German general making threatening noises in the wings. Moving in his particular circle, he would be much more likely to recall that Kaiser and King were cousins, members of the same family, impressively united on high-profile royal occasions, and that such connections suggested an easy companionship between their two countries. Surely the absurd

scenarios envisaged by the popular press were the stuff of fantasy, or
of irrational malice, mainly aimed at selling more newspapers than
their rivals, while military sabre-rattlings from afar, if they cut any ice
at all, could surely be left to those in the War Office or at Sandhurst
whose duty it was to concern themselves with such matters. There is
therefore in his elegy for a vanished world almost a sense of surprised
sadness that what had seemed safe and secure was so brutally
snatched away.

If Rupert Brooke was to become, famously, the laureate of the
coming war, at least in its initial phase, the poet most closely associated with Sitwell's lost arcadia had already published his most influential work almost two decades earlier. This was A. E. Housman,
whose poetry sequence *A Shropshire Lad* was barely noticed when it
first appeared in 1896. As the war progressed it was to have a
remarkable resurgence, because while it evoked an apparently idyllic
rustic past it was a past unmistakably under sentence. Looked at from
the vantage point of 1914 his book seemed prophetic, effectively an
elegy in waiting. The landscape might be beautiful, but it was a
landscape threatened by war, its ploughshares to be turned into
swords, its young men doomed to be called to arms with scant chance
of returning:

> On the idle hill of summer,
>   Sleepy with the flow of streams,
> Far I hear the steady drummer
>   Drumming like a noise in dreams.
>
> Far and near and low and louder
>   On the roads of earth go by,
> Dear to friends and food for powder,
>   Soldiers marching, all to die.

Even more evocative, indeed almost prescient in the light of
subsequent events, was this tiny, haunting poem:

> Into my heart an air that kills
>   From yon far country blows:
> Where are those blue remembered hills?
>   What spires, what farms are those?

This is the land of lost content,
I see it shining plain,
The happy highways where I went
And cannot come again.

In the summer of 1914 the air that killed came in the form of an item of devastating news from a far country that shook Europe just six days after King George V's Birthday Celebrations of 22 June. It was passed to Kaiser Wilhelm while he was out in his private yacht mingling with the fraternizing ships at Kiel, being delivered as a note thrown on board inside a cigarette box. The Kaiser came ashore in an obvious state of agitation and left immediately for Potsdam. It became clear at once that the festivities were over. The British ships made rapid preparations to return to their own waters. The next time the two fleets would meet would be in markedly different circumstances at the Battle of Jutland just under two years later. The countdown to war had begun.

# CHAPTER TWO

# WHEN THE LIGHTS WENT OUT

THE FAR COUNTRY in question was Bosnia, then a newly acquired, restive province of the somewhat ramshackle, creaking Austro-Hungarian Empire. Its seizure in 1908 had left its substantial eastern neighbour, Serbia, outraged and angry, but as a mainly agricultural society without industrial clout Serbia had no chance of challenging the policies initiated in far-off Vienna by going to war. Racial humiliation – both Bosnia and Serbia had largely Slav populations, with closer links to the Russian Empire than the Austro-Hungarian one – had added fury to frustration. In 1911 a Serbian secret society called the 'Black Hand', their purpose evident in their slogan 'Unity or Death', had been formed with the aim of promoting the political unification of Serbia with South Slav minorities in Austria-Hungary and the nearby Turkish territories. Their dream, which would eventually come to pass and then end in bloodshed many decades later, was to create a Serbia-dominated Yugoslavia. Eager to embrace what would now be called terrorism to gain their ends, they had found a suitable occasion on which to make a gesture of protest on Sunday, 28 June.

On that date a senior member of the dynasty which ruled the Austro-Hungarian Empire, the Habsburgs, was due to pay an official visit to the Bosnian capital, Sarajevo. This was the Archduke Franz Ferdinand, heir presumptive to the Austrian throne since 1889, who would carry out his visit after several days in the area attending army manoeuvres. One pleasing consequence for him was that he would be able to make a public appearance with his morganatic wife, Sophie, Duchess of Hohenburg. Not being of the blood royal, she received nothing but cold shoulders in the Imperial court in Vienna, but in Sarajevo could bask more openly in her relationship, almost as though she were a queen in waiting. To add to their happiness, 28 June was their wedding anniversary. But it was also a day of commemoration for the Serbs: the anniversary of the Battle of Kosovo in 1389, when they had suffered a terrible defeat at the hands of the Ottomans, only redeemed by the fact that one Serb hero had managed to exact revenge by assassinating the Turkish Sultan. The 'Black Hand' would be there in Sarajevo in the hope of achieving a somewhat similar coup.

So it came about that as, on a glorious summer morning, the honoured couple drove through the flag-bedecked streets in their open limousine – the Archduke had refused to use a closed one – a bomb was thrown from somewhere in the watching crowd. Nobody in the car was hurt but several others were wounded including the aide-de-camp of the Austrian Governor of Bosnia, General Pitoriek, who was rushed to hospital. When the official party reached the town hall there was an understandably queasy encounter with the local authorities, following which the Archduke, who did not lack courage, decided that he would pay a visit to the Governor's wounded aide.

Unfortunately, the Archduke's car and its escort turned into a street that had not been cleared as part of the original itinerary. The Governor immediately suggested a different route and as the chauffeur halted to reverse, a nineteen-year-old member of the Black Hand called Gavrilo Princip, accomplice of the thrower of the earlier bomb, stepped forward and fired two bullets from a Browning pistol, which effectively started the First World War.

The assassination of Archduke Franz Ferdinand and his consort became one of those events which impressed itself so strongly on people's minds that they would always remember where they were and what they were doing when they heard of it. This was especially the case in Austria, where the death of a Habsburg – especially one next in line to the long-serving, increasingly frail Emperor, Franz Josef – was bound to produce major shock waves. The writer Stefan Zweig was listening to a spa band which suddenly stopped playing and left the podium. An Austrian nobleman, Prince Clary, was stalking roebuck on the Bohemian plains, when his cook came hurrying towards him on a bicycle. A Christian Socialist named Funder was praying in a church in the Vienna Woods when someone slipped in to pass him the news. Yet shock did not invariably mean sympathy. Franz Ferdinand had not endeared himself to the general Austrian population. In Vienna the Prater, renowned for its low-life, high-spirited entertainments – and three troubled decades later for Harry Lime's famous revolving wheel – reputedly continued its jollifications as though nothing extraordinary had occurred.

One young British citizen who would never forget how she heard of the assassination was Beatrice Kelsey, aged twenty-six, the daughter of a Warwickshire farmer and a product of the Coventry High School for Girls, who had been working since February 1913 as a governess to the three daughters of a Viennese family named Berl. The Berls lived in the fashionable Schottenring and were cultured as well as wealthy. They also had a French governess and an Austrian one, so that conversation at dinner could be conducted in four languages: English, French, Hungarian and German. Beatrice Kelsey had led an exciting and privileged life, with visits to concerts, theatres, the opera, museums, galleries, the skating rink in winter, while also enjoying dinner-parties, dances and occasional visits to the Berl country house at Ugersbach.

On Saturday, 27 June 1914 she went with some of the family on a river trip down the Danube to Budapest. On Sunday the 28th she wrote in her diary:

> Grilling heat . . . spent the morning sightseeing . . . At lunch heard the appalling news of the murder of Archduke Franz Ferdinand and the Duchess of Hohenburg . . . All music was stopped at once and a pall cast over everything.

Describing the event at length later, she wrote:

> We had planned to spend our afternoon in Budapest on the Marguerite-Insel, a small island in the river as it approaches the city. With its gardens and restaurants and music it was a favourite place where the laughter-loving Hungarians spent many happy hours in the hot summer afternoons.
>
> After visiting some of the lovely buildings on the opposite side of the river, we returned to our hotel for luncheon, to the accompaniment of the gypsy music, which was such a feature of entertainment in those days. Suddenly halfway through the meal, the music stopped and a hush fell over the room. The headwaiter moved about, speaking in a low voice and, when he reached our table, it was to tell us that the Archduke Franz Ferdinand and his wife had been assassinated . . .
>
> Within an hour or two of the tragedy becoming known Budapest

changed to a city of mourning. All entertainment was cancelled and black streamers and flags at half-mast appeared on public buildings. The few people in the streets moved quietly and spoke in hushed voices.

We decided to cut short our stay and to return to Vienna by train next day. There, as in Budapest, there were signs of mourning on every hand and there was anxious questioning about the new political situation which would inevitably follow the Archduke's death.

Elsewhere the news of the assassination, while it came as a shock, did not always – since it concerned the 'matter of Serbia' – come as a surprise. In British high circles the effect was personal, because the heir to the Habsburg throne had paid a successful private visit to Britain some six months previously. King George V went unannounced to the Austro-Hungarian Embassy early the following morning to express his grief. The Austrian Ambassador, Count Mensdorff, was the King's distant cousin; he gratefully accepted the royal and other condolences which flowed into the Embassy on that gloomy Monday. Prominent among the messages received was one from Britain's Foreign Secretary, Sir Edward Grey, stating: 'The cruel circumstances attending to it add to the tragedy . . . Every feeling political and personal makes me sympathize with you.' As a token of sympathy Court Mourning was ordered for one week.

* * *

That this obscure act of political terrorism in a minor province in the Balkans should have led to a cataclysmic war can still seem bizarre, even absurd, in spite of the countless attempts that have been made to explain it. (Certainly there seems no suggestion in the ritualistic acts of sympathy that followed the Archduke's assassination that this was an event likely to have world-shattering consequences.) Austria-Hungary blamed the Serbian Government for sponsoring the outrage – though this was almost certainly not the case – and sought to exploit it to teach the Serbs a lesson. But the Serbo-Russian connection would almost certainly mean that any threat to Serbia would produce an angry response in St Petersburg, causing the mighty Russian Empire to rattle its sabres in response. The Austrians therefore sought an assurance of help from their best ally, Germany, which famously handed Austria a 'blank cheque' to do as she wished, while not at first seriously expecting the cheque would be cashed. But Russia was allied to France, not at this moment seeking hostilities but ever anxious to reclaim the provinces of Alsace-Lorraine lost to Germany in the Franco-Prussian War of 1870–71, while Britain had, literally, a cordial understanding – an *entente cordiale* – with France, backed by already agreed plans to come to her aid should she be seriously threatened.

The pre-war European balance of power – Germany and Austria yoked together in the centre; Imperial Russia to the east linked with republican France to the west; Britain strong but benign riding off-shore behind her 'silver sea' – had seemed to many a reasonable guarantee of peace. The pieces were roughly equal on the chess-board; who would want to upset the equilibrium? In the event, however, it was as though the links became shackles, the countries involved somehow contriving to drag one another over the edge into the fire.

The fuse burned with incredible slowness through the hot sum-mer days of what would become known as the July Crisis. Key people were not at their desks; many were taking the waters at spas or their ease in holiday resorts. The streets of the great European capitals were curiously silent. Events speeded up when the Austrians pre-sented Serbia with a haughty ultimatum of which the principal demand was that she acknowledge her complicity in the murder plot and institute proceedings against its abettors – which they were sure she could not accept. The fact that she did, if with reservations, curiously served to accelerate rather than slow down the gathering momentum; Vienna wanted revenge however Serbia reacted. The powers began to stir, sensing disadvantage if they were not prepared for eventualities. Why not take basic preparations for war, just in case? Plans argued over for years came off shelves to be discussed over desks. Maps were spread on tables. Railway schedules were brought out, being central to the intensifying drama as all the countries involved proposed to use trains as the key means of getting their troops to their war stations – even Britain, though she also had a Channel to cross. At this stage the word 'mobilization' entered the argument, the term itself becoming a potent factor in the story. To some countries it meant ordering soldiers to their bases and recalling reservists so that they might be properly armed and equipped. In the case of Germany mobilization had a more proactive meaning; it entailed despatching her armies to the frontiers, only awaiting the order to invade.

There was inevitably much confusion, and much anxiety about other nations' intentions, but there was also another factor: opportunism. In particular the German military leadership saw that they had been presented with the chance to grasp a nettle of which they had been aware for some years. They had come to believe that a European conflict would have to be fought sooner or later, since their principal potential continental enemies – Russia and France – were steadily improving their warlike capacity and therefore posing a threat to which they felt the need to respond. The general assumption had been that a crunch point might arrive in or around 1917. Suddenly the escalating problem in the Balkans, and the subsequent stirrings across Europe, offered Germany the chance to make her move in 1914.

Yet there is evidence that this was not the almost casual response to the situation that the above account suggests. The Kaiser took a tough line, calling for Austria to punish Serbia harshly and raising the temperature with rash, belligerent comments. It has been argued that despite this neither he nor his entourage believed that the crisis would result in a major war, and that that was why he continued his annual summer routine by going off on his usual North Sea cruise, with the full encouragement of his Chancellor, Bethmann Hollweg. But other interpretations claim that this was a cover-up for far more malicious intentions and that the famous blank cheque was effectively filled in with a promise to pay from the moment it was sent. Meanwhile even before Sarajevo the High Seas Fleet was secretly mobilizing under a cloak of normality, thus making the Yachting Week at Kiel to a substantial extent a carefully stage-managed distraction. In essence, from the start the match was far nearer the powder keg than has been generally imagined. Germany wanted her war and was determined to have it.

* * *

Now the situation was like that of a ticking time bomb. On 28 July Austria declared war on Serbia. On the 29th Germany asked for a guarantee of British neutrality in the event of a European war. On the following day the British Foreign Secretary, Sir Edward Grey, rejected the German request. Meanwhile on the 30th Russia ordered partial mobilization, prompting Germany to threaten to mobilize unless the Russians called a halt. The Russians did not halt. Instead on the 31st they ordered full mobilization. Austria mobilized on the same day, as did Turkey, though she would delay her actual involvement in the burgeoning crisis until October. Britain marked her card by asking both France and Germany for assurances that they would respect Belgian neutrality; Belgium's neutral status had been accepted by all the major powers of Europe since 1839 and Britain now assumed the role of her prime guarantor. France agreed at once, while Germany prevaricated for reasons that would soon become obvious.

The new, fatal month of August 1914 began. On 1 August France, Germany and Belgium mobilized. On the 2nd German troops entered Russian Poland, Luxembourg and France. On the 3rd Germany and France declared war on each other. On the 4th Germany declared war on Belgium and immediately invaded Belgian territory. That same day Britain mobilized and issued an ultimatum to Germany stating that, unless guarantees of Belgian neutrality were received within twelve hours, Britain and Germany would be at war.

There was a major division in the British Cabinet as to what would constitute the violation of that neutrality. If the Germans merely clipped the southern corner of Belgian territory that might be overlooked, provided the Germans paid for any damage for which they might be responsible. The resolution communicated by the Cabinet to the King on 2 August stated that 'a substantial violation' would be necessary before the Government would feel compelled to take action under treaty obligations. Once it became clear that the German Chief of the General Staff, von Moltke, demanded unimpeded passage through the *whole* of Belgium, effectively the die was cast. Bethmann Hollweg famously lamented to the British Ambassador to Berlin, Sir Edward Goschen, that Britain was prepared to go to war for 'a scrap of paper' – in diplomatic language '*un chiffon de papier*', his dismissive term for the treaty of 1839. When no reply to Britain's ultimatum was received by the appointed hour, she was irrevocably committed to join the belligerents. Indeed, the outcome was inevitable. Britain could not sit in some grandstand watching the continent of Europe tear itself to pieces. She was, in present-day terms, a superpower, and it is not given to superpowers to watch others fight the battles and share the spoils.

In those final days the arguments in Britain raged thick and fast. Numerous eminent scholars raised their objections, among them the well-known historian G. M. Trevelyan, who publicly opposed 'the participation of England in the European crime'. To many the whole idea of a war against *Germany* seemed absurd. On 1 August *The Times* published a letter of which the central thrust was: 'We regard Germany as a nation leading the way in the Arts and Sciences, and we have all learnt and are learning from German scholars. We consider ourselves justified in protesting against being drawn into a struggle with a nation so near akin to our own, and with whom we have so much in common.'

In many places, however, the pre-war mood was dictated by crowds, crowds taken over by war fever, elsewhere caught up in anxiety and concern. Monday, 3 August, was a Bank Holiday, the last of the year until Christmas, and therefore a popular day for festivities and outings. A seventeen-year-old bank clerk, E. C. Powell, arrived back from a trip to the Chiltern Hills to find the city of London 'in a state of hysteria. A vast procession jammed the road from side to side, everyone waving flags and singing patriotic songs.' By contrast, the mood in that ever-popular holiday honeypot only a few miles off, Hampstead Heath, was much less strident. To the local paper, the *Hampstead Record*, the Bank Holiday was 'a dismal affair ... Many attempts were made to infuse gaiety into the proceedings, but even when these attempts were partially successful, incongruity was afforded by the harsh and discordant voices of news vendors shouting out the latest war news.' Similarly the *South London Observer* recorded: 'It has been a black Bank Holiday, people have tried to enjoy themselves but have been conscious of a skeleton at the feast.'

Meanwhile, holidaymakers returning to London from the east coast became aware of another omen of the times as they crossed paths with hundreds of Germans, many of them reservists, hurrying home to the Fatherland.

The evidence so far relates to the capital: how was the move towards war received elsewhere? The Revd James Mackay, a Methodist minister in his mid-twenties living in Newcastle, kept a diary

during the first days of August which focuses on the crisis as seen
from the country's industrial north:

*Saturday Aug. 1st.* Great excitement prevails all over the country.
News has come that Russia is mobilizing and Germany has presented
an ultimatum. People are alarmed everywhere. People are buying
large quantities of foodstuffs especially flour.

 Grave fears are held for our own country. People are talking in
hushed whispers everywhere. Great anxiety prevails.

*Sunday Aug. 2nd.* Coming home from Sunday School I bought a war
edition (my first Sunday newspaper). The situation is very acute.
A special cabinet meeting has been held. The feeling in the country is
electric. We await with great anxiety the statement of Mr Asquith on
Monday. I preached at Worley Street in the evening. I had the national
anthem sung.

*Monday Aug. 3rd.* At 9.30 a.m. left Central Station for Stocksfield with
45 mission members. The weather was splendid but the great dark
war cloud hung over us. We could not dispel our anxiety try as we
would. Despite this however we had a very enjoyable outing.

 At every railway station on the way up a military guard is stationed.
The whole community seems alive with uniformed men. Several
trainloads of soldiers passed us on their way to the city.

 News has come to hand that the Naval Reserve have orders to
mobilize. War between France and Germany has been declared.
Things look very black. Germany's high-handed action makes our
interference almost inevitable.

*Tuesday Aug. 4th.* The great news of the early morning is that Britain
has presented an ultimatum to Germany. The army and Territorials
received mobilization orders.

 11.0 p.m. Went down into the city. Crowds had gathered at the
Central Station and in front of the 'Chronicle' offices, waiting for the
declaration of war to be made known.

For many, perhaps most, however, there was no doubt as to how
Britain, or rather England – the standard name for Britain at the time
– should respond. Hence, for example, the comments, made subsequently, of Miss Mary Coules, who was the daughter of a news editor
of the Reuters Press Agency based in London, but who was on holiday
on the south coast at Worthing as the crisis deepened:

During the first three days of August everybody was asking 'Will England join in?' and we were beginning to dread that we should have to be ashamed of our country – or rather of our government. It was the German invasion of Belgium, of course, that decided it.

We were listening to the band on the parade on the night of August 4th – there was a queer, subdued flutter of excitement among the crowd, and we youngsters guessed that something important was happening. The band struck up – for the first time – the National Anthems of the Allies, except the Belgian, which nobody knew. At the close of 'God Save the King', there was an outburst of cheering, and caps thrown in the air. We raced home to learn the news, which was contained in a single headline: 'British Ultimatum to Germany – To Expire at Midnight'. So it was decided. And that night we discussed the future of the world in the light-hearted spirit of youth, never dreaming what it would mean to this dear England of ours.

Doubts about British participation largely faded the moment the first German boot touched Belgian soil on 4 August. Thus even the hitherto anti-war G. M. Trevelyan would shortly concede that 'the present awful struggle is to save England, Belgium and France from the Junkers, and to save our island civilization, with its delicate fabric, from collapse'.

That this was the crucial factor in bringing Britain into the conflict is evident from Asquith's comment on hearing the news: 'This simplifies matters.' Grey later admitted that without it the country 'would have been split from end to end'.

The future Prime Minister Neville Chamberlain is rarely thought of as being ardent for war, but even he was moved to comment, when contemplating the thought that Britain might not have come to Belgium's aid: 'It fairly makes one gasp to think that we were within a hair's breadth of eternal disgrace.'

On the evening of 4 August Asquith spoke to a packed House of Commons reiterating Britain's demand that a satisfactory answer on the matter of Belgian neutrality should be received from Germany before midnight – midnight in Berlin, eleven o'clock in London. As he uttered the 'fateful and terrible words' implying that there would be war if no such answer was received, the ranks of members responded with wave upon wave of cheering, which continued and increased as he rose and walked slowly down the floor of the House.

The scene was witnessed by his second wife, Margot, who, when all the members had poured out of the House and the building had gone quiet, went down to the Prime Minister's room. Here, however, there was none of the euphoria that had characterized the public occasion in the Chamber upstairs.

> For some time we did not speak. I left the window and stood behind his chair:
> 'So it is all up?' I said.
> He answered without looking at me:
> 'Yes, it's all up.'
> I sat down beside him with a feeling of numbness in my limbs and absently watched through the door the backs of moving men. A secretary came with Foreign Office boxes; he put them down and went out of the room.
> Henry sat at his writing-table leaning back with pen in his hand . . . What was he thinking of? . . . His sons? . . . My son was too young to fight; would they all have to fight? . . . I got up and leant my head against his: we could not speak for tears.
> When I arrived in Downing Street I went to bed.
> How did it . . . how could it have happened? . . .
> I looked at the children asleep after dinner before joining Henry in the Cabinet room. Lord Crewe and Sir Edward Grey were already there and we sat smoking cigarettes in silence; some went out, others came in; nothing was said.
> The clock on the mantelpiece hammered out the hour, and when the last beat struck it was as silent as dawn.
> We were at War.

Meanwhile, Winston Churchill had been waiting in one of the great rooms of the Admiralty, where the windows were thrown wide open to the summer night. At last above the almost palpable excitement of the nation's and the Empire's capital could be heard the chimes of Big Ben, heralding the vital hour. On the first stroke of eleven, wrote Churchill, 'a rustle of movement swept across the room. The war telegram, which meant "Commence hostilities against Germany", was flashed to the ships and establishments all over the world.'

It was the end of certainty; it was the beginning of uncertainty.

A new, dangerous era had dawned. Sir Edward Grey was no great wordsmith in the class of such as Churchill or Asquith, but he has one famous statement to his credit that will for ever be associated with this remarkable period of twentieth-century history. Looking out of his Foreign Office window on the evening of 3 August, he saw the gas lights being extinguished in the streets below and commented, sadly: 'The lights are going out all over Europe. We shall not see them lit again in our lifetime.'

Reactions to the declaration of war were inevitably mixed. While there was much enthusiasm it was far from universal. 'There were no great demonstrations of excitement,' the Revd James Mackay commented, writing in Newcastle in the early hours of 5 August: 'The people took things very calmly.' He himself felt dismayed but determined:

> War with all its horrors is upon us. The nations, enlightened as they are, are ready to fly at each others' throats. The Prince of Peace is forgotten. Oh! How this must wound his great loving heart.
>
> Nevertheless now that war is with us the thing we must do, however much we deplore it, is to fight and we must fight to win. Germany must be so utterly defeated as to be reduced to a second rate power.
>
> Oh! How one grudges the fine young lives that must be lost both here and in France, Russia and Germany. May God's will be done in all this.

Also on 5 August, at a barracks in Scotland where precautionary mobilization was already under way, an infantry officer, Captain J. L. Jack, wrote thoughtfully in his diary:

> About 2 a.m. I receive a telegram stating that Britain declared war on Germany at midnight . . .
>
> One can scarcely believe that five Great Powers – also styled 'civilized' – are at war, and that the original spark causing the conflagration arose from the murder of one man and his wife . . . It is quite mad, as well as being quite dreadful . . .

Some days later a similar viewpoint would be expressed by a young Englishman who would never, even had he wanted, have the opportunity of taking part in the war because of circumstances beyond his control. On 14 August Edgar Wright wrote to his mother:

> It is difficult to believe that half the world is at war – it is absolute folly and childishness. I cannot for the life of me understand how the Liberal government came to declare war. It seems incredible. Naturally the Germans are bitter about it – it seems such a cowardly action. England had everything to lose and nothing to gain by a declaration of war. However it is no use discussing this now.

# CHAPTER THREE

---

# GETTING BACK HOME

THE OUTBREAK OF WAR in the middle of summer inevitably created formidable problems for people holidaying, studying, or indeed working abroad, who suddenly found themselves confronted by the possibility of being stranded on a continent in conflict. As frontiers closed and former friendly powers became alien ones overnight the alarming thought arose that it might be difficult, if not impossible, to get back home. This would prove a particular hazard in the case of men of military age, or those near enough to it to look like potential soldiers. Edgar Wright was in that category. Adding to the anxiety of many was the fact that, though thousands carried passports, it was not mandatory to do so, and so thousands of others did not. There was something attractive and invigorating about being able to cross the Channel and travel around Europe without being encumbered by tedious documentation. In a world that largely believed in free trade the free passage of the individual was something to enjoy, even celebrate. Now suddenly this breezy attitude seemed out of fashion. Perhaps one should have acquired a passport after all.

A remarkable case was that of John Andrew Jellicoe, a second cousin of Admiral Sir John Jellicoe, who had been a longstanding choice to command Britain's fleet in case of war. Aged seventeen and a pupil of Bradfield College in Berkshire, John Jellicoe had spent the summer learning German at Celle, in Westphalia, when the increasing gravity of the international situation prompted him to cable his parents asking for money so that he could take prompt steps to return. The three other students with him, two English boys and one French, thought the crisis would soon blow over and opted to stay. Jellicoe's parents also took the situation lightly, even suggesting he should take a local job if his money ran short. His younger brother Geoffrey, however, thought differently and wrote to his parents from his school in Cheltenham arguing, 'if you haven't sent the money I should certainly send some out at once'. Unfortunately the banks closed just as the Jellicoes decided to accept their younger son's advice, and they were reduced to collecting money from friends and neighbours in order to cable an appropriate sum. At last, after a series of anxious visits to the post office in Celle, John Jellicoe was able to lay hands on the cash sent to him and entrain with his baggage and bicycle, although both had to be left behind when after several changes he had to fight his way on to a crowded train heading for the border. What happened then was written down many years later not by Jellicoe himself but by his widow:

> Eventually they got to the last halt before the border and the passengers were lined up. Passports not being obligatory in those days he had not got one. All passengers were checked and those with passports were allowed to stay on the train and continue their journey. Those without were turned off the train for interrogation. An official came down the line and got as far as the woman immediately in front of him who showed her passport. In those days it was a large sheet of paper not in book form. Having seen hers the official's attention was momentarily called. Quickly the woman turned to Jellicoe and handed him her passport and said 'Be folding that up'. Slowly he folded the passport and seeing him doing this the official passed on to the next passenger. Thus he got over the border and so home.

The telegram announcing his return 'dirty but well', preserved with the rest of the family papers, carries the significant date '4 August', the date on which Britain formally entered the war. After joining the Inns of Court Officers' Training Corps in October 1914, John Jellicoe was commissioned in February 1915, subsequently serving in France and India. A postscript to his widow's account states: 'The French boy and the other two English boys at Celle were interned for the duration of the war during which one of them died.'

* * *

Two days before John Jellicoe reached his destination, the young governess Beatrice Kelsey, who had heard the shocking news of the Sarajevo assassination while at lunch in Budapest with her Austrian family, began her own escape attempt. Leaving Vienna on 2 August armed with a first-class ticket for Charing Cross, she found herself on board a succession of slow, extremely overcrowded trains –'always troop trains, loaded with soldiers and their baggage' – sometimes falling in with other would-be escapers, sometimes travelling alone, even at one time parched with thirst having had nothing to drink for twenty-four hours. There were frequent disturbing incidents:

> 2.45 a.m. August 5th. Train from Würzburg to Aschaffenburg. Quite alone packed in with soldiers in the dark until daybreak. Search for a spy at 5 a.m. He was found (Frenchman, under cover of Red Cross) and was led off to be shot. Also a girl who had locked herself in the waiting room, a Belgian.

At Aschaffenburg she saw a notice stating that England had declared war and that English nationals had until ten o'clock that night to be out of the country. She managed to get on a train for Frankfurt leaving at 9 a.m.:

> Found an Englishman (recognized by golf clubs) in my compartment. Got to Frankfurt at 12 o'clock, hopeless as to how to get on. Very hungry, having eaten only scraps since Monday night (Aug. 3rd).

Later, on 6 August, she was able to attach herself to an English group of about seventy with whom she journeyed overnight to Mainz, arriving at 4.15 a.m.:

> At 5 o'clock we were all marched in to the commandant and examined. Were given a pass on the train and all travelled 4th class from Mainz to Bingenbrucke. There we were all hauled out by soldiers, to the jeers of the reservists. I had a narrow escape from a German bayonet, in trying to shout a message to Mr Brodhead who was on the train. We were told we should be kept in Bingen till the war was over. Cheerful prospect! At 10 o'clock we were marched off under guard to a little hotel and told to stay in our rooms there. We were guarded by sentries all night – Next morning we were searched – Saw a man shot on the bridge. Also two motorists and began to realize our desperate plight.
> Got an order from the commandant to go to Cologne that night. Marched to the station under guard and put on the train. We were taken up the left bank of the Rhine – everywhere trains and all in total darkness. Thousands of men, siege guns etc. going to the front. We

were packed in amongst the men and did not speak or move, for fear of violence.

They received somewhat better treatment in Cologne, where they were taken to a large barracks. The officer in charge, 'who spoke perfect English – had been at Oxford', was 'quite decent', while a soldier assigned to escort them told her that he had lived in Sheffield for three years and was engaged to an English lady who had left the city only the previous Sunday. 'He asked us to send her news of him (I afterwards wrote to her).'

At Cologne they were told a Dutch boat was being chartered to take them down the Rhine to Holland. As in so many other cases profiting from American help – the United States being a neutral power unaffected by the exigencies of war was in a position to offer legitimate assistance – they had their passports visa'd by the American Consul in Cologne, while the Dutch Consul gave them the necessary permission to travel. They boarded the boat at 4 a.m. on the morning of the 11th:

> *Aug. 11th.* My 27th birthday! We left Köln at 5 a.m. thinking we are at last getting towards safety. Got to Düsseldorf at 8 a.m. and were held up for an hour by dense river fog. Went on and at 10.30 were chased by a tug and told to return to Düsseldorf.
>
> We felt we were going to be taken back to Köln.
>
> After much talking and a guard coming on board, as well as the detectives who were conducting us into Holland, we were allowed to proceed – but at Wesel, after a delay of an hour, the military came on board and ordered all men between 18 and 40 to go ashore. We had only a few minutes to say good-bye to them.

After a bitterly cold, foggy night anchored out in the river, the remainder of the party continued, reaching Rotterdam the following afternoon. Here they boarded a Great Eastern Railway vessel bound for Harwich, gratified to have 'a glorious crossing with no unusual happenings'. Beatrice Kelsey achieved her goal of reaching England on 13 August, after taking eleven days over a journey that would normally have taken under two.

\* \* \*

It was on 14 August that Edgar Wright wrote his letter to his mother cursing the folly and childishness of Britain's entry into the war; in it he also admitted the end of his hopes of returning home before the end of it.

Wright, travelling with a business companion, had been in Vienna when the crisis began and was as eager as almost everybody else in his situation to make his way home. Like Beatrice Kelsey, he availed himself of the aid generously offered by Britain's fellow democracy across the Atlantic. 'The American Medical Association of Vienna got tickets for a large party, for London via Ostende and Dover,' he told his mother in his letter. 'We got two tickets from men who decided to stay. Reached here all right, but they would not let us go any further, so about fifty of us put up at this hotel.' The elegant headed notepaper of the Hotel Stuttgarter Hof, Frankfurt am Main, on which he wrote his letter, indicated where Mrs Wright's son was effectively trapped.

In his letter, which he entrusted to a friendly doctor with an American passport to take to England, he explained the predicament in which he and countless of his compatriots now found themselves:

> Naturally the authorities won't let Englishmen go back to augment the British forces. An Englishman with a German wife got police passes yesterday through to Holland, but I suppose they thought he was above the age limit – name of Poole, of Horley. A married couple called Bainton, from Gosforth, are here with us. The police say the lady can leave, but not her husband. If Mrs. Bainton does try to get through, I will send another letter by her.

Despite his unpropitious circumstances he urged his mother not to lose heart:

> Now, my dear Mother, you really must not worry! There is not the slightest occasion for it. I am probably safer here than you are in England. I am in very good health, am having a holiday, and have freedom of the city, which is the most beautiful one I have seen. They may possibly keep us here till the end of the war. Even so you needn't worry – the people are treating us kindly enough. I shall have an opportunity to learn German. Now, even if you don't hear from me again, there is no need to worry about it. It may not be possible to get word through after the Americans have left, but you can rest assured I shall be all right.

Wright, like Edgar Bainton, who was a noted composer, would remain in Germany far longer than either of them could have imagined in August 1914 – spending most of his time in the famous internment camp at Ruhleben, Berlin, which housed so many intellectuals, academics and artists that it was to become almost a kind of barbed-wire university. They would be held there until 1918.

\* \* \*

The problems of getting back to Britain were not confined to those caught in actual or potential enemy territory. On 2 August a young Edinburgh-based actor named William Armstrong wrote a deeply troubled letter to his girlfriend from Lucerne, Switzerland, from which it is clear that returning home even from a traditionally neutral country, far from being routine, had already by that date become a matter of formidable difficulty. He wrote his letter on the special notepaper of the place where he was staying: The Chalets, Seeburg, Lucerne, its telegraph address, 'Polytechnic, Lucerne', possibly suggesting that this was a teaching establishment, or an actors' summer school, where Armstrong had been working either as performer or instructor, or possibly both:

> Angel,
>     Worry about work and one's future is at present over as the war is the one and only thought I have on my mind at present. Things are terribly serious and the question is how we are to get back safely to London. Today there is not a single route to England open and the people are sleeping in Basle streets waiting for trains to take them back home. Lucerne is empty and the hotels are shutting up today when usually the season is at its height and Lucerne is crammed to excess with visitors. The Swiss troops are mobilizing all over the country and the new lounge here at the Chalets is full of soldiers. Last night only forty of four hundred people of our Saturday arrivals reached here and at two in the morning after having had to walk four miles with their luggage. The Ostend people were sent back to London from Brussels and we have no idea where the Paris party of a hundred people are as the wires and phones are monopolised by the military. The most serious thing is that our food supplies are very limited and we are already having meals cut down. Then too the Swiss people are for some silly reason down on the English and we are

feeling the antipathy of the Swiss staff here and the atmosphere is very strained. Don't know what is going to happen and the news that Germany has declared war on Russia today is the beginning of the war proper. Don't know when this letter will get through to you. It is all so unexpected and incredible.

Thanks most awfully for all your letters, angel. I will answer them later but at present I have the war on my nerves to a ridiculous extent.

Yours only and ever

In fact William Armstrong, like John Jellicoe and Beatrice Kelsey, though unlike the unfortunate Edgar Wright, also got back home. However, whereas his first letter was deeply private, a later letter describing his and his fellow-Britons' ordeal was printed at considerable length in *The Times*, turning him almost into a one-day national hero. As if sensing the opportunity of a larger stage, the style of the writing rose to the grandeur of the occasion. Hence this rich opening paragraph:

Imagine, if you can, so sensational a headline as 'Ten Thousand British Tourists Marooned on the Island of Switzerland', and the outcry against such an atrocious geographical 'howler'. Nevertheless, during these last weeks that land of the Alps has proved a veritable island to many thousands of holiday-makers for around its shores a great sea of warring nations has thundered, and there lay no safe passage to the homeland. The sound of the cannon of France and Germany came echoing through Basle, making that great junction a virtual 'cul-de-sac'. Austria was a battlefield, and Italy had closed its sea doors of escape. Some courageous voyagers risked a way of escape by Southern Switzerland and France; but the risks seemed tremendous, and we, the less adventurous, heard breathless rumours of nights passed at primitive frontier stations, of forced marches with luggage, and the melodramatic arrested as spies. For a brief time panic was imminent, but realizing the futility of such attempts, we resigned ourselves to the waiting, consoled by the intelligence that the British Government knew of our condition, and would ultimately arrange for our safe transport.

Meanwhile, 'Repatriation Committees' were set up, with 'our wants and means pigeon-holed and labelled in the most organized of methods'. At last there came the news that the 'refugee' trains would begin running from 22 August:

> Excitement and happiness were intense, and as the ten thousand expected to go back by the first train, a vast 'weeding out' was essential. The most urgent cases were allowed to return by the first train. And many of those were full of tragedy and loss of work and even destitution; but this train did not contain the lady who 'simply had to go back because there was a new maid coming', or the man 'who had to see the dentist because a tooth has lost its gold filling'.

One of a Lucerne group of a hundred, Armstrong was able to leave by the third train on Wednesday 26th. It was joined at Olten by another three hundred from Zurich, and at Geneva by a further four hundred from the Oberland. The complete party, eight hundred strong, left Geneva in a special 'Government Train', and travelling via Lyons, Paris, and Folkestone reached London on Friday, 29 August, after an ordeal lasting sixty hours. But this was no ordinary train journey. Every nook and cranny of space was occupied: 'Everything was organized to the last seat, each traveller being given a definite place which he was compelled to occupy. There was no chance of the old dodge of "one seat for myself, one for the luggage and one for my feet". Soon we had all amiably adapted ourselves to "eight in a carriage".' But if what was happening inside the train was unusual, outside it was almost beyond belief; if the Swiss had been difficult and suspicious, the French, by now their fellow belligerents, offered an unforgettable contrast:

> All along the route the enthusiasm was unexpectedly intense. Every wayside station had its little group of enthusiasts. A small child of three waved its baby fist and lisped '*Vive l'Angleterre*'. At a window an old Frenchwoman is throwing us rapturous kisses. The soldiers are everywhere along the line, and they raise their caps with a smile and a cheer.
>
> But the climax was reached when we passed under the arch of Lyons Station, for here a great crowd of townspeople, military, and railway officials awaited us and cheered us vociferously. They joined us in the thrill of the '*Marseillaise*', and then followed a scene of the wildest hurrahs and handshakes, and the ever present '*Vive l'Angleterre*'. The wonder of it all caught our hearts, and one was not ashamed of tears.

How good it was to be allied to such people. One dared not think what the journey would have been had England stood aloof from battle. We could never have looked a Frenchman in the face.

Reaching the French capital, they were warmly welcomed by the British Committee in Paris, which had laid out a great stretch of tea tables to offer the homebound voyagers welcome and appropriate refreshment. At Pontoise their train halted next to a train of French soldiers: a signal for more expressions of *entente cordiale* and patriotic enthusiasm:

> One gallant throws some autumn flowers into our carriages. '*Où allez-vous?*' [Where are you going?] we ask, and the answer comes back, '*Pour faire la soupe avec la tête de Guillaume*' [To make soup out of Kaiser Wilhelm's head]. A wild shriek of laughter greets the soldier's answer, and he points with much humour to a chalked inscription across his horse van, 'Berlin. *Aller et retour*' ['Return ticket to Berlin'.] They are rich in humour, these French *paysans*.

So to Dieppe, where as they reached the harbour and struggled on to their ship there was 'a scene of much disorder, a struggling mass of weary people and deckchairs and a multitude of luggage'. All berths were soon filled, leaving hundreds to use their cases as impromptu seating accommodation or to stretch out shamelessly on the decks, while others sought hotel rooms on shore as they were not due to sail till the following day. At last the ship vibrated to the thunder of her engines and her bows turned towards the open sea:

> The morning sunlight is yellowing the Dieppe cliffs as we pass out of the old harbour. Every window on shore seems to have its cheering occupants, the siren shrieks its warning . . . again the *Marseillaise*, and the waving of flags innumerable, and the Channel is ours. His Majesty's Royal Navy being required elsewhere, grumbling old ladies looked in vain for the expected escort of battleships and torpedoes and aircraft. Some of us grow tremulous at the thought of floating mines. Folkestone at last, and then that London which in our exile men had told us was a city of the dead, welcomed us once more as of old.

This clearly was not just a homecoming, more a triumph.

* * *

If William Armstrong and his fellow-travellers were desperate to reach England, there were others equally anxious to leave England for France. It might be assumed that transit from one close ally to another would be straightforward, but it did not so prove in the case of a Frenchwoman, Mrs Céline Williams, and her companion Nelly, attempting to visit relatives in Normandy in the first days of the war. She described their experiences in a letter written to the Revd W. L. and Mrs Walter of Sutton Mandeville, near Salisbury, though their journey seems to have begun in Birkenhead.

> We left Woodside by the 40 year old express train to Euston, at 10.45 a.m. Had a comfortable journey as hardly any one seemed to travel in our direction. On arrival we went to Charing X to get information as to further progress. I interviewed a courteous gentleman (I heard him speak 4 languages in 10 minutes), he told me that on the 3rd, they yet issued tickets to Paris, but they had received orders not to do so anymore. In my precarious state of health, I intended spending the night in London, but when he said there was a boat to Boulogne that night, and that no one knew how soon the service would have to be stopped, I decided to push on at all hazard.
>
> We had to take the train to Folkestone by assault, as it was packed by all my French boys going home to their different companies' depôts. Their English friends gave them a rousing 'send off', you never heard such a noise; and they kept such a cheery din on board the boat, that we never took any notice of the sea.

At Boulogne the two women were forced to stay the night in a railway carriage in a siding, there being neither transport nor porters to carry their baggage. They spent the next day in a state of exhaustion going from one official to another, endlessly queuing to obtain the necessary travel papers, which then had to be taken for signature by the major of the garrison 'who was all powerful, all France being under martial law'.

At last by devious means they managed to board a train for Caen on 6 August, together with what she described as

> A downright bonnie lot of men! Most of them between 30 and 38. They wanted to give up their smoking, but I would not hear of it; they told me a lot about themselves. There was amongst them a fellow

with a *mèche de cheveux rouges sur le front* [a lock of red hair], who
evidently had been drinking and was very excited; his comrades told
me he had his Morocco medal, and was threatening great things
against the Germans, and the speaker added: 'I wish we had a few
thousand like him!' Then the same speaker added: *'Nous allons vous
appeler Maman'* [we're going to call you Mum], so of course they
were called *'Mes enfants'* [my children] by me after that.

Attempting to get something to eat during a break in the journey at
Serquigny, she succeeded only in purchasing two pork chops and
some unappetizing bread from a cafe, but on returning to the station
noted that

the place was alive: all the women had bouquets of flowers and told
me they were for the English soldiers who were expected to pass
through the station a little later on.

In fact the visit was only a temporary one, doubtless undertaken
for reasons of family solidarity and reassurance at a time of crisis. On
17 September Céline Williams returned to England to resume her
work in Birkenhead, and it was from there that she wrote her account
on 3 December, by which time her adventures were well behind her,
but clearly still intensely vivid in the mind.

* * *

One of the most dramatic safe returns of this anxious time was
that of the crew and passengers of the Union Castle Line steamer, the
SS *Galician*, which sailed from Cape Town for the United Kingdom
on 28 July. Her crew did not hear the news of the outbreak of hostilities until 7 August, when, as the ship was passing close to the Ivory
Coast, she received a wireless signal transmitting the disturbing
message: 'Germany has declared war.' Being alone and unprotected
out in the Atlantic Ocean in a conflict which most people expected
to be settled at sea was not a happy predicament for a vessel of one
of the leading protagonists, though there was little response her
captain could make other than sail on at maximum speed and hope
for the best. But at least something might be done to avoid advertising her presence. He had a card printed carrying the following
advice:

Owing to a state of war existing between England and Germany, passengers are kindly requested, as a precautionary measure, to draw the curtains over the port-hole at night, and not to leave the cabin light burning when not in use.

*8th August, 1914*

The card survives attached together with some letters, photographs and newspaper cuttings in the collection of a Mrs Ada Calwell, the newly wed Afrikaner wife of an Irish doctor, Gault Calwell, who had been working for some time in South Africa and had now decided to return home. The couple were en route for Belfast, where Mrs Calwell's mother had taken up residence, and it was to her that Ada's letters were addressed.

In her first, started on 8 August, Ada Calwell describes what would be the 'first scare' of many:

> Heard the bugle and bells ringing, and the patter of running feet, then the engine seemed to stop, so I rushed out and saw men rushing up and down the stairs with life belts on. I don't know what I thought. Imagined the German fleet was in sight or something. However I found it was only a fire drill. So we watched them swing out the boats. It was quite interesting.

Union Castle liners could provide passage not only for citizens of British South Africa but of German South-West Africa as well, routine in normal times but a somewhat disturbing anomaly in time of war:

> We have on board a German, Mr Gers, and his wife from Upington, he knows Mrs Hughes. He is such a funny stick, says he is not a German any more. They got up a sort of imitation army, wore high paper caps, and Captain Gers marched them along the deck at one o'clock. It was the source of much amusement, wonderful what childish things people do on board ship. They are still at it. Gault [Ada's husband] is medical officer, and everybody is getting his particular place in the ranks of 'The Gallant Galicians'. Last night it was a sort of leapfrog business.

By 10 August, however, this curious initiative failed, the situation having become 'too serious now to joke about'. The ship sailed on in an atmosphere of mounting rumour and speculation, until on the afternoon of the 14th, by which time they were approaching the Canary Islands, a huge four-funnelled liner appeared on the horizon and steamed rapidly towards the *Galician*. This was, however, no ordinary liner but the German armed merchant cruiser *Kaiser Wilhelm der Grosse*, still retaining her peacetime profile but fitted out as a man-of-war.

They were soon to discover how the *Galician* had been found. The ship's wireless operator – referred to somewhat scathingly by Mrs Calwell as 'the Marconi fellow' – had wired ahead to Tenerife stating that perhaps the ship might want to call there for coal, and had asked 'Was the coast clear?':

> The German boat picked up the message, and said yes, and that they were the *Carnarvon*. So you see how beautifully we were trapped. When the German boat came in sight our Marconi man tried to send an SOS for help to Tenerife; of course the boat caught the message, and said 'Follow us, or we sink you. Wireless, and we sink you.' Our silly old captain gave orders to send a wireless, but the first officer (a real hero) pulled him out by force. Our next message was to take down our wireless.

Perhaps because it was so early in the war, as the two ships came to anchor only a small distance apart, the reaction of the passengers on the *Galician* suggests that, far from being fazed by the occasion, they seem rather to have enjoyed it. A boat put out from the enemy ship:

> It was most exciting seeing them row from their boat to ours. The cinematograph was going all the time, the fellow got quite a number of jolly good films. The two German officers looked very smart as they walked on to the deck. They got all the papers, then the crew got orders to line up, then passengers. The officers (German) counted them all, called us all up by name. Gault and I went down to our cabin, packed a few things, in case there was any chance of taking them with us. The most pathetic incident of the afternoon was two of our passengers being taken prisoner. One first class, one third class. The former was Lieutenant Dean, a young fellow going on a holiday, we all shook hands with him and cheered him, as they rowed away we sang 'Hip, hip hurrah!' It sounded grand.

> Well! Orders from the Germans that we are to be ready at dawn tomorrow, packed and all.

An interview with her husband printed in a Belfast newspaper carried a slightly more colourful version of this episode:

> The lieutenant was one of the jolliest of our party and his removal sent a sort of thrill through the ship. Those who knew him felt the severance keenly – he was such a splendid fellow. When he and his fellow-prisoner [an Army private] were being conducted down the gangway our passengers encouraged them by singing 'For they are jolly good fellows', winding up with a mighty 'Hip, hip hurrah!'. They never flinched in the slightest degree, and the parting salutation was maintained until they passed out of sight.

Shortly afterwards both ships pulled up their anchors and steamed off, on, for the *Galician*, a quite different course, the general impression among the passengers being that they were heading towards the island of St Vincent off the West Coast of Africa. Strict instructions had been left as to how the ship should proceed. Ada's account continues:

> They gave orders there were to be no lights at all except the light at the back. They followed us, also minus a single light. Every porthole was blocked shut. I wish you could have peeped into our cabin while we were packing, the sweat pouring down our faces. Gault was forced to strip. I heard this morning that there were others in the same garb, or minus. We slept in our clothes, or rather *nearly* all of us, and most of us on deck, on the chairs. Gault and I brought up our mattress, so we were fairly comfortable, the night seemed unending as we steamed along at top speed. I bet the old *Galician* has never gone so fast since the day she put out to sea, and I dare say the Germans thought we were crawling.

The general idea among the passengers was that the Germans would put them on board their ship and sink the *Galician*, though there was also a slight hope, or maybe a hopeful rumour, that some British cruisers might come to their aid and achieve a miraculous rescue. Certainly no one expected the denouement that actually occurred. Ada heard the startling news in the following manner:

> Gault went into a heavy sleep towards morning, and when the Steward came round saying 'Purser says passengers must be awakened', he could not wake up, so I went down to my cabin to

wash my face, and a little while after Gault came in and said, 'Old girl, we are released and can go on our course'. I could hardly believe my ears.

Summing up their ordeal later that day, Ada Calwell wrote:

> This is the Germans' signal to us this morning. 'Owing to your women and children, you are dismissed. Good bye.' The *Kaiser Wilhelm der Grosse* is a magnificent boat. The best in the world about 1907. They say she was a German American liner and was got ready in 24 hours, and cleared off before war was declared. She stands rather high in the water and every inch of her is black. She carried big guns, but not many, from what we could see, but she kept them well on us.
>
> Well, it wasn't the Captain who saved this boat. It was the Purser and Mr Gers, the German passenger, he was tactful and collected. When the Germans set foot on the *Galician* the Captain, shaking in his shoes, said 'What are you going to do with us? Are you going to sink us?' and the officer said, 'No, sir, we are not savages.' The officers were all fine. Mr Gers acted as interpreter, and had a good deal of fun out of it.
>
> It was a magnificent sight to watch the *Kaiser Wilhelm der Grosse* before daybreak, as she whirled round and just cut her way gracefully through the waves. We are all very anxious to know where she has gone.

The *Galician* had a hero's welcome on her return to home waters. Dr Gault Calwell told his newspaper correspondent:

> Entering the English Channel, we were literally surrounded by French and English battleships. They seemed to emerge from all quarters. The magnificent French cruiser *Gloire* came alongside our liner, but on being convinced that all was right we were permitted to proceed. During the entire route to Gravesend searchlights played on us from all quarters of the Channel, but we had no further interruptions. The voyage, with the exception of the incidents described, was a very pleasant one.

As for the *Kaiser Wilhelm der Grosse,* her wartime activities were over within the month, but if her career was brief, it was also not dishonourable. It is worth noting that, in a war so soon to be disfigured by atrocity, particularly German atrocity, the officers and crew of this German man-of-war behaved with great decency and compassion.

Confirmation that this was the case exists in the diary of a fishing captain from Grimsby – name unknown – whose boat, the SS *Tubal Cain*, had fallen prey to the *Kaiser Wilhelm der Grosse* in Icelandic waters on 7 August. Two officers came on board demanding the ship's papers and the crew were then transshipped in their own boats to the German liner. The fishing captain recalled:

> When we were all nicely on board, they fired on our ship [sinking her] after having forty five shots put into her, one of the officers coming to me saying she was British, she takes a lot of sinking, but I can't speak too highly of the Officers for their kindness both to me and my crew. We lived well and were treated with the best of respect, they all saying they were sorry they had to do it.

Conditions deteriorated as more ships were sunk and more crews brought on board. Hopes were raised and dashed, tempers frayed and there were serious irritations, but in the end on 26 August the German commander made one vital gesture of goodwill which guaranteed the survival of his prisoners and much of his own crew. A collier had met the ship to replenish her fuel supplies:

> Towards noon we were ordered to our berths, they had sight of a British Cruiser and at 1.00 p.m. we were all ordered on board the collier, and we steamed away, English prisoners and German sailors of the *Kaiser Wilhelm der Grosse*. We saw a lot of shooting as we steamed away, I myself feeling very sorry for all the Officers and the Commander who to the end proved to be a gentleman. And I think it was very plucky to fight a cruiser. I shook hands. They gave us very little time to get off the *Kaiser Wilhelm der Grosse*. We did not see the finish of the fight before they were out of sight.

The British cruiser was HMS *Highflyer*, armed with eleven 6-inch guns and nine 12-pounders, serving in the 9th Cruiser Squadron, against whose fire power no armed merchant cruiser could be expected to survive in a one-to-one sea fight. Severely disabled after a severe action, the *Kaiser Wilhelm der Grosse* was sunk by her own crew to avoid capture.

It would seem that the chances are high that the young lieutenant and the private soldier taken off the *Galician* were among those prisoners transferred to the armed merchant-cruiser's collier before the action took place.

# CHAPTER FOUR

# THE SHOCK OF WAR

SO WAR BEGAN and the peoples of the now belligerent nations reacted in their own very different ways. Some notable voices spoke in protest. In Berlin, Albert Einstein was among the signatories of a 'Manifesto to the Europeans', designed as a response to the bombastically pro-war address 'To the World of Culture' signed by ninety-three intellectuals. In Vienna Sigmund Freud, after an initial surge of patriotism, came out against the concept of 'the warring state', which would inevitably allow itself every extreme of violence in the pursuit of its aims. The novelist and international cultural figure Romain Rolland pronounced himself devastated: 'I would like to be dead ... The European War is the greatest catastrophe in history, for centuries. It's the ruin of our holiest hopes for human brotherhood.' Bertrand Russell called Sir Edward Grey 'a warmonger' and denounced the war as 'the result of a failure to pursue a rational policy of appeasement towards Germany'. But these were largely voices against an unstoppable tide. Even such normally cautious prophets as H. G. Wells endorsed the war with something approaching zest; he wrote in the *Daily News* later in August: 'I find myself enthusiastic for this war against Prussian militarism. We are, I believe, assisting at the end of a vast, intolerable oppression upon civilization.'

In St Petersburg, strange frenzies afflicted elements of the population. A woman in a crowded street, seeing a young army officer in uniform, tore her dress at the collar, fell on her knees with a loud cry and pressed her naked breast against the soldier's dusty boots. 'Take me!' she cried. 'Right here, before these people! Poor boy ... you will give your life ... for God ... for the Tsar ... for Russia!' Another shriek and she fainted; it must be assumed the young officer was not able to take advantage of her patriotic offer.

Sergei Kurnakov, who recorded this event, also witnessed a sustained attack on the German Embassy, a 'great greystone monstrosity', as he described it, 'facing the red granite of St Isaac's Cathedral'. The steady hammering of axes on metal made him look up at the Embassy roof, which was 'decorated with colossal figures of overfed German warriors holding bloated carthorses' and where 'a flagstaff supported a bronze eagle with spread wings'.

> Several men were busily hammering at the feet of the Teutons. The axes were hammering faster and faster. At last one warrior swayed, pitched forward, and crashed to the pavement one hundred feet below. A tremendous howl went up, scaring a flock of crows off the gilded dome of St Isaac's. The turn of the eagle came; the bird came hurtling down, and the battered remains were immediately drowned in the nearby Moika river.
>
> But obviously the destruction of the symbols was not enough. A quickly organized gang smashed a side door of the Embassy.
>
> I could see flashlights and torches moving inside, flitting to the upper storeys. A big window opened and spat a great portrait of the Kaiser at the crowd below. When it reached the cobblestones, there was just about enough left to start a good bonfire. A rosewood grand piano followed, exploded like a bomb; the moan of the broken strings vibrated in the air for a second and was drowned: too many people were trying to outshout their own terror of the future.

In Paris, by contrast, the mood was curiously muted. On the night of 1–2 August a journalist, Jacques Thibault, walking homeward past the cathedral of Notre Dame, saw that the great doors were wide open and the interior lit by hundreds of candles as the dark figures of young men queued outside the confession boxes. Proceeding on his way, when he reached the corner of the Quai de l'Horloge and the Boulevard du Palais, he found the boulevard virtually shaking with a continuous rumble, the sound of hundreds of marching men as regiment after regiment headed for the two railway stations linked with France's vulnerable frontiers, the Gare de l'Est and the Gare du Nord. There were no rifles garlanded with flowers, he noted, and there was no singing of patriotic songs.

The following morning large numbers of young couples waiting to get married queued outside the *mairies* of certain *arrondissements*, exemplifying the urge of countless young men about to be drawn into the conflict to seize the day because night might soon fall.

Emotions of a more visceral kind became apparent when various establishments with alien connections, such as the obviously Austrian Brasseries Viennois, were trashed by bands of young men to the sound of angry shouts and much shattering of plate glass.

Nationally, the patriotic spirit was roused in various ways. Thus the Maid of Orleans, Joan of Arc, famously France's champion against the English, who had burned her at the stake in the centre of Rouen, was immediately invoked as a rallying force against the Germans. Her defiant cry *'Dieu protège la France'*, 'May God protect France', was directed now not across the Channel but eastwards across the Rhine. Earlier in 1914 the cathedral church of St Etienne at Auxerre had commissioned a stained-glass window depicting St Joan directing military operations, its supporting 'text' being the statement attributed to her: 'I have been sent by God the King of Heaven to drive you out of all France.' The English were now France's friends; such mystic energy as the cult of St Joan might engender would be directed at driving out the Germans. Shortly the German bombardment of Reims Cathedral, where Charles VII had been crowned in 1429 in Joan's presence, would add fury to this change of focus.

Elsewhere in France local authorities in the south reported the return of large numbers of monks and priests expelled in an ecclesiastical clampdown in 1905 crossing the Spanish border eager to volunteer, while in the north a trainload of two to three hundred French deserters who had avoided national service during the previous ten years crossed into France from Belgium.

In Germany on 1 August massed crowds sang Martin Luther's great hymn: *'Ein Feste Burg ist unser Gott'*, 'A safe stronghold our God is still'. Since Luther had been both a great Christian and a great German, patriotism and Christianity were seen as being effectively one and the same. On 4 August – the day on which the British Government's ultimatum was being scrupulously ignored – Kaiser Wilhelm himself attended a special service in the cathedral in Berlin, where the preacher took his text from St Paul's Epistle to the Romans, chapter 8, verse 3: 'If God be for us, who can be against us?' The preacher summoned up the memory both of Luther and of the 'old heroes of 1813', who had famously defied the Emperor Napoleon a century earlier during the wars with post-revolutionary France. Crystallizing his message, he proclaimed: 'We march to the fight for our culture against unculture, for German morality against barbarity, for the free, German, God-fearing person against the instinct of the uncontrolled mass.'

All the nations involved entered the war convinced of the rightness of their cause, none more so than Imperial Germany. Thus whereas to the British the Germans came to be seen as dark-age barbarians, suitably derided as 'Huns', Germany interpreted herself as a modern, revisionist power believing in the free co-existence of peoples, and therefore fit to sponsor independence movements in India, Egypt or Ireland. Similarly, she had deduced from France's example that parliamentary government implied atrophy and disorder and so saw higher virtues in a disciplined monarchical state. A leading thinker of the time claimed: 'We signify the morning chorus of a new day not only for Germany, but also for mankind.'

In London vast crowds filled the streets, a particular focus being, inevitably, Buckingham Palace, where the King and Queen and Princess Mary were greeted with 'wild enthusiastic cheers' when they appeared on the balcony about 8 p.m. on 4 August. Reporting this, the *Daily Mirror* added the benign detail that 'seeing the orderliness of the crowd, the police did not attempt to force the people back and went away'. Later 'the cheering was renewed with increased vigour' and soon after 11 p.m., by which time Britain was at war, monarch and consort emerged again, this time with the Prince of Wales appearing in place of Princess Mary. The National Anthem, already sung earlier with much gusto, was sung once again, followed by 'hearty clapping and cheering'. Even after the royal party had withdrawn a number of enthusiasts stayed on 'keeping up the demonstration by shouting and waving flags'.

Crowds; everywhere crowds. There were those, however, for whom crowds were no index of general sentiment, whatever their motivation. Thus in the retrospective judgement of Wyndham Lewis, 'the war-crowds who roared approval of the declaration of war in 1914, were a jellyfish ... For some they were a Great People in their wrath, roaring before the God of Justice, for the blood of the unrighteous. That was not my view of the matter.' Similarly, Osbert Sitwell, who also saw the celebrations of the Armistice four years and four months later, who would fight in the coming war and lose many close friends during it, would look back from that vantage point on the events of 1914 and memorably describe the innocents of that August night as 'cheering for their own death'.

* * *

What helps to make the first weeks of war seem so poignant in retrospect is the naivety, the innocence of so many of the assumptions at that time. One particular obsession that arose was the idea of a rapid seizure of the enemy's capital city, in a gesture not dissimilar to claiming checkmate at chess, with the added implication that once the war got going it would all be quite easy. An officer of the Russian Imperial Guard asked the opinion of the Tsar's physician as to whether he should pack his full-dress uniform for the entry into Berlin at once or have it brought by the next courier heading for the front. For numerous members of the Russian military the standard wisdom was that they would be in Berlin in about six weeks. Osbert Sitwell, quoted above, after reporting as a reservist to the Grenadier Guards, went to say goodbye to friends already in arms and destined for the front, of whom many were never to return: 'Two or three of the most confident I heard instructing their servants to pack their evening-clothes, since they would need them in a week or two in Berlin.' In similar vein, an elderly colonel addressing men of a Territorial battalion in the Midlands told his men in simplistic terms that Britain's plan of campaign, so far as he understood it, was that Lord Kitchener was 'massing a great army to take Berlin'. The concept also caught the imagination of an early married volunteer who would emerge as one of Britain's lesser but still remembered war poets, Robert Vernède, who even before his actual enlistment addressed his wife with an optimistic ode beginning:

> What shall I bring you, wife of mine,
> When I come back from the war?
> A ribbon your dear brown hair to twine
> A shawl from a Berlin store?

Sadly he was not one of those who did come back from the war, nor did he ever get anywhere near Berlin.

At about the same time a German officer, Count Häseler, on leaving for the front, stated that he expected to take breakfast at the Café de la Paix in Paris by Sedan Day, 2 September, the date on which in 1870 Germany had achieved her greatest victory of the Franco-Prussian War. Trucks on some German troop trains carried such optimistic messages as *'Ausflug nach Paris'*, 'A Trip to Paris', almost as though advertising a relaxing weekend excursion.

Meanwhile, a future British lieutenant general, Tom Bridges, returning to his regiment from Brussels, where he had served as a military attaché, on being asked his views as to the war's duration, replied that there were 'financial reasons why the Great Powers could not continue for long'. His wisdom, he claimed, came from the Prime Minister, who had heard it from the former Secretary of State for War, Lord Haldane.

All this underlines the general view that apart from a handful of prescient pessimists everybody expected a short war. Kitchener would emerge firmly among the pessimists: the rapid seizure of the German capital was definitely not in his immediate plans. (That he made his views known very rapidly is evident from a letter by an officer of the Essex Regiment, Lieutenant Arthur Maitland, writing on 16 August: 'I suppose you have seen Kitchener's article in the papers, in which he states that he expects the war to last for 3 years; so don't expect to see me back before the end of 1917!!!') Similarly, Lieutenant General Sir Douglas Haig, about to exchange the post of Director of Training at Aldershot for that of Commander of I Corps in France, writing to Lord Haldane on 4 August, prophesied: 'This war will last many months, possibly years.'

Thus the views of two British notables. Elsewhere the truth would seem to be that certain key figures hoped for a brief war while sensing the reality might be different. 'We must prepare ourselves for a long campaign, with numerous tough protracted battles.' This was the assessment of the German Army Chief of Staff, Helmuth von Moltke, in 1912. Similar ideas pertained in Austria, though the most notable holder of this view was the recently deceased General Alfred von Schlieffen, German author of the famous 'Plan' proposing a swift knock-out attack against France so as to be able to concentrate on defeating the great Russian Bear to the east. He advocated a short war precisely because of his recognition that if it became a long one, Germany could not win. By contrast, the chief of the main staff of the Russian War Ministry from 1912 to 1913, General Mikhnevich, saw positive advantage in a protracted conflict, stating that 'time is

the best ally of our armed forces', since he knew it would take time
for the Russian bear to lumber into action.

'Over by Christmas' has long been one of the best-known phrases
to emerge from this first period of the war. The prevalence of this
belief has been recently challenged, though the future Prime Minister
Harold Macmillan can hardly be deemed to have been at fault when
he stated of himself and his Oxford contemporaries that 'the general
view was that [the war] would be over by Christmas', adding, 'Our
major anxiety was by hook or by crook not to miss it.' The other
memorable, much derided statement of the time was that made by
the German Emperor himself when he told a gathering of his troops
in the first week of August: 'You will be home before the falling of
the leaves.'

* * *

Some Britons were so eager to fight for the nation's cause that they
volunteered at the earliest possible moment. H. C. Meysey-Thompson,
a thirty-year-old ex-public-schoolboy commuting to London to a legal
post in the City, opened what would become his war diary with the
following entry:

> *August 5.* British ultimatum to Germany expired at midnight and war
> certain.
>
> Decide to try and join something, if possible 'Inns of Court' O.T.C.
> Go up to London by morning train and go straight to Inns of Court
> armoury in Lincoln's Inn. Find that adjutant has left for luncheon, so
> go and lunch at 'Cock', returning directly afterwards. Find a long string
> of would-be recruits, waiting to interview second-in-command. Finally
> my turn comes, and I go before an elderly gentleman disguised as a
> major, who, in spite of his uniform, boots and spurs, could be nothing
> but a Chancery barrister. My age, and the fact that it is twelve years
> since I performed any form of military duties make him reluctant
> to accept me, but I impress upon him that I was a marksman at
> Marlborough, and carefully suppress the fact that I never attained the
> rank of lance corporal, and am finally passed.

Applicants with medical qualifications had fewer problems. On
the same day, 5 August, a twenty-nine-year-old doctor, Frederick
Chandler, wrote to his family:

I went to the War Office today and in 2 to 3 hours everything
was fixed up. I am to go with the expeditionary force' as a Civil
Surgeon attached to R.A.M.C. rank as first Lieutenant.

I go to Aldershot Friday. I will write again from Belgium or
wherever I find myself.

Chandler was commissioned as a temporary lieutenant in the
Royal Army Medical Corps on Friday, 7 August; he would be on the
way to the front by late October.

Thirty-year-old Douglas Laidlaw, a married man with two children,
employed as an exchange dealer for a firm of stockbrokers in Glasgow,
was another instant volunteer. In spite of his family commitments he
was accepted at once, and, together with a number of other volunteers from the same background, spent the first night of his service at
a local recruitment centre. He wrote to his wife, Bertha, on 6 August:

Darling Wifie,
Just a wee line to tell you to keep up your pecker. I bet you will
feel a wee bit lonely all by yourself but we will be lonely because we
will miss you so much.

I felt awful at leaving you today altho perhaps I did not show it.

Well Wee Pet I will ring up in the morning and come up to see
you at dinner.

Don't worry about us, we will be all right.

Ta ta Dearest, all my love

Yrs

D

You are a brave wee girl.

As it turned out, he had barely uttered his dramatic farewell before
he was back home, having been being given a month to sort out his
affairs, and would not join his regiment in Inverness until 7 September. Together with most of his Stock Exchange colleagues, he became
a member of the Glasgow Stock Exchange Company of the 5th
Battalion, the Queen's Own Cameron Highlanders, which eventually
served in France as part of 9th (Scottish) Division.

\* \* \*

The patriotic surge following the outbreak of war affected many of
the nation's womenfolk as well as its men. One obvious way for

women of contributing at this early stage was to inspire, cajole or shame those of the opposite, allegedly stronger sex who did not immediately respond to the challenge of the hour, especially married men, who, unlike Douglas Laidlaw, showed hesitation before immediately rushing to the recruiting stations. As early as 28 August the *Daily Mail* carried the following advertisement:

> Doctor's wife, middle-aged, will undertake to perform the work of any tramway conductor, coachman, shop assistant, or other married worker with children, provided that the worker will undertake to enlist and fight for his country in our hour of need. The wages earned will be paid to the wife and family. Apply to Mrs Lowry, the Priory Terrace, Kew Green, London, SW.

The following day, under the heading 'RECRUITING DRIVE/ DOCTOR'S WIFE AS TRAMWAY CONDUCTOR, the newspaper expanded the story:

> 'This is a perfectly genuine offer', said Mrs Lowry's husband, Dr Ernest W. Lowry. 'We feel that recruiting is far from satisfactory, and that if women will offer their services in this way it will wake up the workers to the gravity of the situation.'

To add to the force of his wife's appeal the good doctor cited the example of the capital of the nation's prime enemy: 'I hear that women in Berlin are acting as tramway conductors and doing other labour left by men who have joined the colours.'

Certain women chose to help the national cause more simplistically by going about the streets handing white feathers to men not in uniform. To one civilian, F. A. Robinson, who was a close follower of the war and the war news, this amounted to 'a sort of persecution'. He instantly equated them with the suffragettes: 'These are the women, or some of them, who up till quite recently claimed equality with men, and who by their outrageous conduct and their immodest fashions in dress have done their utmost to bring themselves into contempt.' Yet there is no doubt that they had some success, though they could often anger men who had enlisted but were out wearing their 'civvy' clothes, or distress men who were medically unfit or whose offer to volunteer had been refused.

Other women showed their support of the volunteer spirit with equal fervour if somewhat less dramatically. Hence this letter written on 3 September by Douglas Laidlaw's aunt to his mother, Mary, her favourable attitude being guaranteed by the fact that her own son, Willie, had also joined up. Mary had sent Willie a modest cash donation to cheer him on his way. Aunt Eliza was charmed:

> Many thanks for the 20 shillings you have sent for Willie. It is indeed good of you and will be used to the best advantage for his comfort. Fancy Douglas going on active service. Well he is doing nobly and I am sure you are very proud of him tho' it is very hard for you and Bertha. Still we would not keep them back when the country needs them. I cannot understand any healthy young man who has no one dependant on him, holding back. You would think he would feel ashamed and indeed people here look very pointedly at young men not in uniform.

Supporting the nation's young heroes took many forms at this time. One practice taken up by countless women and endorsed by none other than Her Majesty the Queen was the knitting of socks, a practice which later had to be scaled down when it was realized it put thousands of professional hosiery workers out of a job. Douglas Laidlaw's Aunt Eliza was clearly an early and zealous practitioner in this field: 'Let me know whenever you can when Douglas is going away. I would like to send him some socks if he has not already got them I will have a pair finished tomorrow which would fit him and would soon get another pair done. I have another pair finished but they would be too large. They are warm socks which will be much appreciated when the weather gets cold.'

Aunt Eliza's zeal was such that she felt deeply frustrated at being of the gentler sex at this time of national emergency, a sentiment in which she was far from alone: 'Don't you sometimes wish you were a man and able to go and take a share in the fighting especially when you read of the shocking outrages on the poor Belgians. Well it is too terrible to dwell on, but as there is a God in heaven, a day of reckoning must come for Germany.'

A touching example of a letter echoing similar sentiments occurs in the papers of Eva, Marchioness of Reading, writing, in the second week of the war, to her future husband, the Hon. Gerald Rufus Isaacs, then already in uniform as a staff officer in the Territorials. Born Eva

Mond, daughter of the industrialist Sir Alfred Mond, and at this date only nineteen, she poured out her thoughts to her fiancé:

> My dear, you know that I am immensely proud of you, and I am glad to think that you are soldiering while we are at war; though you know how much I would give to have you with me. My darling I long for you more each day, and I wake in the night and call your name, but the knowledge that you are doing the only thing that is right and worthy of a man, makes it easier to bear being apart from you. I wish I could do soldier work; it would be infinitely preferable to sitting at home making shirts, but still one must do whatever is most useful.

*  *  *

Men and women could make a conscious decision to support the war. Horses could not, but they were vital to its prosecution. They were required not only for cavalry, but for artillery; in every army at this time they were the main 'motor' for moving the guns. It was clear from the first that they would be required in huge numbers. The requisitioning of animals deemed fit enough to bear the rigours of active campaigning began at once. Miss Mary Coules described in her journal an outing in Sussex in the second week of hostilities to observe the results of this, to many owners, deeply distressing policy:

> About the 9th August we went down to the Steyning Playing Fields to see the horses that had been commandeered. Poor beasties! Three magnificent hunters came in from Findon; it must have hurt someone to part from them . . . A rough-looking man came in with two cart-horses, and stayed for about half an hour patting them and giving them sugar. It was very sad. We took a photo, but it wasn't very good, as it had only just stopped raining.

In the cities horses were often taken at sight, in a manner reminiscent of the ancient press gangs seeking sailors for the Royal Navy. Rifleman Graham Williams, a member of the Territorial battalion proudly entitled the London Rifle Brigade, based at this stage in the premises of the Merchant Taylors' School in Charterhouse Square, described how this process worked in the capital:

> Small parties were sent out, under a man with some technical knowledge, to requisition horses for the Transport Section. They

could stop any likely-looking horse encountered, and remove it from the cart or van it had been drawing. The person in charge was given a receipt and a requisition order. The horses were brought back to Charterhouse Square, where they were inspected by a Vet, and, if suitable, were retained, the owners being paid compensation by the Government. Any not accepted were returned to the owners. The horses retained were exercised daily by being led round and round the Parade Ground – formerly the school playground.

The loss of their horses was felt grievously by their owners. George Orwell would always remember the sight of a London cabman bursting into tears when his companion – and his living – of many years was arbitrarily taken from him. But there was, inevitably, a greater shadow over the requisitioning of horses in the nation's cause. Used for the purposes of warfare, they would be as vulnerable as the soldiers who rode or drove them. One distinguished Englishman who was particularly distressed at the thought of their sufferings in the fighting to come was the composer Sir Edward Elgar, famous for his symphonies and oratorios but also destined to be strongly associated with the war effort as the creator of what would virtually become a second national anthem, 'Pomp and Circumstance March No. 1', better known as 'Land of Hope and Glory'.* He saw little glory in what would happen to the horses. He wrote to a friend on 25 August:

> Concerning the war I say nothing – the only thing that wrings my heart and soul is the thought of the horses – oh, my beloved animals – the men – and women – can go to hell; but my horses; I walk round and round this room cursing God for allowing dumb brutes to be tortured – let Him kill his human beings but – how CAN HE? Oh, my horses.

This attitude was not confined to civilians. There would be many cases of soldiers expressing their sadness and distress at the pitiful suffering of horses, and also in other fronts, such as Gallipoli, of mules, caught up in the perils of war.

\* \* \*

* This was not, however, a creation of the 1914 war; the words, by A. C. Benson, were written in 1902 for the coronation of Kind Edward VII.

For most men who enlisted in the first heady weeks there would be a long delay before they saw active service. In the case of the nation's regulars and reservists the prospect was much more immediate. Everywhere there was excitement and hope, yet even the best-case scenario inevitably envisaged much serious fighting, with many deaths, many wounded, many maimed, many missing, before the guns stopped firing. That this was evident to the civilians who could do little except watch their menfolk go amid the accumulating signs of war is clear from the diary of the Newcastle minister, the Revd James Mackay. He wrote under the date 5 August:

> Great excitement and sorrow prevails in the city. All the volunteers have been called out as well as reservists. Soldiers have been leaving the city in great numbers all day.
>
> Went down town to see if I could see any soldiers. The sights were heartrending. Weeping women everywhere. There are no great demonstrations of enthusiasm. Everyone feels the awfulness of the situation and a becoming gravity prevails.
>
> 800 soldiers have been quartered in Tilleys Rooms, Market Street. Armstrong College has been turned into a hospital. At St Thomas's church an unusual scene presents itself. The floor of the Church is littered with straw and about 50 or 60 Territorials are gathered there. Horses by the score are feeding in the church yards.
>
> At the barracks in the evening great crowds have gathered. Soldiers are leaving every hour.
>
> 10 p.m. Went down the city. Enormous crowds have gathered in the streets. At the Central Station there is nothing but soldiers going to and fro. No demonstrations of enthusiasm are given. There is an occasional cheer but things generally are grave.

How did the men themselves, who knew from the start that they might soon be called upon to face the enemy either in the field or at sea, respond to the prospect?

Inevitably there was a wide range of reactions. For one nineteen-year-old naval reservist, Sydney Miller, the thought of returning to the colours with the prospect of active service filled him with delight. Writing only a few months later in circumstances he could never have envisaged, as a result of which he would be out of action for the duration of hostilities, he began his account of his brief but dramatic encounter with the realities of war with an almost palpable nostalgia:

> It was the morning of August Bank Holiday 1914, 3 August – I shall never forget it – my cousin Laurie who was staying in London happened to be digging with me at the time, and as was usual on such occasions we were eagerly discussing the day's programme when a knock at my bedroom door brought us to the realization that it was 9 o'clock and we were still in bed. Hastily jumping out, I found a long, official-looking letter awaiting me, in the corner of which were the words 'Mobilization Order'. With a shout of expectancy I hastily tore open the envelope and eagerly read the letter, at the conclusion of which we both simply danced for joy. In fact for some little time we could not bring ourselves to dress but literally performing all sorts of capers in our pyjamas. However, hastily recovering ourselves, we were soon down to breakfast and in less than an hour we found ourselves at the RNVR Headquarters in Lambeth.

Miller was confident at this stage that he would be soon at sea, since he and his fellow-reservists were immediately given instruction in 'Gunnery and Ammunition, Helm and Compass, head and line; blocks and tackles, anchors and cables, knots and splices, bends and hitches, sails and rigging, cutter and whaler drill, ships routine and in fact, we touched lightly upon everything required of an able seaman'.

For Lieutenant Ralph Blewitt, of 39th Brigade, Royal Field Artillery, in the Army's 1st Division, writing from his barracks in Hampshire on 5 August to the lady he was wooing and who before long would become his wife, relief that the days of uncertainty were over combined with a breezy approach to the prospect ahead put him in the most positive of moods. (The lady in question, a Miss Denys [sic] Henderson of Henley-on-Thames, had recently given him a record of the popular song of the time 'Gilbert the Filbert', which he had had much delight in playing on his gramophone.)

> Well, we're at it in earnest I'm glad to say. They say (and you know how much these reports are worth) that the 2nd Division pushes off on the 6th day and the 1st Div on the 10th. Why don't you and Mrs H. roll over some afternoon. Bring a tea basket and I'll give you tea. Do roll up and hear Gilbert (an awfully good record I've

got). Well, Cheer up, May the best side win, Don't leave the soap in the bath, and God Save the King.

One day later, on 6 August, Lieutenant Colonel G. T. G. Edwards of the 20th Hussars wrote to his sister from the Cavalry Barracks, Colchester, in a less jocular mood but nevertheless one of serene confidence:

> We are pretty busy getting ready to be off but when we go I don't know – it will be a big show and I am likely to be able to go out as CO of the Regiment I have done all my services in. I would not change my position with anyone and please God I hope we shall be able to give a good account of ourselves. The war had to come and it looks as if it has come at the right time for us and I expect the Germans will have to take a back seat when it is all over.

Equally enthusiastic was Lieutenant Arthur Maitland, 2nd Battalion, Essex Regiment (already quoted in this chapter). Impatient at being sent to a country estate in Norfolk, Contessy Hall, considerably further from the war than where his battalion had originally mobilized, he wrote to his mother on 16 August:

> I ought not really to have put my address on the top of this letter, but as so many people know that we are here it does not really matter. I'm very fit except for a certain stiffness in my left arm when I was inoculated the other day; most of us have been done – against Typhoid. We are all hoping to get across to the other side at the end of this week, but we've been hoping that ever since we left Chatham!!

Other soldiers, particularly those with family anxieties, found the prospect of war distinctly less alluring. One young officer to whom the thought of parting from his wife and newly born son proved particularly distressful was Lieutenant Angus Macnaghten, 1st Battalion, Black Watch. A number of hurried, somewhat staccato letters survive from this first phase of the war as he wavered between a desire to see his wife before he left for the front and the anxiety that this might make his departure even more painful for both of them. Despatched south from their base in Scotland – 'a bad journey, 17 in the carriage and 2 reservists in the lavatory' – he wrote to her on the notepaper of Oudenarde Barracks, Aldershot, in an undated letter almost certainly sent in the first week of hostilities: 'I am posted to C Company and am busy getting to know the men. I expect I shall go out with the Regiment alright, so my sweetie must make up her mind to be a brave little darling.'

A second undated letter soon followed:

> I rather fancy we shall be off on Sunday, but nothing is certain. I shall try to come up and see you before we go, but if by any chance I don't see you, my dearest, it will be all for the best, and our thoughts will be with each other just as much.
>
> It is so horrid parting that it is almost better not to meet.

Another undated message stated, plaintively: 'Don't write too loving letters to husband as it makes him feel the parting more.'

It was only when he was in France that he could relax and come to terms with the situation: 'Feeling so cheerful, now the goodbyes are over.'

Yet the pain of saying goodbye could leave an unforgettable impression. Charles Rainbird, a reservist who went to war as a private in the 1st Battalion, West Yorkshire Regiment, left his wife and children in London immediately on being recalled to the colours, to travel to his depot in York. In the remarkable diary account which, not many months later, he wrote as a record for posterity in a German prisoner-of-war camp, he recalled the moment of parting:

> It was a tearful and heartbreaking farewell, at a time when a man finds out that all he loves in the world is being torn from him, and the woman knows that her husband, breadwinner and father of her children is leaving her at his country's call perhaps never to return. You readers who have never felt the loving arms of your little children round your neck, or the loving embrace of your wife, cannot understand the feeling. You readers, who have felt them, understand.

That status or rank did not necessarily reduce the emotional impact of going to war is evident from the attitude of the distinguished veteran of the 1898 Sudan Campaign and of the Boer War, Edward Douglas, Lord Loch, at forty-one substantially older than many of those around him. He would shortly become a senior staff officer but was at this stage second-in-command of the 2nd Battalion, the Grenadier Guards, sister battalion of the 1st Grenadier Guards, whose colour had been trooped just a few weeks earlier. His regular letters to his wife Margaret, the only daughter of the 5th Marquess of Northampton, sometimes at the rate of two per day, would make him one of the most incisive and revealing chroniclers of the war throughout his three years in France. He wrote his first war letter on 12 August while actually en route across the Channel:

> The dreaded moment has come and gone – I am so ashamed of myself for not being stronger and helping you more, but I love you so much that my feelings were stronger than my will. Now we must trust in God to bring us together again and preserve us through the interval. In spite of the Science of Evolution [and] the arguments of learned men I do believe that there is a supreme being in force whom we call God – and I further believe that God is all powerful that he can and does alter and change the destinies of men, when it is right to do so.

# CHAPTER FIVE

# OPENING GAMBITS

THERE WAS A FLURRY of political activity in Britain as hostilities began.

Kitchener's appointment as Secretary of State for War had been strongly promoted by a press campaign headed by the military correspondent of *The Times*, Colonel Repington. 'Lord Kitchener is at home,' he argued in the edition of 3 August, 'and his selection for this onerous and important post would meet with warm public approval.' Similarly, the editor of the *Westminster Gazette*, J. A. Spender, warned that if Kitchener were allowed to depart 'there would tomorrow be such an uproar against the Government as had not been known in our time'. Asquith's preference at this stage was for Lord Haldane, who had held the post between 1905 and 1912, but the case for Kitchener had obvious advantages. During a period when national unity was of paramount importance, it would promote the Government's and the country's cause if this central role were to be offered to someone outside politics who had the extra bonus of being a celebrated and admired soldier.

Of necessity, events moved quickly. On 4 August Kitchener asked the Prime Minister 'if there is any objection now to my making arrangements to leave for Egypt on the P. and O. [steamer] next Friday', i.e. the 7th. He was appointed the following day. Asquith noted that 'K. was, to do him justice, not at all anxious to come in, but when it was presented to him as a duty he agreed.' The attitudes of the two principals in this matter are worth recording. To Asquith, the appointment was 'a hazardous experiment, but the best in the circumstances, I think'. Kitchener's view, as pithily expressed in a private aside, was 'May God preserve me from the politicians.' Asquith's daughter Violet, who would become a well-known and popular figure under her married name of Lady Violet Bonham Carter, later recorded that 'the psychological effect of his appointment, the tonic to public confidence, were instantaneous and overwhelming'.

The nation's first naval moves did not depend on the dispositions being made in the panelled rooms of Whitehall. The Navy already had its own political leadership in Winston Churchill, on whose orders the Home Fleet (to be known henceforward as the Grand Fleet) prepared to steam to its assigned war station at the northern end of Britain – the great anchorage in the islands of Orkney, Scapa Flow.

In the first days of the war a major provincial newspaper printed a map entitled 'Where the Big Fight Will Be'. At the heart of the map was the North Sea: the great area of water between the British Isles and the European Continent. This was assumed to be the supreme battleground, while the champions fighting there for supremacy would be battleships. The map reflected the widespread expectation that if or when war came there would soon be a repeat of the great sea battle of Trafalgar fought in 1805. On that famous occasion the fleet of Britain's most celebrated naval hero, Vice-Admiral Lord Nelson, had brilliantly outwitted the combined fleets of France and Spain and made Britain the undisputed mistress of the seas. In 1914 there was no Nelson – such men are only produced when there are long-running wars in which they can emerge and flourish – but there was the Nelson tradition. This, it was believed, would be strong enough, combined with fine ships superbly commanded by the descendants of Nelson's captains, to defeat the new young navy of Napoleon's contemporary equivalent, the Kaiser.

At the bottom of the map there was just enough room to include most of Belgium and a small area of northern France. What the map's creators could not know was that apart from one furious brief encounter in the war's middle year – the Battle of Jutland – the North Sea would be virtually void of great warships from 1914 to 1918. Nelson's famous message during Trafalgar, 'Engage the enemy more closely', might echo tantalizingly in the minds of Britain's finest sailors, but the enemy's fleet had to appear to be engaged. Meanwhile the area of land at the bottom would be scarred by the northern end of what would become notorious as the 'Western Front', the double line of trenches stretching from the Channel coast to the frontier of neutral Switzerland, tellingly described by the soldier–writer Henry Williamson as 'that great livid wound that lay across Europe'.

THE YORKSHIRE OBSERVER, FRIDAY, AUGUST 7, 1914.

Newspaper map published in the first week of hostilities reflecting the
general assumption that the war would be won at sea

There was great expectation in the Navy as well as in the nation that there would soon be a dramatic, war-winning encounter. There were, however, distinct variations of attitude and ardour, as is evident from the sharply observed diary which a senior naval doctor, Surgeon Captain Leonard Moncrieff, kept in the opening months of the war. He began it at Tilbury where he and many other members of his branch, both regulars and reservists, gathered on the first day of hostilities to be told of their war postings. There was a prodigiously wide choice of ships, from the old so-called pre-Dreadnoughts dating back to the 1890s to the latest super-Dreadnoughts of the *Iron Duke* class:

> *4 August.* Medicine men, RN and RNVR, arrived in dribbles all day. Taken all round a proper comic mixture, the RNVR being all out for blood, the others knowing slightly more nothing like so keen: still nobody's got any idea of what a sticky mess it will be when a scrap comes.

> *6 August.* List of ships we are to be sent to handed round about 7.30 a.m. I draw the *Marlborough*, the latest thing in superdread-noughts.

Moncrieff could hardly have drawn a better ship. HMS *Iron Duke*, completed in March 1914, was the fleet flagship; HMS *Marlborough*, in the same class, had only just been completed in June. But there was a hint of disappointment both when he came to inspect the new battleship's facilities and when he saw what happened next:

> Medical arrangements marvellously civilized for great British Navy only nothing wonderful, saw better in a Yank in 1911.

> *7 August.* Put to sea at 6 p.m. and seem to wander aimlessly about doubtless so that the Admiralty can say we are doing something.

> *8 August.* Still at sea, nothing much doing.

Magnificent and powerful as the Grand Fleet undoubtedly was, there was an understandable concern about the – literally – latent threat presented by the relatively new and still controversial arrival in the realm of sea warfare: the submarine. While being well aware of the challenge of Germany's High Seas Fleet, the British also knew that the enemy had a substantial number of U-boats at his disposal. Still under the date 8 August Moncrieff noted:

One of the ships reports in forenoon a torpedo passed under her quarter. Attack of submarinitis forthwith, we summon numerous destroyers and light cruisers to make look see. We continue to wander God alone knows what we are doing bar burning coal.

*9 August.* Cheerful tidings, submarine *U15* caught bending on surface at 4 a.m. by *Birmingham* and promptly rammed.

'Submarinitis' would, in fact, significantly delay the Grand Fleet's intended occupation of Scapa Flow. For many weeks Admiral Sir John Jellicoe, its newly appointed commander, a highly competent but instinctively cautious sailor, felt obliged to keep 'Britain's Sure Shield' at sea, rather than riding at anchor in Scapa Flow, where conceivably the devisers of Germany's U-boat strategy might see the great ships as easy targets. (Even so a 'super-dreadnought' of the *King George V* class, HMS *Audacious*, a member of the Grand Fleet's Second Battle Squadron built as recently as 1913, was to succumb, not to a submarine but to that other insidious new invention, the mine, when the Fleet was steaming in northern Irish waters in late October. The Navy tried hard to keep the disaster a secret, an aim difficult to achieve since her sinking was observed by the passengers of a transatlantic liner, the SS *Olympic*. Her loss did nothing for naval morale, or for Britain's prestige.)

Meanwhile, as the Fleet continued its patrols, its captains became prey to another anxiety that would become a distinct neurosis as the months went by: the growing suspicion that the High Seas Fleet, for all its flaunted power, might deliberately avoid the expected head-to-head duel with its British rival. Moncrieff had foreseen this in the very first weeks:

*18 August.* What good we are doing I don't know for the Germans don't seem keen on coming out to fight us and there is small wonder for here we are steaming along with the biggest fleet that has ever been seen.

Late August brought an encouraging success, achieved by the Grand Fleet's battle-cruiser squadron under Vice-Admiral Sir David Beatty, assisted by Commander W. E. Goodenough's 1st Light Cruiser Squadron, with Jellicoe's big ships playing no part. On the 28th, in what became known as the Battle of the Heligoland Bight,

Beatty retrieved a situation that was on the verge of being bungled by bad staff work, and accounted for three German light cruisers and a destroyer, at the cost of serious damage to just one British cruiser. Moncrieff wrote the names of the sunken cruisers – *Köln*, *Mainz* and *Ariadne* – in his diary the following day, adding: 'German wireless admits the losses, 340 Germans saved, 250 by their own people and about 90 by ours, reckon over 600 must have been scuppered.'

What he could not have known was that this relatively small-scale encounter made the anticipated clash of the main fleets even less likely than before. While to Churchill the battle offered positive proof that the British were prepared to hazard their vessels in daring offensive action, and get away lightly, it had a profoundly negative effect on the morale of the supreme arbiter of the fate of the German Navy, Kaiser Wilhelm. As Germany's most prominent naval strategist, Admiral von Tirpitz, later recorded: 'The Emperor did not want losses of this sort ... Orders were issued ... to restrict the initiative of the Commander-in-Chief of the North Sea Fleet: the loss of ships was to be avoided, fleet sallies and any greater undertakings must be approved by His Majesty in advance.'

It was not long, however, before the British became aware of this no-risk policy, if only through the leakage of intelligence to the effect that some at least of the enemy's fighting sailors were impatient at the Kaiser's restrictions and eager for a challenge. Hence this entry in Moncrieff's diary a few weeks later:

*18 September* Prisoners reported that the younger German officers want to come out and have a scrap.

From which it seemed evident that for the older and more experienced officers, thoughts of a make-or-break showdown were distinctly less attractive.

'Submarinitis' was soon back with a vengeance, however. On 23 September Moncrieff recorded one of the most tragic naval disasters of 1914, the sinking on the previous day in the North Sea of three cruisers with substantial loss of life. Doubtless to the Germans their despatch was fair revenge for the loss of their cruisers at Heligoland, though at least that took place during a traditional sea battle. This was an early and shocking example of the new-style underwater warfare, in which death and destruction came out of the blue without warning. 'Pretty sickening,' commented Moncrieff, 'they got one first and then the other two as they were standing by.'

On 22 September *Aboukir*, *Hogue* and *Cressy*, light cruisers of the same class, all completed in 1902, were patrolling an area off the Dutch coast known as the Broad Fourteens. They were discovered by the German submarine *U9*, which proceeded to torpedo them in short order one after another. In the case of the second and third ships, the automatic instinct of their crews to stop to pick up survivors made them little more than sitting ducks.

Even as Moncrieff was annotating his diary in *Marlborough* on 23 September, an ardent young submarine captain, Lieutenant Ronald Trevor, who was in command of a newly commissioned submarine, *E10*, was writing in angry dismay about the disaster to his parents, more or less with the attitude of 'I told you so':

> The news is sad but is what we submariners have been expecting for weeks. The commodore has repeatedly warned the Admiralty that those ships ought not to patrol the N. Sea. I hope the fellow who is responsible for putting them there gets hung. They will not realize the submarine menace.

In a letter written on the same day to his favourite confidante, his cousin Daphne, Trevor expressed his frustration not only at the enemy's reluctance to do battle, but also at his own side's distinctly lacklustre attitude to the underwater arm:

> I only wish the Germans would give us the same chance they have had to make a name for themselves. Our Admiralty still seems to think submarines no use in spite of lessons taught at manoeuvres. It is a wonder to us the German submarines have not done a great deal more damage.

In a letter of 29 September to his father he amplified the same theme:

> I hope our fleet will stay in a safe harbour free from Submarine attacks. The Germans have taken a leaf from our book and their submarines are on the warpath. Destroyers and submarines are the only craft that ought to be at large in the North Sea.

Destroyers were built to be sleek and fast; the twelve-year-old cruisers, four-funnelled, longer, wider, slower, should not – and not only in Trevor's view – have been sailing far from their base off the shores of a neutral country, Holland, doing little more than showing the flag.

Early October found Trevor and *E10* on patrol off the North Sea coast of Germany. Writing to Daphne, he described their frustrating situation as

> quietly sitting on the bottom at 90 feet till daylight when we will dive slowly to the surface [sic] and see if there is anything doing. There is an annoying cruiser in harbour which has been there since the beginning of the war and won't come out to be killed, unfortunately the water is too shallow for us to dive up.
>
> I wonder how long this blessed war is going to last. I want to have something to show for all this labour, a couple of battleships at least.

Trevor's concern for dramatic action – like Moncrieff's questioning as to whether there would ever be the expected confrontation of the great fleets – was, of course, extremely understandable, but might be said, in the context of the naval role overall in the war that had just begun, to be missing the point. The Navy's most important achievements at this period were not of a kind to produce banner headlines, but were profoundly effective nevertheless. They were: to begin the process of denying western imports to Germany that would eventually produce the blockade which was as much a war-winning weapon as the efforts of the great armies; to maintain secure trade routes from the outer world to Britain in order to keep the homeland supplied and fed; and – one of the unsung but major success stories of the whole war – to secure safe communication between the ports of southern England and those of northern France. No troopship crossing the Channel was sunk between 1914 and 1918. Whatever the dangers men might face once they had landed, they could feel assured of a safe passage to take them to their destination, and, if they survived, to bring them back. This was as good as a victory, but no newspaper claimed in banner headlines, 'Another good month for the Channel packets', or 'Don't worry, lads, we'll get you to the Front in one piece.' Commenting on this subject in his biography of Winston Churchill, Roy Jenkins stated: 'There was a basic contradiction between the sophisticated theory of seapower and the desire of the British press (and maybe public) to see victories won.' Churchill himself, being the man he was, was eager for such victories. But, in effect, to render the German High Seas Fleet a verbal contradiction by bottling it up in its home ports was tantamount to defeating it.

Such speculations, inevitably, would have carried little weight in submarine *E10* off the coast of Germany, where Lieutenant Trevor waited vainly for a cruiser or a battleship to present itself for sinking; indeed, his frustrations would continue throughout the war and he would never have the lusty sea fight he longed for. Not for the last time, it would seem, his thoughts strayed from his own predicament to what was happening beyond Britain's surrounding seas on the continent of Europe. Enquiring after Daphne's brother, who had enlisted in the Army, he wrote: 'When is Stephen going out to the front?', adding pointedly, 'I wish I was there; there is no excitement in this sort of warfare.'

* * *

The 'front' was of course the Western Front, which phrase was already becoming strongly established in the vocabulary of the war. There had been much excitement and, already, much horror and tragedy in the area covered by that name in the weeks during which Moncrieff and Trevor were coming to terms with the irritatingly unsatisfactory nature of the conflict at sea.

By contrast with the naval war, the emphasis in the land war, from the start, had been on speed. Germany's invasion force in the west, transported rapidly to the frontiers by scores of trains following carefully synchronized timetables, stormed into Belgium and France with that cynical disregard for treaties and frontiers which had made Britain's entry into the war inevitable. At the same time France threw some of her best forces eastwards towards the nearest points of German territory, only to lose thousands of men – still dressed in their ludicrously conspicuous blue and red uniforms – in what became known as the Battle of the Frontiers. This was the result of the implementation of France's fateful 'Plan 17', originally the brainchild of General Foch and adopted in 1913 by the French Commander-in-Chief, General Joffre, as suiting the temperament of an army committed as a matter of dogma to offensive rather than defensive warfare. At its heart was the concept of *guerre à outrance* – 'war to the hilt, to the uttermost' –

built on the belief that dash and *élan* would carry the day against even the most stalwart and resilient enemy. Before August was out a series of calamitous defeats forced its abandonment.

Meanwhile, Germany's offensive followed the latest version of the Schlieffen Plan, her aim being to encircle Paris, and then swing round to the east to grip both France's capital and her fighting armies in a fatal armlock. The French would thus be forced to acknowledge defeat (as they had done in 1870–71, and would do again in 1940), thereby allowing Germany, assisted by Austria-Hungary, to give her unencumbered attention to Russia, confident that her highly motivated and superbly trained troops would rapidly outwit and defeat the largely peasant armies of the Tsar. If all worked out as planned, the war would be bloody, but it would be brief. In a matter of weeks Germany's enemies would be around the table, negotiating terms of surrender.

However, like France's Plan 17, Germany's Schlieffen Plan would become one of history's great failures. The German advance through Belgium, which had been expected to be swift – neutral Belgium was not rated as a formidable opponent – turned out to be, from the point of view of the German High Command, frustratingly slow. There was far more opposition than had been expected. The fortress city of Liège proved a major stumbling block. Massive siege guns had to be brought up to subdue the city's defending forts. Moreover, resistance was offered not only by Belgium's regular troops but, spontaneously and often to substantial effect, by armed elements of the civilian population. This for the Germans evoked ghosts of their 1870 campaign, when so-called '*francs-tireurs*' – free-shooters, i.e. non-combatants under arms – had seriously impeded the Prussian advance through France. Arguably with some justification, they had seen this as being against the understood rules of war: uniformed opposition was acceptable and expected; non-uniformed opposition was illegitimate and irresponsible, therefore worthy of brutal and contemptuous suppression. It followed that the death penalty was virtually automatic for any armed civilian taken prisoner, just as death out of hand was seen on all sides as the appropriate fate for the spy. In its account of this aspect of the 1870 war, the *Encyclopædia Britannica* of 1910 had stated that 'the severity of the German reprisals [was] itself the best testimony to the fear and anxiety inspired by the presence of active bands of *francs-tireurs* on the flank and in the rear of the invaders'.

Now in 1914 it was all happening again, with the Germans reacting the more furiously because they saw this as a blatant repeat performance: bitter history revisited. War never fails to produce outrage, but the immediate German recourse to reprisal in 1914 was particularly horrific for this reason: that once bitten, the Germans would not be twice shy. The word 'atrocity', and its even more strident companion and word 'frightfulness', instantly entered the vocabulary of the British press and populace. This would be a nasty, no-holds-barred war, and since there was no visual distinction between the armed and the unarmed this was a recipe for the killing of anyone who might seem, however remotely, to offer a threat. From civilians as targets it was no large step to use civilians as human shields. Nor were property or heritage safe from the punitive attentions of the invaders' artillery; any building might conceal an enemy and so pose a threat, from hovel or house to library or cathedral.

A basic cause for this overwhelmingly brutal German response to resistance was, of course, panic. The grand plan assumed token opposition, causing minimal delay. Without it the whole equation was under threat. There was no plan B.

There was another unforeseen, more human, factor: trains might run at a guaranteed speed within Germany, but once on alien ground the railways could play no further role. The 'motor' of the German offensive was now the feet of marching men, who, especially in extreme summer heat, could soon become exhausted. Within a very short time, as over-optimistic schemes disintegrated on both the Western and the Eastern Fronts (the Russians were not quite so laggardly in coming into action as the German High Command had expected), the focus on both sides of Europe was not on speedy victories but on brutal and sacrificial fighting. The mass bloodletting for which the war would become notorious began at the point when it became clear that it would go on for some time.

Into this increasingly heated situation stepped the modest but determined strike force of France's near neighbour and nearest ally, Great Britain.

The British Army of 1914, a professional body of volunteer regulars, had long had as its principal duties the policing of the British Empire and the protection of the home country from invasion. However, since the implementation from 1908 onwards of the reforms initiated by Lord Haldane, it had acquired an important supplementary role. Haldane's plan was to produce an elite, modernized, fully trained home-defence force of one cavalry and six infantry divisions, which would also be available for rapid despatch to mainland Europe as a British Expeditionary Force in the event of war. Backing it would be a Territorial Force of fourteen divisions, similarly all volunteers, though serving on a part-time basis and organized on regional lines. This force's prime function was to provide a permanent home garrison, with no obligation to serve overseas, though there was an implicit understanding that its members, despite their amateur status, might be invited to waive their right to stay at home if circumstances required.

In line with these arrangements it was understood from the first that a British Expeditionary Force, to be known instantly to everybody as the BEF, would soon be on its way across the English Channel to play its part in the rapidly evolving crisis.

It duly crossed the Channel – a force with a total ration strength of 110,000 men – its declared purpose to be that of helping and supporting Britain's chief ally, France.

*   *   *

Second Lieutenant Geoffrey Loyd, aged twenty-four, a product of Eton and Magdalen College, Oxford, and subaltern of the 2nd Scots Guards, sailed for France with the 4th (Guards) Brigade, 2nd Division, on 12 August. He travelled not with his battalion but as officer in command of 1 Platoon, 2nd Division Cyclists Company, attached to B Squadron of the 15th Hussars, operating as Divisional Cavalry. He began a diary of the campaign the following day:

> *Thursday 13 August.* Arrived at Le Havre after a good voyage, going dead slow so as not to arrive before 10 a.m. All yesterday was terribly hot and in consequence the night was not too cold. About four ships crossed together, ours being the last. At midnight three whistles sounded and we feared we had hit a mine. But the ship was being driven hard astern to avoid collision with a tug.
>
> Our reception at Le Havre Harbour was beyond words, with such care had the French learned the catch-phrases of our men, and together with singing our National Anthem in English they also kept

1. Monarchs of pre-war Europe assembled for the funeral of Edward VII.

Left to right: Haakon of Norway, Ferdinand of Bulgaria, Manoel of Portugal, Wilhelm II of Germany, George I of Greece, Albert of Belgium. Seated: Alfonso XIII of Spain, George V, Ferdinand VII of Denmark. (Q 81794)

2. Symbol of a lost world: a summer's day at Henley Regatta, 1912. (Q 81813)

3. The family at the centre of the story: Archduke Franz Ferdinand of Austria, heir to the throne of Austria-Hungary, with his wife Sophie and their children. (Q 114774)

4. St Petersburg: crowds on the Nevsky Prospect during the period of partial mobilization: 29 July. (Q 81828)

5. Berlin: a German officer reads out the Kaiser's order for mobilization, 1 August. (Q 81775)

6. London: crowds outside the Houses of Parliament, on the afternoon of Bank Holiday Monday, 3 August. (Q 81792)

7. Ruhleben internment camp, Berlin, on the site of a former racecourse. (HU 57923)

8. The call up of Royal Navy reserves: 2–3 August. (Q 81809)

9. Army reservists waiting for medical inspection: 5–6 August. (Q 67397)

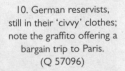

10. German reservists, still in their 'civvy' clothes; note the graffito offering a bargain trip to Paris. (Q 57096)

11. Paris: female solidarity; a woman marching alongside French troops destined for the front. (Q 81765)

12. Requisitioning horses for war service; the photograph taken by Miss Mary Coules as described in Chapter 4. (IWM Department of Documents)

13. Symbol of a new style of warfare; a cyclists' unit under training. Second Lieutenant Geoffrey Loyd, much quoted in the book, was an officer in a cyclists' battalion. (Q 53674)

14. Admiral Sir John Jellicoe, appointed Commander-in-Chief on the outbreak of war, on board HMS *Iron Duke*, flagship of the Grand Fleet, the widely acknowledged symbol of Britain's supremacy at sea. (Q 63697)

15. 'From Rock to Sea for the Honour of Germany': a postcard of 1914 showing the Kaiser, the German eagle and the High Seas Fleet, symbolizing Germany's defiance of the world's greatest sea power. (Courtesy the late Charles Seifert)

16. The German march towards Paris, as envisaged, overoptimistically, in a contemporary German postcard; the French, in their uniforms of blue and red, are shown as being in full retreat. (Courtesy the late Charles Seifert)

17. German propaganda postcard, depicting captured 'francs-tireurs', i.e. members of the local population bearing arms but wearing civilian dress. The fear of 'francs-tireurs' was the cause of numerous atrocities by the invading German troops. (Courtesy the late Charles Seifert)

18. British Highland troops landing at Boulogne, August. Kilted soldiers created great interest among both enemies and allies. (HU 57680)

19. Enter the British Commander-in-Chief: Field Marshal Sir John French arrives at Boulogne, 14 August. (Q 55512)

20. *Entente Cordiale*: British and French soldiers drinking together in the early weeks of the war. (Q 70071)

up a continual passage of jests in English to the great enjoyment of
our fellows.

Glorious day.

When all was ready we marched into a rest camp in a potato field
on the hills about four miles off. Extended over a very large area are
both the 1st and 2nd Divisions, forming the I Army Corps.

Loyd's first full day in France, 14 August – again 'gloriously hot
with everybody in their shirt sleeves' – seemed at first more of a
holiday than a time of preparation for war:

> Supplies being up, I managed to make a substantial breakfast. At
> about 11 a.m. the companies marched about two miles and after a
> precipitous climb down the cliffs, bathed in the sea. I and the doctor,
> Huggan, found a place in the rocks and had the finest bathe either of
> us has ever had in our lives, the water being exceedingly warm – we
> then sat naked on the rocks and gloried in the tremendous sun, letting
> our feet get the full hardening of the salt water.

Reality struck in the evening, however; on leaving their camp for
the station at 8.45 news came from the rear that one of the unit's
wagons had – 'as usual' – broken down:

> The effort to divert the remainder so as to link up with us after
> passing the breakdown was disastrous in the dark. We did not leave
> Havre station until 2 a.m. by which time all was loaded up with the
> exception of three wagons and a corporal of mine, who must have
> lost their way and could be found nowhere in the vicinity. As a result
> we left Havre with all the officers' kits and blankets etc left behind
> with no prospect of ever seeing them again.
>
> Thunderstorm and rain on leaving Havre. Woke up after a
> miserable night to find ourselves approaching Rouen which we
> reached at 6.30 a.m. All the men, as might be expected, are travelling
> in cattle trucks – the whole battalion of Coldstream in one train.
>
> Tubs of water had been laid on all along the goods yard and during
> our half-hour halt we were invited to wash therein. French soldiers of
> the reserve handed us pails of strong black coffee mixed with rum.
> We also were issued a tin of sardines amongst five and some very
> mouldy sour bread.

From the goods siding where their train had stopped Loyd could just see the towers of the cathedral, which brought up nostalgic memories of a visit he had paid to Rouen with a friend during the previous winter.

Loyd's journey to France had been comparatively swift. For others the ritual of going to war took much longer. Gunner Saville William Crowsley, aged twenty-four, of 'E' Battery, Royal Horse Artillery, had been based at Newbridge in Ireland when the war began. His unit had started urgent preparations on 5 August: 'First day of Mobilization,' he noted in his diary. 'Hard work for all. Very busy.' By the 6th they had acquired the horses to make up their required number: '70 horses joined from 'K' Battery at Christchurch. Balance to complete Battery up to War Strength (228) came from Belfast and Curragh.' Crowsley was not greatly impressed, commenting: 'Majority poor.' The following day the reservists joined; there was much clutter, overcrowding and some difficulties in impressing the urgency of the situation on the returnees: 'Harness in Barrack rooms. Men sleeping on the floor. Hard task to get Reservists back to discipline.' However, by Saturday the 8th, the situation was under control: 'Mobilization completed. Battery ready to move, all ranks anxious to move to the front. Mobilization was completed in 3 days: 7 are allowed, very good work all round.'

On 9 August the Battery paraded for a route march under their commanding officer, Major A. B. Forman, and on the following day the 3rd Brigade with its Ammunition Column was inspected at the Curragh by the GOC (i.e. General Officer Commanding) of the 3rd Cavalry Brigade, General Gough. A message was received from their Colonel-in-Chief, Lord Roberts, pronouncing them 'Very Fit!' and wishing them 'Good Luck and God Speed'.

They entrained on 15 August for Dublin, where they marched to the docks:

> At Northwall we embarked on the S.S. *Pancras* (Booth Line). We set sail at 7.30 p.m. with all lights covered or extinguished under sealed orders. Had a good send-off from Dublin, each man receiving a bag containing 1 packet of cigarettes, 1 orange, 1 bar of chocolate, 1 small cake with printing on each bag, viz: 'From your Irish friends, who are proud of you'. Received a Semaphore message from the Dublin Sea Scouts wishing us 'Good Luck and God Speed'.

When clear of the shore got news that we were sailing for Havre, great jubilation as all ranks were under the impression that we were to garrison the East Coast of England.

*Monday 17 August.* Early in the morning the Coast of France was visible about 5.30 a.m. A French Torpedo Boat Destroyer signalled us to stop and owing to the ship's staff being slow in flying the flags, and the number of the ship not being visible, it came within 50 yards of us when the number was hoisted. Our hopes would have been small if the TBD had been German as it had a nasty little gun trained on our bows. A hearty cheer came from the French crew, hats thrown into the air, all ranks returned the greeting, and the boat left us, and we were soon under way again.

Very pretty sight entering Havre, throngs gathered at the docks cheering, children scrabbling for biscuits and souvenirs etc. Landed at 3.00 p.m. and commenced to disembark, horses first, the guns and wagons were very slow coming up from the hold, owing to the difficulty of getting the steam crane to work, and the ship's staff going on strike. Unloading finished at 10.00 p.m. and marched to Rest Camp passing all through Havre on to a very high ground arriving there about 1.00 a.m. the 18th. Enthusiastic reception by French population who smothered us with flowers and cheers etc.

*Tuesday 18 August.* In rest camp all day, had a good look round everything. First taste of French Siege Bread, very hard, brown and mouldy, managed to buy white bread at 11 francs a loaf. Had a walk round in the evening as far as possible with 3 others, not much to be seen as all shops were closed. French girls seeking souvenirs, we had to, more or less, keep badges and buttons under cover. Had supper at a Café, could not get on at all well with the language, returned to camp about 10.15 p.m.

Crowsley, it should be stated, was not the only one to report language difficulties. When a number of new arrivals in the Royal Horse Artillery went into the town to buy eggs at a small grocery store near the docks they failed to get anywhere, as one of them put it, 'until we drew an egg on the counter and tried to cackle'.

Loyd's unit had left Le Havre on the 14th. Crowsley's followed five days later:

*Wednesday 19 August.* Battery entrained at Havre in one train about 500 yards long. Started at 7.00 p.m. and travelled all night via Rouen, Amiens to Hantmount. I rode outside with the gun as the carriages did not look very comfortable. Splendid sight passing up country, could not keep very clean owing to being exposed and smoke from the engine. Watered and fed the horses at places selected by the Major.

*Thursday 20 August.* Arrived at Hantmount about 3.00pm. Very dirty place, coal mines etc. Detrained and by the time we had finished we were all like sweeps. Marched to Quievelon (9 miles) terrific hot day, and bivouacked, marched through Maubeuge and billeted in an orchard there at 6.00pm. Plenty of fruit, had toothache all night, had to walk about until tired out, laid by the camp fire (Thanks to Chocolate!)

\* \* \*

If Lieutenant Loyd had left Rouen in a chastened mood, Saturday, 15 August, found him and his party in a much happier one on arriving at Arras, where they received 'a great ovation, the people flowing on to the platform and showering us with gifts of cigarettes, tobacco, matches, fruit and flowers'. Even the usually thorny problem of billeting presented no problem: 'The desire to please with the French is wonderful, nothing seems to be too much trouble.'

The following day, 16 August, they paraded at 10.45 and set off for Grougis, south-east of Cambrai, a town Lloyd described as 'better able to accommodate our troops in billets' and where they embarked on some vigorous shopping:

> We spent all afternoon in buying up provisions for our company messes. There were many amusing scenes in the village streets, such as officers in mixed kits, shepherds' plaid trousers and khaki jackets, slouch Homburg hats and rush-soled shoes of local manufacture — myself walking down the street with two squawking chickens in one hand.

The holiday mood, however, could not belie certain inevitable anxieties. Now that they were deep in France they were nearer to the action but, moving under often unexplained orders in a foreign country, they had very little idea as to what was going on. Loyd emphasized this point in his diary on 17 August, writing with an undertone of anxiety:

> Although we are only 40 miles from the frontier and about 70 from the firing line not a word of information has reached us. War might have terminated for aught we can tell.

Already present at Grougis was the 2nd Battalion, the Grenadier Guards, with Lord Loch as its second-in-command. Writing on the same day, he expressed a similar concern, if with the assumption that the absence of information suggested that matters were more or less under control. If they were not, surely they would have heard:

> We have no news but whatever happens in the end the Germans have not walked over as quickly as they did in 1870.

Loch's comment reflected an understandable concern in the minds of France's most supportive friends, and in France herself, at this stage of the war. For anyone with a sense of history – and Loch, born in 1873 to a distinguished family with a background of high public service, had had plenty of opportunity to acquire one – the awareness of the dismissive defeat by the Prussia of Bismarck and Kaiser Wilhelm I of the France of the Second Empire and Napoleon III a mere four decades or so earlier was bound to raise questions as to whether what had happened once could happen again. However, when writing to his wife on 21 August – by which time hints were in the air that a meeting with the advancing enemy might not be far off – another famously historic year came to Loch's mind, the year that saw the end of the long nightmare of the Napoleonic wars on the battlefield of Waterloo. The British had not borne arms on the continent of Europe since that year; the fact that for Loch Waterloo was the obvious comparison shows how significant he considered the fighting about to begin would be. This was make or break, the real thing, not an enjoyable summer excursion in the sun:

> The Germans have started their big advance. May God grant us strength to do what is right. We are engaged in a war to a finish as much as ever it was in 1815. The men don't realize what it is or what it is going to be. They are out for a picnic at present but I believe the heart is right and when the pinch comes they will answer to the call.

# CHAPTER SIX

# FROM MONS TO THE MARNE

THE BEF WAS UNDER the command of Field Marshal Sir John French, a veteran of the war in South Africa. The force was divided into two Corps: I Corps under Lieutenant General Sir Douglas Haig, II Corps under Lieutenant General Sir Horace Smith-Dorrien – the latter having been suddenly summoned to France when the intended commander, Sir John Grierson, died of a heart attack in the train carrying him to his corps headquarters. Additionally, there was the Cavalry Corps under Major General Sir Edmund Allenby. The campaign of 1914 would be fought by these four men, under the guiding authority, wielded largely from London though with occasional interventions in the field, of Lord Kitchener.

There had been serious argument as to where the BEF should concentrate on its arrival in France, the choice lying between Amiens – seen by some as too far back from the obvious areas of action – and Maubeuge, just south of the Belgian frontier, where it would take position to the left of the armies of the French. They opted for Maubeuge, which proved to be a historic decision. Maubeuge was not far from Mons, in Belgium, where on 23 August Smith-Dorrien's II Corps, having nudged forward across the frontier, found itself opposite the advancing soldiery of the westernmost of Germany's five armies, the First, under the redoubtable General von Kluck.

Mons was a novel kind of battlefield for the British regulars. At the centre of a thickly inhabited industrial zone stretching from Charleroi to Lille, it provided a serious culture shock for men who had done much of their soldiering in India or Egypt or whose homeland training had been carried out on Salisbury Plain or Dartmoor. Smith-Dorrien's battalions and batteries hastily took up position, to the west and east of the town, in what was in effect a vast coalfield. As well as a scatter of pit villages, there were all the usual signs of mining: pitheads, engine-house chimneys and numerous pyramid-like slag heaps. These heaps of shale and slurry were seen at first as possible artillery observation posts until the boots of men attempting to climb them began to sizzle. For a front line the units west of the town were assigned the southern bank of the Mons–Condé canal, a shallow, unsavoury waterway fifteen miles long, full of slime and chemical effluent. Being crossed by eighteen bridges, it was not thought to constitute a major obstacle to an attacker, while behind it the industrial clutter of the area inevitably obstructed fields of fire. Further south, running obliquely across the countryside, was the main railway line linking Mons with the nearest town in northern France, Valenciennes; holiday trains would steam to and fro along its tracks throughout the coming battle.

Further east, II Corps continued to man the canal as it took a circular loop around Mons, thus producing a front like an extended question mark. Haig's I Corps was aligned to the south of the town, facing east, holding the front as best it could between the British and the nearest French army, further south still, under General Lanrezac. It was to be only marginally involved in the ensuing action, which could be said to have taken place behind it and over its left shoulder. Of the Cavalry Corps, also based east of Mons, only certain units of the Royal Horse Artillery made a notable contribution. Both the BEF's flanks were exposed. There was a clear gap between Haig's right and Lanrezac's left, while to Smith-Dorrien's left only three French territorial divisions stood between his troops and the Channel coast.

Making the best of things, the infantry dug in, sometimes borrowing picks and shovels from the local populace to eke out their own supply. Preparations were hurriedly made to blow the bridges.

According to some accounts, Smith-Dorrien had no desire to be where he was in the first place. He had already planned a line in more open country some way south of the canal but confusion over the C-in-C's orders left him stranded. Other interpretations have it that the two men agreed on II Corps' dispositions and quarrelled about them afterwards. What is beyond question is that Sir John French considered there was no serious prospect of an immediate engagement and, after conferring with Smith-Dorrien, drove off to Valenciennes to discuss the situation with the local French commander. He was away from his headquarters for six hours, prompting some historians to ask why the din of the bombardment of the BEF's first battle did not bring him hurrying back. To complicate the situation it was a Sunday; the first salvoes began to fall as the local inhabitants, dressed in their black Sunday best, set off to or returned from mass. If this was to be a war that would involve civilians to an extent never seen before, as indeed it was, this was a marker set down for the British at their very first action.

The Battle of Mons surprised the Belgians, but it surprised the Germans too. Von Kluck appears to have assumed there was no enemy nearer than fifty miles, so he knew next to nothing about the dispositions of the British Army as the units of his own First Army stumbled into it one by one. The battle also surprised the British. There had been numerous rumours of 'Uhlans' in the vicinity – shorthand for every kind of German cavalry – but no thought that a mighty German force was pounding towards them from the north at the best speed its highly disciplined soldiers could achieve.

Private G. R. Juniper, 1st Battalion, Middlesex Regiment, 19th Infantry Brigade, which had just arrived from England to join II Corps, recorded in a brief contemporary account how the battle began for him:

> We left Le Havre on Friday the 21st for Valenciennes. We arrived there after a train journey of 24 hours, which was very nice as there were only 50 of us in a cattle truck.
>
> We marched away at 8 a.m., to a place about 8 miles N.E. of Mons, where we heard 10 Uhlans had been seen in the early morning. As night was drawing near we had positions to take up on the near side of a canal.
>
> [Next day] Captain Cunningham, thinking that the rushes on the far side of the canal would interfere with our rifle fire, sent two sections under Sgt Shippam to clear the rushes away. As we had just finished a tiring march we had permission to leave our equipment and rifles behind, only taking our entrenching tools with us. We had cleared the rushes away for about a mile, when a Maxim gun opened fire and we showed them how to do a mile in record time. On reaching the Coy we had to take up a position which we held until 2 a.m.

The nearest neighbour to the right of Juniper's 1st Middlesex, almost halfway between Condé and Mons, was the 1st Battalion, Duke of Cornwall's Light Infantry, 24th Infantry Brigade. The battalion's adjutant, Captain Arthur Acland, described his experiences in a journal account written up at the end of September. They had arrived in the vicinity of Mons at a tiny hamlet on the canal called Sardon at 4 p.m. on Saturday the 22nd, and swiftly got down to business, among other things establishing a foothold on the northern side of the canal:

> We put out outposts and dug ourselves in and waited for the Germans. They arrived about 4 p.m. next day. They arrived, as a matter of fact, in small but bold patrols at dawn that day, and at intervals during that day. But at 4 p.m. they arrived in a large solid mass on the road we were holding on the far side of the canal, and proceeded to march on a point we had carefully ranged on. We could only get a few rifles to bear on the spot or they must have lost far more than they actually did. As it was they deployed quickly on either side of the road and came on quickly. Our advance companies had got orders to retire over the canal as soon as any strong attack was made, so they withdrew almost at once, as the Germans were ten to one of us.
>
> As soon as these companies were over, the bridge was blown up, and we got back to a position about 800 yards back, on the far side of a stream called La Haine where the rest of the Brigade was in position. The fight went on till 11 p.m.

This was the twenty-nine-year-old officer's first taste of war, but the experience seemed curiously unreal:

> So did I first hear the song of the bullet and the howl of shrapnel. I can't quite describe my feelings through this show, but I somehow don't believe it dispelled the odd idea that we were on some big sort of manoeuvres, which had been idiotically with me since we started from the Curragh. The burst and hum of the shrapnel surprised me, and the bullets made me duck my head! It interested me, I think, when a bullet flicked the ground just in front of old Warwick as I was riding along a road to get more ammunition. I won't say I was not frightened, I'm sure I was, but I don't think I knew it.

His response might have been very different had he been on the German side, because for von Kluck's soldiers Mons was a terrible baptism of fire. The best-known German chronicler of the 1914 campaigns is Captain Walter Bloem, whose book *The Advance from Mons* tells without exaggeration or distortion the story of the war's first encounters. Of the clash with the BEF at Mons he wrote:

> Reports coming back along the column seemed to confirm the fact that the English were in front of us. English soldiers? We knew what they looked like by the comic papers; short scarlet tunics with small hats set at an angle on their heads, or bearskins with the chin-strap under the lip instead of under the chin. There was much joking about this, and also about Bismarck's remark of sending the police to arrest the English army.

Matters did not work out as had been expected, however. By the end of the day

> the men [were] all chilled to the bone. almost too exhausted to move and with the depressing consciousness of defeat weighing upon them. A bad defeat, there could be no gainsaying it; in our first battle we had been badly beaten, and by the English — by the English that we had so laughed at a few hours before.

What had happened was that they had come up against the superb marksmanship of the British regular soldier. Infantrymen were trained to fire fifteen rounds per minute at a target the size of a head and shoulders at a distance of 300 yards; a miss might deprive them of their proficiency pay. Because of this at Mons 70,000 British troops with 300 guns facing 160,000 Germans with 600 guns achieved a kind of David versus Goliath victory. The Official Military History of 1914 quotes a description of the battle published in 1919 by the German General Staff:

> Well entrenched and completely hidden, the enemy opened a murderous fire ... the casualties increased ... the rushes became shorter, and finally the whole advance stopped ... with bloody losses, the attack gradually came to an end.

That the enemy quickly acquired a healthy respect for British marksmanship is clear from the diary of an officer in I Corps, Captain C. J. Paterson, 1st Battalion, South Wales Borderers, in an entry dated 31 August:

A German prisoner with the Black Watch said that the Russians can't shoot at all, that the French are not good shots, but that the English shoot and kill.

As well as the infantry, the artillery performed to great effect on 23 August. This is from the diary account of E. J. Cummings, an NCO – rank uncertain – serving with 'J' Battery, Royal Horse Artillery, 5th Cavalry Brigade:

> We rose at 3.30 a.m. It was a glorious morning and little did we dream that ere nightfall we should have fought what was perhaps the greatest battle in the World's History. Soon after noon the Battle started and our convoy was heavily shelled when passing down a road for about 3 miles.
>
> Hot, tired and dusty we dropped into action about 3 p.m. Our Commander chose an admirable position with 3 or 4 false crests in the ground line and though it took us some considerable time to range our enemy it was as hard for them. Our guns were almost red hot, our mouths were parched and the heat hung in mists before our eyes yet the order came through with a monotonous regularity: 'Two Rounds Battery Fire, repeat', and like machines we repeated.

It had been a hard and demanding day, but the battery's reaction was one of exhilaration rather than exhaustion:

> Such was Mons, did it damp our spirits or knock any of the enthusiasm out of us, not a bit of it. On the contrary it made us long for another rub at the enemy, even if it meant fighting the same odds.

Brigadier General Sir John Headlam, a senior officer of long experience who had served in South Africa and India, was in command of 5th Division artillery at Mons. In a letter to his wife dated 25 August, he praised 'the gallantry, and perhaps more valuable still the wonderfully high type of the best soldierly spirit shown by all ranks in circumstances which have been I believe unparalleled'. He added: 'I shall always have the greatest pride in thinking that I was one of the 5th Division, and especially that I commanded such a wonderful artillery.'

Summing up the situation overall, Lord Loch wrote to his wife a few days later in an equally buoyant mood:

We are a tiny atom but we have shown we can bite very hard. The Germans did us the compliment of sending three if not four times our numbers against us. We lost heavily but they lost more.

The British losses numbered approximately 1,600 killed, wounded and missing; the Germans a substantially larger if unknown figure. The comparatively low cost gave rise to a popular myth in Britain that had the BEF been able to muster more men it would have thrown back the whole German Army. But this was a first fight only and it would be the only one of its kind.

* * *

Captain W. G. 'Bill' Morritt was one of the Mons battle's 1,600 casualties, in that he ended the day in the third category listed above, that of the missing. His battalion, the 1st East Surreys, had dug in some six kilometres to the west of the town, at St-Ghislain, not far from the meeting point of the Valenciennes–Mons railway and the canal; in fact his company was deployed on the forward side of the canal with, to their immediate right, a rising embankment leading to a railway bridge carrying a local branch line. Morritt described his experiences in a letter to his mother written some ten days later:

> We held [the] Germans all day, killing hundreds, when about 5 p.m. the order to retire was eventually given. It never reached us and we were left all alone. The Germans got right up to the canal on our right, hidden by the railway embankment and crossed the railway. Our people had blown up the bridge before their departure. We found ourselves alone and I realized we had about 2,000 Germans and a canal between myself and my friends.
>
> We decided to sell our lives dearly. I ordered my men to fix bayonets and charge, which the gallant fellows did splendidly, but we got shot down like ninepins. As I was loading my revolver, after giving the order to fix bayonets, I was hit in the right wrist. I dropped my revolver; my hand was too weak to draw my sword, this afterwards saved my life. I had not gone far when I got a bullet through the calf of my right leg, and another in my right knee, which brought me down.
>
> Those who could walk the Germans took away as prisoners. As

regards myself, when I lay upon the ground, I found my coat sleeve full of blood, so I knew an artery of some sort had been cut. The Germans had a shot at me when I was on the ground to finish me off; that shot hit my sword, which I wore on my side, and broke it in half just below the hilt; this turned the bullet off and saved my life. We lay out there a night, for twenty-four hours. I had fainted away from loss of blood and when I lost my senses I thought I should never see anything again. Luckily I had fallen on my wounded arm and the arm being slightly twisted, I think the weight of my body stopped the flow of the blood and saved me. At any rate, the next day civilians picked up ten of us who were still alive and took us to a Franciscan Convent where we have been splendidly looked after.

All this happened on the 23rd August, it is now 3rd September. I am ever so much better and can walk about a bit now, and in a few days will be quite healed up.

Unfortunately the Germans are at present in possession of this district, so that I am more or less a prisoner here. But I hope the English will be here in a week, when I shall be ready to join them.

I am sending this letter by a civilian who is going to Ostend; I hope you will get it.

The letter duly arrived. Sadly, Captain Morritt's hopes for himself were not to be realized. At some point he was found by the Germans and became a prisoner-of-war. The records show that he died in Germany, on 27 June 1917, aged twenty-four. He is buried in a Commonwealth War Graves Commission cemetery in Hamburg.

* * *

Lieutenant Geoffrey Loyd, in I Corps, did not take part in the fighting of 23 August, though he observed it keenly from a distance:

Steady booming of artillery all along our line and from Havay I could see the plain stretching towards Mons and Binche, with cavalry dotted about and great white puffs of smoke hanging in the air from shrapnel bursts.

He was aware of 'an almost irresistible desire to go out and join in', which some of his comrades did, but the following day he commented:

Perhaps it was fortunate that I did not take part in the skirmish of the Divisional Mounted Troops yesterday. Apparently the Squadron, supported by the other two platoons of cyclists commanded by Hall, fired on a German patrol at Villers St Ghislain, and while retiring to the hill in rear towards Harmignies where the infantry should have been in support, were caught on the road by German artillery fire at about 1,500 yard range with terrible accuracy, shells bursting among the bicycles and dismounted men and led horses. As a result of this shell fire which burst low, out of the 30 bicycles of No 2 platoon only 15 returned – one man having his machine blown to pieces beneath him.

Hall was among the officers wounded, a Lieutenant Blacker was hurt severely enough to be evacuated to England, but died of his wounds soon after, while 'poor J. M. Tylee', a cavalry officer of the 15th Hussars, was killed by a piece of shell hitting him in the throat. At first it was assumed that Loyd too was among the fatalities, though the first he heard of this was when he received 'the universal congratulations of the 3rd Coldstream both officers and men, who had heard a report that I was killed'.

Loyd was a perceptive young officer, not merely concerned with the fortunes of his own side, but also well aware of the effects of approaching war on the local inhabitants:

In face of a German advance all Belgian families have left their houses and put up shutters, leaving cows unmilked, chicken eggs lying all about, and all presenting a sad spectacle. In one such house, during the pause for dinner at 1 p.m., I was bitten on the hand by a wretched disconsolate dog, left chained at the front door. I sought out the doctor of the Coldstream to cauterize the marks, but I saw that he was too sleepy to do so. However, I found Roger Bentinck shaving himself by the reflection off a cigarette case, and with his leave took off my two days' beard, etc, which proved a great relief.

He wrote this on 25 August; on the same day he underwent his own (at this stage modest) initiation:

While retiring with the Brigade Staff, rather too leisurely under a steady shrapnel fire, a shell burst on the far side of the Mons–Maubeuge road by my platoon and flew over us in a swarm of pieces. I confess to have ducked my head while the pieces whistled past it, and one man of my platoon was raked across the shoulder-blades — fortunately, although the companies looking on thought every minute that we should be wiped out, no other shell burst with accuracy.

'Retiring with the Brigade staff': looked at with hindsight, this can be seen as the key phrase in Loyd's account. The BEF had performed well on 23 August, but were now facing the inevitable consequence of an engagement fought with such a disparity of forces. The momentum of the advancing Germans might have been halted, but only briefly, and the only option for the Allies was to fall back before it. Thus the Battle of Mons was now being succeeded by what would become known, equally famously, as the Retreat from Mons. Suddenly, instead of heading north, the BEF was retiring south, or more strictly south-south-west. The hurried departure of the nearest French army, that of General Lanrezac, without the courtesy of informing Sir John French of his intentions, made this outcome doubly inevitable. What exacerbated an already deteriorating situation was that Haig's I Corps and Smith-Dorrien's II Corps were out of contact and so were unable to offer mutual support. As I Corps made good its escape on the eastern side of the River Oise, II Corps, in rather less good order – understandably after a stiff defensive battle – withdrew on the western side at a slower pace and with the enemy virtually on its heels. Separating them even more effectively as the retirement continued was the Forest of Mormal, a compact mass of oak and beech 9 miles long and 3–4 miles broad. It had routes through it, but mostly forest tracks, and the British had no adequate maps. Sir John French tried to retrieve the situation by ordering the two corps to halt on the night of 25–26th on the line Le Cateau–Landrecies at the forest's southern edge.

However, the Germans disrupted the C-in-C's plans by making their own bid to seize Landrecies. Reputedly they entered the town under cover of night led by some of their men dressed in French uniforms to catch the British off guard. Once roused, however, the 4th Guards Brigade fought head to head with the enemy while the rest of I Corps continued its retreat. The 3rd Battalion, Coldstream Guards in particular came out of the fracas with an enhanced

reputation; their exploit at Landrecies was one of the episodes of
1914 singled out for honourable mention in Charles Carrington's list
of key events quoted in Chapter 1. The Official History's verdict,
however, was that 'the seriousness [of the fighting] was at the time
somewhat exaggerated'. Second Lieutenant Loyd, writing later the
same day, reported the episode with great admiration, though the figures he gave of enemy losses were to prove grossly inaccurate:

> Guards wiped out the German attack upon Landrecies with great
> coolness after being under a terrific rifle and shrapnel fire from 8 p.m.
> in the dark until 2 a.m. and killed not less than 800 of the enemy
> whose casualties were estimated at 2,000, their dead lying in heaps
> across the road. The Coldstream lost about six killed and 150
> wounded, while of officers poor Archer Windsor Clive and Hawarden
> were killed, together with R. H. Vereker, Grenadier Guards, who was
> shot in the head and killed instantly by one of our soldiers in error
> from a window.

The Official History's figures of losses are, for the 3rd Coldstream,
120; for the opposing Germans, 127.

By 4 a.m. on the 26th, all was quiet again on the line of I Corps.
But in the darkness no one knew what threats might be impending,
so much so that as early as 10 p.m. on the 25th I Corps had tele-
phoned French's GHQ, with the message: 'Attack heavy from north-
west can you send help?' GHQ promptly directed Smith-Dorrien to go
to the aid of I Corps, or at least to detach the recently arrived 19th
Brigade. Smith-Dorrien refused, wisely, because on the following day,
the 26th, he needed his maximum force and his undivided attention
for what would become the most important action in which he was
ever engaged.

The Germans were so close as to be almost infiltrating his rearguard. As II Corps approached the small township of Le Cateau,
50 kilometres south-west of Mons and 10 kilometres west of the
southern end of Mormal, Smith-Dorrien brought his divisions to a
halt and, acting entirely on his own initiative, ordered them to turn
and fight. The Battle of Le Cateau was to prove a turning point in the
campaign, at least as crucial as Mons though far more costly, with
7,812 officers and men killed, wounded and missing. Fittingly, it was

fought on the anniversary of the Battle of Crécy in 1346, and would not be unworthy of being ranked with that famous medieval encounter.

But it was also in part an ugly little battle, with its moments of panic and, in the eyes of some participants, unsoldierly behaviour. There were reports of men in such a hurry to get away, following an order to retire issued in mid-afternoon, that they left behind guns, wagons, horses and wounded, while even some of Britain's famed infantrymen were throwing away their rifles, ammunition, equipment and running for their lives.

For Major Herbert Trevor, 2nd King's Own Yorkshire Light Infantry, 5th Division, this was the action that for him revealed the true nature of modern war. In his letter of 2 September (quoted in the Prologue, on page xxi), he wrote to his sister:

> Le Cateau on the 26th was too terrible for words. We fired 300 rounds a man in my Company and did a good deal of execution that day, but we were in an absolute trap – it's a marvel that anyone there is alive and untouched. I lost my horse and a good deal of kit after the battle but am now all right with two good animals. Since the 26th I've been commanding the battalion as Bond and Yates were killed (as far as we know) and we lost 17 other officers including my Captain and 3 subalterns.

Trevor came out of the battle with a healthy respect for the enemy, describing the German Corps he faced as 'a good lot':

> I cannot help admiring all their monkey tricks, They seem to be supplied with everything and us with nothing. It is always German aeroplanes, star shells, motor cars shoving forward machine guns, generally a few more guns than our side wherever we happen to be. We are absolute amateurs.
>
> I'm glad to say that we're supposed to have behaved with conspicuous gallantry at Le Cateau and the General has since told me on several occasions that he thought our fellows were splendid, but war is a rotten game and none of us would be sorry if it was over. It is terrible for the inhabitants of these parts. I should be much happier if it were in England so that people could realize what it was and take necessary action for the future.

Regarding the 'conspicuous gallantry' of Trevor's battalion, the
Official History supports his claim:

> That night [the evening of 26 August] the 2/K.O.Y.L.I. mustered
> only 8 officers and 320 rank and file, but it had held up the Germans
> at the only point where they penetrated into the British position, and
> thus gave the rest of the 5th Division a clear start in their retirement.

It also clarifies the fate of Yates, though giving his name differently: Major C. A. L. Yate, who had commanded the battalion's firing
line in the heat of the action, was not killed but was captured together
with many others in the enemy's final rush. Taken to a prisoner-of-
war camp in Germany he immediately attempted to escape and was
found near Berlin with his throat cut. He was awarded a posthumous
VC, another tribute to the Yorkshire battalion's key role at Le Cateau.

In fact the KOYLI's achievement was symbolic of the whole battle,
the aim of which was to break free from the harassing Germans. As
was well known in the Army, General Smith-Dorrien and Field Marshal French were far from the best of friends, and the latter would
eventually secure the former's dismissal from his command; but, after
Le Cateau, French paid him this handsome tribute in his official
Despatch:

> I say without hesitation that the saving of the left wing of the army
> under my command on the morning of 26th August could never have
> been accomplished unless a commander of rare and unusual coolness,
> intrepidity, and determination had been present to personally conduct
> the operation.

\* \* \*

One of Trevor's complaints was of the constant presence of German
aircraft. There were also aircraft under British command at Le Cateau,
among them a French-built 'Henri Farman' biplane (usually shortened
by the British to 'Henri') piloted by Lieutenant W. R. Read, Royal
Flying Corps, recently seconded from the King's Dragoon Guards. The
RFC, formed only two years before and numbering 105 officers, 755
men and 63 aeroplanes, was regarded almost as a joke when it made
its debut in France in August 1914. Within days, however, it became
apparent that information about troop movements gathered during

aerial reconnaissance could be of great value. Without the RFC's help, it has been claimed, the Mons Retreat might have been more like a massacre.

Read not only reported his findings to his commanders, he kept a detailed diary. On 25 August he noted: 'All our troops are in retreat, using every road available and making for Le Cateau.' One constant complaint among the British was that they never knew what the French were doing. Read had the answer: 'The whole of the French cavalry were retiring on Cambrai.' Returning from his reconnaissance at 1 p.m. he was given orders to move south to Saint-Quentin: 'As soon as we landed a heavy rain-storm came on and swamped everything. I feel so sorry for poor Henri. It is doing him a good deal of harm, this rain and hot sun.'

Inevitably, 26 August required a longer than usual entry:

> Off on reconnaissance at 7 a.m. with Jackson to report on engagements in the Le Cateau and Espagnol area. The whole sight was wonderful – a fierce artillery engagement for the most part; we were getting the worst of it. We had all the German army corps against our little force. We could see nothing of the French. I watched one of our batteries put out of action, shell after shell burst on it and then there was silence until more men were sent up and it opened up again.
>
> Le Cateau was in flames. We were shelled by anti-aircraft guns so I kept at 4,500 feet. We were also giving the Germans a bad time – their cavalry and infantry nearly always advanced in masses, offering as they did so a splendid target and getting mown down by the score.

An attempt to land at II Corps headquarters at Bertry was less than successful. 'We skidded and soon as we touched ground the landing chassis gave way; as a result Henri pitched on his nose.' Jackson was thrown out about ten yards ahead, while Read was left in the machine; both were shaken but not hurt. There was no time to attempt a repair as shells were already falling over the town. In the town itself everybody who could was leaving as fast as possible. At headquarters General Smith-Dorrien spoke to him, asking where he had come from:

> When I told him I had broken my machine he was very kind and said, 'Well, you must not be left here, you are wanted with the Flying Corps,' and then, like the sportsman he is, found someone to give me

a seat in a staff car. I think we got away only just in time as shells
were bursting all round the town. We went to Maretz where roads
everywhere were crowded with troops retiring. It was not a good
sight, the look of dejection and despair everywhere. Poor fellows,
they had had no sleep or food for three nights and days, being driven
back and pressed always by the advancing army. The Germans have
us on the run and we are fighting a rearguard action against big odds.

* * *

Le Cateau not only stopped the German harassment of the British, it
also threw von Kluck's First Army off the scent. Not appreciating the
direction of the BEF's withdrawal, he turned off westwards towards
Amiens. Thus Smith-Dorrien was able to state subsequently: 'After Le
Cateau, we (II Corps) were no more seriously troubled during the ten
days' retreat, except by mounted troops and mobile detachments who
kept at a respectful distance.' At the time he was able to comment in
more jubilant terms to his wife, writing on 29 August: 'The French
say that my big fight on the 26th which I fought against orders
checked the Germans so much as to render Paris safe for the present.'

Nevertheless, withdrawing from contact with the enemy was not
what Britain's regular soldiers had trained for; they had come here to
confront him, not to walk away from him. This, plus the unhappy
coincidence of a blistering heatwave, helped to turn the Retreat from
Mons into a grim and dispiriting experience. Lieutenant Roger West,
a product of Rugby and King's College, Cambridge, who had immediately found a post as an Intelligence officer on the outbreak of war
and had crossed to France with 19th Brigade, caught the general
mood in an account written up soon afterwards:

From now on there was nothing for it but to trek away to the
south in a seemingly never-ending retreat. Never any rest, rarely any
food, a series of nightmare days and nights, when the dust-grimed
columns moved on. Our guns, hopelessly outnumbered, stayed behind
and guarded the tired Infantry, till the last moment, when they would
limber up and toil to the next position.

West spent most of his time on a motorcycle, rounding up lost
groups of soldiers, checking roads to ensure they were clear of the
enemy, and, necessarily, foraging on his own behalf:

I rode on ahead of the Brigade to the next village, and entered a cottage to get some food. There was a shrivelled-up old woman and a little girl about twelve years old. They managed to make me some coffee and an omelette. 'Better the English should take all than save anything for the Prussians,' they said, and refused to be paid. Then I went out to wait till the troops came up and sitting down on the cobbled pavement was asleep in a moment.

Local reaction was not always so charitable. Lieutenant William Synge, 1st Battalion, King's (Liverpool) Regiment, recorded that as the retiring columns left one town 'there was an old man, who stood at the corner of the street and cursed us heartily, calling us cowards for running away and every name under the sun'. There was no possible response to such recriminations.

'It was the same old jogging along,' commented E. J. Cummings, summing up the retreat's third day, 27 August, 'the same dust which almost choked us and the same sun which seemed to scorch us.' However, he for one saw little loss of morale, continuing: 'Still everyone seemed to be happy, the only thing we did not like was the absence of cigarettes and tobacco.'

Infantrymen had the hardest task, slogging endlessly down the cambered French roads. As between gunners and cavalrymen, it was arguably worse for the latter; guns did not become exhausted, horses did, and so did their riders. Also on 27 August Lieutenant Rowland Beech, 16th (Queen's) Lancers, wrote in his notebook:

Started about 1.30 and rode at a walk as far as the woods above Homblières (east of St Quentin), about 15 miles. Practically all the men were fast asleep on their horses, either held in the saddle by their lance-sling, or else continually falling forward on the horse's neck. Halted for 3 hours, holding the woods to the front and flanks, but saw nothing. We got a certain amount of oats and bread; also I bought some brandy for the horses, which were getting very weak. Domino fell down nearly every time I got on to him and I all but decided to discard him. Went on to Harly, where we got supplies, but hardly had time for food before we moved on again. We wasted a lot of time looking for Jack Riddell and Horny, who were supposed to be in one of the houses getting food ready. Was now absolutely done up – the worst moment of all.

Writing the same day, and striking the same note, was Gunner
Crowsley, Royal Horse Artillery.

> At 5.00 a.m. we had a long march to Harly and rested there till
> 2.00 p.m., all ranks being very much depressed owing not only to the
> fact of us continually retiring, but at the total absence of any infor-
> mation, we appear to be blindly driven back.

On the 31st it was a similar story:

> Started at 10.30 a.m. Went to bivouac about 8.30 p.m. All ranks
> grumbling about the suppression of all information, weather still very
> hot. We knew that we were marching towards Paris, owing to the
> retirement of the whole army, and we heard rumours as that the
> French Government had been shifted to Bordeaux, or that our base
> had been shifted to Nantes, which all seemed to point to a disaster.
> All we could get from the Officers was that the French Corps of
> Cavalry should have now been with us, but nothing turned up. We
> were occasionally told that we were going back some distance to rest,
> or to the base to be refitted, but the way we were brought out of
> villages at the dead of night with such a rush, we all knew the Germans
> were too close to let us rest.
> Horses were suffering from improper rations, want of grooming,
> continual marching, sore backs and withers, sore galls, leg weary, etc:
> men too riding fast asleep in their saddles.

Horses were not only the prime means of transport, they were
much valued companions, their reactions to danger not markedly
dissimilar from those of the men who rode or drove them. At one
point after observing his horse's reaction to shellfire, Crowsley was
moved to comment:

> To say a dumb animal has no sense is all rot, as my horse, quite
> on its own, got down in the ditch (which was not above a foot deep)
> and then on to the bank where I was sitting and crouched under the
> wall for shelter.

For Lieutenant Beech there were occasional moments of satisfaction. Thus on 29 August:

> At 8 p.m. we left Jussy and I blew the bridge up – a biggish iron
> girder bridge. All the windows of the houses nearby fell out. Private

Adams, who was watching, fell off his bicycle, and there was a cloud of dust you couldn't see through. Went and looked at the bridge; it had fallen right into the canal.

There were also less satisfactory days. On 31 August, after an unhappy example of local hospitality – 'Hope the Germans gingered up the lady of the farm; she grudged everything we had from her' – they crossed the River Aisne at Le Port Fontenoy and eventually arrived at Chelles – 'a village right down in a valley' – at 10 p.m.:

> Spent the night here, the men lying in the street and holding the horses. No supplies but found sufficient oats for the squadron. This was another bad night, as we didn't expect to get away without being shelled.

\* \* \*

The Germans might have lost touch with the BEF immediately after Le Cateau but it was not long before they were back in contention. One of the fiercest, and most famous, clashes during the retreat was the action at Néry on 1 September. The night before, 'L' Battery, Royal Horse Artillery, had halted at this small village south-west of Compiègne with the rest of the 1st Cavalry Brigade. At 4 a.m. the forward troops of the German 4th Cavalry appeared out of the fog and mounted a surprise attack. The British artillerymen reacted with amazing speed, getting three of the battery's six guns into action, though two were disabled almost at once. The remaining gun, however, continued to defy the enemy, until only the Battery Sergeant Major and one wounded sergeant were left and their ammunition had run out. Nevertheless three German guns were put out of action and the arrival of reinforcements forced a German withdrawal.

The cost was high; twenty-three of 'L' Battery's officers and men were killed, and thirty-one wounded. Subsequently three VCs were awarded, while the French celebrated the action by conferring one Légion d'Honneur and two Médailles Militaires. But the action at Néry was more than a gallant little gesture causing a temporary pause in a ten-day withdrawal and doing good things for morale. At a time when the cavalry was about to lose its primacy as a weapon of war, it was to win iconic status. Major General Sir Edward Spears, a former cavalryman and Head of the British Military Mission to Paris in 1914, later wrote:

> To the cavalryman of the first war the tale of 'L' Battery at Néry was a shrine concealed deep in his heart where he could pay a proud though secret tribute of affection and respect to his beloved Horse Artillery, his very own gunners who had never been known to let him down.

Néry was a brutal hour that became a legend.

Lieutenant Geoffrey Loyd's sharpest clash with the enemy at this period was during a rearguard action in the vicinity of Villers-Cotterêts on the same day as Néry, 1 September. This took place in another of northern France's great forests, the Forêt Dominiale de Retz, which proved a particularly difficult place to fight in, with broad rides alternating with areas thick with oak trees, thus providing a confusing mix of easy visibility and deep cover. The day inspired an unusually long entry in Loyd's diary:

> We entered the forest with the Irish Guards in extreme rear. XV Hussars and we linked up and were patrolling the rides.
>
> Suddenly a patrol of German lancers entering a ride from the west cut the column in half not many yards from us between the Irish and Grenadiers. We killed several, heavy firing commenced, the Guards fixing bayonets, German Infantry came up in masses and an engagement commenced in which the Guards lay down where they were in the road, utilising what cover there was with splendid discipline. At one moment George Morris commanding the Irish Guards and still on his horse ordered his men to cease firing and stand up while he strongly reprimanded them for firing indiscriminately and told them to be steady, the whole while he and his men were under a heavy rifle fire.
>
> I extended my platoon and joined the firing line, killing one German myself – at the same time leaving men to bring on the bicycles. I was able to keep them together and without panic, move away to the east. We came upon Brigade Headquarters prepared for a last stand surrounded by machine guns. The General, Scott-Kerr, was shot in the leg, George Morris in the arm, and his horse killed. At one time after having collected my men and bicycles I was unable to find my own and walked all the way back down the firing line to the last of

the Irish at the end of the column but not finding it, had to return. This I did in the wood as the fire was too hot on the road which was dotted with dead, and picked up two of my men whose bicycles also were missing. We pushed on together, eventually we got back to the platoon, and leaving headquarters I led them by rides in the wood to Villers-Cotterêts, Sharpe walking with me having lost his bicycle.

I called the roll and found that out of my platoon we had eight missing and 4 dismounted, out of a total of 30.

We were ordered to the rear and worked our way back reaching Antilly after dark, where we found the transport and bivouacked by the church. Late that night the Squadron came in, but I was too exhausted to join them at supper. I passed a bad night because of the cold and dew after the excessively hot day, and because I had only a great coat as covering.

Colonel the Hon. George Morris lost his life in this action, while Brigadier General R. Scott-Kerr was severely wounded. Altogether this fierce fight in the forest, against a substantially larger German force, cost approximately 460 officers and men.

Wednesday, 2 September, offered a brief time for recuperation after such strenuous efforts. Finding themselves in the village of Meaux, where the deserted grocers' shops had already been broken into, Loyd allowed his men a certain legitimate if disciplined foraging:

I took my platoon in and we helped ourselves liberally to boxes of biscuits, sardines and other things, so that when we left each of my men had one large biscuit tin on his bicycle besides other items pleasing his fancy.

* * *

Inevitably, given the rigours of a sustained retreat in high summer, there were many casualties of a different kind from the normal, a category that became a particular concern for Lieutenant Roger West. He spent much of his time in the late stages of the retreat riding the roads on his motorcycle, sometimes alone, sometimes with a fellow-officer, Lieutenant Fletcher, marshalling columns of troops and looking out for anybody, or any animal, following in their wake:

The end of our column was always brought up by a sad straggling line of men, lame and footsore, stumbling onwards, interspersed with wretched horses, gaunt, wounded and dying, yet limping along, compelled by that gregarious instinct which forbade them to be left behind. Captain Jack [already quoted, see p. 21] thought that such horses, given rest and food, would become quite fit again. So we had to do our best to get these miserable scarecrows along, and those that stopped were to be shot.

At the tail of the line was riding Major Vandeleur of the Cameronians, also keeping stragglers on the road. We found two Cameronians beside the road trying to cook their breakfast, dinner or tea, or whatever meal it was, ideas of time being lacking. One was removing his boots to ease his tired feet and both were dead weary and practically refused to come along when told. Suddenly the ever-resourceful Major Vandeleur arrived. Far away down a long ride in the forest a few horsemen came into view. We got our glasses and saw that they were some of our troopers, trotting in a bunch through the trees. 'Here come the Germans', said the Major. 'They don't take prisoners. They'll have their long lances into you fellows if you don't hurry.' The effect was magical. The fellow with his boots off pushed them on again without doing up the laces, stumbled up to Fletcher and myself and asked us to take him along. The other one stuck his cooking into various pockets and followed suit. They clambered on the back and we roared away through the forest. We caught up their comrades some way ahead and deposited them with severe reproofs for their criminal behaviour. They were very repentant, but they were absolutely exhausted, and it is doubtful if they kept up long with their unit.

Happily there were also uplifting moments to record:

We overtook some of our Infantry, a portion of the Royal Welch Fusiliers marching along and singing – actually singing – as they went. The Royal Welch Fusiliers always were a musical crowd (and I found out later the more it rained the louder they sang).

Nevertheless, the overall situation was having a serious effect on the efficiency of the whole BEF. In his letter of 4 September Lord Loch painted a deeply disturbing situation:

We had a long consultation tonight and came to the conclusion that the army was not in a condition to attack, to retire fighting rearguard actions or to sit down and fight a defensive battle. In other

words at the present time we are useless as an army. With this
decision I am not quite in agreement. I think the men are better than
they think. The strain on Commanders and Staff has been awful and
many have gone under. One senior Staff Officer has committed suicide
– another has broken down and had to be invalided etc. Lawrence
Drummond could not stand the strain of even a few days and went
home.

The losses of the 2nd Corps in killed, wounded and missing are as
follows: 3rd Division Officers 154, other ranks 4,791. 5th Division
Officers 163 other ranks 4,240. The 5th Division have also lost 28
18-pounder guns, one 60-pounder gun and one howitzer and 18
machine-guns. The 3rd Division has also lost guns but how many I do
not know at present. Up to the present none of these casualties have
been replaced – Lord W seems to have said in the House that they
have but they have not. I know efforts are being made and they are
trying to get the first reinforcements up but owing to the congested
state of the railways none have yet arrived though they might have
joined yesterday.

Loch knew precisely the sensitiveness of the information his letter
contained and that there was no possibility of its being sent to
England by the normal means:

Now I have given you some idea of our state and written a very
indiscreet letter which cannot go unless I can get the King's Messenger
to take it.

* * *

As the September days passed, still the retreat went on. By now even
the Royal Horse Artillery NCO E. J. Cummings was losing his earlier
optimism. On the 6th he wrote: 'Still retiring. We go into Chaumes
which is really a suburb of Paris. We are all to put it mildly "fed up"
with retiring and longing to have a rub at the "Kultur Models".'
His entry for 7 September, however, caught a sudden change of
mood; at last the products of German 'Kultur' were not having it all
their own way. He noted: 'Today the French Armies came up on our
right and we started to attack.' Loyd too was delighted to find that the
campaign had suddenly changed direction, applauding 'the difference
in our troops who showed a fine and unusual spirit directly they

found themselves marching east'. Meanwhile Crowsley was writing of 'our great joy' at witnessing the first signs of a general advance. Lord Loch was in similarly upbeat mood now the tide had turned: 'We are now advancing and the difference in everybody is wonderful.'

The change in Allied fortunes had been due to a series of developments and decisions which together produced what would become instantly famous as 'the Miracle on the Marne'. Up to that point it was the Allies who had had to look over their shoulders as they marched the baking summer roads. Now it was they – in particular the French, with the BEF playing a supportive, though distinctly subsidiary role – who were dictating the course of events, forcing the Germans away from Paris and thereby depriving them of the chance to achieve the quick killing in the west of Europe which would allow them to turn their attention to their other great enemy in the east. The German High Command would have much rethinking to do and the Kaiser's soldiers would not be home before the falling of the leaves. Effectively, this was the turning point of the war.

Out of this moment of high drama there emerged heroes, and villains. On the Allied side the supreme hero was the French Commander-in-Chief General Joseph Jacques Césaire Joffre, who for many months to come would be idolized worldwide for his success in turning the tide in 1914, being honoured by such titles as 'Father of the Country', 'Executor of God's Will', 'Benefactor of Mankind', even 'Saviour of the World' – though his lustre would dwindle markedly in 1916 in the wake of the less satisfactory campaigns at Verdun and the Somme. On the German side the obloquy fell on their Chief of Staff since 1906, Field Marshal Helmuth von Moltke – nephew and namesake of the military genius who had masterminded the Prussian victory over France in 1870. Deputed with the implementation of the Schlieffen strategy, he made, from the German point of view, the crucial mistake of responding to unexpected developments rather than sticking to the hallowed plan's central doctrine. At a time when iron will was required, he vacillated. Thus he diverted troops to the east when Russia advanced more rapidly than expected, and he responded unnecessarily to Germany's unanticipated success in Lorraine when he should have given the fullest possible commitment to the main thrust through Belgium and northern France. In the event there was never any chance of the Germans gripping Paris in the fatal headlock they had hoped for. Plans for the Kaiser's planned triumphal entry into Nancy were hastily abandoned. As the situation deteriorated, Moltke, the more ineffective for being far from the scene of action in Luxembourg and sensing he was rapidly losing control, wrote plaintively to his wife on 7 September:

> Today our armies are fighting all the way from Paris to upper Alsace. I would give my life, as thousands have done, for victory. How much blood has been spilled and how much misery has come upon numberless innocent people whose houses have been burned and razed to the ground.
>
> Terror overcomes me when I think about this, and the feeling I have is as if I must answer for this horror, and yet I could not act otherwise than as I have.

On 14 September, just one week later, Moltke was compulsorily retired and his place was taken by the grim, hard-line, deeply Prussian General Erich von Falkenhayn.

Meanwhile, Joffre, having sacked one incompetent commander, Lanrezac, and now enjoying full support from two others who were far more focused and determined, General Franchet d'Esperey and General Foch, was increasingly emerging as the master of the battlefield. Ever taciturn, never one to bluster or panic, or to allow the pressures of war to interfere with his belief in the virtue of regular meals and a good night's sleep, he was clearly a man fulfilled, recognizing and relishing his finest hour. He would later describe how he initiated the battle that would end Germany's hopes of victory:

> On September 5th, 1914, as commander-in-chief of the French forces facing the invading German hosts along the river Marne, I issued this order to the gallant troops whose valour was to decide the future of France:
>
> 'As we are about to begin the battle upon which depends the fate of our country it is necessary to remind all that the time for retreat has ended. Every effort must be made to drive back the enemy. A soldier who can no longer advance must guard the territory already held, no matter what the cost. He must be killed in his tracks rather than draw back.'
>
> How gallantly our troops responded to the call of 'La Patrie' all the world knows. Paris, the heart of France, was saved. The Germans

were driven back to a line where they dug themselves in. Their dreams of quick conquest were over.

\* \* \*

Meanwhile, for the soldiers of the BEF this was a time to forget the sense of distress and anger at being forced to march away from their intended enemy and to adjust their perspectives to the next stage of the campaign.

One officer whose initial jauntiness had given way to a more sober view of the nature of conflict was Lieutenant Ralph Blewitt, 39th Brigade, Royal Field Artillery. In a letter to his future wife dated 5 September, he had written:

> About this 'Romance of War' one hears such a lot about. Do you know anything about it? Can't spot it here; one is usually too tired to think of anything except getting a few cornsheaves to doss down on. However, I suppose it exists somewhere . . . We have done no real fighting in the battle sense of the word only some pretty dirty rearguard actions but we live in hopes of a pukka show in a day or two.

Blewitt often wrote his letters over several days before posting them. This one has a page of a signal pad attached to it with a scribbled message in unusually large handwriting; dated 8 September, it suggests that the news of the tide-turn had come late to the writer's part of the front, but its message was plain and clear:

> Just raised an envelope and am sending this off. The Germans are bolting at present and we legging it after them for a change. Awfully dirty, would give anything for a good bath.

Lieutenant Blewitt was an officer who could always manage a touch of humour, almost nonchalance, even in adverse and difficult circumstances. But the Retreat from Mons had been a gruelling experience, which had brought many to the verge of collapse. The Official History quotes one officer as stating: 'I would never have believed that men could be so tired and hungry yet still live.' There were certain instances of serious looting, one commander, Lieutenant Colonel Edwards, 20th Hussars, being so incensed by this that he paraded his regiment and warned his men that anybody caught in the act would be tried and probably shot. One soldier *was* shot, for desertion; condemned on 6 September, Private Thomas Highgate, 1st Battalion, the Queen's Own Royal West Kents, was executed at dawn on the 8th. The message from both these instances was clear: misbehaviour of whatever kind would be met with the full force of military law. Yet overall the rigours of the Retreat had been bravely, even gallantly borne. An Intelligence Corps colleague of Lieutenant Roger West, Captain Edgar Cox, wrote later in September:

> No one at Home will ever know the extraordinary way in which the Tommies came though that retreat. They were absolutely battered by four guns to one. They had to retreat day after day with a victorious enemy at their heels, yet they stuck to it and never lost heart.

# CHAPTER SEVEN

# BUSINESS NOT AS USUAL

EVENTS IN FRANCE might have suddenly turned for the better but Captain Edgar Cox, close to the secrets of the BEF's Intelligence operations, was profoundly worried. His letters of the first weeks of war bear witness to an acute anxiety in the BEF that they were desperately, perhaps crucially, short of troops. He wrote on 24 September:

> We want every trained man we can lay our hands on. The German resources in men are enormous. Just now we are holding our own, but if Russia is slow and the enemy are able to transfer fresh troops from east to west, we shall be forced to fight on the defensive again until we get more men, men, men!

Three days later he was hammering the same point:

> If Russia is at all slow, we shall have to bear the brunt of the whole German forces for several weeks more. The losses will be enormous and we shall want every single man. I would like to tell every single fellow who hasn't joined up how our forces are fighting out here. It's no use saying it's their job to fight. In a war like this it is everyone's job to fight, everyone who can.

On the whole, he was preaching to the converted. The surface impression of the home country as seen from the battlefront might seem curiously calm. The prevailing doctrine of the time was that in Britain the population was carrying on as before: 'business as usual' was the standard mantra. Yet, in fact, normality was out, and for a long time to come. Recruiting posters bearing such slogans as 'Rally Round the Flag/ Every Fit Man Wanted' had been produced with amazing speed following the outbreak of war, while terms of enlistment and instructions how to join, under the heading 'Your King & Country Need You', had rapidly appeared on Britain's innumerable red pillar boxes. Soon the same message, reinforced by the stern features and the pointing finger of Lord Kitchener, had brought volunteers hurrying to the recruiting offices nationwide, ready to transform themselves into fighting men to wage war on behalf of King and Country.

For the received view of this subject there could be no better exponent than A. J. P. Taylor, who in his book *English History 1914–1945*, the concluding volume of the *Oxford History of England*, wrote, 'War produced a great surge of patriotic enthusiasm; all less passions were laid aside', while also hailing Kitchener's New Army as 'the greatest voluntreer force ever raised in any country'. It is important to acknowledge, however, that recent research has suggested caveats to this view. Since one of the first results of the war was a dramatic fall in employment, many men volunteered not so much to have a crack at the Kaiser as to get a job. As the historian Adrian Gregory has written: 'Economic distress had always been the British Army's recruiting sergeant and the slump at the start of the war was, in the *short term*, probably the most severe bout of economic distress in the twentieth century.' An instinctive enthusiasm might have brought many to the colours, but, Gregory claims, the main rush to enlist occurred after the Battle of Mons, or, more accurately, after the publication of the Mons Despatch on 25 August, which clearly showed that the war was becoming serious. 'Men did not join the British Army expecting a picnic stroll to Berlin but in the expectation of a desperate fight for national defence.'

One young officer commissioned straight from Cambridge in October, Geoffrey Donaldson, was present at a recruiting session in the Midlands, where he noted a distinct mix of motives:

> Our recruits included mechanics and the like from Coventry, but also farmers and labourers from Stratford and Warwick. For the most part they enlisted with the assumed blasé indifference of the average Englishman, with some such remark as 'my pals have enlisted so I thought I might as well'. Just a few produced the 'King or Country' stunt. Of those rejected by the doctor the majority went away very sadly, but a few were obviously relieved.

Yet there is also much evidence to support the traditional view. Donaldson was one of a mass of recruits from Cambridge. Oxford responded with equal enthusiasm. In his Introduction to *The Oxford University Roll of Service*, which listed the 14,561 members of the University who had served during the war, the Merton Professor of English Literature, Sir Walter Raleigh, vividly evoked the atmosphere of August and September 1914. During the long vacation, a Committee of Military Delegacy sat in a dingy little room in Alfred Street to interview all Oxford men who applied for commissions. Raleigh recalled: 'A torrent of young life surged through that little room, eager, and even gay, light-hearted but not light-minded, fully conscious of all that was involved in the test that was now at hand.' More than 2,000 candidates were interviewed, the great majority receiving commissions.

Yet some would-be volunteers with, as they believed, suitable officer potential were turned down for reasons that would seem derisory barely six months later. A notable case was that of the future author of the powerful war drama, *Journey's End*, R. C. Sherriff. When he heard of Kitchener's appeal, and of the announcement that suitable young men were required for training as officers, he was excited and enthusiastic:

> An officer, I realized, had to be bit above the others, but I had a sound education at the grammar school and could speak good English. I had had some experience of responsibility. I had been captain of games at school. I was fit and strong. I was surely one of the 'suitable young men' they were calling for.

Wearing his best suit, he went to the headquarters of the local county regiment, where he was sent to a room where a dozen young men like himself were waiting to be interviewed:

> The adjutant came in. He sorted out some papers on his table and called for the first applicant to come forward.
> 'School?' inquired the adjutant.
> 'Winchester,' replied the boy.
> 'Good,' said the adjutant. There was no more to be said. Winchester was one of the most renowned schools in England. He filled in a few details on a form and told the boy to report to the medical officer for routine examination. He was practically an officer. In a few days his appointment would come through.

The next applicant was from another famous public school. He too sailed through triumphantly.

My turn came.

'School?' inquired the adjutant. I told him and his face fell. He took up a printed list from his desk and searched through it.

'I'm sorry,' he said, 'but it isn't a public school.'

I was mystified. Until that moment I knew nothing about these strange distinctions. I told him that my school, though small, was a very old and good one – founded, I said, by Queen Elizabeth in 1567.

The adjutant was not impressed. He had lost all interest in me. 'I'm sorry,' he repeated. 'But our instructions are that all applicants for commissions must be selected from the recognized public schools, and yours is not among them.'

It would take some months for Sherriff to achieve his ambition, the catalyst being the fact that the casualty figures of the first campaigns were so high that such canons of selection no longer applied. 'It was a long hard pull,' he wrote, 'before I was at last selected as an officer. Only then because the prodigious loss of officers in France had forced the authorities to lower their sights and accept young men outside the circle of the public schools.' He was to serve as an infantry officer in France until he was wounded in 1917.

Another determined would-be soldier who eventually enlisted after a whole series of rejections was Reggie Secretan, who left his public school, Oundle, in July 1914 when just turned nineteen, with the intention of training as an engineer. On the outbreak of war he instantly put such ambitions on hold and hurried up to London from his home in Hertfordshire, on a motorcycle belonging to a friend who was absent abroad, with a view to joining up as a dispatch rider. To his surprise he was rejected, partly because his borrowed motor-cycle was too old, but also because he was short-sighted. Undeterred, he tried again, some eight or ten times in all, yet although A1 in every other respect his defective eyesight produced the same negative result, repeatedly announced to his family with the message 'Same old luck, won't have me!' He finally applied to the Motor Transport section of the Army Service Corps at Grove Park in London, and was accepted. He wrote home: 'I am so bucked! I am a real soldier at last!' This was just before Christmas, the process of enlistment having taken almost five months. By 1 January 1915 he was in France as a despatch rider attached to GHQ, writing of his appointment that it was 'a jolly good job, and I like it awfully'. He would later be commissioned in the Infantry, but sadly would lose his life as a second lieutenant in the Hertfordshire Regiment on the first day of the Third Battle of Ypres, 31 July 1917.

For many would-be volunteers the motive behind the decision to enlist was an instinctive patriotism, an almost romantic urge to rush to the nation's aid at a time of challenge. *'La patrie en danger'* – the homeland in peril – was a continental, specifically of course a French, concept, but its Anglo-Saxon equivalent was in the air in Britain in 1914. What C. E. Montague would define as the urge to reclaim the world for 'straightness, decency [and] good-nature', or, in Rupert Brooke's equally idealistic terms, to lay down one's life gallantly in some foreign field that would remain 'forever England', seems to have predominated over the idea that war might mean actually facing and killing the enemy's soldiers in hot or cold blood. For twenty-two-year-old Bruce Seymour Baily, however, trying to persuade a father worried as to whether his son was robust enough to become a soldier, a readiness to kill was a basic part of his argument. He had already visited a London gunshop and practised firing a revolver on a range, before writing to 'My darling Dad' on 31 August, pleading to be allowed to consult a military doctor:

> I feel I shall never be happy again if I do not at least do that. Nothing would please me better than to die fighting for my country. If I am not fit they will not have me, but I shall at least have tried, and will not deserve one of those white feathers some ladies are going to present to fellows they see loafing about. Do please say I can do this or I shall never respect myself again. It is worrying my conscience a very great deal . . . You can depend on it I shall not disgrace myself if I am accepted . . . *I would love to have a go at the Germans. I could do for a few before I should be hit* [author's italics]. Do please say I can take my chance . . . It is for the old country Dad.

Presumably he received an encouraging reply for within a week he had enlisted in the 5th Battalion, Wiltshire Regiment and was based at Tidworth. He would serve throughout the war mainly in Mesopotamia, only leaving the army in 1922.

Kitchener's initial appeal was for men aged between nineteen and thirty, though this soon changed. There are numerous stories of men who in their eagerness to join up adapted their date of birth to suit the regulations. One sixteen-year-old Yorkshire volunteer, Arthur Wadsworth, having been turned down at Bradford, immediately walked to Leeds, where he successfully enlisted, having shrewdly aged three years in the course of the day. A famous case is that of the future band-leader and icon of the ballroom-dancing world, Victor Sylvester, who enlisted at fourteen and was promptly discharged when this was discovered. Examples of men who lowered their age to take the oath are perhaps harder to find. One such was Jesse Sheldon, aged thirty-seven, a collier with a wife and five children from North Staffordshire, who enlisted on 29 August, giving his age as thirty-four – thirty-five being the official maximum at this point. Sheldon's case, like Secretan's, would have an unhappy outcome. After three years' service in the Middle East, first in Gallipoli and then in Mesopotamia, he was discharged as medically unfit on 19 October 1918, and collapsed and died in the backyard of his home on the 29th. Because of various administrative delays, he achieved the melancholy distinction of being buried on 11 November, Armistice Day. His widow could never understand why he felt the need to leave his job and family, when he had no obligation to do so, to fight for a cause which would ultimately demand so great a sacrifice.

\* \* \*

The patriotic surge of 1914 won widespread public approval, countless recruits being acclaimed as heroes before they had touched or even seen a rifle, but in many cases it was too much for the authorities to cope with; neither uniforms nor weapons nor accommodation nor properly qualified officers and NCOs were on hand to deal with a situation which had not been foreseen. A vivid portrait of a new division struggling to be born emerges from a letter by Captain Eric Craig-Brown, a staff officer with experience in the Boer War, who found himself posted to Dorset in September. He wrote from the division's temporary headquarters, the Red Lion Hotel, Wareham, on Sunday the 20th:

> My dear Mother
> Got here about 6 o'clock and found my new General in this Hotel: Major-General W. R. Kenyon-Slaney CB. Also the only other member

of the Staff of the Division, viz:- Captain E. C. Packe of the Royal
Fusiliers. Everything is new and everything has to be found out by
continual questions. My first job was to construct some sort of
inventory of the Division and I am gradually getting it done. I have
visited each of the 3 brigades today, one here, and 2 at Wool. It is a
beautiful clear cool day so I bicycled to Wool and back this afternoon.
It will be a slow slow business getting these new armies to take on
the Germans, but I must say the men are extremely orderly and well
behaved.

Few have uniforms and those that have are in a motley mixture of
khaki and redcoats. The new battalions are *very* short of officers and
NCOs, but almost complete as regards men.

As a regular soldier with a long track record he felt it wise to
discourage an eager family member, or possibly a family friend, who
was eager to join the colours:

From what I have seen I should not advise Archie to enlist in one
of the new battalions at the present time. They have no arms,
equipment or uniforms, and what training they get is of the most
elementary kind and by 'dug-out' N.C.O.s who are out of date in drill
etc. A heart breaking business for a keen man who wants to get on.

Concluding his letter, he summed up his division's state of readiness for action in the terse sentence: 'We have no office, clerks,
stationery, at present and are just scraping along the best way we
can.'

Craig-Brown's difficulties in Dorset were paralleled many times over
in the south of England's greatest training area, Salisbury Plain, where
camps sprang up in all directions. Writing on 29 September, Major
A. N. Kennedy commented to a fellow officer about the hazards and
satisfactions of creating and administering one of them (unnamed, in
the vicinity of Codford St Mary):

We are hard at it and I fancy we shall be much older men if not in
years at least in experience before we get things shipshape. It's a
funny show all round this organizing of an Army entirely consisting of
recruits. One CO has already resigned saying that he felt himself
'utterly incompetent to deal with the situation'. One of the few
Captains has been retired for 24 years. Altogether it is an experience

or rather *the* experience of one's life, but the men are ripping stuff, they are now well supplied and well fed, and if we can only keep clear of disease ought to do all right.

One recruit who did all his basic training on Salisbury Plain was Private Reg Bailey, a commercial artist in civilian life, who had enlisted in the 7th Battalion, Royal Berkshire Regiment, and soon found himself one of a thousand men drafted there from Reading. At first they were posted to Ludgershall, where they accommodated themselves as best they could in the village's various facilities. He wrote to his family:

> I've got a corner place in the Laundry to sleep in. We have had a horse blanket served out between every two men, besides our blankets, so have slept a treat.
> It's a fine healthy life on the whole and everybody seems to have knuckled down to it. As there are no uniforms amongst us some of the chaps are screamingly funny. One of our Corporals is a broken down Shakespearean actor, and another wears a very old bowler hat and filthy frock coat and sand shoes. Some of our chaps are billetted in a Wesleyan chapel and a few of them sleep in the pulpit. We are going to have some pants and shirts and other things served out today. I think they are going to serve us with blue uniforms until we go to the front, because khaki is running short.

Shortly afterwards they were informed that they were to move to Sherrington Camp at Codford St Mary, 'a worse place than this, so we are told, about twenty miles from here':

> We are now under canvas out here. I don't know exactly where we lie on the map but we're about 7 miles from Warminster and 14 from Salisbury. The nights now are fearfully damp and cold but today they have served us with some overcoats so it'll be a bit more comfortable at night.
> The last 3 or 4 days have been glorious and the country around here is magnificent. The country is simply swarming with Kitchener's Army from all parts of Britain. One has to line up as at the theatre if one wants a drink at the solitary pub. The 7th Berks are said to be the smartest up to now in K's army. I'm expecting to be made a

lance-corporal. I heard that the lieutenant said I was the smartest driller in the platoon and has given my name in.

By mid-October, even though the glorious weather of September had been succeeded by several days of rain, Bailey had still retained his enthusiasm:

Everything in the tent is more or less damp: blankets, kits, while the overcoats are soaked through, and yet everybody is cheerful and singing and laughing and joking can be heard from all sides. It's fine to think that all these thousands of chaps, coming from comfortable homes and decent beds and meals should take everything in the spirit they do.

* * *

Norton Hughes-Hallett, fresh from his public school, Haileybury, and the school's Officer Training Corps – and an outstanding cricketer, having already played for Derbyshire in the County Championship – also witnessed the New Army's teething problems from the viewpoint of an early volunteer. He too was posted to Salisbury Plain, to Tidworth Barracks, where he briefly found himself part of the newly formed 9th Battalion, Worcestershire Regiment:

*10 September 1914*

Dear Mam and Dad,

Sorry I have not written before, but we get so little time, as we are on parade from 6.30–7.45, 9–1, 2–5. There are such scores of men, and so few officers.

*14 September 1914*

Dear Mam

Hardly anyone has uniforms, in fact five people are in our tent and none of us have them. They are training us as officers to get commissions. One in our tent got a wire five minutes ago, giving him a commission.

PS. Don't worry so about bedding etc as everything is alright.

Two days earlier he had written home briefly in some excitement: the supreme iconic figure of the time was about to pay a visit:

> Kitchener is coming here on Sunday. Thousands of men are pouring in, of all classes . . . They think we shall be in Belgium before Christmas, which will be a pretty good move.

When he reported on what he had learned from the Secretary of State's visit, there was no loss of enthusiasm, but a more measured note had been struck, as the great man had stated that he hoped to get them out to the front in December, but had also warned that the war would last two years.

Shortly afterwards Hughes-Hallett was transferred from the 9th Worcestershire to the 7th King's Shropshire Light Infantry, another Kitchener Army battalion, which he found in an even worse state of preparedness than his previous unit. He wrote on 11 October:

> The officers are all 2nd Lieutenants and a pretty poor-looking lot. Though one or two are not so bad to talk to.
>
> An aged subaltern of yeomanry without any knowledge of infantry has arrived, looking fresh from the Crimea. Still he is a bit more imposing in his old age, than most of the crew here, who are quite hopeless, though the two in my company are both over 25 and quite nice. The CO, Sir Robert Cockburn, is quite hopeless as he is so slack. Still, I daresay, if we get a few decent officers, it will be better.

The arrival of a new CO a few weeks later produced only a partial solution. 'He is a bit of an improvement,' the eager recruit commented, 'though suffering from lumbago.'

It would not be until September 1915 that Second Lieutenant Hughes-Hallett achieved his ambition of participating in the fighting on the Western Front.

* * *

Animosity towards 'aliens' is a standard reaction in any war. It was especially virulent in 1914. The outbreak of war immediately put people of German or Austrian origin under a cloud; however long they had lived in Britain or however innocent their occupation, they were immediately seen as potential traitors, enemy aliens, even as spies. The musical world was especially rich with its German connections. Sir Edward Elgar himself owed his breakthrough from obscurity to the manner in which his much-loved choral masterwork *The*

*Dream of Gerontius,* after a disastrous first performance in England, had been seen for its true worth in Germany where it had been rapturously received. Now this most harmonious of international alliances was to be brutally disrupted. One distinguished musical patron, Sir Edgar Speyer, was forced to renounce his connection with London's famous venue, Queen's Hall, and was ultimately expelled from the country for alleged collaboration with the enemy, when all he had done was to send food parcels to starving German relatives. A close acquaintance of Elgar and also a friend of Siegfried Sassoon, Frank Schuster, managed to survive by offering his elegant London house overlooking St James's Park, his car and his chauffeur to the Belgian Ambassador to assist in coping with the flood of refugees arriving in the wake of the German invasion.

Others sought sanctuary by changing their names. Most poignantly of all, a certain English-born widow with a distinguished German surname felt obliged to call herself and her children by its English equivalent. This was Mrs Isabella Jaeger, whose husband had been memorably celebrated in the most famous of Elgar's Enigma Variations, 'Nimrod'. Nimrod, according to the Bible's Book of Genesis, was 'a mighty hunter before the Lord'. Jaeger was the German word for hunter, so Elgar had deftly played the biblical card to amuse and tease his friend. By changing her name to Mrs Hunter the former Mrs Jaeger effectively disowned her connection with this beautiful and much loved piece of music – ironically now played regularly before that most British of ceremonies, the two minutes' silence in Whitehall, London, on Remembrance Sunday. Doubtless few people recall that this remarkable variation celebrates a gentle and eminently civilized German, one of the greatest friends of this country's most 'English' of composers.

Anti-alien feelings were cleverly exploited in 1914 by a particularly objectionable, if influential, self-appointed tribune of the people eager to make capital and cash out of an already tense situation. This was the uniquely odious Horatio Bottomley, editor of the well-known magazine *John Bull.* Trickster, fraudster, con-man, one-time MP, brilliantly successful journalist, and, ultimately, jailbird, Bottomley knew how to milk popular sentiment and he did so with a vengeance from the moment the war began. He would shortly boast that he was second only to Kitchener in persuading men to enlist, declaring himself to be 'England's recruiting sergeant', though the intensity of his persuasion tended to vary according to the size of the audience and the amount of his fee. Before that, however, he launched a furious attack on anyone with real or apparent German connections, even, in the case of one impeccably English public figure, for employing a German butler and his wife, who were clearly, in his view, spies; a former cook was cited as having seen the said butler cleaning a revolver in his pantry.

Bottomley even produced his own special term of odium for the times: 'Germhuns'. 'Huns' was already up and running as a popular name for the hated enemy; Germhuns added an extra tinge of unpleasantness, as though anyone of German origin was the carrier of some fell disease. Reeling under Bottomley's attacks, well-known firms such as Lyons or the producers of Bovril felt obliged to publicize the fact of their ethnic probity, while eminent hotels, among them the Savoy and the Ritz, published announcements to the effect that there was not a single person of German or Austrian origin, whether naturalized or not, working in their establishments. It was small wonder that Elgar's friends felt the need to take swift evasive action.

The chill wind spread rapidly to other areas. Lord Haldane, the man responsible for a major reshaping of the British Army from 1908, was thought to be pro-German; he had been educated in Germany and had been rash enough in peaceable times to describe Germany as his 'spiritual home'. Another figure in high places under heavy attack was the First Sea Lord, Churchill's highest-ranking professional partner at the Admiralty, Prince Louis of Battenberg. Although born in Graz in Austria, he had assumed British nationality in 1868 when he joined the Royal Navy at the age of fourteen. Despite this, British xenophobia helped to force him out of office in October 1914, his switch to the un-Teutonic-sounding linguistic equivalent 'Mountbatten' not being enough to save him from popular denunciation. At a time when allegedly some patriots thought kicking a dachshund in the street a major step towards the winning of the war, he clearly had no chance of survival.

The kickers of dachshunds would gain one other remarkable scalp in 1917, when the royal house disposed of the cumbersome and politically hazardous combination 'Saxe-Coburg-Gotha' – hardly ideal at a time when Germany was attacking Britain with Gotha bombers – and took instead the politically safe name of the House of Windsor.

* * *

Those who had, in pre-war days, joined the Territorial Force – one of Lord Haldane's most important creations during his time as Secretary of State for War – whose prime purpose, by definition, was home defence, the protection of the nation's own territory, were soon to find themselves under pressure to waive their immunity from foreign service. W. L. Green, a non-commissioned officer in a Midlands Territorial unit, wrote to his father from Derby on 12 August, describing a battalion parade at which their brigade commander had addressed his men in extremely forceful terms. He was clearly shocked by the news that so far only 5 per cent of those present had agreed to serve overseas:

> He said that every man must consider the welfare of the Empire first and that wives, children, sweethearts and business must go to the wall. He pointed out that he as well as all the other officers were having to leave their families and businesses. Next day NCOs were called to a meeting at which we decided to follow our Colonel into active service or anywhere on earth.

This was such an important issue that it clearly could not be left just to the politicians or the generals. The Bishop of London, the Very Revd Dr A. F. Winnington-Ingram, was brought into the fray. On 31 August, at Bulswater Camp near Bisley, standing on an army wagon, he addressed a parade of 5,000 Territorials, his speech clearly being of such effect that it was instantly rushed into print as a pamphlet under the appropriate title for the times, *A Call to Arms*. Himself a military chaplain, he began by assuring his audience that he had not come uninvited to speak to them, but had in fact been ordered to do so by his divisional general, following a similar event the previous day at which all the battalions present had been got up to fighting strength, so that the brigade they belonged to was 'in consequence ready as a unit to go forth on foreign service'.

The Bishop took as his text the Biblical verse 'If I forget thee, O Jerusalem, let my right hand forget her cunning', the core of his message being that England was 'our Jerusalem' and that her sons must do all they could to defend her. If this meant going overseas to meet her enemies, should the need arise, let there be no holding back:

> I am speaking in the presence of the Commander-in-Chief of the Home Forces, and I understand that in any case you will be trained for a month or two to get ready. Well, at the end of that time, if the tide of victory has gone for us, perhaps the Territorials will not be wanted. If the tide has turned against us, and the Germans are upon us, then I think you will see the great advantage of slipping across the silver streak and meeting the enemy over there. Will it not be best in that case to cross the silver streak and meet the invader on the other side rather than have, for the first time for a thousand years, an invader's foot staining the soil of Britain?
> (Applause)·

Earlier, having raised the mood by quoting the speech before Agincourt from Shakespeare's *Henry V*, the Bishop went on to urge his audience to think of themselves as men about to refight that other famous across-the-Channel battle, Waterloo. His final sentence had its own splendid ring: 'Train yourselves, get ready, and, when the moment comes, in the name of GOD strike home.'

A note at the end of the pamphlet claimed that in response to the Bishop's appeal, given in the two camps of Cowshot and Bulswater, six more battalions volunteered for foreign service, and the Bishop received the thanks of the Commander-in-Chief.

Winnington-Ingram's robustly patriotic stance raises a question which was bound to be deeply troubling at this time. How did the Church, or rather the various Churches, react to a war which from the start was clearly going to be fought with maximum rancour and with much recrimination, and in which the doctrine 'love your enemies' was one of the earliest casualties? The newly installed thirty-one-year-old Vicar of St Paul's, Worcester, had no doubts. His parish magazine for September contained the following statement: 'I cannot say too strongly that I believe every able-bodied man ought to volunteer for service anyway. There ought to be no shirking of that duty. Those who cannot volunteer can pray.' At least, however, the writer was a cleric who would put himself where his words might have conceivably helped to send numerous others. For this was the Revd Geoffrey Anstell Studdert Kennedy, who would become a legendary padre of the Western Front, known to the troops as 'Woodbine Willie' for the regularity with which he appeared in zones of danger bringing good cheer, consolation and prayers as appropriate, and a constant supply of cigarettes. If, as was apparently the case, he later regretted the almost glib simplicity of his 1914 appeal, he did all he could to atone for it and would be remembered and honoured by thousands of men.

Studdert Kennedy's nickname is eloquent; Woodbines were his method of getting close to the men. In a war in which the phrase 'a fag after a fight' was a mantra, in which the first thing you did for a wounded man was put a cigarette between his lips, being free with the smokes was far more effective than handing out texts. One of many basic problems facing all chaplains in the field would be that the task of concentrating the thoughts of men under the threat of death on matters relating to their immortal souls was never going to be an easy one. Church parades were often resented, though there would frequently be a higher attendance, with many men taking communion, before a major offensive. But chaplains finding themselves face to face with men in a private as opposed to a public ritualized situation had to be very wary of their approach. This was a lesson learned only after much difficult practice. In a preface to a post-war history of chaplaincy (which for some reason was never published), Canon C. E. Crosse, formerly Senior Chaplain to the 7th Division, wrote:

> It was useless to go to France with a cut and dried gospel because it was unintelligible to men placed in such abnormal conditions.
> Before a padre could be of much use he had to throw overboard his natural temptation to be spiritual profiteer.
> A chaplain who knew his duty could accomplish much not in the way of teaching the mysteries of religion but in improving the general morale.

It is hardly surprising that such wisdom was unavailable, either on the far or the near side of the 'silver streak', in the first phase of the war. Thus, according to a recent biography of the distinguished Methodist divine, the Revd Dr J. Scott Lidgett, following the onset of hostilities many Anglican clergy regarded the crisis as a welcome opportunity to reverse increasing secularization and the decline of their own influence and prestige evident before 1914; the war would enable them, they thought, to identify the Christian community with the nation as a whole.

The author cites Winnington-Ingram as the most extreme of the patriots, and, though some clergy and Oxford dons were deeply concerned by any encouragement to vengeance and hate, the majority supported him. 'Frustrated in their wish to join the battle as combatants, many priests engaged in pro-war rhetoric from their pulpits.'

There were distinctly variant views among the Free Churches. Thus the interdenominational paper *The British Weekly* was prone to a jingoistic approach: 'United We Stand' was its headline on the first Thursday of the war, while by contrast Scott Lidgett, as Editor of the *Methodist Recorder*, deliberately headlined the recent Wesleyan Conference and reserved his comments on the crisis for the inside 'Notes and Comments' page. There he admitted that the German invasion of Belgium had left Britain with no alternative than to join the belligerents, but he put particular stress on the duties of the Churches in the new situation. He called for constant prayer, ministry to the distressed, sharing privations, avoiding the exploitation of opportunities for personal gain, and 'stern repression of every spirit of hatred'.

Elsewhere Lidgett was to write that war 'may be the indispensable means of avoiding yet greater evil' and in some circumstances to abstain from war might be 'a meaner act than participation in it; no Christian nation bound by treaty obligations could buy peace by complicity with wrong'. An unhappy postscript to this thoughtful search for a suitable response to an impossible situation was that Scott Lidgett's only son was to lose his life in France in the severe fighting of March 1918. But there would be no railing at the Almighty at such a blow, rather the quiet sharing of a grief known by then to countless thousands.

All this was the iceberg tip of a subject that would give rise to endless anguish and argument as time went on, though 1914 was perhaps too early for the unanswerable question that would perplex many people in many countries as the human cost mounted: 'Why doesn't God stop the war?'

\* \* \*

During August 1914 as many as a hundred patriotic poems a day reached *The Times*, and though thereafter the number declined, several thousand had been received by the following August.

On 19 August, just fifteen days after the start of hostilities, *The Times* published one of this avalanche which clearly must have stood out from the ruck: a rousing poem entitled 'The Call'. Its message was as clear as it was proud: that a nation long devoted to what would today be called organized games now had a new and more important game to play, on a different kind of field, to a different, though not dissimilar, code of rules, and, by definition, for higher stakes. Not, in this case, to win or lose, but to live or die: and to live or die for a significantly greater team, England:

> Lad, with the merry smile and the eyes
> Quick as a hawk's and clear as the day,
> You, who have counted the game as the prize,
> Here is the game of games to play.
> Never a goal – the captains say –
> Matches the one that's needed now:
> Put the old blazer and cap away –
> England's colours await your brow.

The author was Robert Vernède, a gentle, scholarly, married man aged thirty-nine, educated at St Paul's School, London, and St John's College, Oxford, and a poet who would never have made many literary ripples had he not volunteered to fight in a war well beyond his and countless others' comprehension and eventually, in 1917, had died in it. From the vantage-point of almost a hundred years on, his interpreting of war as basically just a more serious form of sport can seem absurd, even ludicrous; but it would not have seemed so to many of those readers of *The Times* who digested Vernède's poem along with their kippers and kedgeree on that August morning in 1914. 'Lad', for some, was a term that might have awakened memories of A. E. Housman's poetic sequence, *A Shropshire Lad*, now suddenly, after two decades of obscurity, about to come into its own. It would not be long before Housman's prophetic vision of 'the lads that will die in their glory and never be old' would became the essential stuff of memorial services for the fallen of the Somme and other such holocausts, but for the moment the echoes the poem would have evoked were of a different provenance.

'Athleticism' – a term widely used to define that view of sport which was seen to be particularly and essentially British – had been part of the imperial culture for decades. Games, particularly as institutionalized in the 'public schools' (now known more correctly as independent, i.e. private, schools) to which the upper, governing classes sent their sons, were not merely recreational, played with the aim of producing '*mens sana in corpore sano*': a healthy mind in a healthy body. Their purpose was also to convey the message that braced muscles were as important as trained minds for those whose manifest destiny was to take on the white man's burden, in particular the Englishman's burden, of administering a world-wide Empire on which the sun never set. A classic statement of this imperial doctrine was that of Headmaster Haslam of Ripon School, Yorkshire, as enunciated in his address on Speech Day, 1884:

> Wellington said that the playfields [sic] of Eton won the battle of Waterloo, and there was no doubt that the training of the English boys in the cricket and football field enabled them to go to India, and find their way from island to island in the Pacific, or to undergo fatiguing marches in Egypt. Their football and cricket experiences taught them how to stand up and work, and how to take and give a blow.

Now, in 1914, there was a new challenge to take or give a blow, so 'The Call' of the moment, as interpreted by Vernède, was to dispense with caps and blazers, symbols of the games of peace, and to make ready for the new 'death or glory' sport of armed conflict. The poem ended with a Nelson touch, in acknowledgement that the war would be fought at sea as well as on land:

> Hark once more to the clarion call –
> Sounded by him who deathless died –
> 'This day England expects you all.'

However, the prime target of Vernède's exhortation is evident from the key lines of the first stanza:

> Never a goal – the captains say –
> Matches the one that's needed now:

Scoring a goal was the vital aim of Britain's most popular team and spectator sport, football, also known as 'soccer'. Vernède's message was, in brief – if more elegantly put – get off the football field, head for the battlefield. However, the expectation that all footballers, of whatever class or social background, would instantly trade in their shorts and shirts for uniforms was not to be realized. As the new season got into its stride – defensibly so in view of the prevailing doctrine of 'business as usual' – there arose a situation of extreme rancour between the amateurs, to whom their sport was a testing of resolve and a stimulus to high achievement, to be willingly relinquished for the national cause; and the professionals, who played their sport for money, and, moreover, were watched by countless thousands whose only contribution to the game was to stand on the sidelines and either cheer or groan – an activity singularly unlikely to stiffen any sinews for the rigours of war.

In this way the year 1914, far from producing a united front to the enemy in this area of national activity, witnessed an angry class war between those who believed that continuing to play professional football was an insult to soldiers fighting and dying in France and Flanders, and those who thought that, whatever was happening overseas, the ordinary working man should be allowed at least some residual means of relaxation and escape. Surely ninety minutes once a week of playing for or watching your favourite team from the terraces did not necessarily imply a lack of support for, or an indifference to, 'our lads' at the front.

The row dragged on for months, producing increasingly angry reactions from both sides. The ever-forthright Captain Edgar Cox put his oar in from France; referring in a letter of 8 November to football as 'still the rage', he stated:

> I would like to drop a Jack Johnson [soldiers' slang for a particularly nasty German shell: see Glossary] into every football ground in Britain,

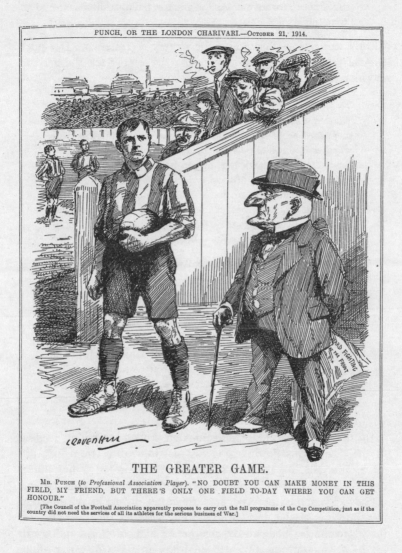

PUNCH, OR THE LONDON CHARIVARI.—OCTOBER 21, 1914.

## THE GREATER GAME.

MR. PUNCH (*to Professional Association Player*). "NO DOUBT YOU CAN MAKE MONEY IN THIS FIELD, MY FRIEND, BUT THERE'S ONLY ONE FIELD TO-DAY WHERE YOU CAN GET HONOUR."

[The Council of the Football Association apparently proposes to carry out the full programme of the Cup Competition, just as if the country did not need the services of all its athletes for the serious business of War.]

Mr Punch's rebuke to Britain's professional footballers for their failure to cancel the 1914 season

not to kill but to frighten. It was the greatest pity that the clubs were
told to go on playing.

Clearly stung by such protests, the writers of Tottenham Hotspur's
Official Programme for their game of 5 December felt the need to
mount a spirited defence:

### Why is Football Attacked?

The fact is, the agitation against football is being conducted by
prejudiced people who dislike and oppose professional football
whether in times of peace or times of war. It would certainly
appear that the attack is made on football because it is the
working men's game, otherwise the same campaign would be
employed in relation to horse-racing, hunting, golf, theatres
and music halls. We cannot understand why footballers, and
those who obtain rational recreation from looking on, should
be singled out and sneered at as being shirkers.

### What a Stoppage would mean.

The real facts entirely disprove the charges made by the anti-
football crusaders. The Bishop of Birmingham says:– 'To stop
the game would be not only to deprive tens of thousands of
perfectly innocent and healthy enjoyment but also to throw
thousands of men (many of them fathers of families) out of
work.' Should football be stopped it would mean that between
70 and 80 men would be affected at Tottenham alone, and a
good many would then be without employment altogether.
Football is still being played in France, Germany and Austria.
Why should it be stopped in England?

In the end the anti-football campaign proved too strong, leading
to the formal closedown of professional football as from 24 April
1915. The issue for that day's game of *Oriental Notes*, the 'official
organ' of the Clapton Orient Football Club (now Leyton Orient)
acknowledged 'the unprecedented difficulties [which] have attended
our sport this season', but did so proudly, wishing 'those members of
the O's team who [had already] answered the call of King and Country
... a safe and speedy return to civil life, after having successfully
accomplished that to which duty [had] summoned them'.

In fact the club had little to be ashamed of: overall, forty-one
members of the Clapton Orient staff enlisted for war service, helping

to form a footballers' battalion of the Middlesex Regiment. Nor was the club backward in supporting the ethos of the time; writing of those who had already taken up arms, the 24 April programme stated: 'They have learned, on the football field, "to play the game", and that knowledge will be ever useful on the much more important field of battle.'

Meanwhile, in Scotland the controversy had been, if anything, substantially more virulent, with the famous Edinburgh team Heart of Midlothian being traduced as 'White Feathers of Midlothian' for continuing with the normal season. The response was remarkable: the founding of the 'Heart of Midlothian Battalion', a brotherhood of sportsmen to which seventy-five football clubs contributed members and which joined the British Army as the 2nd Edinburgh City Battalion, or more formally, as the 16th Battalion, the Royal Scots Regiment. By December 1914 Private George Blaney of the proud new unit wrote in a forceful rhyming couplet:

Do not ask where Hearts are playing and then look at me askance.
If it's football that you're wanting, you must come with us to France!

They duly sailed to France and eventually joined that other brotherhood of the battalions that went 'over the top' on the historic first day of the Battle of the Somme, 1 July 1916.

The alternative winter game was rugby football. It had split into two in 1895, Rugby League settling in the industrial north, while Rugby Union favoured the south and a substantial number of public schools. In the years before 1914 numerous clubs such as Harlequins, Blackheath and London Scottish developed links with the Territorial Army, while many rugby players at school or university automatically joined the OTC. The hands-on toughness of the game was seen as offering better preparation for soldiering than soccer, and its players were proud of the fact. Ronald Poulton, captain first of Harlequins and then of England, was an early enlister in 1914. He wrote in August to his parents: 'Germany has to be smashed, i.e. I mean the military party, and everybody realizes, and everybody is volunteering. And those who are the best trained are the most wanted, and so I should be a skunk to hold back.' So many did the same that by the beginning of September club Rugby Union was at an end throughout England.

Yet special matches continued. Thus in December the Public Schools and Universities Battalion narrowly defeated a Canadian military side in front of a crowd of 3,000 at Richmond. *The Times* noted that the ring seats along the touchline were almost solidly military – 'rows and rows of khaki caps and khaki figures leaning forward with hands on knees, rows of canes waving in time to the tunes of war cries that rose and fell'. The canes give away the class: as the historian who has researched this subject stated: 'the contrast with the crowd of "loafers" attending soccer matches could not be made clearer'.

Yet while rugby might raise the warrior temperature of the nation, it had one grave disadvantage. It could not be exported to the battlefields. The oval ball had no chance on ground where the round one could produce a decent game, even in areas pocked by shellfire. So football, footer, soccer, was far from finished. If it was the ordinary man's favourite game, it was also that of the fighting man – and of the enemy's soldiers too. It would play a notable part in the later history of 1914.

The other spectator sport of the masses, cricket, attracting vastly greater crowds than it does today, was not under pressure because it was obviously nearing the end of its season as hostilities began. Even so, its obligation to conform to the pressures of the time was sternly spelt out in a letter dated 12 September, in a magazine called *T.P.'s Weekly*, by the nation's most legendary batsman, Dr W. G. Grace:

> The fighting on the Continent is very severe and will probably be prolonged. I think the time has arrived when the county cricket season should be closed, for it is not fitting at a time like the present that able-bodied men should play day after day, and pleasure seekers look on.

Before the end of 1914, cricket quietly bowed out, long before football accepted the inevitable. A tucked-away announcement in the *Illustrated Sporting and Dramatic News* of 19 December stated:

> War or no War, there will be no county cricket next year. We have this from the lips of Lord Hawke, President of MCC, speaking last week at a Yorkshire County CC meeting, and again, a few days later, at the annual meeting of the Worcestershire County CC. Lord

Cobham, who was again elected President, made the same announcement. These straws show the direction of the wind.

\* \* \*

One inevitable consequence of the British urge to excel was that they had long been in the forefront in the matter of exploration. In the nineteenth century they had played a major role in the opening up of Africa. From the start of the twentieth century they had turned their attention to a new target: Antarctica. However, their hopes for supremacy in this far-flung part of the world had been dashed in December 1911 when Captain Scott's Polar Expedition lost the race to the South Pole to the Norwegian Roald Amundsen. Subsequently Scott and four other members of his party, thwarted by appalling weather, lost their lives on the way back. This was seen as a national tragedy, yet it was a tragedy with an aura of greatness about it, its essential element being a gallant struggle against appalling odds, so that it could become, almost, a kind of victory. If there was a motto, or text, for such high-risk ventures it was that famous line from Tennyson's *Ulysses*, 'To strive, to seek, to find, and not to yield'. The words were duly inscribed on the memorial cross erected at Scott's Antarctic base in honour of the fallen explorers.

Now in 1914 Sir Ernest Shackleton, an Anglo-Irishman with a substantial Antarctic track record in his own right, was planning to claim a new laurel for Britain: the first crossing of the Antarctic continent. Churchill came out against Shackleton's plan, calling it a 'sterile quest': 'The Pole has already been discovered. What is the use of another expedition?' But King George gave Shackleton his encouragement, presenting him with a flag for planting as and where the expedition might deem appropriate, while *The Times* saw virtue in Shackleton's intention 'to re-establish the prestige of Great Britain ... in Polar exploration'. Acquiring the necessary financial backing had taken months, the successful outcome being achieved just as the storm clouds gathered over Europe. In fact, Monday, 29 June, produced two striking headlines in London's *Daily Graphic*: the report of a Scottish millionaire's massive gift to Shackleton, and the news of the assassination of Archduke Franz Ferdinand in Sarajevo.

By the beginning of August Shackleton's ship, the aptly named

*Endurance*, was crewed, supplied and ready to go. She sailed from London's docks on Saturday the 1st. But the die was not yet cast. While on Bank Holiday Monday, 3 August, the *Endurance* rode at anchor off Margate, two expedition members departed to rejoin their regiments. Shackleton summoned his crew, announced that anyone who wished to do so could leave, and, with general approval, telegraphed the Admiralty, offering to place 'ship staff stores and provisions at your disposal recognizing the claims of my country before all other considerations respectfully submitting that if required the expedition be used as one unit'. He added: 'If not required I propose continuing the voyage forthwith . . .' The Admiralty declined his offer, effectively giving the green light for the expedition to continue. Anxious to leave no stone unturned, Shackleton sought a personal meeting with Kitchener, but Britain's new warlord showed scant interest in availing himself of the famous explorer's services. In any case at forty Shackleton was above the age of the volunteers the Secretary of State was now seeking for his new armies, and as something of an oddity would be very difficult to employ. In the event Shackleton's Scottish financier, Sir James Caird, solved his client's moral problem. The explorer reported Sir James's wisdom to his wife: 'There are hundreds of thousands of young men who could go to the war and there are not many I think who could do my job.' He decided to proceed.

This expedition, like Scott's, was to end in failure, but it was to emerge as, in its way, magnificent – and, curiously, in a manner that would link it to 1914. Shackleton never reached the Antarctic continent. His ship was caught and crushed in the Polar ice. In open boats he and his crew managed to reach an uninhabited protuberance of rocks in the southern seas named Elephant Island. Leaving the bulk of his men there, Shackleton and a select handful struggled through terrible trials to South Georgia, where, after conquering the final hazard of that island's formidable mountain range, they stumbled into the whaling station of Grytviken. All this had taken so long – nothing had been heard of Shackleton for the best part of two years – that his first question, on being recognized, was: 'Tell me, when was the war over?' The answer was chilling: 'The war is not over. Millions are being killed. Europe is mad. The world is mad.' He eventually made his way back to Elephant Island and retrieved every single member of his crew, at a time when, by a strange irony, squeamishness about losses had been long abandoned elsewhere.

The news that Shackleton and his crew had survived reached Britain on 1 June 1916, the day following the Grand Fleet's one major clash with the German High Seas Fleet, at Jutland, a naval battle of a kind that would never occur again and in which thousands perished. Over time Shackleton's story gained increasing respect. If his expedition had been a failure, his all but incredible journey back to civilization and safety was seen as an achievement of the utmost determination, grit and valour. One of his best officers, Captain Thomas Orde-Leese, would, indeed, make a very plausible comparison between Shackleton's brilliantly managed escape from near catastrophe and the British Expeditionary Force's own heroic withdrawal after its first clash with the Germans in 1914. 'The British Army failed at Mons,' he wrote,

> and carried out a retreat of unparalleled masterfulness, which was nothing but glorious ... The retreat of Sir Ernest Shackleton against overwhelming odds was none the less honourable and equally as successful in its own little sphere.

There could be no higher accolade.

\* \* \*

Long before this, the retreat from Mons had acquired a curious celebrity, almost a sanctification, in, by all normal standards, a most unexpected context.

On 29 September 1914 the London *Evening News* published a short story called 'The Bowmen'. Its author was Arthur Machen, a fifty-year-old writer born in the Welsh Marches who has been variously described as a visionary, a mystic, a poet and a seer. However, he would claim no supernatural inspiration for the story that would win, within a remarkably short time, an amazing international reputation, so much so that its actual authorship would be all but forgotten as his modest fable came increasingly to be seen as historical fact.

In brief, Arthur Machen's beguiling story, intended as a moralebooster for a populace increasingly dismayed by disturbing news from the Western Front, created the myth of the Angels of Mons. As the British fight back against the advancing Germans on that dramatic first day, 23 August 1914, a young soldier remembers a motto he has seen (curiously, on a plate in a vegetarian restaurant), *Adsit Anglis Sanctus Georgius*: 'May St George be a present help to the English'. He utters this out loud, to find that his cry is taken up a thousand-fold by a throng of ghostly figures, described by Machen as 'a long line of shapes, with a shining about them. They were like men who drew the bow, and with another shout, their cloud of arrows flew singing and tingling through the air towards the German hosts.' The assailants fall in their thousands, their generals deducing that the English must have used some new poison gas, 'as no wounds were discernible on the bodies of the dead'.

From this overtly fictional beginning there arose a vast if flimsy structure of credulity, which in a very short time led to claims that there had indeed been divine intervention on the battlefield, and that Machen's shining ones were clear evidence that God was on the side of the British. In some ways the speed with which the story circulated and was believed was symbolic of a desperate need for reassurance at a time when, for a nation somehow confident of an easy victory, things seemed to be going so badly wrong. In fact the country needed all the encouragement it could get, for at the front the fighting was showing signs of moving into a new and more challenging phase.

# CHAPTER EIGHT

# SIEGE WARFARE ON THE AISNE

THE BATTLE OF THE MARNE, by denying the Germans the quick victory they had planned for, made the war a long one. With hindsight, it can be seen that the Battle of the Aisne made it the kind of war it was.

Stopped in the valley of the Marne, the Germans made for the next valley to the north, that of the River Aisne. This should have been the occasion for an all-out counter-attack by the Allies, a seizing of the hour to press home their advantage. Such was certainly in the minds of the more ardent French commanders. With an almost Napoleonic flourish, General Foch wrote 'Vitesse! Vitesse!' at the foot of his orders. Similarly, General Franchet d'Esperey passed the message to his troops: 'En avant, soldats, pour la France!' But such exhortations to men with jaded minds and wearied limbs fell largely on unheeding ears. The psychological downturn of the one thing a soldier is never trained for – running away from the enemy – was not easily overcome by fine words. Nor was the situation helped by a sudden change in the weather. Drenching rain and wet, slippery roads were as dispiriting in their way as the scorching heatwave from which they had just emerged; if the choice were between dust and mud most soldiers would opt for the former. Meanwhile, as the infantry dragged their feet in exhaustion, the cavalry and the artillery could only advance at the speed of their long-suffering horses. As for the soldiers of the BEF, had they even been aware of such slogans as 'Vitesse!' and 'En avant', they were likely to be met with succinctly dismissive Anglo-Saxon rejoinders. The names of French generals meant little to the Tommies sweating through the August heat or slogging through the September rain. The only general whose name they latched on to was, it seems, the commander of Germany's First Army, von Kluck, who apparently was known to the Tommies as 'One O'Clock': e.g. as in the alleged statement by a man of the Duke of Cornwall's Light Infantry at Mons:

'I reckon them Surreys put the wind up One O'Clock....', though doubtless there were other unchronicled uses of the German general's unfortunate one-syllable name.

Cyril Falls's view of the British performance at this period was scathing.

> Most British historians have done their utmost to make as good a story as possible of the BEF's advance. In fact it was a crawl. The chief blame must undoubtedly fall on the head of Sir John French, who never seems to have sensed that he was moving into what was virtually a void, and never drove his troops forward.

For his part, Haig was dismayed at the sluggishness of the British advance, which was not helped by the fact that the cavalry and the infantry had somehow managed to get into a hopeless tangle. He noted in his diary on 9 September:

> I met the 5th Cavalry Brigade (Chetwode) moving at a walk and delaying the advance of our Infantry. I trotted on and saw Chetwode ... I explained to him that a little effort now might mean the conclusion of the War! The enemy was running back. It was the duty of each one of us to strain every effort to keep him on the run.

Nevertheless there were some serious if small-scale encounters. Captain Arthur Acland, 1st Battalion, Duke of Cornwall's Light Infantry, who had been involved in the first clash at Mons, was caught up in what he described as 'real hard fighting' in the last phase of the Marne: a 'rough and tumble' on 9 September which prompted him to state, 'I think there will never be a hotter corner than the one the CO, Major Price, and I, and A Company, got into.' Part of 14th Brigade, commanded by Brigadier General S. P. Rolt, they found their attempts to advance halted by 'pretty hot fire' in an area where there was thick woodland ahead of them:

> We could not tell where the enemy lay. As the hottest fire seemed to come from our right we faced in that direction and charged through the wood. We came out, after about fifty yards, to the far side and there we came under a perfect hail.
>
> There was nothing for it. The enemy were on the edge of another wood about eighty yards away with wire between us and them. We silenced the people opposite us pretty soon, but we could not deal

with those on our left. As soon as we held our fire the Germans opposite got at us again. Of course, it was a matter of time only to when our ammunition gave out and, at the rate we had to fire, that would not be long. If one moved a hand or head it drew a shower of lead, so we lay rather 'doggo' and only retaliated when their fire grew too hot to bear in silence. After about half an hour the CO asked me to go back to report to the General and ask for more troops, as we had lost heavily. I got back to the General in wonderfully quick time! Here I was told there were no more troops to be had. I was told to go out to the right and tell the situation to the 15th Brigade, who were coming up on our right at this time. So I went off and explained matters and the 15th attacked up on our right and eased things for a bit. If it had not been for them and the 13th Brigade to our left, we should have had a far worse time. As it was the regiment hung on until just before dark, when, having run clean out of ammunition, we had to retire to a position in the open a short way back. At nightfall we collected on a road at the back of our position, the 15th Brigade covered us with outposts, and we slept by the roadside, very weary.

For the most part at this period, however, desultory skirmishes were the norm, glancing blows, the enemy's main force never being quite in contact. The gunnery NCO E. J. Cummings wrote under the date 10 September:

D., E. and J. Batteries of Horse Artillery working in conjunction with each other managed to smash up a German Convoy. Later we captured 2,000 prisoners. I think you will agree it was a good day's work.

*Sept 11th.* We advance over the Battlefield today and view with interest the damage we have done. Bodies, horses, wagons etc are scattered over the fields and we have to throw them into the ditches on either side of the road, in order to proceed.

His diary entry for 13 September, however, can be seen with hindsight to strike an altogether more significant note:

Today, Sunday, I think, a terrible battle starts. The artillery as usual are playing a large part in it. The Germans have an almost impregnable position and are making a determined resistance.

Thus the insight of an artillery 'other rank'. The following day, 14 September, Field Marshal Sir John French came to the same conclusion. He wrote in his diary a brief sentence which has been tellingly described as 'the epitaph' for the first phase of the 1914 campaign: 'I think it is very likely that the enemy is making a determined stand on the Aisne.'

\* \* \*

Independently but correctly the young gunner and his Commander-in-Chief had come to the identical conclusion. There was going to be very serious fighting. Some battles are named retrospectively; this battle had its name ready and waiting from the start. It would last far longer, and would be far more of an ordeal, than any of the armies involved had at first expected.

It would not be listed among the most famous battles of the First World War, indeed it would often be given short shrift by historians eager to deal with better-known and more sacrificial encounters. But the Battle of the Aisne would, in one very important respect, set the pattern for the style of warfare that would dominate throughout the next four years, for it was here that the term 'The Trenches', destined to enter the nation's folklore as one of war's defining concepts, had its first significant outing.

A key factor that has done little for the standing of this battle is that it was fought far from those areas of the Western Front with which the British are best acquainted. While visitors by the thousand walk the sites of Belgium and northern France, few think of heading south to the country of the Aisne.

Should they do so, they would find a very unfamiliar kind of battlefield. The valley of the Aisne is utterly unlike the flat territory of the Flanders Plain, or the Chilterns-like rise and fall of the Somme country. The river, running east–west, is slow and sluggish, so much so that navigation has to be assisted here and there by stretches of canal, while the valley itself is quietly agricultural, with a scatter of tiny villages, most of them on or near the riverbank. To the south of the river, the countryside is unremarkable: fields, copses and gentle undulations to the far horizon. To the north, however, the ground rises to dramatic forested heights, from which spurs and shoulders thrust out, making this a good territory to defend but an extremely difficult one to attack. Moreover, the summit, far from being a jumble of crests and hollows and wild afforestation, has been so well groomed by man and nature that it carries along it for most of its length the famous highway known to history as the Chemin des Dames, the 'Ladies' Road', built at the instruction of King Louis XV for the ease and pleasure of his daughters on their journeys from Compiègne to visit the château of the specially favoured Duchess of Nemours. To have their own well-laid roadway behind their lines would be of great use to the Germans in the coming battle. Beyond the summit the ground plunges down to another valley, that of the Ailette, with another steep rise beyond that, and, nine miles further north, the cathedral city of Laon – which would shortly become German head-quarters for this sector of the front – dominating the surrounding country for miles around.

There would be fierce fighting here again in 1917, and yet again in 1918, with British units heavily involved, so that the 1914 encounter would become known as the First Battle of the Aisne, the later encounter becoming officially the Second.

This was the arena in which the opposing armies now found themselves with no alternative than to fight a vital battle. It soon became obvious to those concerned with the strategy and tactics of the new situation on the Allied side that, in effect, they were about to conduct a siege.

As it happened, on 13 September, the British almost achieved a coup that might have broken the siege before it became established. Haig's I Corps pushed its brigades up the spurs leading to the Chemin des Dames ridge at a point where there appeared to be an exploitable gap between the Germans' First and Second Armies. They could not know, however, that the fall on 8 September of the fortress of Maubeuge, which had been holding out since 25 August, had released the VII Reserve Corps for service on the Aisne. Its thrusting commander, General von Zwehl, had promptly ordered his troops south at breakneck speed. By 11 a.m. on the 13th von Zwehl's all but exhausted men (a quarter of his force had dropped out during the march) had reached the crest of the ridge, closing the gap – one is almost tempted to write 'slamming shut the last gate' – as they did so.

One notable observer present who was well qualified to analyse the new situation was a certain officer of the Royal Engineers, whose duty, as officially assigned to him by the British Government, was to report his findings to the outside world by writing regular despatches from the front. Colonel Ernest Dunlop Swinton had won a distinctive reputation before the war as both a military historian and as a writer of stories, though it might be better to define them as parables, intended to raise matters of importance in relation to the art of war. (One notable fable dissecting the failures of the Boer War, entitled 'The Defence of Duffer's Drift', had attracted notice even in political circles, while a series of shorter stories, published under the title *The Green Curve*, had been a source of much discussion among serious-minded officers since 1908.) Shortly after the opening of hostilities Swinton had been sent to France by the Secretary for War, Lord Kitchener, to act as a war correspondent. The French had gone back on previous arrangements and forbidden the battlefields to all professional journalists. However, although they barred civilians, they were prepared to accept some suitably qualified army officer, and Churchill, on the basis of his admiration for 'Duffer's Drift', suggested Swinton for the role. Swinton seized his opportunity enthusiastically and produced a stream of vivid and widely syndicated despatches under the *nom de guerre* of 'Eye-Witness present with General Headquarters'.

He soon saw the true character of the Aisne fighting, pointing out, in particular, that the Germans were using techniques which, he deduced, had been specifically evolved against the possibility of their having to lay siege to the French capital. In his report of 21 September he wrote:

> The present battle may well last for some days more before a decision is reached, since, in truth, it now approximates somewhat to siege warfare. The Germans are making use of searchlights, and this fact, coupled with their great strength in heavy artillery, leads to the supposition that they are employing material for the siege of Paris.

Unable to use these resources as planned for the purposes of urban warfare, the Germans were now using them defensively in the field.

Four days later Swinton returned to the same subject, suggesting that the reason for the emergence of siege warfare conditions was owing 'first, to the immense power of resistance possessed by an army which is amply equipped with heavy artillery and has sufficient time to fortify itself; and, secondly, to the vast size of the forces engaged, which at present stretch more than half-across France'. He concluded: 'To state that methods of attack must approximate more closely to those of siege warfare ... is a platitude; but it is one which will bear repetition if it in any way assists to make the present situation clear.'

A not dissimilar view of the situation was taken by Lord Loch, in the letter he had written to his wife on 14 September:

> We are fairly hung up on the Aisne and have not been able to advance at all or at least very little. My own opinion is that we are going to have a big battle here. Our pursuit of the Germans when they were on the run was feeble and slow and they had time to collect their people. Now when they find they have been able to check us on the Aisne they are bringing more troops down to fight. I estimate that we have 10 Corps in front of us and the French armies on each side of us. This gives us a superiority in numbers and we hope in morale but it means a big battle.

He was also seriously concerned about the problems of coping with a battlefield with a river running through it: on which side should they put their guns?

> At the present moment we are in a tactically bad way as the Germans can bring gun and rifle to bear on our infantry and we cannot support them with our guns. If we put our guns on the south side of the river, the range is too great, if we move them to the north they cannot fire or at best cannot direct their fire owing to the rising ground on top of which we cannot establish ourselves. At least that is the situation as regards II Corps. I Corps is better as they have got fairly well established on the north side and I hope may help us tomorrow.
>
> The French on our immediate left are also stuck but those further west are getting on well. The French Corps on our right is being very heavily counterattacked. The Germans completely outnumber us in guns and all our casualties practically are from gun fire.

Loch added a personal codicil naming three of his friends who had just been killed – one on 13 September and two the very day he wrote

to his wife – ending with the heartfelt comment: 'Oh this beastly war
I do wish it would end.'

* * *

How the Allies were to respond to this situation – how, in fact, they
were to invest this unexpected new-style Troy glowering down at
them from the Aisne heights – was the dilemma which overhung the
whole battle. At first they did what they were expected to do in any
such situation; they launched a series of attacks. But before that there
was the necessary preliminary stage: getting their infantry across the
river, almost all of whose bridges the Germans had attempted to
destroy, and where any movement in the open was likely to be clearly
visible to the enemy's observers on the heights above.

As Loch indicated, some elements of I Corps had already made the
crossing. The newly constituted III Corps now attempted to follow
suit on the night of 12–13 September, at Venizel, south-east of
Soissons. The Germans had attempted to blow the bridge there with
four substantial charges, but one had failed to explode. The engineer
sent forward to examine the bridge reported that, although the main
girders on each side of the principal span were cut, the reinforced
concrete of the roadway would probably be sufficient to allow infantry to cross, provided great care was taken, though there was no
guarantee that the bridge might not collapse at any moment. It was
decided to make the attempt, with the men being sent across in single
file and the contents of the ammunition carts being passed over by
hand.

One officer who viewed this prospect with considerable alarm was
Second Lieutenant the Hon. Lionel, later Lord, Tennyson, 1st Battalion,
Rifle Brigade, 4th Division, notable for the dual distinction of being a
relative of the famous poet and a future cricket captain of England.
He had not been long at the front and had spent much of his time
since his arrival as a kind of unofficial staff-officer to his brigade
commander, the unpredictable Brigadier General Sir Aylmer Hunter-
Weston, known to the troops as 'Hunter Bunter', and not regarded as
one of the most sagacious and reliable of the BEF's corps of general
officers. Tennyson was suspicious that the bridge had not been
thoroughly reconnoitred and that the country beyond had not been
checked to see if it was under German surveillance. His diary, written

at the time but brought up to date a few months later, showed that there was acute anxiety among the troops as they approached the bridge:

> It seemed to us all an absolute risky slapdash proceeding, which luckily for us turned out alright, though if we had not been so lucky and the Germans had not imagined they had destroyed this bridge, we should none of us been left to tell the tale. However, about I a.m. the whole of 11th Brigade went over the bridge one by one in the middle of this pitch black night, in the pouring rain. The bridge which was some 60 feet above the river quivered and shook as every man went over, and eventually the whole brigade got across, though it was a pretty dangerous proceeding. The men were so tired they fell asleep as they stood or marched, and one felt oneself walking along and reeling like a drunken man. As soon as the whole brigade were across the river we advanced across the open ploughed and stubble country, through the village of Bucy-le-Long with bayonets fixed, to the top of the ridge of hills overlooking the Aisne.
>
> As it turned out, if we had not crossed tonight over the river, and this flat open country, we must have lost hundreds of men doing it, as the Germans had a wonderful position, and never till this day shall I know why they had no outposts out tonight, except they thought they had blown up the bridge. Even the village of Bucy-le-Long, they informed us, was full of half drunken and dead tired Germans who never awoke.
>
> We arrived on top of this ridge about 4.30 a.m. I was now able to snatch two hours sleep till 6.30 a.m.; though it was still pouring with rain, it did not keep me awake, as I was beat to the world.

Early across the river, they were also early into action; indeed Tennyson's entry for Sunday, 13 September, is a searing account, fuelled by anger at what he saw as the spendthrift carelessness of those issuing the orders and by dismay at a serious example of that most frightening of phenomena, casualties caused by one's own side's guns – now known, with considerable irony, as 'friendly fire'. First, however, there was a curious encounter with an unusual sort of 'native', showing the kind of bizarre episode that can occur when the tide of battle suddenly sweeps over hitherto peaceful country-side:

At 6.30 a.m. I had a tin of bully beef just outside a cave which we went into, and found an old hermit in there with great long nails, hair and beard, a regular sort of person one reads of in fairy stories. We had him out and searched him, but could find no traces of him being a spy, and though we kept him under supervision the whole time we were there, the inhabitants said he had lived there for years.

As they made their advance, the problem as to which side of the river the British should deploy their artillery was seen as one of more than academic interest only:

C Company after breakfast were ordered to watch our right flank, and my platoon were put in advance of the rest of the company, along the edge of a field, on outpost. I sent out one or two sniping parties who came back and reported they had picked off from the top of a hayrick several Germans who were digging a trench.

Everything went more or less calmly till 9.30 a.m. when our own guns spotted us in our waterproof sheets, as it was still raining, from the opposite side of the river, and thinking we were Germans started shelling us with lyddite. Of course our General I imagine had never let these gunners know that we had crossed the river. These shells were particularly well aimed, and though we tried to signal to them who we were, the shells came thicker and thicker until my captain, Jimmy Brownlow, signalled to me to retire to where he was. Across this open field we went, doubling as fast as we could, and the shells falling all amongst us. We lost a very good corporal, Acting Corporal Gregory, a signaller, who had his head blown off right close to me, and three more men severely wounded as well as one or two others killed, and several more wounded, the names of whom I cannot remember. My servant Welch, who was close to A/Cpl Gregory when he was killed, had all his hair stained absolutely yellow by the lyddite, which was still that colour for weeks afterwards, and he couldn't get it off.

I had great luck just before we managed to get under cover as I was hit in the back on the burberry by a bit of a shell, which burst between a rifleman called Hall and myself, but never hurt either of us. Everything went quiet now for a bit, and our guns stopped shelling us, and we got the wounded removed, and buried poor young Gregory.

About midday the Germans started shelling us, but nothing came particularly close.

The hazards of the day were, however, far from over; even though the battalion had barely established itself in unknown terrain and had come through a night and a morning of severe risk and stress, it was instructed to make an attack:

> At about 4 p.m. A and B Company were ordered to advance at about the N in Le Moncel, while C and I coys were in reserve. As soon as these two companies got to the crest of the hill, all the German batteries started opening fire on them, having got the range perfectly. About 30 of our fellows were killed and another 70 or 80 wounded, as well as Captains Nugent, Harrison, and Riley, the last named very slightly. Sergeant Dorey, my old platoon sergeant of no 7 platoon, when I was in B Company, was killed, and Rfmn Spindler and many others I knew killed. Sergeant Walker, who had done so well at Ligny and had been recommended for the DCM and Médaille Militaire, had his leg almost blown off in this advance, but hanging by a bit of bone. It is hardly credible but he took his pocket knife out and on the field where he lay cut his leg off, and bound his leg up and when it grew dark he was still conscious when he was brought in on a stretcher. Sergeant Roberts of B Coy was badly wounded also.

For Second Lieutenant Tennyson there was no easy acceptance that all this was part and parcel of the ritual of battle. He continued, angrily:

> This stupid advance did no good, and we were forced to retire about 300 yards again. The Germans went on shelling us up till about 10 p.m. and sent over occasional shells during the night. Had something to eat in a cave about 9 p.m. which was full of wounded and dying, which was a horrible sight that I shall long remember. Dropped off to sleep in this open field about 10.30 p.m. but was aroused about 1 a.m. to go and dig trenches on the ridge where we lost so many men about 4 p.m. today.

So ended for the 1st Rifle Brigade the first day of the Battle of the Aisne, 1914.

\* \* \*

Another hazardous crossing of the Aisne was at a village some kilometres to the east of Venizel which rapidly won itself a certain celebrity: Pont-Arcy. Major Henry Daniell, 2nd Battalion, Royal Irish Regiment, 3rd Division, in a letter to his mother, offered her a graphic, if a deliberately light-hearted, account of what he had experienced and seen there:

> The actual crossing of the river was rather hazardous and yet rather amusing. The bridge had been blown up but a plank bridge for infantry over the gap had not been removed by the Germans. We had to run over this while a German gun played on us at a range of 1,000 yards; it was all right if one bolted just after the gun had fired, but it more often happened that the men miscalculated the time – often I saw the guns blaze into a crowd of men as they were running over and yet only one of my men was hit. I was directing them, as they arrived on the far side where they had to bolt down under cover under a bank and there was much fun and merriment as they arrived safely under cover.

Daniell does not date the day of his unit's crossing, but under the date 15 September Gunner B. C. Myatt, 109 Battalion, Royal Field Artillery, newly arrived in France, saw the grim hazards this tiny fragment of the front presented and was less amused. He wrote in his diary:

> A great infantry battle all night. The Germans were greatly strengthened here and our troops had to cross a canal, a railway and a river, all close together, and all the bridges were blown up. There was a girder left on one of the bridges which our infantry ran across under heavy machine and rifle fire. They gained the other side and held it but they were in a horrible position. They could neither go forward or back, but they held their ground. All the time it was raining terrible and our troops were in an awful state.

In such circumstances, for a military chaplain, the call of duty might mean recrossing the river almost as soon as having crossed it. On 14 September the Revd Frederick 'Fritz' Smithwick, chaplain to 5th Brigade, 2nd Division, after experiencing several hours of 'jolly unpleasant' shelling on the northern bank, had barely reached his assigned destination at the little village of Verneuil when he was summoned back to perform one of his, by now, all too frequent religious rituals. The occasion, and its aftermath, produced the following sombre entry in his diary:

> A message came for me to bury a RE officer and a sapper the other side of the bridge at Pont-Arcy. I jumped on my horse and rode off about four miles.
>
> On reaching the bridge I was nearly knocked over by a party of sappers flying from the bridge which was being shelled. I had to cross and I am glad to say the shells went wide.
>
> I buried Lt Miller RE and the sapper and returned to Verneuil.
>
> After a very scratch meal we went up to the château which had been turned into a temporary hospital.
>
> The horrors I saw tonight I will never forget.
>
> Over 200 wounded are here and some of the cases are terrible.
>
> I hear Col. Montresor was killed. Col. Dalton is badly wounded and hardly likely to recover.
>
> I spent some hours doing what I could amongst the wounded and returned to a room in the château for a little rest.
>
> The guns are still firing and a night attack evidently is proceeding. Please God this will not last long.
>
> It is terrible.

One young officer who found himself deeply moved by the gallant efforts of his comrades to harass the enemy and maintain their attack was Second Lieutenant Geoffrey Loyd. He wrote on 15 September:

> The British Army at this moment is making history. With a small force extended upon a large front clinging to the slopes of a position chosen by the enemy and well prepared several days before after terrible losses and absolutely no reserves, it is defying a force which has three Army Corps against the 1st, 2nd and 3rd Divisions, and which could mass a force and march straight through us, did it only know the true state of affairs.

* * *

If the Battle of the Aisne was indeed a siege battle, as it clearly was, if of an untraditional kind, the corollary of that fact was that it was also bound to become a battle of trenches: serious ones, not the overnight scratchings in the ground which had been the norm during the days of rapid movement after Mons. The original policy of head-on attacks having produced little success, from about 18 September the situation became one of hanging on and hoping, while taking increasingly energetic precautions against the attentions of guns which were no longer in movement but static and registering on targets with a deadly accuracy. In a report to the King on 2 October, Field Marshal Sir John French wrote the following prophetic sentences:

> I think the battle of the Aisne is very typical of what battles in the future are most likely to resemble. Siege operations will enter largely into the tactical problems – the *spade* will be as great a necessity as the rifle, and the heaviest calibres and types of artillery will be brought up in support on either side.

For the spade, read trenches. As the battle continued, more and more the focus was on trenches. Looking back from the vantage point of 26 September on a period of twelve days and nights in the line – in which another disadvantage, a lack of adequate clothing, had come to the fore – Major Daniell wrote in his letter home:

> Five of our nights in the trenches we spent in pelting rain, most of the men had no greatcoats and as the cold was intense I do not know how they kept their health, but they have done so, as there has been next to no sickness. We have been sitting in the trenches exposed to shellfire, and where our artillery has been unable to reply or give us any assistance, during the day we have kept very few men in position, the rest have been underground.
>
> Every man had to dig a hole in the bank, and completely disappear like a rabbit. Some days they could not even come out for any food. Casualties have occurred daily except for one day. In spite of this all the men are well and in excellent spirits. Such a filthy dirty lot as we were you cannot imagine. For ten days I was unable to take off my clothes or get a complete wash and I had to keep on the same wet boots for five days, fortunately some new government boots and socks came over to us and I was able to get a change.

'To dig a hole and disappear like a rabbit': the phrase flows easily from Major Daniell's pen. He is making light of things, yet – as a moment of reflection will confirm – there is a terrible irony in the fact that a proud regular battalion like the 2nd Royal Irish Rifles has suddenly been reduced to such indignities. He would not be the only

officer to use such a simile as the war hardened and became bogged
down over the next few weeks. Lieutenant Rowland Owen, for
example, 2nd Battalion, Duke of Wellington's Regiment, 5th Division,
wrote home on 30 September: 'We are now living in a wood in little
rabbit scratches, roofed over with straw – I am getting terribly sick of
it.' Lieutenant Arthur Maitland, 2nd Battalion, Essex Regiment, wrote
in similar terms the same day, though he at least managed a humorous variation on the theme:

> I spend my day and night in a trench. I have got a hole, partly
> burrowed out and partly roofed over with branches, just big enough
> to lie down. . . . As a matter of fact I think our position is too strong
> for the Germans' liking, they shell us constantly but we laugh at them
> from our burrows like rabbits.

More seriously, Lieutenant Angus Macnaghten, 1st Black Watch,
offered the following thumb-nail account of his current routine, in a
letter he wrote to his much-loved young wife in early October:

> I am very fit and well, but wearying for home. It is a ghastly job,
> and I often have to bury one of my poor fellows after dark in a
> nameless grave. Have to wait till dark to avoid being shelled. I'm
> always up half the night patrolling my sentries etc. The rest I spend in
> a little hole in the ground, just like a rabbit. We all dig ourselves right
> into the earth, unless we are lucky enough to be near a cave, of which
> there are quite a number here.

Yet as at almost any time throughout the war, there were always
those who could make light of their situation, however adverse. One
such was Captain Arthur Acland, 1st Battalion, Duke of Cornwall's
Light Infantry, whose experiences at Mons or the Marne had done
nothing to weaken his resolve or cool his ardour. His account of
conditions on the Aisne survives as part of a letter written by his
sister on 30 September to either a relative or a close family friend:

> I had a line from A[rthur]. written on the 21st at 5 p.m. They
> were all in a wood, and he writes 'I'm sitting in a little palace of my
> own making. It's made of several poles cut from the wood we are
> occupying, two huge gates borrowed from an adjoining garden, much
> brushwood, straw, and 4 waterproof sheets. A thick carpet of straw
> and a few bundles as an arm chair, and no one could be cosier under

the circumstances. A certain continuous banging and booming becomes a bore, altho' one does get extraordinarily used to it. About this time of day our gunners and those of our friends seem always to exchange compliments. One can almost tell the time by it!' So for the moment they seem to be having a slight rest.

\* \* \*

Digging and trenches soon became dominant themes in the entries in Second Lieutenant Tennyson's ever-eloquent diary (which frequently included map references for greater clarity):

*Monday, Sept 14th.* 2nd Day of the Battle of the Aisne
    Started digging trenches on this ridge about the N in Le Moncel about 1 a.m. and dug hard until 4 a.m. when we stood to arms. The Germans who were about 800 yds off were pretty busy all night firing across our way a good bit . . .
    Germans started shelling us about 5 a.m. again tremendously, and as our trenches were very narrow, and we were very crowded in them we spent a most miserable day. They had our range to a nicety, only just managed not to pitch one in our trench, but the suspense of hearing the shells coming just before they burst is awful. They came very very near us all day, but we only had about four men wounded.

There then occurred a tragic incident that could only have happened when the kind of warfare for which the Aisne would become notorious was so new and unfamiliar that even experienced officers failed to appreciate its hazards:

    About 10 a.m., there had been a lull for some reason or other and no shell had come over for about twenty minutes, when to my surprise I saw our Colonel Biddulph and Sir Evelyn Bradford in command of the Seaforths who were on our left coming up to our trenches with a map in their hands. They called Jimmy Brownlow, my captain, out of the trench and they all three stood looking at the map. I heard the words 'General Advance', but at that moment two shells burst in rapid succession right in the middle of these three. Sir Evelyn Bradford, who by the way used to play cricket for Hampshire, was instantly killed, Jimmy Brownlow had two great holes blown in the back of his head, and we never thought he would live the day out, though thank heaven he is still alive in February [1915] when I am copying this out of my diary, and our Colonel had his hat blown off about 30 yards. We got Jimmy into the trench and managed to get him back to the cave for medical assistance. I was now in command of C Company and for the rest of the day the Germans shelled us with their heavy siege guns unmercifully until dusk, when we were relieved by another company until 8 p.m.

Even this did not bring an end to Tennyson's extraordinary day. As they were being relieved there was 'a scare of a night attack by the Germans', resulting in his being sent down to warn the rest of the battalion:

I was fired on three times in running down to tell them. However no night attack came off. Dug trenches all night till 4 a.m., when we stood to arms.

Thus ended, for Second Lieutenant Tennyson, the second day of the Battle of the Aisne.

* * *

Tennyson's diary for the following days records the arrival of other elements which would soon become part of the culture of trench warfare. On 23 September the trench raid, albeit in rudimentary form:

A party of Germans crept up just before daylight this morning, and stabbed one of our sentries in I Company, and killed him. These Germans are pretty plucky fellows as they had to come right up to the end of one of the trenches to do this, but the sentry must have been asleep.

On 2 October the night patrol:

Started digging a forward trench about 300 yds ahead of our present forward trench, about 50 yds from the edge of the turnip field. We dug till midnight, and put up barbed wire in front of these trenches, got sniped a good bit during the evening, but nobody was hit. I went out with our listening patrol about 200 yards into the turnips, being about 400 yards from the German trenches. It is very creepy work lying in these turnips at night, as the overgrown turnips look exactly like men advancing at night, and one hears all sorts of sounds among the leaves rustling. The Seaforths' listening patrol was on our right though they would not come out very far into the turnips.

Perhaps the main differences between that patrol and countless later ones were the distance between the trenches – usually quite wide at this stage – and the rustling of leaves. There were not too many trees with rustling leaves when trench warfare got into its stride.

Finally, on 6 October, the communication trench:

> At dawn we moved back to our previous forward trenches by a wonderful communication trench about 300 yards long which we had dug. If the farmer is not a fool here he will keep these trenches after the war, and would make a fortune by tourists coming to see them, as even our General who is not given to praise anyone much said they were very fine trenches, and the best he had seen.

* * *

The twenty-four-day encounter on the Aisne had a number of moods, varying between a kind of sullen torpor and moments of extreme violence. Private Charles Rainbird, 1st Battalion, West Yorkshire Regiment, which was on the extreme right of the British sector next to the French, experienced the battle at its most ferocious, when his unit found itself in particularly dangerous straits on 19–20 September. In fact these two days saw the beginning and the end of his fighting war. The diary account he scribbled at the time and then wrote up soon afterwards is a remarkable document, part vividly observed historical narrative, part *cri de cœur* to the family he fears, with some justification, that he might never see again.

*19-9-14*

Halted last night in a field, and had to stand in pitch darkness in the worst rainstorm I have ever experienced. At dusk tonight we advance to attack the enemy, three miles away. I have no doubt it will be hard work, but as the artillery have been shelling them for a week, perhaps we shall do it. We are the 6th Division, and we have the support of part of the 4th Div. I don't know exactly how many are opposed to us, a considerable number, I believe. Well, Au Revoir all, God bless you. We have marched and fought our way from St Nazaire to this place, Bourg-et-Comin. I may not write any more, Nemo Mortalium Omnibus Horis Sapit. [No man knows the hour of his death.] If I come through alright, I'll tell you all about it; the Gs' shells are dropping in the village now, so we must move forward. General Congreve says we are to occupy the trenches, facing the Gs' artillery, and hold them at all costs. Ah, me; Wife, Children, Mother, all farewell: Charles.

*20-9-14*

Dawn

The Trenches, Bourg-et-Comin

The last for some of my comrades, for we have been in action since 8.30 last night. A and B double companies in the front trenches, have been firing continuously since we relieved the Coldstreams' D and C companies in support. I have lost many an old comrade since last night. I am scribbling these notes during a lull, and eating bully and biscuits.

There then occurred another instance of the nightmare predicament of being caught in 'friendly fire'. Lest it be thought Rainbird might have allowed his imagination to run riot when describing this episode, it is fair to say that the Official History, under the heading 'Disaster to the West Yorkshire', tells, if in more measured terms, much the same story. Its account reads as follows:

> Soon after dawn the Germans attacked the Moroccans immediately on the right of the British line and drove them back. Lieut-Colonel F. W. Towsey commanding the 1/West Yorkshire Regiment, which was the right battalion of the British Army, thereupon sent out a company to cover his exposed right flank. The Moroccans soon rallied and came forward again, when, not knowing what had happened, they fired into this company, inflicting some thirty casualties.

This is Rainbird's version, though note he calls the Moroccans 'Zouaves', a name often used by both French and British:

*20.9.14. 8.30 a.m.* As dawn was breaking this morning there occurred one of those hellish mistakes which occur in every war. We saw through the half-light a large body of men evidently retiring on

our right. Our Colonel ordered my Company 'D' to swing round so
as to cover their retirement if they should prove to be allies. After
advancing about 200 yards we saw that they were allies (Zouaves)
when, to our horror they suddenly turned and opened fire on us. Oh
God, it was awful, every one of us exposed to a raking fire and no
cover; they had evidently mistaken us for the enemy. My mates were
falling all over the place and there were 37 killed in less than two
minutes. Naturally, our boys opened fire on them, in spite of the
CO's shout of 'Don't fire!' I dropped one fellow as he was in the act
of firing, then we received the order: 'Retire'. Our support trenches
were about 200 yards away, 500 yards behind the front firing line. As
we turned to retire I caught my foot in some obstacle and, pitching
forward on my head, was for a second or two stunned. On regaining
my senses I saw my comrades had regained their trenches, and was
about to follow them, when I heard a shout from my right; looking
round, I saw one of my mates named Luby crawling along on his
knees or rather one knee, and dragging the other leg behind him. He
had been shot through the thigh and the bone was broken. Seeing
that he could never reach safety in his wounded state, I ran over to
him and, dropping my rifle, swung him over my shoulder and started
for the trenches. My God, how the bullets did whistle, for they were
still firing at us, but my luck was in and neither of us was hit again, and
I am glad to say I got back to the trenches with him. I was pretty
exhausted as he was a 14-stone man and I had all my equipment on.
General Congreve, who had witnessed our lucky escape, asked my
CO for my name and number. So perhaps I was mentioned in
dispatches. Many a VC has been won for less.

There was more to come for the poor 1st West Yorkshires that
day. The battlefield briefly quietened but then the Germans attacked
again, forcing the Moroccans back a second time. Once again the
West Yorkshires took a fearsome pounding, this time with enfilade
fire from the Germans. Rainbird was uncertain as to what might have
happened because he was writing up his account in the German
prisoner of war camp in which he found himself soon after the events
described. He was captured in the confusion following the battalion's
second ordeal of that day.

\* \* \*

Any battle is a complex of innumerable elements and experiences, and one such as this one, fought not, as it were, in 'dedicated' territory, devoid of civilians and totally occupied by the matters of war, was bound to have an especially wide range of participants and victims. Later battles like the Somme or Passchendaele were fought each in its own arena, its own stadium *de guerre*, but this one was fought across an ordinary populated landscape and was thus prone to what would now be described as 'collateral damage'. The diary of Second Lieutenant Loyd includes two notable examples, the first being the tragic fate of a local aristocrat who paid the price for his determination not to be ousted from his home ground. Thus on Monday, 14 September, Loyd wrote:

> The unfortunate Marquis de Verneuil, of about 44 yrs of age, remained in his Château all day while German shells played upon it and did considerable damage. Verneuil itself was well nigh a shambles before dark.

The almost inevitable sequel followed on Thursday the 17th:

> The unfortunate Marquis Rillar de Verneuil was hit by a shell in the side yesterday while burying men and horses in his garden and died and was buried today. A French interpreter was instantly killed by his side.

His diary for the previous day included another poignant event, witnessed when coming back to his temporary quarters after a day of hostile artillery fire and harassment by both sides:

> As I returned alone and began to climb down the slope I saw a touching incident in the garden of the cottage in which we were living. We had been in the next room to the body of an old gentleman who had owned the house and who had died at a ripe old age four days before from heart failure. I saw the old ladies of the house, who had bravely cared and cooked for us the night before, and a party of my platoon and the French interpreters all bareheaded in the performance of burying the old man under a fruit tree in his own small garden. A Church burial in these sad times would have been beyond possibility. It must have been a drear funeral, during the greatest artillery duel the British Army had held during the war.

It is hardly surprising that in a passage written on Friday, 18 September, describing a search along the canal bank near Pont-Arcy cutting unnecessary wires and examining bridges for electric contacts, Loyd should have pointedly commented on the 'dreadful relics' of the execution of the German guns, in particular 'horses lying on all sides, some cut in two with only the forequarters and head to be seen'. It was precisely the kind of scene imagined by Sir Edward Elgar when he had written of his fears for his beloved horses only a few weeks earlier.

*  *  *

All this raises an important question: what did those involved think of the kind of warfare that characterized the early fighting of 1914, up to and including the Battle of the Aisne?*

There is a fairly general assumption that the regulars who bore the brunt of the first campaigns went off cheerfully and uncomplainingly to challenge the enemy, ready to do their duty for King and Country whatever the cost, and that it was only when the civilian volunteers of 1914 took the field that – in the old expression – 'war was found out for what it was'.

The papers of Captain C. J. Paterson, 1st Battalion, South Wales Borderers, offer an interesting case history.

*Wednesday, 16th September.* I have never spent and imagine that I can never spend a more ghastly and heart-rending forty eight hours than the last . . . We have been fighting hard since 8 a.m. on the 14th and have suffered much . . .

We have been under fire of all sorts, rifle fire from snipers, shell from the enemy, shell (bursting short) from our own guns and we have not lacked experience. The sights were ghastly. Wounded crying all night and no one to help them. The doctors have done all they can, but the casualties are heavier than they can easily cope with . . .

He then continued, reflectively:

Here I sit outside my Headquarters trench in the sun. The rain which we have had without a break for the past two days has now stopped and the world should look glorious . . . [A]ll should be nice

* See the Prologue for an extended discussion of this subject.

and peaceful and pretty. What it actually is is beyond description. Trenches, bits of equipment, clothing (probably bloodstained), ammunition, tools, caps, etc. etc. everywhere. Poor fellows shot dead are lying in all directions. Some of ours, some of the 1st Guards Brigade who passed over the ground before us, and many Germans. All the hedges torn and trampled, all the grass trodden in the mud, holes where shells have struck, branches torn off trees by the explosion. Everywhere the same hard, grim, pitiless signs of battle and war. I have had a belly full of it. Those who were in South Africa say that that was a picnic to this and the strain is terrific. No wonder if after a hundred shells have burst over us some of the men want to get back into the woods for rest. Ghastly, absolutely ghastly, and whoever was in the wrong in the matter which brought this war to be, is deserving of more than he can ever get in this world.

One other young officer who had no love for the kind of warfare in which he found himself on the Aisne was Lieutenant Rowland Owen. In his case the evidence comes not from a diary, but from letters to his parents. As early as 13 September – at the start of the Aisne fighting – he was writing:

> It is a very sickening thing to be under a shellfire, and we have had a good dose in the small time the war has been on ... I have not seen any Russians or Austrians, but I have of the other three forces, and there seems to be a unanimous feeling that nobody would mind how soon this war came to a close.

He was even more vehement writing sixteen days later, on the 29th: in a passage in which the 'John' referred to is his fire-eating naval officer brother, with whom he feels increasingly out of sympathy:

> I have not met a single man (or horse) of the English, French or German armies who is not dying for the war to finish! John and the Kaiser alone want to keep on. I often feel that this war has done a lot towards the world's peace. You see, if all goes well, we ought to win the victory which swallows up all strife, like Waterloo; and that ought to keep the peace for, say, 50 years. By that time the really universal feeling against war will manage to make soldiers a thing of the past. Rather rough on John, but still.

If this passage is startling, his next paragraph is equally fascinating in that it shows its author had a remarkable awareness of the bases of Germany's war strategy; without mentioning Schlieffen it is clear that he knew what the Schlieffen Plan was all about:

> I don't really see that this war can go on much longer. I always imagined that Germany had been informed by her internal ministers that she must not make war unless she could guarantee to
> 1) finish in 6 weeks or
> 2) win such a decisive battle within that time as to let them do pretty well as they liked.
> Now, after about 8 weeks, things have gone against them, *and* our fleet is blockading them as tight as blazes; I don't see that they can go on for long, especially if we bring off a great victory.

Sadly Owen never lived to see whether or not there was a great victory; he survived the year but was killed leading a charge in the Ypres area – at a point of vicious contention of which no one had heard at this early stage, the notorious Hill 60 – in April 1915.

Other officers reacted quite differently. Captain Eric Fairtlough, an artillery officer, currently seconded to the Army Signal Service, was one of many who, while recognizing the inevitability of hard fighting and serious losses, saw no cause for alarm. Thus on 17 September he wrote to his 'Dearest Mother':

> We have been having a big battle for the last three days and it is now still going on. Pretty heavy casualties, those of the Germans enormous. We have taken a lot of prisoners. Everything is going well and we are steadily driving back the Germans.

On 18 September he wrote more expansively to his father:

> For the last four days a tremendous battle has been going on along the front of the British Army. We have held our own and driven back the Germans who have now entrenched themselves and things have calmed down with both lines watching each other. The Germans are up to every low trick. A party put up a white flag and when our fellows went out to capture them opened fire and killed several; they surrendered later and we publicly shot two German officers in front of their men.

The Germans have some 8-inch siege guns with high explosive shells which are rather unpleasant. I saw a gun team completely destroyed by one, still fortunately they fire at long range and their fire is necessarily rather wild, but occasionally they do hit something. The weather has been very wet and cold. The situation is entirely satisfactory.

Equally positive throughout was the ever buoyant Brigadier John Headlam, artillery commander, 5th Division, even though he had lost some of his closest friends, including a member of a well-known military family, the Goughs. He wrote to his wife on 29 September:

It's extraordinary how *well* the men are, one of my brigades has got a new Doctor, so he thought he'd inspect the whole of the men – and he found *one* sick out of 650 – and he said it wasn't only that the rest were not ill, but that they were in such an extraordinary state of health. I am more and more convinced every day that a war such as this is a fine thing for character in individual or nation, and that all the suffering will be amply repaid to the nation if we go on in the spirit in which we have begun. Of course it is dreadfully sad for individuals – the Charlie Shaftoes for instance, or poor young Gough's mother and wife – but of course he might have broken his neck any day out hunting.

Thus the opinion of several officers; what of the 'other ranks'?

The diary of John McIlwain, a platoon sergeant in the 2nd Battalion, Connaught Rangers, 2nd Division, tells the story of a fellow NCO who was seriously disturbed by the conditions pertaining during the Aisne battle. McIlwain's diary is an unusual document in that it is a mixture of contemporary annotation and retrospective comment added when typing up his account in 1936–7, which explains the variation of tense in his evidence. Hence his 'scene-set' to this passage:

We have many casualties with the heavy shelling and our lack of protective dug-outs. Our CO, Major Sarsfield, is killed by having a lump of his thigh torn off by a piece of shell. It was impossible to save him. Our only 'rest' is when we go back from the caves to shelter in whatever kind of cover we may dig for ourselves on the hillside. The heavy shelling has caused a few cases of demoralization. The case of Sergeant R. for instance.

At first Sergeant R. had given the impression of being someone who would take anything the war could offer in his stride:

> He was a vigorous, alert young non-commissioned officer of a type useful in peacetime soldiering: qualified as a gymnastic instructor; a martinet in the gymnasium in Aldershot. He first forced himself on my notice on the Marne by yelling at me to take cover from the German snipers who were fighting such a skilful retreat among the woods in the valley. R. himself was crouched on the ground abusing such men of his company as were finding it necessary to move about; they were 'attracting enemy fire', he said. At the moment I was in the company of my own company officer who had brought me up to the brigade major for instructions relative to the advance of my platoon. The gentlemen, of course, ignored R, but I couldn't resist a jibe at his expense. The German bombardments at Verneuil were more than R. could bear. Repeatedly he deserted his trench for shelter in the cellars of the houses down the hill. Twice Sergt Major Bruen caught him and ordered him back to his platoon. The third time he pulled him out of a house, placed him under arrest and with him the unfortunate Sergt. McN. who happened to be with him. At a court-martial later both were reduced to the ranks and sentenced to two years imprisonment. Men who had been knocked about by R. in the gymnasium naturally jeered at him for his panic condition.

The advantage of hindsight in this case is clear from McIlwain's account of what happened thereafter:

> The sequel is interesting. R., of course, after a few months in prison, joined our first battalion in France in 1915. Later, with that battalion he went to Mesopotamia. He was a Cork man, and in 1917, when in Kinsale, I saw his photo in the *Cork Examiner*, illustrating an account of how, again a sergeant, he had won the DCM for a particularly daring deed when fighting the Turks. He had evidently learnt his lesson.

McIlwain's testimony is the more impressive because he was soon to recognize his own fallibility in the face of such extraordinary pressure:

One dark rainy night, in pain and weariness, I report sick and go down to the casualty station, which is the church in Verneuil. The sergeant in charge gives me a blanket to lie on the stone floor. I can't sleep. All night the wounded are being brought in and taken out. There is one doctor. By candlelight, he operates on men moaning and screaming. In the morning I have to see the doctor. I cannot recall the preliminaries, but I shall never forget the conclusion. 'You have rheumatic pains,' said the wearied doctor. 'I have sounded you, and your heart is not affected. Your temperature is normal. I can't do anything for you. This place is for wounded soldiers.' Like Sergeant R., I had had *my* lesson. I thought of the awfulness; of the howling artillerymen and others getting shrapnel probed out of their shoulders and back by the wearied surgeon, the last doctor left, carrying on by himself day and night. I took my aching body up the hill again determined to stick it out till I was carried away alive or dead.

Other evidence, however, suggests a more robust reaction to the pressures of the new warfare. The diary of Gunner B. C. Myatt, now, following his late arrival at the front, fully involved in the fighting, suggests he was taking things more or less in his stride:

*September 29th.* Well I think hell was let loose last night. The German infantry advance in mass to try and push our fellows back, but they completely failed and they left thousands of dead about and they also gave our infantry an awful twisting. The ambulances are passing now taking hundreds of our fellows wounded, but there you are, it's all in war.

I think they gave the Germans a lesson they won't forget in a hurry. They are finding out that we are not such a contemptible little army as they thought we were when they started.

\* \* \*

What of the enemy during the Battle of the Aisne? That it was no picnic for the enemy is clear from evidence written into the diary of Second Lieutenant Tennyson, who was doubtless gratified to learn that if the British were having a hard time of it, so were the Germans:

*Thurs, Sept 24: 12th Day of Battle of the Aisne*
Lectured the Company this morning, and read them extracts from

letters found on wounded Germans written to their relatives as follows:

1. Letter of Lieut A., dated from Reims, 11 September 1914:

'My Dear, As you see I have been away from my regiment for several weeks engaged in a very bloody battle, which has lasted since Sunday. I have been wounded. My regiment which started with 60 officers has now only 5. More than 2,000 men are hors de combat, with the result that my gallant regiment is only a fragment. It is the same with the gallant Saxons fighting at our side.

'I beg you not to speak of our great losses which can only lead to useless rumours being spread. To speak candidly, the army to which I belong has passed through terrible experiences during the last four weeks, let us hope it will soon be over.'

2. Letter from Lieut B., of the 26th Regiment Field Artillery:

'For the last five weeks we have undergone colossal fatigue, lack of sleep, and desperate combats. The Xth Corps has been constantly on the move since the 1st day of the campaign. My battery especially is always with the Advance Guard. Our horses are for the most part worn out, and we are now using Belgian and French ones. There are moments when they simply cannot go on, then they simply lie down and frequently have to be shot. From 5 a.m. in the morning to 8 p.m. at night we are under the enemy's fire without being able to rest or drink. I was so tired I could not keep on my horse even at a walk.

'There was a murderous battle which lasted from Sunday 6 to Wed. 9 Sept. The 10th and Guard Corps were the chief sufferers. Let us hope that we shall soon have a decisive battle and so end these masses of carnage, even in bivouac at night our troops are not safe.'

3. Translation of extracts from a letter found on a prisoner of the 74th German Infantry Regt (X Corps):

'I've just been living through days that defy imagination. I should never have thought men could stand it. Not a second has passed but my life has been in danger, and yet not a hair of my head has been hurt. It was horrible, it was ghastly, but I have been saved for you and for our happiness, and I take heart again, although I am terribly unnerved. God grant that I may see you again and that this horror may soon be over. None of us can do any more, human strength is at an end. What I have suffered in the terrifying battle which extended along a front of many miles near Montmirail, you cannot possibly imagine. For four days I was under artillery fire, it is like hell, but a thousand times worse.

'Our 1st battalion which has fought with unparalleled bravery is reduced from 1,200 to 194 men. These numbers speak for themselves.'

Tennyson commented: 'These letters pleased the Coy enormously, as things seemed to be going well for us.' Not everybody would agree with the second half of his statement, but if nothing else the quoted letters suggested that the Germans too were finding the new style of fighting very different from their expectations.

* * *

Thus the German perspective on this remarkable battle. A somewhat unusual British perspective is to be found in the papers of the artillery subaltern Ralph Blewitt, who had memorably noted the demise of the 'Romance of War' at the end of the Mons Retreat. He wrote little or nothing at the time, the only letter he sent to his confidante Miss Henderson being less focused on what was happening around him than on his hopes for a consignment of cigarettes. But one year later, on 14 September 1915, he wrote for her a vivid account of his first day in the Aisne fighting, which had clearly left a searing impression – and a need to admit his own failures and inadequacy at a time of severe trial. Perhaps the frankness came the more easily because now he was addressing her, rather less informally than before, as 'My Darling Girl':

A bloody day it was too. I suppose the division lost more on that single day than any other since. It also saw them at their best. That day the battery first came under fire, its baptism being a salvo of four eight inch toys [sic] slap in the middle as we were just wheeling to come into action. One officer was sick on the spot!!! Jones's horse was killed under him, mine was blown (or shied) aside and I fell off! In the ensuing mêlée both my guns got turned over coming down a steep bank. I saw one but didn't know about the other as I was leading the battery at the time and when I finally got them into the next position I found my section was gone. Before we fired a round in the new position the Infantry came back through us and we loaded up with fuzes and expecting the Bosches [i.e. the Germans] to be following. However as they didn't roll up the Major thought we'd better get back to the crest behind and went on to find a spot, telling Jones or me to bring on the battery. The teams came up and we got them away somehow, the ground being frightfully heavy plough [sic]. I gave Jones my horse as he had to get on to the Major and I waited with a couple of gunners to get away on the last wagon. However the team had been killed earlier and they didn't roll up so we left the darn thing there and did a two mile run back with bullets thick all over the country. I've never heard anything to approach the rifle and MG fire on that day. We got to our new position and we subalterns went out in turn to the forward crest to try and find out something or observe something. Forward observation wasn't the clear cut game it is now and I'm afraid I was so scared and absolutely ignorant of where our feet [i.e. infantry] were or where the Bosches were that I didn't do as much good as I might have. However I had a look for my guns but found them gone. One of my sergeants – an excellent fellow now an officer – had stayed and got them away and he joined me in the evening. We shot a good deal chiefly into the Blue. About 6 I was sent off to find a place for the night and found young Fetherstonhaugh with his transport. He gave me an English cigarette!!!! and a glass of white wine. No smoke or drink in my life ever was or will be half as good as those.

21. Eve of the battle: men of the 4th Royal Fusiliers resting in the Grand Place of Mons, 22 August. (Q 70071)

22. Not the best of friends: Field Marshal Sir John French and Lieutenant General Sir Horace Smith-Dorrien in a roadside conversation, date unknown. (HU 961060)

23. The Mons Retreat:
British cavalry retiring.
(Q 60706)

24. Exhausted troops
resting during the Mons
Retreat. (Q 51468)

25. Battle of the Marne:
elements of the 1st
Middlesex under fire; nine
horses were killed and a
water-cart riddled with
shrapnel. (Q 51489)

26. Recruiting at a London recruitment centre; eyesight test. (Q 30067)

27. Under training: mixed uniforms in a camp at Mytchett, Hampshire; the first and third soldier are wearing temporary uniforms known as 'Kitchener blue'; the one in the middle is wearing khaki. (Q 53596)

28. Territorials (members of the Queen Victoria's Rifles) undergoing fitness training on the edge of Hampstead Heath. (Q 53596)

29. 'Our tent': camp of the Liverpool Scottish on the edge of Edinburgh; R. A. Scott-Macfie collection. (IWM Department of Documents, Q 114676)

30. A boat of Belgian refugees arriving at Folkestone; photographed by Miss Mary Coules. (IWM Department of Documents)

31. Turn of the tide: members of the 1st Cameronians advancing northwards towards the valley of the Aisne. (Q 52486)

32. Trenches on the Aisne: 1st Cameronians in a rudimentary trench; Ste-Margerite, 24 September. (Q 51501)

33. The Race to the Sea: troops of the 1st Cameronians during their journey north towards Belgium, preparing to move after their overnight bivouac in a wood near St-Rémy, 5 October. French cavalry passing in the background. (Q 51503)

34. Men of the Howe Battalion, Royal Naval Division, posing for the camera of a Belgian civilian at Vieux-Dieu, near Antwerp, 6 October. (Q 14772)

35. Refugees fleeing from Antwerp to Holland. (Q 52339)

36. The last train to get out of Antwerp. The next one was attacked by the Germans; the naval personnel who had boarded it ended up either as internees in Holland or as prisoners of war in Germany. (Q 14782)

37. British infantry of the 7th Division marching into Ypres, 14 October. (Q 70235)

38. A British 18-pounder field gun, the mainstay of the Royal Field Artillery, in action south of Ypres, 19–20 October. (Q 109609)

39. London buses bringing soldiers up to the front. (Q 51506)

CHAPTER NINE

# THE BID TO SAVE ANTWERP

THE AISNE BATTLE had just begun to acquire an air of permanence when the armlock in which both sides were caught suddenly loosened, the opposing forces disengaged and there ensued a significant episode which was to become legendary as 'The Race for the Sea'. In fact, it was no such thing. As one historian has put it: 'It was a race that neither competitor wished to win since to reach the coast would spell deadlock and initiate siege warfare from Nieuport to Switzerland.'

That, as it transpired, is what did actually happen in the end. What persuaded the Germans to break loose, however, was the realization that their only hope of retrieving the initiative they had lost was to outflank the French and British and thrust decisively past them towards the French heartland: in effect, to improvise a supplementary variation to the Schlieffen Plan and attempt a second make-or-break strike in the direction of Paris. One reason why Colonel Swinton had assumed that the Aisne battle would continue for some time was that, with the two opposing armies spread out across so large an area of countryside, any effort by one side to out-manoeuvre or march round the other would be fraught with difficulty. Now the Germans were attempting to do precisely that, and with characteristic determination; indeed, it might be argued, in the circumstances, with desperation. The Allies reacted at once, parrying as the enemy lunged, parrying again as the enemy lunged again, with the result that the focus of the fighting moved progressively further north like a spreading forest fire. In the end the inevitable outcome occurred: a hand-to-hand slogging-match virtually within sight of the Channel coast. If the Germans were to win this round, the war might indeed be over by Christmas, though not as Britain's August optimists had expected. If they failed, the consequences would be: logjam, stalemate, a stand-off until the next season, and, worst of all, a long war.

A central strand of this process was a major shift of ground by the BEF. As agreed by the Allied high commands, the British now transferred north, effectively returning to where they had begun. They would thus be able to resume their original position to the left of the French armies, as had been the case in the build-up to Mons. By definition, in so doing, they would also be in nearer contact with their own bases, their own ports, their own sources of reinforcement and supply, and their own homeland. So it came about that in the first weeks of October, with considerable relief, they relinquished their trenches on the Aisne, and by devious routes, by secret moves often at night, sometimes by train, sometimes by boot and hoof, headed for that area of France and Belgium which they would soon come to see as their own dedicated sector. In due course, that sector would substantially increase (though it would never approximate or even approach the geographical spread of the area held by the French), but in essence they were about to take possession of the 'Western Front' as it would come to be known in British history, mythology and culture.

The Royal Horse Artilleryman E. J. Cummings recorded his unit's migration north, while also usefully dating the time when some at least of the BEF got wind of the enemy's intentions:

*Sept 23rd.* The Battle still rages although we have every reason to believe that the Germans are retiring. We are reserve Battery but in the firing line. Late in the evening we march to Fismes and have a rest for 10 days the first we have had since we came out here.

*Oct 2nd.* We move off at 6 p.m. on a series of marches both night and day, passing through the following places. Villers-Cotterêts, Crépy-en-Valois, Mondidier, Amiens, Doullens, Frévent, Hesdin, which we reach on 11th Oct.

*Oct 12th.* Rose at 5 a.m. and moved off at 8 a.m. We got in touch with the Huns about noon, but they were very wary of attack, so we had to stand by in readiness. The 1st Brigade were in action on our right.

*Oct 13th.* Rose at 4 a.m. and manoeuvred until noon. Our cavalry were in action and successfully repulsed a German attack.

*Oct 14th.* We rise at 5 a.m. and move off at 7 a.m. in a pouring rain. We hear many sad tales as we pass through the villages. We cross the Franco-Belgian frontier late in the evening.

*Oct 15th.* The Germans are hastily retiring and we are as hastily pursuing. We bivouac at Messines about 10.30 p.m.

*Oct 16th.* We receive a check as the enemy have got into another of their entrenched positions.

Captain Paterson, 1st Battalion, South Wales Borderers, which moved much later than Cummings' 'J' Battery, described the situation as it developed on his sector. He wrote the following under the date 10 October:

> Last night there was cheering and singing, German and Austrian National anthems, from the German trenches. Now what can that mean, I wonder. Does it mean they have had a victory somewhere, or that they have been told so, which is a very different matter, or that there has been an issue of beer in the trenches. Another curious thing is that we have been given maps of the North-West of France and South of Belgium and that we have been asked whether we have sufficient horses to move our Transport. Also the 2nd Army Corps has gone somewhere and the siege guns too have gone from behind us. I wonder if we shall move to Belgium. I hope so, as we are all sick of this village and valley and neighbourhood.

A week later, on Saturday, 17 October, supposition had become certainty; they were on their way:

> Entrained and got off at 8 a.m. No one any idea where we are bound for. Just before entrainment I was given the Way Bill showing destination 'ETAPLES', but (clever devils) on arrival at Etaples we found we were to go on to practically the North-East of France to a place called CASSEL, where we detrained on the morning of the 18th and marched to HONDEGHEM, where we went into billets. We got a very nice house for Battalion Headquarters surrounded by a moat, and full of beautiful old things in the way of brass and furniture.

But their good fortune did not last. On the 20th they moved on, with the result that, as in the case of Cummings' account, a succession of new names appeared in his chronicle, names that would soon become as familiar to the soldiers of the BEF as they are to students of the Great War today: Poperinghe, Elverdinghe, Boesinghe, Pilkem, Poelcappelle, Langemarck.

In the meantime, however, another name had dominated the

headlines: that of a Belgian city that became as famous for a time as its sister fortresses of Liège and Namur had been in the war's first weeks, only to disappear into virtual oblivion as the focus of war moved elsewhere. There seems little doubt that the shouting and singing in the German trenches noted by Captain Paterson on 10 October were largely in celebration of the fall of Antwerp.

\* \* \*

As the German First Army swept across Belgium and into France in August, the ancient port of Antwerp at the mouth of the River Scheldt was to all intents and purposes bypassed, left behind as an unclaimed trophy either to be ignored, or seized later, if it should prove troublesome. Troublesome it soon became when, King Albert having withdrawn his army's 65,000 troops into the city, on 24–25 August the Belgians re-emerged to harass the First Army's rear columns, with a view to relieving pressure on the British and French engaged at Mons and Charleroi. The First Army's commander, General von Kluck, reacted determinedly by detaching four divisions to grasp this nettle.

When, undaunted, the Belgians attacked again on 9 September, the German High Command decided that enough was enough and assigned a force of five divisions, with 173 guns, under General von Boseler, to seize Antwerp and take it out of the war.

The port was guarded by an outer and inner ring of fortresses and garrisoned by 80,000 reserve troops in addition to elements of the Belgian regular army. Launching their onslaught on 28 September, Germany's siege guns soon silenced the forts. With the city in imminent danger of falling, the British Government took serious fright and decided that something must be done to halt, or at least delay, that fall.

What then happened was to become one of the more colourful, if controversial, episodes in the First World War career of that ever-active volcano, Mr Winston Churchill. Other high-profile figures of the period would also be involved, yet despite this and the hurried commitment of a mass of men to the cause, the bid to save Antwerp would soon be written off as futile and a failure and largely forgotten. It was, in one sense, an early example of a First World War 'sideshow', a concept of which there would be few successful examples. It has even been described as a Cinderella story, though clearly one without a happy ending. But it would seal the fate of many brave and fine young servicemen: some to lose their lives, some to find themselves interned indefinitely in neutral territory, others to be doomed to a long captivity in an angry and vengeful Germany.

Churchill's basic role as First Lord of the Admiralty was to deal with the challenges and pressures of the war at sea, but that did not prevent him from dabbling from the outset with the war on land. Fully aware of the importance of maintaining control of the Channel ports, he had paid frequent visits to Dunkirk, where he had established both a naval air squadron and, also under naval command, several armoured car squadrons, these being created by the requisitioning of as many Rolls-Royces as he could lay hold of and furnishing them with armour plating. In effect these were in essence embryonic tanks; but for the fact that they had wheels not tracks, they were almost the shape of things to come. On the night of Friday, 2 October, Churchill was once more en route from London to the coast when his special train was halted, and as rapidly as possible, consonant with the exigencies of railway safety, reversed. On arriving back at Victoria Station he was rushed to a meeting in Lord Kitchener's residence in Carlton Gardens, where the Secretary for War had assembled a handful of other luminaries including Sir Edward Grey and the First Sea Lord, at this stage still Prince Louis of Battenberg; the Prime Minister was unable to be present as he was conducting a recruiting drive in South Wales. The meeting had been called in response to a telegram from the British Minister to Belgium stating that the Belgian Superior Council of War had taken the decision to abandon Antwerp and evacuate their forces to Ostend. This was clearly in British eyes a policy of despair that could not be allowed to go unchallenged. The upshot of the meeting was that Churchill was empowered to go to Antwerp with all possible speed, to stiffen the sinews and raise the morale of an apparently failing ally. By 1.30 the following morning, 3 October, he was on his way, not merely carrying, as it were, a portfolio of arguments and exhortations, but also promises of immediate armed support.

For this there was no need to plead to the War Office or to pester an already harassed Sir John French in France. Churchill had his own solution to hand: a newly formed fighting division consisting of naval personnel already training to serve as infantry because there were not

enough ships to accommodate them. Being surplus to the require-
ments of the Fleet, they were therefore available to be deployed
elsewhere.

The 'Royal Naval Division', consisting of two Naval Brigades and
one Brigade of Marines, was ultimately to become one of the most
renowned formations of the war. It was to play a distinguished role at
Gallipoli and, redefined as the 63rd (Royal Naval) Division, would win
notable battle honours on the Western Front, fighting there from the
late stages of the Somme battle through to the last campaigns of
1918. However, its initial blooding, at Antwerp, was to offer it little
chance of success and therefore none of glory. Thrown into a situation that was deteriorating even as they were sent to save it, its
undertrained officers and men were reduced to making what show of
resistance they could and hoping to fight another day.

One problem the division had from the start was that it was
composed in large part of deeply reluctant land warriors; men who,
having joined the world's greatest Navy, were not happy to become
adjuncts to the nation's distinctly modest Army. As Ernest Myatt, an
ordinary seaman in Collingwood Battalion (naval names and ranks
were employed even though the men were to fight as soldiers), put
the point in his eloquent and thoughtful pocket diary:

> Most of the old hands were rather fed up, they had set their hearts
> on going to sea, as everybody was told when they joined up. 'You will
> be in the first fighting line in case of war.' Yet here we were under
> canvas and turned into a Naval Brigade, and only about 100 of our
> crowd sent to sea.

Myatt's military training had started painfully, on the train journey
from London, where the Collingwood Battalion was raised, to their
intended camp at Walmer, on the Kent coast:

> I got a smack on the face from a carriage door and got laid up in
> hospital for three weeks as soon as I got there and very pleased I was
> to get out. Then I started the camp routine, up at 5.30, parade at
> 6.30, physical drill until eight o'clock, breakfast, out again at 9.0,
> probably a route march or platoon drill until 12.30, out again at 2
> until 4 – then leave till 8.0 and then bed. Occasionally things were

varied by, say, turning out at 4.30 a.m., knocking off at 12 or 1 and then turning out for a night spasm from 8.30 till 10.30.

Others were less aggrieved at the prospect of being transmuted from mariners into soldiers, among them the enthusiastic nineteen-year-old reservist Sydney Miller. His initial naval training in London had gone well, giving him 'the infinite satisfaction of passing the elementary examination for an ordinary seaman', thanks in no small measure to the officer in charge of the instructional classes, Lieutenant Commander King, whom he considered 'a very fine man – service to the bone'. Nevertheless he greeted without displeasure the news that 'the Admiralty proposed converting us into a Naval Brigade, for which we were required to join a Naval Camp at Walmer, Kent, in the shortest possible time':

> This was of course received with intense excitement, which was only perhaps damped by the melancholy duty of wishing 'Goodbye'. That evening I went up to Business [the nature of which is not specified] and wished them 'Goodbye'. We had a small cake and a pot of coffee between us, and altogether spent a very pleasant time, which was perhaps marred by a little 'contretemps' with Mrs Thompson, who had some imaginary grievance with the department. My farewell at home was very brief but I of course felt it immensely. Well to cut a long story short, we left London Bridge the proudest fellows alive, for weren't we going to serve our King and Country?

They were not to stay in Walmer long, some of the Royal Fleet Reserve and Royal Naval Reserve men being moved to nearby Betteshanger to form a separate brigade. Miller now found himself in 1st Section, 4th Platoon, 'A' Company, Hawke Battalion of what would shortly become the 'Royal Naval Expeditionary Force'. 'Thus commenced', he wrote, 'the happiest of weeks I have ever experienced.'

Meanwhile, at Walmer, according to Ordinary Seaman Myatt, training continued in a somewhat haphazard way until Sunday, 4 October, when it became evident that something was afoot:

> I happened to be on guard that night and had done my two hours spasm from 2 to 4 and was just turning in till 6 when I heard the Colonel running up and down in a very excited manner calling out for the bugler. This was most unusual as the usual turning out time on a

Sunday was 7 o'clock. It transpired that we had to leave Dover at 2 o'clock for Dunkirk. When the news got round, the Camp was all excitement, nobody was ready, nobody was told what to take with them, leather gear had to be served at the last minute, only half the men had water bottles and haversacks, two very important items on active service. But we couldn't be surprised at these things as everyone except a few officers who had seen active service was inexperienced. I think only about 50 per cent had fired a rifle and that morning we were served out with five rounds of ammunition, quite a number didn't know how to load; these little things were disgusting considering we were going into a hostile country.

Whatever Myatt's views on the call of duty, the suddenness of it was particularly annoying on a personal level. It left him, as he put it, 'fearfully wild, as the surprise had absolutely upset my arrangements for the day, as I had intended meeting rather a nice girl I had met while in Walmer and quite anticipated a nice time like I had had on several occasions previously, anyhow I wrote rather a pathetic farewell'.

They marched from Walmer to Dover, arriving there about 3 p.m., and were then ordered on to one of the piers: 'and there we stuck until at 12 o'clock there were about 7,000 of us altogether and three boats to take us across'.

Able Seaman Sydney Miller and the Betteshanger contingent were also heading for the coast:

It was about 6 o'clock on Sunday morning October 4 that the eagerly expected news arrived and we were acquainted with the fact that we were that day to embark from Dover for the front. After a morning of packing and making final arrangements we struck Camp amid much enthusiasm and marched to Dover. Everywhere we were most enthusiastically received – both civilians and soldiers hastening to give us a farewell cheer. Such scenes of greeting will ever remain in my memory – they made one feel how glorious it was to be able to serve one's country. It was during these demonstrations that I chanced to see a footer friend of mine in the crowd at Dover – he was in the uniform of a lance-corporal, and though of course I could not get at him, yet his look of envy only served to make me more elated than ever.

Miller too, like Myatt, found himself enduring a long wait on the pier at Dover, made worse by the fact that he and his comrades had had no food since 11 o'clock that morning and were becoming ravenous. When, at about 10 p.m., as they were just beginning to embark, a packet of cheese and biscuits was issued to each man, he was too far gone to partake and gave his away. However, his spirits revived when at last, shortly after midnight, the quickening reverberations of the ship's engines made it clear she was ready to leave:

> We slipped anchor and were 'en route' for the front. Imagine our feelings! Personally, I cannot describe mine, they were indeed a mixture of pride, hope and infinite joy at being given this early opportunity of joining the gallant forces, who were defending our interests – nay, our very existence – against a nation which respected neither International Law nor the recognized Laws of Civilization.

In the case of Able Seaman Roy Ashenden, his attitude to their embarkation was, in the first instance at any rate, rather more light-hearted. He began an account written for his family a few months later about what he called 'our Antwerp "spasm"' (spasm seems to have been a popular 'buzz' word in the division at this stage) with the sentence: 'Of course we all considered the whole thing as a gigantic bit of fun when we left Dover on that Sunday night and were eagerly looking forward to coming to grips with the Germans.'

His eagerness was, however, briefly challenged by the discomforts of the voyage:

> After we had got all the gear onboard we were sent into a kind of horse-box in the very bowels of the ship and crushed up like sardines. I didn't at all like that so as soon as the ship got under way I crept past the men on watch and climbed up among the kitbags where I 'entrenched myself' and passed a very comfortable night.

Myatt by contrast only achieved two hours of fitful sleep and was up on deck by 4 a.m.:

> Being daylight the coast of France was in sight and it was a nice morning, this somewhat cheered me up. We stood outside Dunkirk for several hours, eventually we were towed in amid great excitement from the people and soldiers on the quay. This was the first time I had left England and various things amused me: the French soldiers in

their various coloured uniforms, red trousers predominating, looked most startling after our khaki, especially for active service. After a great deal of shouting on the part of our French pilot we drew alongside about 12 o'clock. Then there was more excitement about unloading, most of the stuff was simply heaved overboard and several kitbags were dropped in the ditch, the rest were stowed in the train drawn alongside.

We were fallen in and fallen out all day, and more ammunition was served to us, in all we had about 100 rounds each. This was rather a shock to most of us, as it pointed out that we were likely to see a bit of fighting, though as a matter of fact I very often said we never should see any, and at the very earliest in the New Year.

Ashenden was a member of a machine-gun crew; they were anxious to get their weapon ashore in one piece but they saw that as the limit of their responsibility:

We got our machine-gun out of the boat as fast as possible and then made ourselves scarce in the town as our officer told us that if we didn't we should probably be made to help in unloading the boat. There must have been a lot of gear on board as it took 2,000 men all day to do it.

Unlike many of his comrades, Ashenden had some command of French, so he soon found himself in communication with the local populace:

The Frenchmen entertained us with all sorts of horrible tales and speculated on our destination. You can imagine how I enjoyed myself yapping away to them.

About ten o'clock we entrained and were told that we should probably be attacked by Uhlans in which case we must jump out of the train, take cover under the nearest bush or hedge and await orders.

At this point we were still uncertain where we were going, so I jumped out and asked the driver and he told us, of course, Antwerp, pardon! Anvers.

'Anvers', as Ashenden recognized, was the French name for Antwerp.

Ordinary Seaman Myatt and his comrades also discovered their intended destination at this time, though their mood was not enhanced by the fact that as soon as they had got on the train 'all lights were put out, as the Engine driver who had come from Antwerp in the morning had been fired on; this was very pleasing, we all told ourselves – we were in for it now'.

One of the trains that trundled east from Dunkirk that night included among its passengers as a newly enlisted officer, who had joined the division at the personal behest of Winston Churchill, the well-known poet Sub Lieutenant Rupert Brooke. In a lively account written shortly afterwards to his much-loved friend Cathleen Nesbitt, he described how they spent the afternoon unloading and then sat in a great empty shed, a quarter of a mile long, waiting for orders. This period of quiet was shortly superseded by what seems to have been a time of panic:

> After dark the senior officers rushed round and informed us that we were going to Antwerp, that our train was sure to be attacked, and that if we got through we'd have to sit in trenches till we were wiped out. So we all sat under lights writing last letters: a very tragic and amusing affair. My dear, it did bring home to me how very futile and unfinished life was. I felt so angry. I had to imagine, supposing I was killed. There was nothing but a vague gesture of goodbye to you and my mother and a friend or two. I seemed so remote and barren and stupid. I seem to have missed everything. Knowing you shone out as the only thing worth having . . .

At last the trains began to move. For Able Seaman Sydney Miller the night that followed would leave a profound if somewhat bewildering impression:

> To attempt to describe the journey of 108 miles would be almost impossible, as my head was in a whirl and the whole affair seemed like one long dream. Suffice it to say that our journey bordered on the German lines and an attack was therefore highly probable. Consequently the trains were in complete darkness, no smoking, talking or noise of any description was permitted, and we had to remain absolutely on the 'qui vive' during the nine hours of this memorable journey. Fortunately – as events afterwards proved – we were not attacked. The Belgians had somehow or other received word of our arrival, as at every town or village that we passed, little

groups of heart-broken Belgians silently welcomed us. To describe the scene as pathetic in the extreme is hardly expressive enough. Perhaps the reader can conjure up in his mind three great black leviathans – packed with our brave lads, waiting on their rifles for a possible attack – piercing their way through the darkness of the quiet, picturesque meadows of Belgium, at intervals to be silently – but none the less affectionately – welcomed by the poor inhabitants. To add to the pathos of the scene, the moon shone out brightly as if attempting to mock them in their distress, and plucky little Belgian Soldiers who were guarding the railway track silently shook our hands and gave us presents of fruit, water and postcards. Everything was carried out with such silence and impressiveness that it touched us deeply, and I shall always picture that dark, quiet scene of suffering and homeless families and brave Belgian soldiers remaining at their dismal posts, and extending us their welcome as we passed.

Myatt's account was much more laconic, being less concerned with the journey than with the remarkable scenes that met them when they reached their destination:

Off we started, in our carriage there were about 10 of us, just room to sit down and only hard boards, so this was another night when we had only two or three hours sleep. We arrived at our destination about 3 a.m.; of course, except for a few cafés the place was in darkness, as we already knew from English newspapers that the town had been shelled by Zeppelins. But when the news got around that we had arrived all the people hurried out to welcome us and a very substantial welcome it was too; everybody tried to give us something, hot coffee, loaves of bread, tins of meat and various other things and as we went along heads popped out of windows and people in various types of night and partial day attire appeared offering more scran.*

Brooke's account also describes a triumphant arrival. 'We *weren't* attacked that night in the train,' he wrote. 'So we got out at Antwerp, and marched through the streets, and everyone cheered and flung

---

* Scran: food in general, a meal in particular: a term used in both the Army and the Navy dating back to about 1870.

themselves on us and gave us apples and chocolate and flags and kisses, and cried *Vivent les Anglais* and 'Heep! Heep! Heep!'

In similar vein Ashenden described their arrival as being 'much to the delight of the people who loaded us with all sorts of good things, principally in tins which we put into our haversacks'. Shortly he and his machine-gun crew were given transport in a London General motorbus, in which 'we careered about from trench to trench and at last found a resting-place about six miles outside the city at a place called Vieux-Dieu'. This journey was to provide the young able seaman with an early insight into the realities of the conflict into which they were rapidly being drawn:

> It was on the road to Vieux-Dieu that I first realized what a terrible thing war is. Away on our left and right we could hear the booming of the big German guns and could see the flames here and there. Down the road came the last string of refugees and the incident I am alluding to was the sight of a poor old woman who was sitting down by the side of the road with a tiny kiddie. I spoke to her and she pointed to her bundle of clothes and said, 'That's all I've got left in the world, Monsieur, that and the little one. She's the child of my son who is dead at Namur. The Belgian soldiers have had to destroy my house because it was in the way of the guns and now I've no home and *la petite* to support. What am I to do?'
>
> Englishmen at home read our papers over their eggs and bacon in the morning and probably say 'how terrible' and forget about the war, it is only over here that they understand the awfulness of it.

Sometime between seven and eight o'clock Myatt's party arrived at some big houses on the outskirts of the city that had been deserted by their owners and were packed into one of them, where they thought they would be 'alright for a bit of sleep'. However, they had only rested for about an hour when

> to the surprise of everybody we were turned out again, served with more ammunition and marched about five miles with the guns going off all around us. Eventually we halted and more ammunition was served out, so we had about 250 rounds per man, and what without sleep and no decent grub, this weight about killed us.

As they waited, tired, hungry and confused, for further orders they were suddenly confronted by the sight of the person who above all was responsible for their being where they were: 'While here Winston Churchill passed in his motor, and naturally we all cheered even though he was the man who had landed us in this hole.'

Churchill's own account suggests that he was either going towards or returning from the village of Lierre where members of a Royal Marines unit were actually engaged in close fighting with the enemy. Had they known how the First Lord would subsequently spend the night, perhaps the young sailors' cheers might have had a wry edge to them. In his book *The World Crisis* Churchill wrote:

> Here, for the first time, I saw German soldiers creeping forward from house to house or darting across the street. The Marines fought with machine-guns from a balcony. The flashes of the rifles and the streams of flame pulsating from the mouth of the machine-guns, lit up a warlike scene amid crashing reverberations and the whistle of bullets.
>
> Twenty minutes in a motor-car and we were back in the warmth and light of one of the best hotels of Europe, with its perfectly appointed tables and attentive servants all proceeding as usual!

The luxury of a fine hotel was doubtless agreeable, but to the First Lord this was irrelevant. Something else was motivating him as he rushed dramatically about Antwerp and its environs: the determination of a powerful if volatile personality to do all he could to retrieve a seriously deteriorating situation, the challenge of which so excited him that he even conceived the idea of throwing off his political role and assuming command in the field. Thirty-six hours after reaching the beleaguered city he cabled the Prime Minister suggesting that he should resign as First Lord of the Admiralty and take personal charge of the Antwerp situation, under whatever title or rank that might be deemed appropriate. His arguments so persuaded Kitchener that the normally hard-headed Secretary of State declared his readiness to grant Churchill the rank, presumably a temporary one, of Lieutenant General. However, more cautious, or arguably more conventional, voices demurred, among them that of Asquith himself, who recorded that the thought of Churchill, as a mere ex-lieutenant of Hussars, suddenly acquiring authority over a range of major generals, brigadier generals, colonels, etc., 'while the Navy was only contributing its little brigades', received scant support among his colleagues in London, indeed was received in Cabinet 'by a Homeric laugh'.

Yet Asquith was far from scathing in his own personal reaction. He wanted Churchill in his ministerial inner circle, not cavorting about the Continent, but he also admired the qualities of dash and vision which marked him as a man so different from himself. So the First Lord's plea was unavailing. Command was given to a rising professional soldier, Lieutenant General Sir Henry Rawlinson – though he never got near enough to the city to exercise it – and on 7 October Churchill was brought home. There was a family as well as a political aspect to this abrupt return, in that his wife Clementine gave birth to his daughter Sarah on that same day.

\* \* \*

Neither Rawlinson's appointment, nor, it has to be admitted, Churchill's leadership in the field – if he had been allowed to attempt to replay the role of his famous ancestor the Duke of Marlborough – did affect, or could have affected, the outcome of the Antwerp crisis. On the day the British arrived, the Belgian Government left the city for Ostend, thus taking the heart out of the local population's will to resist. Given the Germans' superiority in sheer numbers as well as military capability, their advance into Antwerp was unstoppable, so that despite all their efforts the only course left to the British forces pushed unceremoniously on to the stage was to make their exit as best they could. This was not quite the retreat from Mons, but it was a retreat nonetheless, and moreover, for those involved, a humiliating cut-and-run without the thought, which had buoyed up so many as they had trudged southwards in August, that it was only a matter of time before they would turn towards the enemy and exact their revenge. Now it was a case of reaching the Channel ports and getting back home, or of being killed or captured.

Able Seaman Sydney Miller's account offers a vivid snapshot of the retreat as experienced by those caught up in it, with its confusions, uncertainties and disturbing effects on morale, against a background of hazards and horrors for which they were utterly unprepared. His earlier enthusiasms had clearly been modified by a sharp dose of reality:

It now became pretty obvious that our plan was to evacuate the town and rumours were flying about that our safety depended entirely on us crossing a certain improvised bridge across the Scheldt before dawn. However, rumour or no rumour, on we plodded, choosing the darkest lanes and paths, and even then hugging the shadows. Cutting across fields in utter darkness, across main roads, diving round here, then there, always in the shadows and always preserving absolute silence. To describe the retreat as weird would be scarcely sufficiently expressive. Perhaps the reader can picture a continuous scene of utter darkness – relieved perhaps by occasional silhouettes as we emerged into semi-darkness, and illumined periodically by the flashes of angry cannon: a spectacle of absolute silence – almost uncanny silence – save perhaps for the muffled tread of hundreds of feet, relieved by the spitting of occasional fire: and the unearthly shriek of the projectiles cutting the air with terrific velocity, followed by the fearful crash as they reached their destinations. A scene of almost continuous destruction, desolation and debris, strongly contrasted with fields of beautiful green which had almost providentially escaped a similar fate. A spectacle of absolute hopelessness, which struck one with unmistakable force – ironically arousing a feeling of one's utter uselessness and inability to revenge or avoid such terrible destruction. I wonder how many times that Retreat reminded me of the famous picture of Napoleon's Retreat from Moscow?

For Sub Lieutenant Rupert Brooke, the retreat was also the moment of disillusion. Before that there had been sights to shock but also to admire; things to be seen that were almost of beauty:

Once or twice a lovely glittering aeroplane, very high up, would go over us: and then the shrapnel would be turned on it, and a dozen quiet little curls of white smoke would appear round the creature – the whole thing like a German wood-cut, very quaint and graceful and unreal. Eh, but the retreat drowned all those impressions . . . The sky was lit by burning villages and houses; and after a bit we got to the land by the river, where the Belgians had let all the petrol out of the tanks and fired it. Rivers and seas of flame leaping up hundreds of feet, crowned by black smoke that covered the entire heavens. It lit up houses wrecked by shells, dead horses, demolished railway stations, engines that had been taken up with their lines and signals, and all twisted round and pulled up, as a bad child spoils a toy. And there we joined the refugees, with all their goods on barrows and carts, in a double line, moving forwards about a hundred yards an hour, white and drawn and beyond emotion . . .

We went on through the dark. The refugees and motor-buses and transport and Belgian troops grew thicker. After about a thousand years it was dawn.

It is strange to think that this was Rupert Brooke's one close-up view of the war he would become famous for welcoming, in the sonnets which would be imperishably associated with Britain's response to the challenge of 1914. For he survived Antwerp and got home – to die the following year, not by an enemy's hand but from blood poisoning, while on his way to another, longer-lasting 'side-show' with which Churchill would always be associated: Gallipoli. In fairness, it is important to state that Brooke came back with the scales removed from his eyes, so that he could write, again to his beloved Cathleen, sometime in November (in a letter of which this is the last, incomplete paragraph):

I'm rather dismayed, my dear one, about the way people in general don't realize that we're at war. It's – even yet – such a picnic for us – for the nation – and so different for France and Belgium. The millions France is sacrificing to our thousands. I think – I know – that *everyone* ought to go in. I pray there'll be a raid, or, at least, a score of civilians killed . . .

\* \* \*

Meanwhile, for the troops in retreat, facing the obvious possibilities of death or capture, a third option now emerged, beguiling in one sense but deeply unsatisfactory in another – that of eluding the enemy by escaping into neutral territory. The area of the Low Countries between Antwerp and the Channel ports is geographically and politically a confusing labyrinth. The River Scheldt might be a Belgian river at Antwerp, but on its way to the sea it becomes effectively a part of Holland, with the Belgian–Dutch border zig-zagging almost waywardly on its southern bank, in places coming extremely close to the principal rail route by which the British forces were about to attempt what might be described as their own 'race to the sea'. Thus it came about that for many of Churchill's young

champions their fate following the fall of Antwerp was to become
internees in the neutral Netherlands, safe from the enemy but of no
further value to the nation's cause.

They knew that if they crossed the Dutch–Belgian frontier, the
Germans could not follow them: to do so would be to invade a
country whose neutrality, unlike that of Belgium, had not been
violated. Ordinary Seaman Myatt's account names one officer who
announced that he 'was going to make his best way into Holland and
anyone who cared to follow him could do so'. An order came from
somewhere that rifles and ammunition should be thrown away. But
Myatt refused to obey, 'it seemed so absurd'. It soon became clear
that there was wide opposition to what was essentially a defeatist
policy, and that 'instead of going into Holland we should try and
make for Ostend as H[olland] was a neutral country and that it
would hardly be the right thing to go there unless forced to do so,
it would sort of be running away, rather an easy way of getting out of
things but very un-English'.

Yet for many, internment in Holland came to seem the only
possible option. Able Seaman Ashenden's generally spirited account
to his parents peters out rather dourly, its author being well aware
this was not the outcome he had wanted or hoped for:

> We struggled on terribly tired, we hadn't slept since Sunday and
> felt dead. Men dropped down and were left and nobody stopped. All
> the way we were followed by Uhlan Cavalry who, however, were not
> in sufficient force to cut us up. Never have I seen a dirtier or more
> weary rabble than we were. We walked 48 miles in 19 hours all of us
> carrying our 200 rounds of ammunition. When at last we reached
> Hulst, Holland seemed the Garden of Eden. The rest I think you
> know.
>
> Our Commodore reckons we marched about 72 miles with only
> one-and-a-half hour's rest from Vieux-Dieu via Antwerp, St Gilles-
> Waes, then the Ghent Road and a circuit to Hulst.

As with Ashenden, so with Miller: it was internment that brought
his hopes of a glittering patriotic career to an untimely end. It was
internment, in a barracks in the extreme north of Holland at Groningen, that would allow him the time to write his remarkable account
of his experiences, beginning with the high hopes of August and

effectively ending a mere two months later with the realization that for him and so many of his comrades their war was over. For being interned in a neutral country was like being neutered as a soldier; they were not prisoners, but effectively they were, with no option but to wait for others to win the war.

So internment – the last thing on their minds when they crossed the Channel ready to confront the enemy – left scars. Miller's description of how it came about is low-key, detailed, quietly rational, a sharp contrast to the exuberance and optimism with which his account began.

After an exhausting march, much of it obsessed with a craving for food and water, and including a false alarm that had weary men diving into the ditches on the side of the road – suddenly alert and 'different beings from the poor and weary men of a moment or two before' – they trudged into the town of St-Gilles, on one of the railway lines linked with the coast:

> Arriving at the station, our Commander endeavoured to procure a train for us, in order to convey us to Ostend, but apparently learned that the last train was now leaving with refugees. The Belgian officers wanted to clear the train of these poor creatures in order to make room for us, but our Commander would not hear of it. He therefore informed us that much to his regret we should have to 'about' and make our way to the frontier, a distance of perhaps five miles or thereabouts.

A further wearisome march ended in what with hindsight must have seemed an inevitable conclusion:

> About half past eleven or perhaps nearer midnight, the Commander gathered a few fellows round him and explained sotto voce the position. He said we now had the option of choosing two things. Firstly: – remain the night this side of the border and sleep either just where we were, or in a house or building farther away from the border, and risk a probable night attack by the enemy. Then when daylight came, to consider what was to be done. Or secondly, give up our arms and cross the frontier, relying on the Dutch Government to clothe and feed us. This sudden choice of two scarcely agreeable propositions at first rather disconcerted us, as we were all fully under the impression that we should here be able to get away to Ostend or

Dunkirk by train. However, after careful consideration most of us decided on the latter course, for the following reasons.

We were utterly exhausted, hungry and thirsty and without sleep, consequently unfit to repel or put up a decent fight against a night attack. Moreover we had no cavalry or artillery, whereas the enemy was known to have abundance of both. Further, most of us were without ammunition and proper accoutrements, as many had ditched them in the retreat. Again there was no prospect of getting any food, we were one battalion of 350 absolutely 'done up' men and absolutely cut off from the main British Army. All things considered therefore our decision though disagreeable was discreet and necessary. We therefore handed in our arms and crossed the frontier.

Still not entirely persuaded, they underwent a brief change of mind when the lieutenant commanding their company confronted them, telling them he considered they were doing an exceedingly rash thing and that 'if he only had half a dozen men he would get through':

On the base of that, a friend of mine name Appleby and myself collared our arms from the Dutch sentry, and were on the point of joining our Lieutenant. However, when the above arguments were clearly placed before us, we decided that the course decided upon by the Battalion was the wiser; moreover we should have been more or less a hindrance to our Lieutenant, as we were quite exhausted. We therefore again gave up our arms and crossed the frontier. Most of the fellows had already crossed, so after managing to collar some straw from a neighbouring farm, we made as good a bed as possible in the road and then flung ourselves down, and were in a trice fast asleep.

Straw also supplied their sleeping accommodation when, after some uncomfortable days of being moved hither and thither by not overly benevolent Dutch guards, they reached their permanent home-to-be at Groningen. 'It was Sunday morning,' wrote Miller, from the perspective of January 1915, when he wrote up his account, 'just a week after leaving Walmer, and what a series of adventures we had experienced in a week!'

\* \* \*

What of Ordinary Seaman Myatt and his comrades, who had rejected the prospect of internment in favour of a bid to make it back home?

They had slogged on, short of sleep and food and suffering increasing exhaustion. They passed through a series of villages, the only one Myatt could remember being Saint-Nicholas, where the Belgians came out to cheer them on their way. They halted for tea, but then got the news that they were virtually surrounded by Germans, with only one way of escape, so instead of stopping for the rest they longed for they marched on through the night:

> We were expecting to be fired on any minute and nearly dropping with fatigue, and with doubling at every half mile, it was a damn rotten experience I don't want to go through again.
>
> About 10 o'clock having marched for 24 hours we came to a railway and were told to lie down. Here we stayed for perhaps ½ hour, one message came through there was a spy woman on the railway with us, if anyone saw her to strangle her and don't make a noise. I had a look but couldn't see her, I had seen her once before I heard this. A train came along, not a train we are used to, simply cattle trucks and open wagons, there were perhaps 2,000 refugees on board, anyhow room was made for us. Like myself everyone thought that once we got going we were quite safe, we all did our best to go to sleep. Several shots were exchanged for the first 4–5 miles and several stops. Eventually a long halt was made at Morbeck [sic] and quite a great amount of firing took place. The order came along 'Marines to the front' and we at the back of the train saw what appeared to be a pitched battle. Even we weren't safe, several shots came towards us, I think there were quite as many people under the train as on it. What I shall never be able to understand is why the Germans didn't blow us to hell. It transpired afterwards that there were thousands round us, we saw them and machine guns turned on us, they did fire these over us. Evidently our Officers thought the best policy, on account of the refugees (several of whom had been killed, including two or three babies in arms) and the fact that most of our men had no ammunition, was to surrender, after about (from all accounts) 30 of our men had been killed, and quite as many Germans including their Colonel.

Visited eighty years later the railway station at Moerbeke was still intact, but no longer part of the Belgian national network, the tracks running through it being merely sidings serving a sugar-beet factory. The station building, abandoned and empty, was pockmarked in places with what looked suspiciously like bullet holes, possibly though not certainly relics of the brief outburst of fighting that took place there back in 1914. Undeniably it was a place with atmosphere, where it was not difficult to imagine the overcrowded train stalled with its mix of terrified civilians and exhausted and bewildered sailors. One grim twist is that it seems that the majority of those who scrambled out of it to the right got across into Holland, while those who got out on the left were captured by the Germans. Myatt got out on the left. His diary (written in minuscule notebooks which he continued, if with increasingly briefer entries, into 1916) begins this phase of his story with the first of many humiliations he and his fellows would suffer over the long years ahead:

> We had to down all arms, the new rifles that had only had one shot fired out of them and all gear, hands up and march, then they took all knives, even a pair of nail scissors they took off me, the reason of this, as I heard later, was that some Scotch regiment had murdered their guards with their Jackknives and escaped. Then more marching, on the way passing thousands of German troops, guns and transport wagons. After about 2–3 miles, with chaps going to sleep while walking – I was – a great amount of fighting started in the rear, we all had to fall on our knees and hold our hands up. The reason of this was that Hansen whom I think had lost his head, fired his revolver and shouted 'scatter' then fell on his knees and said the Lord's Prayer. Immediately the Germans fired a volley into us, no-one was hurt near me but several were killed in the rear, some were bayoneted. Poor Hansen was shot the next morning, there is no doubt it was his own fault, as it was impossible to escape. After things had calmed down more marching for about 1 mile until we came to a fairly sized church (name of village Exarde) where we were all locked in and although we only had chairs to sleep on and nothing to cover us with, we slept our first sleep for 48 hours . . .

These men would become among the longest serving prisoners of the war, those who survived not returning until 1919. Many would find themselves not only living on starvation rations in camps but also working in mines, and not just in Germany but as far to the east as Latvia, to come back home thinned to the bone by privation and haunted by experiences so distressing that they would never divulge them to their families, silent witnesses to the suffering and havoc that can engulf people of whatever nation or background when the floodgates of war are opened. Politically and militarily the Antwerp affair was over in a matter of days, but it would cast a very long shadow.

* * *

The Official History, listing the losses of the Royal Naval Division in the Antwerp Expedition, gives the numbers of those taken prisoner as 5 officers and 931 other ranks. Those interned added up to the substantially larger figure of 37 officers and 1,442 other ranks. Casualty statistics are by contrast relatively small: killed, 7 officers and 50 other ranks; wounded, 3 and 135.

As so often in his career, Churchill's proclivity for dramatic action divided opinions, not surprisingly in the case of so high-profile a venture, with hopes suddenly raised and as swiftly dashed. In the considered view of Asquith's daughter, the future Lady Violet Bonham Carter, 'No event in his whole career, with the exception of Gallipoli did him greater or more undeserved damage.' Most of the press was hostile, even scathing, but his colleagues in government gave him a more benign reception, seeing value, even inspiration in his efforts to raise the morale of the Belgians and prolong the city's defence. The rarely eloquent Sir Edward Grey found a deft way of expressing his approval by writing to Churchill's wife, who was just recovering from her confinement, during a meeting at the Committee of Imperial Defence:

Dear Mrs Churchill
  I am so glad to hear that you and the baby are well.
  I am sitting next [to] Winston at this Committee, having just welcomed his return from Antwerp.
  And I feel a glow imported by the thought that I am sitting next to a Hero. I can't tell you how much I admire his courage and gallant spirit and genius for war. It inspires us all.

# CHAPTER TEN

# THE FIRST BATTLE OF YPRES

WHILE THE SIDESHOW at Antwerp was running its course, the BEF was deploying north from the Aisne to the area where it would be engaged in the last great encounter of 1914. This would become known as the First Battle of Ypres; in fact it was the first of four, each with its own special impact on the development of the Western Front war. The second, in 1915, introduced the world to that early weapon of potential mass destruction known as poison gas; the third, in 1917, turned a small Belgian village called Passchendaele into a byword for all that was horrific in twentieth-century warfare; the fourth, in 1918, resulted in the final ousting from Belgium of the Kaiser's armies and the beginning of the countdown to the departure of the Kaiser himself. The first was arguably the most important of all. Had the Germans won, the BEF might have had to concede defeat and retreat to the Channel ports, as was the case twenty-six years later in 1940. What might have happened in such circumstances in 1914 must remain one of the great 'what ifs' of modern times. At the very least we would have had a quite different, possibly even worse twentieth century.

One important point must be made at the outset: the First Battle of Ypres has become so much part of British folklore that it is all too easy to forget that this was a 'coalition battle', fought with the French and the Belgians, and that overall the French were the senior partner and played the more important part. Thus there was some dismay when the British Commander-in-Chief, on being raised to the peerage following his return home at the end of 1915, took his seat in the House of Lords on 29 February 1916 as 'Viscount French *of Ypres*'. It was felt by some at least of his continental allies that his claim to that most bitterly fought-over of battlegrounds had not been fully earned. One French observer, Captain Bernard Serrigny, a close aide to General Pétain, claimed that on 3 November 1914 the British withdrew their divisions after two days' work to let them rest and play football. Whether this was true or not, Field Marshal French's commitment was sometimes seen by his coalition partners as a not always reliable commodity, and French himself as not quite the leading player he should have been on the British side.

There is, however, a more benign view of this collaboration, suggesting that, although there might have been moments of resentment or even anger, on the whole the First Battle of Ypres proved to be a remarkable example of a hurriedly assembled coalition working rather better than might have been deemed possible. Hence this judgement by the interwar historian C. R. M. F. Cruttwell, himself a former serving officer on the Western Front:

> The defence of Ypres [in 1914] is the most perfect example of real comradely co-operation in the west. The troops of the two nations were intermingled, even in small detachments, as hard necessity demanded. Foch, never failing in confidence, loyalty, and tact, exercised a very powerful influence over French, often by suggestion rather than by direct advice, and won the hearty affection of all those who were brought into contact with him. The defence of Ypres wiped out all those feelings of mutual distrust which had been so prevalent in the first month of the war.

* * *

For the BEF one important new factor as the Ypres battles began was the arrival from Britain of a new division to reinforce the six already in the field. The 7th Division had been formed in the New Forest area between 31 August and 4 October from three regular battalions still in England and nine units from relatively near overseas stations. It landed at Zeebrugge and Ostend on 6 and 7 October, its original purpose being to assist the attempt to save Antwerp. However, it arrived too late for that enterprise and so was moved south, through country crammed with fleeing refugees but offering few opportunities to engage the enemy, joining the BEF on 14 October and thus providing the first British soldiers to garrison the city of Ypres. The 7th Division's base in the south of England had been the peaceful New Forest town of Lyndhurst, in Hampshire. It has been suggested that Ypres on their arrival 'seemed as peaceful and welcoming as

Lyndhurst after a long route march through the New Forest. The quaint, old-fashioned Flemish town, lying sleepily by the side of a tree-shaded canal, seemed very remote from war.' This was inevitably a situation that would soon irrevocably change. In fact, almost unnoticed, on 13 October the cavalry of the German IV Reiter-Korps entered the city of Ypres, requisitioned 75,000 Belgian francs, held the Burgomaster to ransom, and departed. Just nine days later on 22 October the great artillery barrage began which over the following months and years would turn Ypres into a smoking ruin. The long martyrdom of Ypres, and of the countless thousands who perished in its defence – still remembered with honour to this day – began at this point.

One other Division, the 8th, would cross to the Continent as the battle approached its end. It would take its turn in the trenches, but, because it disembarked on 6 and 7 November, it would take no major part in the war until the Battle of Neuve-Chapelle in March 1915.

Meanwhile, a major player in the drama of 1914 had arrived from the south: the Indian Corps, consisting of the Lahore and Meerut Divisions, and the Indian Cavalry Corps had disembarked at Marseilles on 30 September. They would play a vital role in the events of First Ypres but at very high cost.

If the British had new forces to deploy, so had the Germans. Von Moltke's successor, Erich von Falkenhayn, aware of increasingly stiffening resistance as he attempted to push his forces north, called into existence a whole new army, the 4th. This would be proclaimed to the world as consisting largely of eager young students, volunteers fired with patriotic enthusiasm, but the truth, as Professor Hew Strachan has claimed, was somewhat different:

> In reality most battalions had only one volunteer in ten; the majority of the soldiers were older men who had either completed their military service or who had never been called up at all. Their equipment was incomplete and only recently delivered: a month before they entered the line some battalions had received only half their complement of rifles. They were short of maps and entrenching tools ... The senior officers were old, brought out of retirement, advocates of the technical ideas of the 1870s ... And all these problems were even worse when related to the more demanding

technical and tactical tasks of the artillery: practised only in direct fire and lacking the telephones to link the batteries to their forward observers, the field guns were to prove woefully inaccurate.

Strachan adds a telling comparison:

> Britain's new armies were no better. But Kitchener, anticipating a long war, did not permit their use until a whole year later. Falkenhayn needed a victory in 1914: there was no virtue in preserving these corps for a contingency which he could not afford to entertain.

\* \* \*

To the British Official History, the First Battle of Ypres was not one battle but several. Included in it were a number of subsections such as the Battle of Langemarck, the Battle of Gheluvelt, the Battle of La Bassée and the Battle of Nonne Boschen, while it officially lasted from 19 October to 22 November. In terms of the quality of the fighting, it was soon seen as being substantially more severe than anything that preceded it. Captain Andrew Thorne, a staff officer in the 1st Guards Brigade, had written frequently to his wife about the grim conditions pertaining in late September and early October before the move north to Flanders. On 4 November he wrote to her tellingly: 'We sigh in vain for our dear old "Funk Hole" and the Battle of the Aisne.'

Three days earlier he had written to her about a subject that must have been on many soldiers' minds as the intensity of the fighting increased:

> I have always meant to tell you but have forgotten up to now to say, that if I don't come back you mustn't ever think of dressing in widow's weeds. I trust this isn't a dismal thought but my very earnest wish. I'll interfere no more than to say that, My Best Beloved.

In the same letter he looked back to the already distant days of the world before the war:

> I can remember the walk round the Downs last spring. . . . It seems ages and ages since then. Why, it is now November and I never had expected the war to last till then. I wish there were more signs of peace but I am sure there are none at present, and we must

just hang on as long as we can. It is not pleasant but absolutely necessary.

\* \* \*

In one sense the First Battle of Ypres can be seen as almost six weeks of solid fighting. But it is also possible to focus on certain key days within those six weeks which were major turning points, of which it could be said that had there been a less satisfactory outcome the whole course of the battle, and of the war, might have been completely different. Saturday, 31 October, was one such date. This was to be a particularly notable occasion in the history of the one West Midlands battalion, and also of the young artillery officer already quoted in these pages, Lieutenant Ralph Blewitt.

On this day General von Falkenhayn, now Germany's leading strategist, scraped together such reinforcements as he could find, to launch an all-or-nothing attack from the south-east along the line of the Ypres–Menin road. Central to the action was the little village of Gheluvelt, whose only claim to fame would be the events that took place that day. By midday the British Line was showing every sign of yielding to von Falkenhayn's pressure. In a gesture intended to steady his retiring troops, General Haig mounted his horse and led his staff and escort down the road, as though on parade. However, about 1 p.m., as if by malign coincidence, a single shell hit Hooge Château, the headquarters of Major General Monro, GOC (General Officer Commanding) of 1st Division, just after his fellow divisional commander Major General Lomax, GOC of 2nd Division, had arrived to discuss the deteriorating situation. Monro survived, but Lomax was severely wounded, dying some months later in England. Field Marshal French, sensing disaster, appealed to General Foch for aid, stating that if he did not come, there would be 'nothing left for him but to go up and get killed with the British I Corps'.

That this was seen as a crucial day by the Germans is evident from the fact that the Kaiser himself had arrived on the scene to celebrate what he saw as a certain triumph. The message to his generals was: 'This breakthrough will be of decisive importance for the war – on this account it must and will succeed.' A special group of five fresh German divisions with a sixth in reserve, formed under General von Fabeck and backed by 260 heavy guns – as opposed to the BEF's fifty-four – had been assembled, their orders being to smash through the British forces confronting them, advance up the Menin–Ypres road, overrun the Wytschaete ridge, seize Ypres and open the road to the Channel ports.

* * *

At this point, as good a way as any to unfold what subsequently happened is to resort to a modest publication issued in Kidderminster by G. T. Cheshire & Sons in or about 1928, entitled *The Worcestershire Regiment in the Great War*. The unit which was to emerge as the hero of the day was the regiment's 2nd Battalion, one of five making up the 5th Brigade in Major General Munro's 2nd Division, the others being the 2nd Oxfordshire and Buckinghamshire Light Infantry, the 2nd Highland Light Infantry, the 2nd Connaught Rangers, and the 9th Highland Light Infantry. This is how the book's author, named as H. FitzM. Stacke, set the scene:

> Daybreak of October 31st was calm and clear. The 2nd Worcestershire, in their reserve trenches west of Polygon Wood, were roused early by the crash of gun-fire. The troops turned out, breakfasts were cooked and eaten, weapons were cleaned and inspected. Then for several hours the companies lay idle about their billets, listening to the ever-increasing bombardment and watching the German shrapnel bursting in black puffs above the tree-tops.
>
> The 2nd Worcestershire were almost the last available reserve of the British defence. Nearly every other unit had been drawn into the battle-line or had been broken beyond recovery; and to an onlooker the last reserve would not have seemed very formidable. The battalion could not muster more than five hundred men. Ten days of battle had left all ranks haggard, unshaven and unwashed; their uniforms had been soaked in the mud of the Langemarck trenches and torn by the brambles of Polygon Wood; many had lost their puttees [i.e. their leggings] or their caps. But their weapons were clean and in good order, they had plenty of ammunition, and three months of war had given them confidence in their fighting power. . . .

Such fragments of news as they heard from retreating soldiers or walking wounded were not encouraging. The enemy was advancing in overwhelming numbers against the remnants of five British battalions, between them mustering barely a thousand men, who were clinging on to inadequate trenches on both sides of the Menin road. Worse, Gheluvelt itself had been lost and a great gap had opened in the British line. There was nothing for it but to call on the last available battalion to throw themselves into the gap and try to save the day.

Brigadier General C. FitzClarence, VC, was in charge of the front in the vicinity of the Menin Road. He commanded the 1st (Guards) Brigade, so that technically, the Worcestershire battalion, being part of the 2nd Division, were not under his orders. However, Major General Lomax had directed FitzClarence to instruct the Worcester battalion to enter the fight should he see fit to do so. Soon after midday, FitzClarence sent for an officer of the Worcestershires to take orders. Major Hankey duly despatched his Adjutant, Captain B. C. Senhouse Clarke, who returned stating that the battalion would probably be wanted for a counter-attack, but that meanwhile one of its four companies was to be detached to prevent the enemy from advancing up the Menin Road. 'A' Company was detailed to undertake this duty. At 12.45 it advanced to a position on the embankment of a light railway north-west of Gheluvelt, where it remained during the following two hours, firing at any enemy who attempted to advance beyond some nearby houses.

At 1 p.m. Major Hankey was summoned by General FitzClarence and was given definite orders. The battalion was to make a counter-attack to regain the lost British positions around Gheluvelt. Fitz-Clarence pointed out the church in Gheluvelt as a landmark for the advance, and delegated his Staff Captain, the already named Captain Andrew Thorne, to guide the battalion on its way.

At 1.45 Major Hankey sent forward the battalion scouts, under Lieutenant E. A. Haskett-Smith, to cut any wire fences that might lie in their way. Extra ammunition was issued, but all kit was lightened as much as possible, packs being left behind. Bayonets were fixed and at 2 p.m. the battalion moved off in file, led by Major Hankey and Captain Thorne, keeping under cover until they reached the south-west corner of Polygon Wood – later to become known as 'Black Watch Corner'. Ahead of them lay the open valley, crossed by the little stream known as the Reutelbeck, beyond which rose a bare ridge, Polderhoek, which hid from view the Gheluvelt Château, though to the right they could see the village church, rising above the smoke of the burning buildings surrounding it.

Stacke's account vividly evokes the area over which the 2nd Worcestershire were to make their attack:

> The open ground was dotted with wounded and stragglers coming back from the front. In every direction German shells were bursting. British batteries could be seen limbering up and moving to the rear. Everywhere there were signs of retreat. The Worcestershire alone were moving towards the enemy. But the three companies tramped grimly forward, down into the valley of the Reutelbeck.
>
> Beyond a little wood the Battalion deployed, 'C' and 'D' Companies in front line, with 'B' Company in second line behind – about 370 all told. In front of them rose the bare slope of the Polderhoek ridge. The ridge was littered with dead and wounded, and along its crest the enemy's shells were bursting in rapid succession. Major Hankey decided that the only way of crossing that deadly stretch of ground was by one long rush. The companies extended into line and advanced.
>
> The ground underfoot was rank grass or rough stubble. The two leading companies broke into a steady double and swept forward across the open, the officer leading on in front, and behind them their men with fixed bayonets in one long irregular line. As they reached the crest, the rushing wave of bayonets was sighted by the hostile artillery beyond. A storm of shells burst along the ridge. Shrapnel bullets rained down and high-explosive shells crashed into the charging line. Men fell at every pace: over a hundred of the Battalion were killed or wounded: The rest dashed on.

The outcome of this story was as remarkable as it was heroic. The German musketry was intense and professional, but behind this line of fire-power the enemy infantry, mainly young troops in newly formed units who had lost a number of their officers, were in some disorder and gave way at once to the Worcestershires' determined attack. Then, suddenly, British voices were heard among the cacophony of shouts and shells as, quite unexpectedly, the Worcestershire men found themselves mingling with the remnants of the 1st South Wales Borderers, who had held the grounds of the Gheluvelt Château all day in spite of being hemmed in by the enemy on all sides. Major

Hankey went immediately to meet the commander of the South Wales Borderers, Colonel H. E. Burleigh Leach, to recognize him as a personal friend. There ensued one of the great moments of the 1914 campaign. 'My God, fancy meeting you here,' said Major Hankey, to which Colonel Burleigh Leach replied: 'Thank God you have come.'

The Germans made no further attempt that day to retake Gheluvelt. They may have thought the Worcestershire attack was the first wave of a stronger force, an impression perhaps amplified by the heavy fire that the British artillery maintained on the ground to the east.

Out of a total strength of eleven officers and 450 other ranks, the casualties of the day were three officers and 189 other ranks.

If 31 October was a red-letter day for the 2nd Battalion, Worcestershire Regiment, it was also an extremely important day in the military career of the artillery officer Lieutenant Ralph Blewitt.

His contribution to the task of holding back the advance of a supremely powerful and confident enemy was fortuitously recorded in the detailed and informative memoir of the Western Front war by the future Brigadier General H. C. Rees, CMG, DSO, at this time, with the rank of captain, commanding officer of the 2nd Battalion, the Welch Regiment. Rees's battalion had suffered so badly early on the 31st that he would later write that on that day it was 'annihilated', adding, 'no other term can describe the casualties'. But he had a clear view of the battlefield and was determined to assist in what way he could with such troops as he still had under his command. Nearby were the guns of the battery of which Blewitt was a key member, his commander being a Major Robinson:

> At this time, Corder and myself were the only two officers who had survived the fighting at Gheluvelt, and we had about 25 men. These men I spread out as a firing line across a turnip field a little in front of the guns and went to interview Robinson. I suggested that he should open fire on some houses about 500 yards away on the south side of the Menin Road which were obviously full of snipers. He said he had got a few rounds of high explosives up for trial and I remarked that it seemed a priceless opportunity. He blew the houses about pretty badly and then continued with shrapnel on the slope just beyond them. This effectually put a stop to the rifle shooting which was getting rather trying.

It is at this point in Rees's account that he alludes, in a character-istically understated way, to the remarkable intervention of Lieuten-ant Ralph Blewitt:

> Lt Blewitt of this battery came up to say that the Germans appeared to be bringing up a gun to the barricade in the middle of Gheluvelt and asked permission to take an 18 pounder on to the road and have a duel with it. Having got permission, he man-handled the gun out on the road. The German gun fired first and missed and Blewitt did not give them a second chance. He put a stop to any trouble from that quarter for the rest of the afternoon.
>
> If the Germans had pushed home their attack during the afternoon, there was nothing to stop them.

For this action Lieutenant Blewitt was formally mentioned in despatches and awarded a DSO: or, more formally, created a Com-panion of the Distinguished Service Order. It appears that he seems to have offered no comment on the episode at the time. His next letter to his beloved fiancée, far from being full of heroics, is curiously laid back, almost as though the fighting had become rather a tedious chore:

> It's a peculiar life, rather wearying and *very* dirty. We were very amused at a Cavalry brigade that came up to relieve one of the Infantry Bdes that had been rather badly mauled about, all full of cheer – any fighting to be had here? – sort of spirit. I expect they got what they wanted.
>
> *Later* Just had a furious biff into La Belle Belgique, hope it did some damage at the other end, but I'm rather sceptical about this map shooting for physical results, tho' the country is so littered with soldiery that any shell is bound to frighten someone.

His letter also included the following statement, perhaps a little surprising from a man who had carried out a deed of extraordinary skill and valour just over a week earlier:

> Well there's no particular news and extraordinarily little humour about these days.

Yet three years later, clearly under family pressure – and at a convenient time when he was employed as an instructor at a gunnery

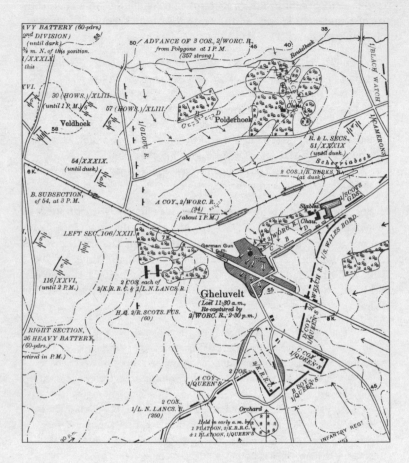

The Defence of Gheluvelt – The Critical Day: 31 October 1914

Detail of map compiled for the Official History of the War,
to accompany *Military Operations. France and Belgium, 1914*, Volume II

Note the line of march of the 2nd Worcestershires, from their start point at the top of
the map to the edge of Gheluvelt village; the position of 1st South Wales Borderers east
of the Château; and the location (centre) on the Menin Road of the German gun attacked
by Lieutenant Ralph Blewitt's battery at 3 p.m.

training school in England – Blewitt wrote a long description of the circumstances which had led to his being awarded the DSO, though still managing to do so without any bravado or bluster, indeed without mentioning the award at all. Headed 'Memories of Ypres 1914' and dated 'Oct 30th: 1917', his account began: 'It is a far cry to try and remember the events of one day 3 years back, but as you are so keen I'll try and put down what I can remember.' In one particularly interesting passage, he described how he saw the then Captain H. C. Rees, already quoted above, retiring from the battlefield with the relics of his battered battalion:

> About this time, I don't know at all what time of day it was, the first group of men properly under control came back, and I saw it was Rees in the Welch Regiment; he had I suppose about 15 or 20 men with him. The Major asked me who he was, and whether I knew him, and whether he was the sort of man who would come back. As he had got a DSO only a few days before I was able to convince him that he was one of the best and that there was no question of his coming back unnecessarily. Rees then came over to the battery. I have rarely seen a man in a more pitiable state, he was muddy and unshaven of course, but barely able to walk for sheer weariness, his equipment had for the most part been shot off him, and he was absolutely stunned and almost speechless. By good luck we happened to have some hot tea going in the battery at the moment, and a cup and a slice of bread and jam, and a cigarette worked wonders. His regiment had apparently been in a sunken road through the other side of Gheluvelt. They had been shelled continuously from dawn, and he and the men with him were the remains. After profuse thanks for the first meal (!) he had had that day, on the Major's suggestion he took his command forward to a half dug trench which was on the crest about 200 yards in front of the battery, and manned it much to the satisfaction of the battery. I did not see Rees again that day as far as I can remember.

Yet Rees clearly saw more of Blewitt that day; indeed, his temporary battalion headquarters put him in a prime position to observe the action for which the young gunnery officer won his award. The following is from Blewitt's somewhat reluctantly written 1917 account:

Just at this time there were one or two shell [sic] bursting among the trees round about but not really close, but on putting up my glasses to observe the next round, I saw a flash over the barricade [as referred to above by Rees] and realized at once that it was a gun – at the moment I had the impression that it must be a How [i.e. a howitzer] – even before the crash which followed a few seconds later. However as is so often the case with their *Heitgeschloss** it was all noise and smoke and no damage was done. However, no time was to be lost and we shot down the road all we knew, H.E., P.S., and occasionally a timed round, about fourteen rounds in all I should think, after which in the absence of any hostile *obus* [French for 'shell'] arriving to prove the contrary I thought one might stop for a moment to see the result as at the moment all was smoke. When it cleared there was the joyful sight of the barricade with a hearty hole in it, through which one could see a gun down on one wheel and no sign of life at all.

We then spent a few rounds making a bigger hole in the barricade, and also put a few rounds down the road up to two or three thousand yards back in the hope of catching someone. One can't tell of course, but I always hope that those few rounds might have severely frightened someone who might otherwise have taken part against the Worcesters who were counterattacking at the time.

Disclaiming any great virtue on his own part, Blewitt put down the success of his ruse to good training and a good crew:

I can't give a better example of what one is always trying to rub into everyone here at the School, that in laying there are two essentials, viz:- accuracy and speed, and how either without the other may on occasions be absolutely useless. My layer at the time was one Bombardier Steel, to whose efficiency I think solely we all – the detachment and I – owe our lives. The detachment as far as I can remember was: Sergt (now B.S.M.) Howes, a sturdier man than whom never stepped, as No.1., Br Steel, layer, Br Priestley (killed a few days later) No.6., while I think Gunners Hobson and Delamere (both at later times my servant, the first wounded by a French battery a few days later, and the latter gassed as a Sergt, in the Bty this year)

---

* Strictly not *Heitgeschloss* but *Geschlossheit*, meaning consistency, or in this case accuracy. Blewitt was evidently not impressed by the performance of the enemy's artillery.

made up the crew. Who the sixth man was I can't remember, but a damn fine crowd they were every one of them.

Despite the all-round excellence of his crew, it was Blewitt as officer in charge who was given the award, not without justice since it was he who put forward the idea of what was, in artillery terms, a life-or-death duel which might easily have turned out quite differently. Published in the *London Gazette* on 1 December 1914, the official citation read as follows: 'Ralph Blewitt, Lieutenant, Royal Field Artillery. For gallant and skilful handling of a single gun in support of infantry on the road to Gheluvelt on 31 Oct., being all the time under heavy fire. This action was of greatest use to the infantry.'

* * *

Although First Ypres was more challenging still than the Marne and the Aisne, there were those who throughout remained confident and determined, allowing nothing to dampen their ardour or dislodge their belief in ultimate success. Captain Eric Fairtlough had been dismissive of all setbacks during the Aisne confrontation, and he was equally positive in his reaction to the later battle. This was certainly the case in his letters to his father, Colonel Howard Fairtlough, who was a holder of the Queen's South Africa Medal and had been awarded the CMG for his services in the Boer War. Far from sitting at home in honourable retirement, Fairtlough senior was by this time actively engaged in helping to raise and train a battalion of Kitchener's New Army, the 8th (Service) Battalion, the Queen's Royal West Surrey Regiment, with whom he would cross to France in September 1915, to be killed on the 26th of that month leading his men into action during the Battle of Loos. Eric Fairtlough's letters to his father read like serious communications between officers, being largely without the usual gossip or pleasantries characteristic of so many exchanges between the civilian world and the front. Hence this one, written on 28 October, and marked by Howard Fairtlough as being received on the 31st. Significantly, it was written following encouraging news of recent advances on the Eastern Front. Also notable is the fact that although Eric Fairtlough was an artillery officer temporarily serving with the Signal Service the wisdom he passed to his father was almost exclusively about trenches:

Dear Father,

Thank you for your letter of the 19th October which I received yesterday. I am glad you have such a fine battalion and know that you must be enjoying being back in harness again.

The news here is most satisfactory especially after the Russian success and people are talking of an early termination of the war. . . .

A few things that the war has shown and that may be useful to you are:

(1) It is impossible to advance in any close formation under modern artillery fire.

(2) Trenches must be narrow and at least four feet deep. The narrower the better.

(3) The importance of accurate shooting and good fire discipline. This is where we have a great pull over the Germans.

(4) Trenches must always be dug as soon as a position is taken.

The Brigade has done very well and has received several congratulatory messages.

I am as fit as a fiddle and have never felt better. Hope you are the same.

Yr loving son
    Eric

Writing to his mother he was still positive, but more anxious to reassure, as in this letter of 4 November, written in the knowledge that two of his brothers were already in uniform and had just been sent to France:

Dearest Mother,

I received all your letters up to Oct. 27th yesterday (5 in a bunch) and the cigars. The pipes have arrived and parcel no 7. Gerard and Lance must be glad to get out here. I feel most awfully grieved for you having all away from home except Vic, but you must be brave and remember we are all doing something for our country. You must not be anxious about them as I don't expect they will be employed in the firing anyway just at present. There is talk of an early termination of the war, as they say the Germans will be exhausted after the great effort they are making now. We have been having a strenuous time, but have hopes of a rest soon as lots of fresh troops are coming up. There is little news as every day is like another. Everybody is pleased and says things are quite satisfactory.

On the following day he sent a cheerful postcard:

> I saw Gerard this afternoon, both he and Lance were very well. I
> motored some way back to a village where they were billeted. Perhaps
> I might see them again, but it is some way off. I am very well and in a
> comfortable billet for the night. The news is good today. Love to all.

To an aunt who was clearly worried about the situation, he was
even more reassuring:

> We have had a hard ten days with a good number of casualties.
> The Germans made several determined attacks but we beat them off
> and as we are reinforced everything is all right. I hear you are very
> pessimistic about the result. I am certain things are all right and it is
> only a matter of time, in fact several well informed people think that
> the Germans are retiring on the Rhine and the terrific attacks to which
> we have been subjected are to cover this movement.

* * *

Another officer who played a full part in the First Battle of Ypres was
the already much-quoted Second Lieutenant Lionel Tennyson. As a
veteran of the Marne and the Aisne, he was well used to 1914-style
campaigning, but even he was not prepared for what he experienced
during the horrific fighting of this later action. His day-by-day
account of a long period in the line in the last days of October and
the first fortnight in November – during which there was no named
set-piece battle, just a succession of apparently random local attacks
and counterthrusts accompanied by ferocious shelling and much
deadly sniper-fire – offers a remarkable snapshot of the messy, confusing, terrifying state that the Western Front had got itself into at
this time. There are no long perspectives; this is about close action
at its unpleasant worst, with a constant drip-drip of casualties and
fatalities, so that, almost certainly, it was only by virtue of having
fallen in the dark and damaged his leg badly enough to be sent home,
that he survived. His 1st Battalion, the Rifle Brigade, was in the far
south of the British sector, in an area that would shortly become well
known for being relatively peaceful – 'cushy' in the language of the
time – and indeed, in a matter of weeks, would become a main focus
of the Christmas Truce. At first they were entrenched on the Franco-

Belgian border, near the River Lys and in the vicinity of Le Touquet and Frelinghien, subsequently moving to Ploegsteert – 'Plugstreet' to the Tommies – and its associated area of forest, the Bois du Gheer, always called 'Plugstreet Wood'. 'Cushy' this sector was not, at this stage, and there was no quarter from either side:

*Thurs, Oct 29th.* Today was the coldest night and day we have had since we left England, and we were all absolutely frozen. The Germans we could hear digging trenches all night, near the river in front of the church of Frelinghien. This town was shelled tremendously by our guns about 11.30 a.m. this morning, which must have done great damage. We heard the distant guns of our 7th Division and the French coming up to the north of us which were supposed to be driving the Germans across our front. Our guns went on shelling the German positions nearly all tonight, and about 9 p.m. we heard and saw them round a fire on the edge of the town, singing round a gramophone. Suddenly from somewhere a long way behind our trenches, we heard a tremendous shell whistle over our heads, and burst straight in the middle of this glee party, and must have blown them and the gramophone all to glory. It was one of the best aimed shots I have ever seen in my life, and as a fellow in my platoon remarked, 'I heard them all two moments ago singing "Der Vaterland, der Vaterland",' and most of them, he said, went there a good deal quicker than they expected.

Rifleman Davey in the Company was killed today, shot through the head, through one of the loopholes of the barricade on the road to our left.

*Fri, Oct 30th.* Terrible battle began about 8.15 a.m. this morning directed at B and C Companies. Such a shelling as the Germans gave us for a few hours I have never seen. This lasted till about 3 p.m., and we were pretty glad when things started quieting down a bit. About 1.30 p.m. we noticed they were massing ready for an attack, and about 2 p.m. they advanced across the open in front of our trenches in two great solid lines, their officers keeping in the background and advancing behind their men. They were fairly mowed down by our guns, machine-guns and rifle fire, and soon broke in disorder and ran in all directions. I saw one German fellow when they started running in every direction, he ran right across our front without being hit, and when within about 5 yards of safety in a trench, one of our shells got the poor fellow fair and square and blew him to glory.

Our men are keeping up their spirits awfully well, and are very cheerful considering what they have been through, though they are rather done in for want of sleep.

Tennyson had no love for his general officer commanding and made no secret of the fact in his diary, but neither did he have a high opinion of the Germans' leadership:

> *Sunday, Nov 1st.* Congratulations arrived this morning from Major General Hunter-Weston (*note* he is now a 'Major General' as he got accelerated promotion a few days ago but what for, nobody knows), congratulating us on our courage and tenacity. This was very encouraging!!
> The Kaiser himself is reported to be commanding the very army opposite us, which is also very encouraging, as he usually makes a hash of things.

So the days and nights dragged by with one harrowing experience after another. On 2 November Tennyson reported 'a terrible night attack by the Germans; their machine gun and rifle fire was simply terrific, and bullets came over in thousands'. On the 5th, 'They have shelled us in a terrible manner all day, the noise being deafening.' Friday, 6 November, was equally unnnerving: 'Terrible shelling of our trenches by the Germans all day long; sometimes one literally feels one is going mad, but I trust one doesn't get as bad as that.' At least the indefatigable army postal system brought a welcome letter from his mother that day, with cigarettes for himself and his men. A clutch of newspapers also arrived, usually providing agreeable relief, but not on this occasion:

> Saw in one of these papers that Paddy Wallis and Freddy Pollock, both great friends of mine in the Coldstream, had been killed, also George Paley, who used to be our 2nd in Command at Colchester before the war, and was now on the staff, had been killed, also 'Bird' Landale, an Australian by birth, and an awfully nice fellow, was killed also. We used to be in the same division at Eton.

This was not the only time he interrupted his accounts of action to include such thumb-nail obituaries of his friends.

Saturday, 7 November, produced an especially eloquent entry:

Today is my birthday, and long shall I remember it! The Germans attacked us again this morning about 5 a.m. till 9 a.m., but we managed to drive them back again. Literally thousands of shells have been bursting all around us, as well as machine-gun fire directed against us.

The battle today continued till about 5.30 p.m. when a night attack started. The Germans used a fair shower of their rockets, lighting up all the ground between our trenches and theirs. About 7 p.m. I was standing on a road which ran between Mitford's and my platoon, showing my platoon sergeant where to dig a communication trench between the two trenches, and he being very dense could not understand where to start it. I therefore got down into the trench to show him. I had not been down there 10 seconds, before six shells burst in quick succession, in exactly the place where I had been standing and must have killed me had I still been there.

Never shall I forget this Nov 7th and my twenty-fifth birthday as long as I live, it being one of the worst days we have had since we left England.

By contrast 10 November was a 'fairly quiet day', and at last they were able to leave a trench system where they had been for fourteen days without relief. The 1st Battalion, King's (Liverpool) Regiment took over, but the battalion was 'tremendously sniped' by the Germans as they made their exit: 'Luckily nobody was hit, as all their bullets went high.'

They had been told they would have two days' rest, but this turned out to be an illusion; 11 November was not to be the respite they had hoped for. After a first bath since 29 September and a change of clothes, Tennyson was hoping for a reasonable break from the tensions and hazards of the trenches; however, orders came about 6 p.m. that they were to move off about 7 p.m. to relieve the Inniskilling Fusiliers, 'at a place about 4 miles to our left front called Ploegsteert Wood':

No rest for the weary! Terribly wet night again, and the mud was simply too awful everywhere. We marched as far as the village of Ploegsteert, where we halted, ate and slept for 3 hours in the church there, all the men sitting in the pews, and lying on the floor, etc. The spies must have reported that we had been in the church, as it was shelled next day, and 3 shells went straight through the roof. After 3 hours rest, we pushed on into Ploegsteert Wood, where we took over the rottenest trenches I have ever seen in my life.

It was here, on 12 November, that Second Lieutenant Tennyson had his accident:

> This is the worst place we have been in for mud, holes, ditches etc. Nobody knows where anyone else is in the wood, and consequently shoot a lot at each other. People seem to be facing in every direction. When about a quarter of a mile from the reserve trenches, I fell into a deep trench, or ditch, in the darkness, while leading my company back, and I thought I had broken my leg. The pain was awful and I had to be practically carried back by two men in our company to our trenches. Here I spent the night in great pain, and hardly any sleep.

The medical officer's verdict, next day, was that the leg was 'pretty badly injured' and the process was launched that, over the next six days, would take him back to England.

* * *

Elsewhere the First Battle of Ypres was going through its final throes.

In his description (quoted in Chapter 1) of the fate that lay in store for the finest of British soldiery parading back in June at Aldershot, Charles Carrington stated that before the year was out 'the Worcesters would have tipped the scale of destiny by the decisive counter-attack at Gheluvelt', and that 'the Oxfordshires, the old 52nd Light Infantry, would have broken the Prussian Guard, as their forerunners had broken Napoleon's Old Guard at Waterloo'.

The achievements of the Worcestershires, on 31 October, have already been described. On 11 November it was the turn of the Oxfordshires: more formally the 2nd Battalion, Oxfordshire and Buckinghamshire Light Infantry, 5th Infantry Brigade, 2nd Division. On that date the Prussian Guard was called up to make a massive final attempt to break through the Allied defences. This was the occasion when in the words of one of 1914's earliest chroniclers, Lord Ernest Hamilton, the soldiers of this elite force 'in their advance displayed the invincible courage for which they have ever been famed' – a courage which he hailed as 'sublime'; but 'the losses among these gallant men was prodigious', and their attack failed. The regimental history preserves a first-hand account by Lieutenant, later Lieutenant Colonel, C. S. Baines, which gives a vivid picture of the close fighting in Nonne Boschen Wood, which the Oxfordshire men entered after a series of short rushes across open ground. Perhaps surprisingly, his description of what happened at this stage of the action suggests that Germany's praetorian guard, far from showing the aggressive spirit described by Hamilton, was showing every sign of having lost its motivation. The wood was seen to be full of Germans, but these were not as they were expected to be, disciplined, organized and controlled; on the contrary they appeared to be in a state of considerable confusion:

> There seemed to be crowds of them, because they were in no sort of formation and were wandering aimlessly about; and most of them put their hands up as soon as they saw us . . . I have no idea how many there were or what happened to them. Starting through the wood, we strung out into a very thin line, two men at intervals of twelve to fifteen yards. Many of the trees had had their tops or branches knocked off by shells, which, together with the thick undergrowth, made progress difficult. We moved forward like a line of beaters and kept coming upon bunches of Germans. Some loosed off their rifles without bothering to take careful aim, thank goodness, then turned tail and ran. Others surrendered without more ado. I took pot-shots with my revolver at those who ran. I fired fifty-two rounds through my revolver, and burnt my left hand on the barrel in reloading. It is not difficult to understand when I say that the longest range at which I fired at a German was about thirty yards and the huge bulk of the average Prussian Guardsman made an easy target, even on the run.

Nevertheless, the losses were extremely heavy on the Allied side too; among the fatalities was Brigadier General C. FitzClarence, VC, who had played so prominent a part in initiating the Worcestershires' Gheluvelt action of 31 October.

A last German attempt on the 17th, equally unsuccessful, effectively brought the battle to an end, although its formal date of closure was later given as the 22nd.

\* \* \*

The Oxfordshire and Buckinghamshire's performance on 11 November acquired a memorable footnote – literally – in that the Official History, on page 427 of its second 1914 volume, recorded a brief episode, for which the regimental history also found space, which showed that even on days of serious crisis and hard fighting humour could break through. During the bombardment that morning the brigade major of Brigadier General Count Gleichen, who was based in the Belgian château the British named Stirling Castle, burst into his general's quarters clad only in a towel, with his clothes on his arm, saying, 'May I finish my dressing here? They're shelling the bath-room'.

The incident was taken up by the Christmas edition of *Punch*, which reworked it into a cartoon entitled: 'The Joy of Billeting in a French Château', though the brigade major's quotation was slightly sanitized, doubtless for reasons of *delicatesse*. The text reads: 'Time 6 a.m. Brigade Major: 'I say, sir, may I finish dressing in here? They're shellin' the north bedrooms!' The brigade major was Captain J. T. Weatherby, DSO, of the 2nd Oxfordshire and Buckinghamshire battalion. (See following page.)

\* \* \*

The First Battle of Ypres took the lives of a number of officers quoted in these pages.

Lieutenant Angus Macnaghten, 1st Black Watch, died on Thursday, 29 October, or, more strictly, was posted missing on that date; his body was never found. His son, newly born in 1914, would write many years later of 'frantic efforts by my mother, my aunts and my mother's uncle [an Army colonel] to follow up all possible lines of enquiry which might lead to his discovery, all, alas, totally in vain'. There was also what he called 'an unfortunate sequel in 1931, when an old friend of my mother's, Miss Enid Hudson, suddenly came forward with the claim that she had caught a glimpse of my father some years before in the Balkans. This led to renewed enquiries, all without result.' This was far from being the only case of grieving relatives hoping for many years that a soldier of whose death there was no incontrovertible evidence might suddenly reappear – eminently understandable in the case of a war in which there were so many anonymous dead, and so many whose bodies were blown to

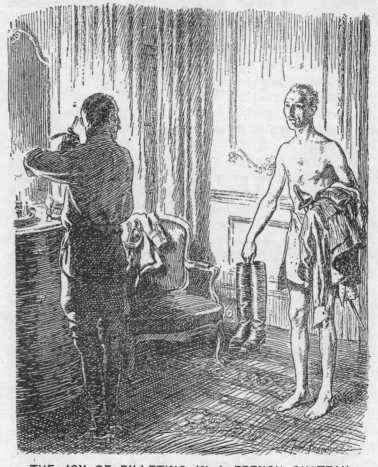

THE JOY OF BILLETING IN A FRENCH CHATEAU.

*Time, 6 a.m.*

*Brigade Major.* "I SAY, SIR, MAY I FINISH DRESSING IN HERE? THEY'RE SHELLIN' THE NORTH BEDROOMS!"

A delicate moment in the midst of an enemy bombardment: from the Christmas edition of *Punch*, 23 December 1914

atoms or buried as a consequence of shellfire or lost in the ebb and flow of battle. Macnaghten's name is on the Menin Gate Memorial to the Missing, Ypres, with 29 October 1914 as his assumed date of death.

Captain C. J. Paterson, Adjutant of the 1st South Wales Borderers, was wounded on 29 October, while carrying orders for his commanding officer, and died of wounds on 1 November. The Foreword to his privately published war diary claimed that throughout it 'there is little thought of personal comfort or of personal sacrifice, least of all of personal glory, only an absorbing sense of duty and desire to "play for his side".' Paterson's grave is in the Ypres Town British Military Cemetery, a matter of yards from the Menin Gate along the Zonnebeke road.

Second Lieutenant Geoffrey Loyd died of wounds on 13 November. His commanding officer, Captain the Hon. W. A. Nugent, who commanded the 2nd Divisional Cavalry to which Loyd's Cyclists' unit was attached, took the time to write a long and detailed letter describing the circumstances to Loyd's father, Mr A. K. Loyd, which was subsequently copied into his son's papers.

> I can't tell you how sorry I am to have to be the bearer of very sad news, but your son in the Scots Guards who was attached to the Mounted Troops 2nd Division was killed in action yesterday. At the time he was with the Cyclist detachment on duty with his platoon. He was just coming back into a dug-out to his brother Officers – when a shrapnel burst over him [sic] – penetrating behind the shoulder blade and travelling on into his stomach. He was immediately taken to a dressing station close by – and thence to an English temporary hospital – where Capt. Nelson and another officer of my Squadron met him – and did all they could for his comfort, and had him placed in an Ambulance, and taken to a proper hospital. I regret to say he died on the way. He was hardly conscious at any time – but expressed a wish early after he was wounded that we should write and let you know. When Nelson met him he was more or less under the influence of morphia – and his servant 'Irons' we sent with him to Hospital, and he told me he never quite recovered consciousness – so I hope he was spared suffering.
>
> I have seen both his brothers this morning – and they have gone down to the Hospital to be present at the last. I cannot express in

any words my sorrow at your sad loss. He is indeed a loss to us. He
was a really promising young officer – of abilities quite out of the
common. He had obtained and deserved the French legion of honour
– and I had hoped to see his name in despatches very shortly, besides
during the three months he has been with us – and we have got to
know him, he has become a real friend to us all . . .

I can say no more to express my sympathy with you, and all your
family in your sad loss, which we share to no small extent.

Loyd was buried at Communal Cemetery, Poperinghe, Belgium.
He was posthumously gazetted Lieutenant (as noted in *The Times* of
27 November), and was mentioned in despatches by Sir John French
on 17 February 1915. Nugent himself, who was the second son of the
10th Earl of Westmeath, and heir presumptive to the earldom, was to
lose his life on 29 May 1915 of wounds received in action.

Another, more notable death had taken place two days before
Loyd's, on 11 November. Captain A. E. J. Collins, 5th Field Company,
Royal Engineers, aged twenty-nine, had won permanent celebrity as a
cricketer when in 1899, as a schoolboy of Clark's House, Clifton
College, Bristol, he had achieved in an inter-house match the
remarkable score of 628 not out. It was a record that has never been
equalled, nor is likely to be. But, in the case of his death – also to be
commemorated on the Menin Gate – equally significant as the score
was the school which had educated him. It was Clifton College that
had produced arguably the best-known writer of imperial verse after
Rudyard Kipling, in the person of Sir Henry Newbolt, whose famous
slim volume *Admirals All* had captured the public imagination in the
year that Collins entered Clark's House as a new boy, 1897. Newbolt's
best-known poem, much admired, later to be much mocked and
lampooned, was a mix of the not dissimilar – as he saw them –
ingredients of cricket and war:

> There's a breathless hush in the Close to-night –
> Ten to make and the match to win –
> A bumping pitch and a blinding light,
> An hour to play and the last man in.
> And it's not for the sake of a ribboned coat,
> Or the selfish hope of a season's fame,

> But his Captain's hand on his shoulder smote –
> 'Play up! Play up and play the game!'
>
> The sand of the desert is sodden red, –
> Red with the wreck of a square that broke; –
> The Gatling's jammed and the Colonel dead,
> And the regiment blind with dust and smoke.
> The river of death has brimmed his banks,
> And England's far, and Honour a name,
> But the voice of a schoolboy rallies the ranks:
> 'Play up! Play up! And play the game!...

For the sand of the desert read the flat Flanders plain and the muddy shell-pocked wastes between Ypres and the sea; the 'Gatling' was an early machine gun, largely overtaken by this time by the Maxim. It is an intriguing thought that the playing field best known to Newbolt was the one on which the young Arthur Collins made his record-breaking score. Doubtless he, like Newbolt's schoolboy hero, like Captain Paterson referred to above, was a man with 'an absorbing sense of duty and desire to "play for his side"'.

Clifton College, like so many other public schools, would pay a high price in the war. Over 3,000 Cliftonians served, of whom 578 died, a younger brother of Collins among them; a third brother, not a Cliftonian, also died. All the members of the 1914 Clifton Cricket XI 'played the game': five were killed, one died of disease, four were wounded. Five VCs, 180 DSOs, and 300 MCs were won by Clifton old boys. Moreover, the school also won the distinction of providing the nation during the war with fifty-two brigadier generals, twenty-three major generals, and one Army Commander, Lieutenant General Sir William Birdwood. It also produced the man who would succeed Field Marshal Sir John French as Commander-in-Chief in December 1916, holding that position to the end of the war as General, later Field Marshal, Sir Douglas Haig.

\* \* \*

There is a necessary postscript to this battle: a German one. Scholarship might question the myth of the *Kindermord von Ypern*, usually interpreted as the 'Massacre of the Innocents at Ypres': the notion of the flower of German youth marching blithely into battle to be cut down brutally and en masse whether by shell-fire or by the coolly efficient rifle fire of the British regulars. But it has its historical support – as, for example, in the memoirs of a German cavalry officer, Captain Rudolph Binding, who wrote under the date 27 October 1914:

> These young fellows we have, only just trained, are too helpless, especially when their officers have been killed. Our light infantry battalion, almost all Marburg students . . . have suffered terribly . . . In the next division, just such young souls, the intellectual flower of Germany, went singing into an attack at Langemarck, just as vain and just as costly.

The myth also has its special memorial. Curiously, there are few memorials to the British performance in 1914. As in so much else in relation to this year, the war's first campaigns are virtually swept aside, as though they were merely a prelude to more tragic events to come. But the German sacrifice of the best of its young is commemorated on the edge of the tiny Belgian village specifically named by Rudolph Binding: Langemarck. Strictly the cemetery there refers to the whole war, but its distinctive gatehouse records in a series of bronze panels the names of thousands of students, clearly the innocents of those costly attacks during the First Battle of Ypres.

In his book *The Culture of Defeat*, published in 2003, the German historian Wolfgang Schivelbusch reaffirmed the important claim that all nations, whether successful or otherwise in war, require their potent, unassailable myths. Thus the United States requires the story of Pickett's Charge, the sacrificial Confederate attack during the Battle of Gettysburg which was almost like a precursor of the Somme; the British need their Charge of the Light Brigade; and the Germans need Langemarck. If the Menin Gate is the most eloquent British memorial on the Western Front, this is surely the German equivalent, specifically recalling the tragic events of 1914.

\* \* \*

As for the British, there is no doubt that First Ypres, while it added a glorious page to the history of the old Regular Army, was also the consuming fire which burnt out its heart. In the words of the Official History of 1914, published in 1925:

The British Army has fought many a defensive battle with success: – Crécy, Agincourt, Albuera, Waterloo, Inkerman; and Ypres proved that the men of 1914, recruited haphazard by voluntary enlistment, were fully the equals of their forefathers in valour and determination. They were more than the equals, not only of the flower of the youth of Germany in the volunteer units of the new Reserve corps, but also of the picked representatives of the German nation selected by the process of universal service.

[But] the cost was overwhelming. In the British battalions which fought at the Marne and Ypres, there scarcely remained with the colours an average of one officer and thirty men of those who landed in August 1914. The old British Army was gone past recall, leaving but a remnant to carry on the training of the new Armies; but the framework that remained had gained an experience and confidence which was to make those Armies invincible ... If they had done naught else, the men of the Expeditionary Force would have done far more than could have been expected of their numbers.

On Saturday, 28 November, when the battle was over, Major 'Ma' Jeffreys, of the 2nd Battalion, the Grenadier Guards, wrote the following inventory in his diary, summing up his unit's losses from the Retreat from Mons onwards:

No draft for the Battalion yet, but the men are getting new clothes, which are badly wanted. Our casualties since the beginning of the War have been:

> 17 Officers killed
> 15 Officers wounded
> 739 Other Ranks killed and wounded
> 188 Other Ranks missing
> Total 959

Practically the strength of a whole Battalion. The missing must nearly all be dead for, except at Villers-Cotterêts and on 6 November there could have been no prisoners, and the Germans abandoned their wounded prisoners, taken at Villers-Cotterêts, when they retired. On 6 November we know of no prisoners, but some wounded may have been left when we threw our right flank back. Some of the missing were probably hit direct by big shells, or buried. Others may have dropped in the woods and not been found.

'No draft yet', he had written on 28 November. On 30 November Jeffreys welcomed 'a draft of 465 men', which by the following day were settling in encouragingly well. 'They are mostly older class reservists with a certain number of serving soldiers from 3rd Battalion, including a few joined in August. A fine lot of men and the Battalion again about 900 strong.'

Yet by now there were hints of a new human cost to this situation, one not only related to the standard statistics of men killed, wounded and missing. It was at about this time that those concerned with the medical and mental condition of the many thousands who had become the casualties of the first campaigns began to realize that they were confronting a disturbing phenomenon of which they had not previously been aware. By December, alarming reports were even beginning to reaching the War Office in London that large numbers of soldiers were being evacuated from the BEF with 'nervous and mental shock'. Some 7–10 per cent of all officers and 3–4 per cent of all ranks were being sent home suffering from nervous or mental breakdown. Dr William Aldren Turner, an experienced neurologist, was sent to France to investigate. He found that as far back as October, when the fighting concentrated in the vicinity of Ypres, there had been a rash of cases of men who became paralysed under shellfire or were reduced to a state of collapse by exhaustion and strain. Turner was not able to stay on to continue his 'psychological work', so the mantle was passed to a Dr Charles Myers, a Cambridge physiologist, who had recently joined the staff of the Duchess of Westminster's Hospital established in the Casino at Le Touquet, just down the coast from Boulogne. It was he who would very shortly introduce the phrase 'shell-shock' to the world in an article in the medical journal *The Lancet* in February 1915.

On 19 November the Hon. Lionel Tennyson was promoted to the rank of Lieutenant. At the time he was recovering from his injury in the comfort of a private hospital in Mayfair, London. Yet though he was far from the war it would not quite let him go. He himself had no difficulty in getting a good night's rest, but, he noted in his diary, 'I kept on being woken up, by fellows yelling and talking in their sleep, all imagining that they were still fighting.' With hindsight, it might well be that these were some of the earliest cases of soldiers wounded more in the region of the mind than the body, of the kind that were currently attracting the interest of Dr Turner and Dr Myers. For his own part, Tennyson clearly had no problems: 'Nobody knows what the feeling of being at home and comfortable after all our hardships is like, but there is no nicer feeling that one can imagine, when one has seen what war is really like.'

# CHAPTER ELEVEN

# ENEMY AT THE GATES

For Lieutenant the Hon. Lionel Tennyson the contrast between the horrors of the front and the peacefulness of the home country, even though he was in a hospital in the centre of a teeming capital city, was profound. But Britain was not a nation at ease; on the contrary, her people were edgy, nervous and apprehensive.

To the British the year 1940 has always been seen as the supreme year for invasion scares. But there was a similar anxiety in 1914. If not an invasion, then there might be a naval raid. Everybody knew the Germans had the ships to deliver seaborne attacks, and the Royal Navy could not be everywhere. Such fears were not without foundation, as events would prove. The East Coast, inevitably, was the area that seemed most vulnerable. Within days of the outbreak of war, visitors were deserting the seaside resorts en masse. As early as 8 August, Clementine Churchill was writing to her husband from their holiday home in Cromer, Norfolk:

> Yesterday the local authorities in a frantic attempt to stem the ebbing tide of tourists had the following pathetic appeal flashed on the screen of the local cinema show. (I am not sure of the words, but this is the gist.)
>
> 'Visitors! Why are you leaving Cromer? Mrs Winston Churchill and her children are in residence in the neighbourhood. If it's safe enough for her surely it's safe enough for you!'

Churchill's sympathies, however, were rather on the side of the fleeing holiday-makers. His concern was increased by the fact that the family motor car was temporarily, as Mrs Churchill described it, 'a lame duck':

> It makes me a little anxious that you should be on the coast. It is a 100 to 1 against a raid – but there is still the chance, and Cromer has a good landing place near.

I wish you would get the motor repaired and keep it so that you can whisk away at the first sign of trouble.

Such fears would recur throughout the months that followed.

* * *

The fall of Antwerp gave a fresh impetus to the anti-alien sentiments that had flared up in the war's first weeks. In view of the implicit British belief in the superiority of their own servicemen it seemed obvious that defeat must have been the result of treachery, a treachery that must by definition have its counterpart at home, with dark forces ready to betray Britain as they had clearly betrayed Antwerp.

In its edition of Saturday, 17 October, the *Daily Mail* published an eye-catching message of warning, titled in thick Gothic-style lettering, of which copies in poster form, 23 inches by 40, could be obtained free by applying to the newspaper at its address in Carmelite House, London, EC. Its (slightly abbreviated) text, targeted fiercely at the enemy whether without or within, read as follows:

### Remember Antwerp

Every Borough and Urban Council should at once make out a list of all owners of property who bear German or Austrian names, irrespective of the question whether they are naturalized or not.

War Vigilance Committees should be formed in every ward of every borough and urban district.

Members of such Vigilance Committees should be appointed as a special police force with the duty of examining the houses, gardens, outhouses, &c., of all Germans and Austrians ...

It is the duty of every Briton who knows a German or Austrian to acquaint the police of his presence and to satisfy himself that the person is registered as an alien enemy ...

Let every Briton remember the fate of Antwerp; how Germans established themselves in that city and betrayed it.

Let him never forget that in the event of invasion every German or Austrian of army service age has his rendezvous to which he will go unless he is put under an armed guard in a camp.

Let no feelings of personal friendship with any German or

Austrian, even though he is your next-door neighbour, over-
ride your duty to your country, which is to regard every
German or Austrian here, capable of bearing arms, as your
enemy, who is waiting his opportunity.

Every man who is not for us is against us. It is better that
every German, naturalized or not, shall be safely put under
lock and key than that one British soldier should die through
the treachery of the enemy in our midst.

To reinforce its message the newspaper also carried a story reporting the 'great glee' of German and Austrian waiters in a West End
hotel on hearing of Antwerp's fall: 'Remarks were made, there were
broad smiles, and evident pleasure was displayed without any dis-
guise.' Another story, headed 'Enemy in our Midst', included an inset
box with the text REFUSE TO BE SERVED BY AN AUSTRIAN OR GERMAN
WAITER, and a letter from a patriotic reader stating:

All my friends and myself have today formed ourselves into a
society, the 'All British Service' (wearing a white badge) and we
hope to rid ourselves of this German spy-waiter pest. Surely we
have enough men waiters of our own. If not, why not employ
some of the out-of-work waitresses?

Under three weeks later incontrovertible evidence of Germany's
malign intentions was provided by the appearance off the Norfolk
coast of a small force of German warships which proceeded to open
fire on Great Yarmouth. A Royal Army Medical Corps doctor, Captain
W. S. Scott, attached to the Shropshire Yeomanry, then undergoing
training in East Anglia as part of the Welsh Border Mounted Brigade,
became a witness – if from some distance – of this disturbing attack.
Some weeks earlier he had noted in his diary an instruction from his
Brigadier General, at an inspection parade on Bungay Common, 'for
the regiment to hold itself in readiness to move at any moment as
heavy firing in the North Sea was expected' – presumably as a prelude
to a raid or an attempt at invasion. Scott thought this precaution
unnecessarily alarmist: 'He evidently is oblivious of the fact that the
landing of a hostile army on this part of the E. coast would be a very
dangerous and protracted affair owing to the shallowness of the water
and no sane enemy would attempt to land under these conditions.'

Now, however, it was clear the enemy was within sight and just off-shore, poised to strike.

This is from Scott's diary entry for Tuesday, 3 November:

> Up at 7.15 a.m. At 7.30 set out for my surgery at Seafield House. On the way there I saw Rogers of A Squadron watching the horizon to the N. and he told me he had seen some curious flashes at intervals apparently out at sea opposite Yarmouth. I saw three big flashes myself. They looked exactly like large bushes flaring up momentarily with red flame. As I entered the surgery I heard a sound like a cannon report. At breakfast the Colonel suddenly appeared at the dining room door in deshabillé and called Capt. Hayes to him. Soon after Lambart entered and said some German vessels were bombarding Yarmouth and that the *Halcyon* – a Lowestoft gunboat – had returned with her steering gear damaged and one man wounded.

The regiment was swiftly on the move, and, travelling by way of Lowestoft, had reached Carlton Colville station en route for Yarmouth when it was ordered to return to Lowestoft, 'the German attack (if it was an attack) having failed'. Later, with a fellow officer, Scott had a look at the *Halcyon*, a twenty-year-old gunboat of the *Dryad* class, with a displacement of 1,070 tons and a complement of 120, when she came in:

> The only thing I saw was a dent on her side and some tears in the canvas surrounding the bridge. At lunch I heard she had a hole in her funnel and after lunch I went out and saw the rent about 6 to 9 inches in diameter. A sailor was busy hammering away in repair of it. At lunch the Captain of the *Halcyon* was lunching with the port Commander. He had evidently been slightly wounded as he had some sticking plaster on the back of his head. People were lining the rails looking at the *Halcyon* across the river. Otherwise things were as usual. Perhaps the promenade crowd was more numerous than usual. They had much to see in the way of big cruisers and destroyers in the offing. It is curious to think that I was one of the few here who saw the flash of the enemy's guns, a sight which has rarely been seen for many a long day.

What Scott had seen was part, not of an invasion attempt, but – as it would be described in the German official history – of a 'demonstration against the English coast' by a squadron of four battlecruisers and four light cruisers. In brief, it was an exercise in psychological warfare, intended less to kill and destroy than to frighten and dismay, to remind the citizens of Britain of their vulnerability and keep their nerves on edge. Steaming parallel to, and about ten miles off, Great Yarmouth, the German warships fired at the town without actually hitting it, then ceased fire and made off to the eastward. The *Halcyon*, it transpired, had been at sea when at about 6.45 a.m. an early-morning fog lifted to reveal six or eight German warships some 7,000 yards off. She made for Lowestoft at full speed with the Germans blazing away at her until about 7.30. The general verdict was that she was lucky not to be seriously damaged or sunk. The Germans themselves did not get off scot-free. Their *Roon*-class cruiser *Yorck*, with a displacement of 9,350 tons and a complement of 633, struck a mine and lost half her crew on her re-entry into German waters in Jade Bay.

The response of the Army was as described. The Navy, fearing this might be a diversion to distract attention from more serious attacks further north, took more drastic action, moving ships rapidly up from Spithead and the Nore, while three submarines from Gorleston, just to the south of Yarmouth, put to sea at the first sound of the enemy's guns. One of these was *E10*, commanded by Lieutenant Ronald Trevor (see Chapter 3), the other two being *D3* and *D5*. In the words of the British Naval history: 'Unhappily as they were hurrying to the scene *D5* struck a floating mine ... and though two fishing-drifters, *Homeland* and *Faithful*, regardless of the danger, rushed to the rescue, nearly all hands were lost.' Trevor, writing the following day, described what happened in a letter to his cousin Daphne: 'We went out with *D3* and *5*, the latter was sad to say blown up. I saw her go down, the water shot high in the air, up went the bows and down she went in a few seconds.'

The young lieutenant's reaction was similar to that of countless other servicemen in this war as the casualty lists steadily increased: 'One's pals being killed day after day has become so monotonous that you simply say "poor chap" and live only for the present and try not to think of what it all means.'

But the British public was not used to deaths on their own shores, so their anxieties continued unabated, if anything increased by the thought that what had happened at Yarmouth could happen anywhere. Indeed, fear of invasion and of the enemy within, of omnipres-

ent spies in all shapes and disguises, was threatening to add up to a
kind of national neurosis. Never were young men who had not
enlisted less safe from the angry accusations of white-feather-touting
women or comfortably over-age men. When Prince Albert (the future
King George VI), who had joined the Grand Fleet at the beginning of
hostilities, had to be invalided ashore with stomach trouble that was
ultimately diagnosed as a duodenal ulcer, he could not be allowed to
appear in London in civilian dress. He was appointed to a sinecure
post at the Admiralty for the express purpose of putting him in
uniform, so that he might be spared such demoralizing attentions. (It
should be added that his elder brother, the Prince of Wales, already
serving on the Western Front as an officer in the Guards, might have
cut a more dashing figure with the public, but was himself deeply
frustrated by the Army's firm intention not to let him near any
significant action – not, said Kitchener, for fear of his being killed, but
because of the prospect of his being taken prisoner.)

Even though they might at times have about them elements of
almost palpable absurdity, rumours of invasion were always taken
seriously. This was true of high places as well as of the nation's public
houses and living rooms. Thus on 7 November, just four days after
the Yarmouth affair, Admiral 'Jacky' Fisher, now First Sea Lord in
succession to the recently departed Prince Louis of Battenberg, in a
letter to Vice Admiral Sir David Beatty (effectively Admiral Jellicoe's
number two as Commander of the Grand Fleet's Battlecruiser Squadron), could write as follows:

My dear Beatty,
    ... Just off to see the King who wants me urgently, he says.
Probably Prince Albert has got a stomach-ache! ...
    The latest German scare from our Minister at The Hague is that
150,000 Germans will land, half at Dundee, the other at Oban, and
the feint of 20,000 men at Norwich four days sooner! This is to be
on Christmas Day when we are all supposed to be drunk ...
    Neither you or Jellicoe can be in on the job – you can't get there
in the time, nor indeed to cut them off with your rear well strewed
with mines and covered by submarines, as it will be a flying escapade,
I expect, on the part of the Germans.
    Yours till death
        Fisher

Barely a week later, even Dr Scott, the sceptical RAMC officer of the Shropshire Yeomanry, had to admit that an enemy strike was on the cards. Moreover, to his rising anxieties about its possibility were added serious concerns about the careless leakage of plans being formulated to counter it, and doubts as to whether there were leaders of sufficient calibre available who could cope if it actually happened. There was no hint of scoffing in this entry in his diary:

> *Sunday, 15 November.* Great rumours of a coming German invasion. Circumstantial accounts of information from Admiralty Intelligence Department of projected raid of 50,000 men and 42 transports accompanied by 30 flat bottomed motor Boats, starting on Monday night; objectives Lowestoft and Harwich. Brig-General and C.O. of Yeomanry apparently spent the afternoon looking for points of defence along the coast. I heard that the Mayor and Corporation of Lowestoft sent a deputation to the Captain of the Port to say that they considered the defences here inadequate. There are really no defences!
>
> It surely would be madness to sacrifice the Yeomanry in opposing directly a landing here. Their proper function is to hold the roads inland till the infantry have time to get to Bury St Edmunds. I hear that 300 infantry have been sent to Beccles to dig trenches – and not before it was time, either. The Brigadier who stayed in the Royal Hotel for the night spent some time in the lounge with Kirby discussing details of defence in a loud voice, several strangers being present. The great fault here is that there is no real man at the helm with brain enough to organize defence thoroughly and systematically. Problems of defence are left almost entirely to regimental officers. I hear that General Sir H. Smith-Dorrien was in London lately and asked for more men as the troops in the trenches are exhausted. The War Office can send very few men now as they are scared by the chances of invasion. Altogether the immediate outlook is not happy.

On the following day, 16 November, Scott reported with considerable relief a 'strong NE gale with some rain. Very cold.' There was advantage in this sudden change of weather:

> This gale should keep the Germans in. Hear that the Channel fleet has kept in Lough Swilly, N. of Ireland. Now it is said to be within 5 hours steaming of Lowestoft. Excitement re raid quietening down.

The arrangements at present seem to be that if bombardment takes place the regiment is to proceed at once to Carlton Colville station or perhaps further on to North Cove near Worlingham on Beccles Road. If troops are without the protection of shell fire the regiment is to make an attempt to hold various points on shore and oppose landing directly – the transport to be in various side streets.

It was doubtless as a result of the same or similar rumours that on 20 November the historian F. S. Oliver, writing to his brother in Canada, reported as follows, adding London to the equation as the apparent ultimate target:

We have had by far the worst scare of invasion this week that there has been yet.

Apparently the tides on the 17th, 18th and 19th are the most favourable for a long time to come for the disembarkation of an invading force in Essex and Suffolk, and the authorities came to the conclusion that an invasion was going to be tried seriously . . .

The idea was that the Germans were going to make a desperate effort; their vessels were to draw out our southern main battle fleet and keep it engaged while they ran 250,000 first line troops right across the North Sea at full speed to the English East Coast and struck, if possible, a blow at London. They were not going to bring any cavalry, but only motor cars and motor bicycles in great numbers. They were not going to bring any heavy artillery – some reports said that was because they had already got it hidden away here – but only field guns. They were to be put on flat-bottomed barges and hauled ashore at high tide. Anyway, whether this was wholly true, or wholly false, there was a tremendous stir. The Southern command was denuded of troops, which were hurried up to the neighbourhood of Harwich, Colchester and Huntingdon.

That fear of the enemy at the gates was widespread at this time is evident from a letter written on the same day, the 20th, from the Royal Naval Barracks, Portsmouth. The writer was Sub Lieutenant Rupert Brooke, posted there 'for a short space', as his letter indicated, before rejoining his Royal Naval Division, the intended recipient being his fellow poet Walter de la Mare. Brooke was clearly much disturbed at the possibility of a German assault, but nevertheless felt himself ready for the challenge if it should come:

We're waiting here for the invasion: ready to go off at any hour of day or night. It's queer that the Admiralty seem so certain of it happening. I've a kind of horror at the idea of England being invaded, as of some virginity violated. But I'd enjoy fighting in England. How one could die!

In view of all this mass of rumour and speculation, it was clearly no coincidence that on 21 November a young gunner of the Royal Garrison Artillery, Alan Sugden, under training at Newhaven on the Sussex coast, wrote the following unusually long entry in his diary. After weeks in tents in wretched conditions he and his comrades had finally been admitted to billets in the town, their base being the nearby Fort; Amy was his much-missed fiancée, far off in his home town of Rotherham, Yorkshire:

Well, we did have a night last night. I was going off to sleep about midnight when the Alarm was sounded by the trumpets in the streets accompanied by a terrible hammering on the door. I rushed down. It was an NCO and he shouted 'Rush off to the Fort'. I hurriedly dressed and we set off at the double. On we rushed towards the Fort, our heavy boots sounding like a stampede of horses. All the women and men of Newhaven rushed to the doors and cheered us as we raced past. Women shrieked as a report spread that the Germans had landed, the poor women clinging to the soldiers as we rushed on, then followed us as best they could. As I raced along my thoughts turned to Amy and those at home. All lights had been turned off and it was pitch black. There were searchlights playing in the sky from the sea and the land. Well, when we arrived at the Fort gates half dead with fatigue (it is no joke to run 1½ miles with heavy clothes on) an officer met us and said, 'Well boys, you have done it in excellent time. Get back to your beds as quickly as possible.' Off we trooped back. The people of Newhaven were not half jolly thankful when they met us coming back. I most certainly thought we were in for it. So did everyone else. A woman and a very young girl stopped me (neither had much clothing on) and asked what was the matter. They were very much upset and said 'We ought to be good to the soldiers and do all we can to help them'. Strange that in all that excitement I did not forget my watch, baccy and fag papers and noted at the Fort that I was fully dressed and not a button undone. I did not sleep much after that lot. Beer has gone up ½d a glass. Rotten.

Nor was that the end of this little flurry of action, which presumably represented Southern Command's attempt to keep such troops as it had left at its disposal on the 'qui vive'. Sugden wrote on the 22nd, this time in a letter to his Amy:

> A sentry was shot dead last night and no trace of who did it. In spite of what the officer said last night I know there was some cause for alarm. There is something wrong. Rumour states that there is an airship knocking about. All searchlights are playing in the heavens.

Justified or otherwise, being called out against the possibility of invasion did not occupy the young gunner's thoughts for long. His letter concluded:

> I am simply dying of love and would give all I possess only to be able to kiss you again dear.
>     Yours with all my love
>       Alan

* * *

Gunner Sugden's 1914 papers are valuable from another point of view. They paint a picture of recruit training in Britain in the first months of the war which hardly accords with the standard assumption that the country was resounding to the cheerful din of happy volunteers devoted to the cause of King and Country, eager above all to win what was known, and allegedly widely coveted, as 'the passport to France'. On the contrary, the men Sugden trained with were largely Territorial gunners, who, unlike the heady enthusiasts of August, had no particular desire to renounce their right to serve only in Britain. In a letter sent shortly before the invasion scare recorded above, Sugden told his fiancée: 'Out of 2,000 Terriers (Territorials) here, only 32 volunteered for active service. Their officer was so wild he broke his sword over his knee.'

One factor which was particularly bad for morale and patriotic ardour was that deep into the autumn Sugden and his fellow gunners were still living in tents. A massive hutting programme had been under way nationwide for some time with a view to providing accommodation for some 850,000 troops. However, shortage of labour as a result of unrestricted enlistment had combined with poor workmanship and the lack of seasoned timber to put this programme well behind schedule. This might not have raised too great a problem had the good weather of the summer continued, but in mid-October a period of almost incessant rain began. This not only meant discomfort and misery, it was also a serious challenge to the health of men used to having a decent roof over their heads. Many men fell sick; in fact before the end of January 1915 there would be over 1,500 cases of pneumonia, including 301 deaths. November saw outbreaks of serious unrest in some of the training camps, with mass meetings and strikes. Ugly moods in camps could also generate unease in the communities next to whom they were being trained. So what Sugden experienced at Newhaven from mid-November was far from being exceptional.

On 14 November the gunners were moved from one unsatisfactory camp to an even worse one, open to everything the elements could throw at them, and the more exposed because of its closeness to the sea. Sugden wrote in his diary on the following day:

> We were moved last night from the Valley Camp on to the top of the hill and unfortunately we have been put in a rotten tent. The wind is blowing at a terrible rate and raging like mad. Half the tents are down on the floor and all the large tents goodness knows where. 3 poor devils have come limping in to the tent wet through to the skin, their tent having been blown away. That is 12 of us now and everything rotten and damp. The wind is howling outside and threatens to tear up the tent, us as well. The tent will go sure as death. The gale is terrible. The tent is going. Men are clinging on to the walls holding her up whilst others keep driving in the pegs.

As if this were not enough there was also the standard hazard of all basic service training, the brutal NCO, hugely resented because the men he was mistreating were not conscripts, but volunteers:

> Our sergeant major is an absolute pig. He swears and strikes the men and yesterday he actually kicked Meeklah. It is a cowardly thing to do as he knows the men dare not strike back. A gunner could get 6 months in prison, perhaps 2 years. It made my blood boil when I saw it, but if he ever kicks or strikes me I shall go for him whatever the consequences and shall half kill him before they get him off me. Well, as the sergeant major left the square all the men hooted at

him like mad. The officer was not half wild. He shouted about and told us if anything like that occurs in the future everyone is going to smell hell. They seem to forget that we have all given up our jobs to do our best for the country and do not expect to be treated like a lot of ragtags.

By now the gunners were being dispersed to various war stations. One group had already gone to Sheerness, then another draft was dispatched to Gibraltar. 'I am among the next lot to be moved but it is 100 to 1 I shall be at some Fort in England, probably Newcastle or Woolwich. As near as I can judge, love, I shall be on the move about next Friday.'

He was right. On 11 December he noted: 'Going tonight so shall be on the way all night. Hurrah. I shall be glad of a change.'

But once again good fortune deserted him. He wrote a day later:

Glad did I say? Good grief, we are out of the frying pan into the fire. We commenced our journey at 4.30 yesterday and arrived at Tyne-mouth at 4 a.m. No joke, mind you, 8 in a compartment for 12 hours and believe me we were not supplied with any rations whatever. Well, when we got to the station at Tynemouth we had to stick in the train until 7 o'clock. We were all split up and along with a squad of 30 we were marched through the rain and in the dark for about 1 mile and stopped in front of the Grand Hotel, a magnificent building. 'Here's a go,' thought I, 'we are going to be billeted', but what a sell, the place had been taken over by the government and there was not a stick of furniture in the place but there were 200 of the roughest lot of men I ever clapped eyes on. 11 of us are crowded in to one small room and of course are sleeping on the floor. The meals are put out in the Saloon Hall on dirty tables, one mug between two. Here once again you have to fight for your meals, wait until one man has done with his plate before you can get your dinner. The whole business is absolutely repulsive but I shall of course have to make the best of a bad job.

However, for once Sugden had a touch of good fortune. On Sunday, 14 December, he wrote: 'Things have taken a much brighter outlook but as in all cases they looked very black at the outset. For one thing we have got a good fire and moreover kept it going all

night. We pinched some coal and a box from a cart and are now very
comfortable.'

* * *

As it happened, Gunner Sugden had arrived in the north-east just
before the next assault on British shores.

On Tuesday, 16 December, German warships attacked three east
coast seaside towns, Whitby and Scarborough in Yorkshire, and
Hartlepool in County Durham. The Yorkshire ports were undefended
and so were unable to respond; twenty-four civilians lost their lives.
But Hartlepool had its own garrison and therefore could be considered a legitimate target. Its Territorial gunners, members of the
Durham Royal Garrison Artillery, responded rapidly, firing their three
6-inch guns to good effect, subsequently winning praise for their skill
from the Germans in their report of the action. But the bombardment
wrought havoc and there were heavy casualties, among them the
first soldier to be killed on British soil by enemy action, Private Theo
Jones of the 18th Battalion, the Durham Light Infantry. Also killed in
the first stage of the attack were Anne and Florence Kay, sisters, of
'Rockside', Cliff Terrace, their house being a tall three-storey building
on the headland near the Heugh Lighthouse Battery, target of the
first shells from the leading German battlecruiser, which were fired at
the town at 8.10 a.m. A near neighbour, Miss Ethel May Giepel, was
killed at about the same time.

Five warships of the German High Seas Fleet were on the prowl in
the North Sea that December morning, all of them battlecruisers:
*Seydlitz*, carrying the flag of Vice-Admiral Hipper, in command, *Von
der Tann*, *Blücher*, *Derfflinger* and *Moltke*, of which the first three
attacked Hartlepool. With an escort of destroyers and light cruisers,
they had left Wilhemshaven at 5 o'clock on the evening of Tuesday
the 15th, and sailing at the speed of 25 knots had headed for the
Yorkshire and Durham coast, which was unprotected by minefields.
Fortunately British Intelligence had reported the fact of their putting
to sea, though clearly there was no immediate information as to their
precise intentions. At eight o'clock Lieutenant Colonel L. Robson of
the Hartlepool Artillery Defence, who was at his fire command post
at the Lighthouse Battery, was warned by telephone that three
ships were approaching the town, travelling fast. They were flying the

White Ensign and answered the signal put out by the Hartlepool defences. However, as soon as Robson sighted the battlecruisers with their distinctive bows, virtually in the shape of ocean racers, he recognized them as German and immediately opened fire.

Norman Collins, at seventeen an alert and highly patriotic young man living in Hartlepool, had already attempted to enlist as a Kitchener volunteer, but had been turned down. The main reason was that he was under age, but there was also the matter of his employment; he was an apprentice in the drawing office of a marine engineering company contracted to build shallow-draft monitors for the Royal Navy and cargo ships for the merchant service. Work did not start until 9 a.m, so at around eight o'clock he was at home sitting down to breakfast in the family home getting ready for a normal day's work. Suddenly:

a tremendous explosion rocked the house followed by an inferno of noise and the reek of high explosives, and as I made for the door clouds of brick dust and smoke eddied around.

The seafront was only 50 yards away and I ran towards it. On my left a short distance away stood the Lighthouse and our home was near the shore end of the concrete breakwater which pointed for 500 yards almost due east. The battery was near the Lighthouse and during normal firing practice we received prior warnings to open our windows to avoid the glass being shattered by the blast from the guns.

Now it was the real thing and I was amazed to see three huge grey battle-cruisers which looked to be only a few hundred yards from the end of the breakwater. Their massive guns were firing broadsides and in the dull light of a winter's morning it was like looking into a furnace. I could not hear our own guns above the blast of the German guns as they belched clouds of flame and behind me the air was torn to shreds by explosions.

The great guns of the warships continued to belch flames continuously and as a landing seemed imminent I retraced my steps up Rowell Street and turned left towards the Baptist Chapel.

A great hole appeared in its stone façade as I approached it.

A few soldiers were running towards the Heugh battery and women carrying babies were milling around in a state of shock. One offered a child to a soldier but he declined it. He was obviously hurrying to repel the invasion.

Buildings near me were in ruins and as I rounded the corner of Lumley Street I saw the body of Sammy Woods, a school friend of mine, a shell having burst just as he stepped out a second before I turned the corner.

Hartlepool was, as it still is, two towns in one: Hartlepool on the coast, West Hartlepool inland. Collins became aware that West Hartlepool was now taking much of the shelling, with many people trying to get away, most making for the open country to the north, some of them carrying their most precious possessions. He noted: 'One realist had a mattress on his head as he staggered past.'

He decided to head for his workplace, the Central Marine Engine Works, in the hope of getting some advice as to what to do. As he approached it he saw the 'curious sight' of 'hundreds of pit-props . . . flying high in the air like handfuls of matches thrown by giant hands'. These were made from tree-trunks imported from Scandinavia and elsewhere for use in the Durham coal-mines, assembled in tall piles covering many acres of land, each piece of timber weighing half a hundredweight or more. 'Shells dropping among the stacks of timber blew them into the air like feathers. About the same time the gasometer received a direct hit and blew up, cutting off supplies to the town.'

Collins reached his office to find it empty. Then, almost as suddenly as the attack began, it was all over. He timed this as about 8.52 a.m. 'Finally there was only the occasional explosion occurred and then silence.'

There was, of course, no knowing if the end of the bombardment meant the end of the episode. Had it been a prelude to something more sinister?

Not knowing whether a landing had taken place I thought I had better find out what was happening and whether my parents and brother were alive as they were very near the German ships and the Heugh battery when I had left the house.

Arriving back home I found it empty but still standing and a neigbour informed me that during the height of the bombardment my mother had been making cups of tea for everyone in the vicinity and my father was last seen pulling an invalid chair with a disabled person away from the area.

I began calling on relatives near at hand, and apart from a relative by marriage who had lost a limb in Victoria Place, we suffered no serious injuries. This was fortunate as we had all had narrow escapes.

Happily there had been no attempt at invasion. A proclamation was shortly issued by the Mayor informing the inhabitants that 'the situation is now secure'. It also warned people not to touch unexploded shells. Despite this, there was much collecting of souvenirs. Collins himself kept several jagged-edged shell fragments which had come through the roof of his house. More poignantly, he found a dead donkey which had been grazing in the field that was used as the home ground of the Hartlepool Rovers Rugby Football Club, and claimed the piece of shell that had killed it.

While the Hartlepools turned out to be the prime focus of the attack, this was not immediately evident to other forces guarding the coast who could feel equally threatened by the approaching German warships. Allan Ferrie was serving as a junior officer of the North Riding (Fortress) Royal Engineers at South Gare, near Redcar, on the Yorkshire shore just across the bay from Hartlepool, separated by the estuary of the River Tees but a mere 4 miles away from the point where the first German shells had struck; indeed, the battlecruisers, as they slowed to concentrate on their bombardment, were considerably nearer to South Gare than to the Heugh Lighthouse, and might at any moment make it a second, indeed easier target. Ferrie rushed off a letter to his mother later that day describing what was clearly seen by him and his comrades as a very lucky escape:

I am still a little shaky, and hope never to come through another such ordeal. It was expected; word came late last night, and it was timed for between 7.30 a.m. and 8.30 a.m. I did not hear of the message till this morning, when I was called at 6.30 a.m. (having been on the first relief last night). Such messages have come in from time to time, though perhaps none of quite so serious an aspect as this one was. At all events we turned out – it was still dark – and stood to arms.

At 8.05 a.m. several other officers and myself went in to breakfast. Five minutes later – I had just finished porridge – some one said: 'Was that a gun? I remarked that I thought it was a door slamming, but I made to go out to ascertain. Before I had reached the door, there was no doubt. We rushed for the door and flung on our arms. Capt. Hedley made for the battery and I was in charge of the engineers. I ran for it and shouted at the top of my voice. Soon they were lined up. It was a tremendous situation. By this time the guns were booming – broadside after broadside – and it was like nothing I have ever heard before. May I never hear such a battle again, and may I never again see these sharpened tongues of flame make lurid such another misty dawn.

We waited expecting every instant to bring a shell whirling into our midst. One shell would have made an end of all for every one of us there. After about half an hour fire slackened and then one of our light cruisers, which had left Hartlepool in the early morning came out towards us from the fight. She was disabled. We could see three holes in her forward just above the water-line, and she was down at the bows. In the channel and just a few hundred yards from our barracks she stopped. Another light cruiser followed and stood by, but after a little went out again. By this time – about a quarter to nine – it was all over, and I believe the enemy had gone north.

The light cruiser that came disabled into the river was the *Patrol*. About 1 p.m. this afternoon at high water she proceeded to Middlesborough. There were on her two killed, two seriously wounded, and two slightly wounded. The vessel that lay beside her was the *Forward*. She was somewhat damaged, though as far as I could make out not badly. She cruised about outside for an hour or thereabouts after the engagement was over, and then disappeared from view.

As it happened, Ferrie's battery had been provided with a grandstand view of the brave but less than successful naval response to the German attack.

Hartlepool was defended by a flotilla of seven small naval vessels: the light cruisers *Patrol* and *Forward*, a division of four 'E' class destroyers, and the submarine *C9*. The destroyers, *Doon*, *Waveney*, *Test* and *Moy*, had been deployed as early as 5 a.m., being sent to patrol five miles off the harbour entrance and parallel with the coast. It was a very misty morning. At about 8 a.m., when the destroyers were a little to the north of the Heugh Lighthouse and steering north, the *Doon* observed three blotches of smoke away to the southward. She at once altered course to the south, increasing her speed. At 8.05 a.m. three large battlecruisers were sighted slightly on the starboard bow steering westwards. These were, of course, the German raiders.

The enemy immediately opened fire, the first salvo falling ahead of *Doon*, correct for range but not direction. The destroyers altered course to the north-east, increasing to full power and spreading, while the Germans turned to the north to try to cut them off from Hartlepool. The *Doon* was hit by the third salvo; the *Test* and *Moy* were also hit. The *Doon*'s wireless was destroyed before she could report to HMS *Patrol*, which was still in harbour, but the *Test*'s message, 'Enemy in sight', did get through. However, events were unfolding so rapidly that there was still no clear concept of what was taking place, *Patrol*'s answer being, 'What enemy? Am slipping to support you.'

*Patrol* and *Forward* were berthed in the Victoria Dock, around the headland to the east of Hartlepool proper, being dependent on a tug to get them swiftly out to sea. *Patrol* was pulled out first, with *C9* following, but when shells began to fall on and around the dock the tug refused to provide the same impetus for *Forward*, which had to make her exit as best she could unaided.

Any questions the captain of *Patrol* might have as to what was happening were resolved when at 8.28 *Test* reported – correctly in essence if not quite in detail – 'Enemy are two Battle-cruisers', with *Waveney* adding at 8.30, 'Two battleships, Dreadnought class.' In a matter of minutes her crew could see for themselves what they were in for. In the words of the contemporary report from which the above details are taken, 'There was nothing for *Patrol* to do but to go on!!' The report continued:

> During the whole of the time that *Patrol* was steaming down the fairway channel, she was passing through a zone of very heavy and rapid fire. Fragments of shell from bursts were flying over the ship. A shot which passed close across the bows hit and smashed to bits a lighter on the mud behind her. Just after this the Captain and the Navigator, who were on the upper bridge, were knocked down by the concussion of a burst close to or by the wind of a projectile just above their heads. The effect was only momentary and they were quickly on their feet again. At 8.35 a signal was made that *Patrol* was 'heavily engaged with two battle-cruisers'.
>
> Almost immediately the ship was hit by two 11-inch shells practic-

ally simultaneously. One of these punched a clean hole in the port
side, going out on the waterline on the starboard side. Shortly after
she was hit again, this time by a 5.9 shell.

Despite this, the *Patrol* fought on, firing at the distant silhouettes
of the *Von der Tann* and the *Blücher*, which then turned on the British
cruiser, the first salvo falling 500 yards over, the second just over, one
shot being in the wake about 10 yards or so astern of the ship.
Undeterred, *Patrol* at 8.40 signalled to the destroyers to attack with
torpedoes.

At this point she ran aground, the situation not being helped by
the fact that all this was happening at dead low water. As she put her
engines alternately full speed astern and full speed ahead to try to get
clear, she again came under heavy fire from the two German battlecruisers – *Seydlitz* was not involved at this stage – so that at 8.46 she
signalled that she was badly injured. Hence the inevitable outcome:

> It was realized that it would be impossible to recross the bar and
> return to Hartlepool, and as another report was made that water was
> 3 feet deep on both mess decks and gaining, and the ship was rolling
> in an unstable manner, orders were given to turn out all boats: the
> men leaving their guns with the greatest reluctance, and the ship made
> for the Tees to the nearest shelter and a defended port.

There was what seemed a final threat when the *Von der Tann* and
the *Blücher* were observed to be turning together to port, as though
they intended to close *Patrol* and finish her off. But at 8.59 a.m. they
ceased firing and steamed off into the mist at high speed.

The odds were, of course, absurd. HMS *Patrol*, with a displacement
of 2,940 tons, was clearly no match for the *Blücher*, 15,000 tons, the
*Von der Tann*, 21,000 tons, and the *Seydlitz*, 24,610 tons, each ship
with weapons appropriate to her size. It can fairly be said that she did
her gallant best in impossible circumstances.

Second Lieutenant Ferrie was correct in his assumption that *Patrol*
was making for Middlesbrough. He was incorrect in his apparent
assumption that his part of the coast had been spared enemy attentions. A second letter home written on 18 December stated:

> We were bombarded by the Germans; I did not know it before. Just
> before this onslaught on Hartlepool they gave us some broadsides.

The shells all went clean over us. On the North Gare – a stump of a breakwater right opposite – I can see with a naked eye how a mass of concrete has been torn away. Many shells passed right on and landed three, four and even five miles inland on the north side of the river. A land battery is a difficult target.

He was clearly eager to deflect any criticism that might arise about his battery's 'spectators only' role in the action:

Our guns could not reply on account of the uncertainty as to which was enemy and which friend, the obscuring of the vessels by the morning mist, and on account of the comparatively short effective range which our (much lighter) guns have.

That the attack on Hartlepool, while a cause for anger at first, and of long-lasting grief in the case of families of the victims, became also a matter of pride and curiosity is evident from a later letter to his mother by Ferrie in March 1915. 'I am sending you another and larger fragment of German shell from Hartlepool. Immediately after the bombardment, one could get specimens in Hartlepool for the asking; now a piece like what I am sending costs about ten shillings.'

If the sense of being exposed to attack by the enemy was strong in Hartlepool, which was at last able to offer some retaliation, it could be stronger still in those towns which had no means of defence. A resident of Scarborough, Mr I. Jordan Fraser, replying to a friend in London who had written offering sympathy to him and his family, expressed what was clearly a widely held resentment felt towards the Government for failing to protect their community, reserving his special anger for the former Secretary of State for War, Lord Haldane, who was widely if mistakenly presumed to have pro-German inclinations. Fraser's letter, dated 27 December, was written, not from Scarborough, but from the popular Yorkshire spa of Harrogate:

It was with real pleasure I received your letter this morning, letting me know of your anxiety about us, thank God we are all right, and were it not for the hideous Satanic cruelty of it I would not have lost the sight 'for nuts' [sic]. In all conscience, we were near enough when on dressing at 8 a.m. that morning, a 'Shell' burst over the House but only left its ugly fragments, or rather some of them, which I now possess, at the front gate some 10 yds. off: some of these honoured the house opposite by tearing thro' the window! Not having taken 'Punch's' advice to those about to marry, viz. *Don't*, I did not get my little revenge. I wrote a very pertinent letter to the 'Daily Mail' asking the Military Authorities why this dastardly bombardment was allowed, and absolutely nothing done to meet it: pointing out, it *could* have been prevented, or at the least curtailed, but my 'better half' advised me not to send it and I didn't. It's a fact it could have been prevented by two or three 'Guns' on the foreshore properly handled by a Squad of Artillery, but no 'Gun' happened to be on either side for many miles!! An outstanding case of War Office dementia, and I should like to tell this German admirer in the Cabinet, Haldane, of my opinion.

Well, as you imagine, most of our Scarbro' friends are here and will be for some time. We have taken a small House, as others have done, and will return when the British Lion has this autocratic savage Emperor by the throat.

So much for the local reaction: what was the reaction elsewhere? What impact did the attacks of 16 December have on national and naval morale?

The day undoubtedly went to the Germans, who, in the words of C. R. M. F. Cruttwell, 'could . . . boast of violating our coastal immunity, in the most spectacular way since the Dutch fleet sailed up the Medway' – and that was in 1667. They had also succeeded in laying a new minefield north of Scarborough, which for many weeks remained a serious danger to shipping. Worse still, the British attempt to exact immediate revenge, by confronting Hipper as he headed for home, failed badly. Acting Vice-Admiral Beatty with four cruisers and Vice-Admiral Sir George Warrender with six dreadnoughts combed the North Sea trying to bring Hipper to book. However, confusing reports plus the intervention of an untimely storm allowed the enemy to escape, while a six-hour delay on the part of the Admiralty in acceding to Commodore Roger Keyes's request to deploy his submarine flotilla, then patrolling off Terschelling, against the returning force proved the final factor in guaranteeing its safe landfall. All this was greatly to the anger and disappointment of the British public and deeply galling to the Royal Navy. It was not a good omen as the year neared its end. British invulnerability at sea was proving to be another of 1914's lost illusions.

The nation rallied to the support of the violated towns warmly and in arguably quite unexpected ways. On Saturday, 19 December, the amateur football teams Dulwich Hamlet and West Norwood played each other. The compilers of the programme for the match used the attack on ordinary civilians at their ordinary tasks to make a stirring appeal for more volunteers to join the nation's forces, emphasizing their message as seemed appropriate by printing key words and phrases in bold type:

> To those of us to whom the war is but a distant nightmare, and strange to say there are some men and lads who do not seem touched by it, the slaughter of peaceful folk during their daily tasks, of schoolboys on their road to school, will surely have brought home the fact that it concerns us all, that it is **our duty to every one of us** to help slay this monster that dares to threaten the peace and freedom **not of Britain only but of the world**. So the instant cry goes up for **Men! Men! Men!** It is only **by numbers of brave efficient soldiers** that victory will crown our cause.

The attack on the coastal towns of Yorkshire and Durham did not call for any action from Gunner Alan Sugden and his fellow members of the Royal Garrison Artillery in nearby Tyneside. It did, however, affect his personal life and his plans. He had been looking forward eagerly to Christmas leave with his beloved Amy, but on 19 December he wrote in his diary:

> We understand all leave is now stopped. Notices are issued in Tynemouth that a bombardment is expected and that people are safest in their homes. They will be warned if it is advisable to flee and if so they must go in the direction of Newcastle.

Three days later, on 22 December, he was confiding in his diary yet again:

> I expected four days' leave and had got a letter written to Amy what train to meet.
>
> I was terribly excited about it. We've just had it that we are not going. This only applies to the Siege Battery. All the other blokes are getting it,
>
> We heard firing out at sea. I hope they have blown the Germans below. I could forgive them a lot but never for stopping leave and closing the pub at 8.

# CHAPTER TWELVE

# GLOBAL WAR

WHILE AT ONE END of the scale the war was becoming close and personal, even to the extent of literally threatening people's homes, at the other end it was spreading its tentacles worldwide. What had begun as a struggle of neighbours within a continent was steadily becoming global. Before 1914 was out it was certainly more than the 'Great European War' which many people called it at the time.

British forces were soon engaged in many areas far from home.

While the 1st Battalion of the South Wales Borderers (whose adjutant was the forthright Captain C. J. Paterson until his death from wounds on 1 November) had been involved from August onwards in the fighting on the Western Front, its sister battalion, the 2nd, had found itself caught up in a fierce minor sideshow in China.

Following the anti-European Boxer Rising of 1900, China had been forced to yield what were known as 'concessions', i.e. areas of territory over which the Chinese surrendered their control, to the powers which had brought the rebellious Chinese to heel. The concessions, based around Tientsin in north China, were French, German, Austrian, Italian, American and British, all manned by small national garrisons; in the case of the British there were two battalions, the South Wales Borderers as already named and the Indian Army's 34th Sikhs. In his unpublished autobiography written in the 1960s, Major General Aubrey Williams, a captain in the Welsh battalion in 1914, looked back on his posting to China, from 1912, with considerable pleasure. There was much time for sports of all kinds and the atmosphere among those who manned the concessions was relaxed and friendly. 'We got on best with the Germans and Austrians, as they took part in our sports and visited our Mess fairly frequently, and we similarly visited them.'

The prospect of war in distant Europe changed all this overnight. The Germans' principal foothold in China was at Tsingtao, on the coast, a fortified naval base in the leased concession of Kiaochow, which was virtually a German Hong Kong:

> Being stationed near the Germans, we heard that they were mobilizing all their reserves at Tsingtao. Their Commander, Major von Kinlow, was well known, and many of us went down to the station to see him and his staff and his Headquarters off. He said that they were going off for annual manoeuvres, but we knew better. He wrote a letter to our Colonel thanking us for all the Regiment had done for his troops, in teaching them football, and the welcome the officers had always given to his officers; and that he was afraid we would now be enemies – but he hoped that after the war, which seemed imminent, we would become friends again.
>
> The next time we saw him and his officers and men again was on the 7th November, about 12 noon, when they were marched out of the Fortress of Tsingtao as prisoners of war.

The British, however, were not the leading contributors to this outcome. Garrisoned by 4,000 men, plus one aircraft, Tsingtao was put under siege by the 23,000 men of the Japanese 18th Division and stood no chance. Japan, which had contracted an alliance with Britain in 1902, had used the terms of that alliance to declare war on Germany. This was on 23 August, but even before Japan formally became a belligerent the 18th Division's experienced commander, General Kamio, had been ordered to prepare an attack. Kamio showed impressive skill when investing the city; to Williams this was an object lesson in how to wage war:

> The siege warfare was a great experience for me. It was conducted by the Japanese very methodically in stages. First an artillery covering position was prepared for over a hundred six–inch howitzers, and under cover of a bombardment the whole line advanced a suitable distance by sapping to the first attack position, and so to a second attack; the artillery being moved up closer so as to get the full advantage of its power.
>
> Generally two companies of ours were in the line, and two back in pressure positions; then these two were leap-frogged forward to the next position. Most of this time we were all under the fire of the German guns, and particularly from their searchlights we had trouble while digging.

The battalion's losses during the siege, by Western Front standards, were minimal: fourteen dead and thirty-six wounded. Williams was a close observer of one of the deaths:

> One night when lying out in the open with my platoon, covering the rest of D Company doing the digging and the entrenching, I was directing the firing of my men at the flashes of the German machine-guns. I was next to Private Pavit, who had been one of my cross country runners in the battalion sports. I was telling him what to fire at. After he had had a few shots, he was just about to fire again when there was a shattering splash of a bullet, and he rolled over on me saying 'Sir, I am killed'; and he was quite dead, the German bullet had struck his rifle just in front of his face, and ricocheted into his brain. No-one need ever tell me that a man does not know when he is killed.

The formal entry into Tsingtao took place on 16 November, the British being represented by one company of each of their two battalions. Ten days later the battalions sailed for Hong Kong, the Japanese giving them a rousing send-off. On 12 December the Borderers re-embarked for England, their unusual contribution to the tapestry of 1914 concluded. Williams' later theatres of service would emphasize the war's global nature: he would serve in Gallipoli and Palestine before being posted to the Western Front in 1918.

On the same day as the British departure from Hong Kong, the victorious Japanese were given an enthusiastic reception in Tokyo. For them effectively their fighting war *was* over by Christmas, their total losses, of fewer than 2,000, already having been incurred. They rapidly refocused their attentions elsewhere. In January 1915 their 'twenty-one demands' forced major economic concessions from China under threat of war. In this first conflict, to the European Allies they were a distant if valued partner, but they had put down a marker and made clear that they had other ambitions than those relating to the imperatives of Europe.

One other battalion which had a brief contact with warfare east of Suez while its sister battalion, the 2nd, was engaged in France, was the 1st Royal Dublin Fusiliers. They were present when the German light cruiser *Emden* bombarded the Indian port of Madras, though they suffered no casualties.

While the German armed merchant cruiser the *Kaiser Wilhelm der Grosse* was conducting her relatively brief campaign against shipping in the Atlantic, the German light cruiser *Emden* was about to embark on a much longer rampage in the Indian Ocean. When hostilities began she had been part of Germany's East Asiatic Squadron based at Tsingtao, but even before that fortress came under threat the squadron's commander, Admiral von Spee, had taken his ships to sea to carry out the policy assigned to him, in case of war, of spreading panic through the Pacific trade routes. Strictly, he should have scattered his forces, delegating his cruisers to make mayhem as they could, on the principle that the greater the spread the greater would be the panic, while the Allies would be given more targets to pursue. This was a basic tenet of what was known as 'cruiser warfare': in other words, there should be a number of foxes on the run, not merely one single pack. However, instead von Spee proposed to keep his squadron together and in particular to take it south-eastwards in the direction of Chile, which, though neutral, was thought to be well disposed towards Germany, and which could provide him with the vital element without which he could not function, coal. Captain Karl von Müller of the *Emden*, however, disagreed sharply with his admiral's plan and requested, and was granted, permission to go it alone.

Müller made for the Bay of Bengal and, starting on 10 September, achieved a huge haul of prizes, capturing over twenty ships, while, as the historian Cyril Falls put it, 'his cheeky bombardment of Madras and Penang provided fine material for German humorists at British expense'. At Penang he torpedoed a French destroyer and a Russian cruiser, the Russians' only major unit in the Indian Ocean. Her crew had no lifeboats posted and only twelve rounds on deck by their guns, while sixty prostitutes were under employment below. Their captain was engaged in similarly unprofessional practice ashore. He was subsequently stripped of his title and commission, and spent three and a half years in prison. On five of the ten occasions when the *Emden* needed to replenish her coal supplies, she was able to do so from her own prizes. On 9 November, however, she was attacked and forced to beach on the Cocos Islands by the Australian cruiser HMAS *Sydney*, von Müller becoming a prisoner of war. His exploits were admired almost as much by the British as by the Germans. Moreover, the *Emden*'s lustre survived her sinking. Von Müller had put a landing party on Direction Island in the Cocos group. They seized a schooner and sailed to the Yemen. After crossing to the Red Sea, they braved the desert and despite attacks by hostile Arab tribesmen made their way to Damascus and thence on to Constantinople.

While the *Emden* was using the Indian Ocean as a labyrinth to hide in, an Expeditionary Force of 5,000 troops was being ferried across it from India towards the Persian Gulf. Officially known as Indian Expeditionary Force (IEF) 'D', its destination was Mesopotamia, later to be renamed Iraq, at this time part of the Ottoman Empire. Its basic purpose was to secure oil supplies, in particular those flowing through the Anglo-Persian oil installations at Abadan, which, being on the edge of the Persian frontier, was under potential threat from Ottoman (i.e. Turkish) forces, should Turkey enter into the war, as was anticipated, on the German side. It was also intended to encourage the Arabs to rally to the Allied cause and stiffen the sinews of some of the more influential local sheiks. By the time war was formally declared, on 5 November, the force was already in position at the mouth of the Shatt-al-Arab, the confluence of Mesopotamia's famous rivers, the Tigris and the Euphrates. Following a successful landing, with naval support, on 6 November, and the arrival of the rest of the 6th Anglo-Indian Division, the force was given leave to advance further inland.

The diary of Private William Bird, 2nd Battalion, Dorsetshire Regiment, offers a striking picture of the campaign as seen from the level of the ordinary soldier:

> *15th November.* Today we heard the enemy were holding a position 4 miles away, so we advanced across the desert in the mud. Suddenly they opened fire on us from some date trees with maxim guns and rifles. We fought them out [of] their position, advancing over a mile without the least bit of cover. At 400 yards we charged their trenches. Shouting and cursing we went at them, and they ran for their lives. We captured men, ammunition and other kinds of material. The trenches were littered with dead and wounded. We lost a few ourselves, but not many considering the awful conditions we had to advance over.

Two days later there was another clash, this time on a larger scale, resolved when the British resorted to traditional infantry techniques, supported by their latest artillery:

At 200 yards we fixed bayonets and charged, and then the enemy lost heart, they jumped from their trenches and ran for their lives. They ran in large bunches and our big guns cut lanes through them, and thus ended another victory for us, yet 2 hours beforehand it looked as if it was impossible to shift them.

The following day, 19 November, they were told what was to be their next target:

Tonight we are moving off after the enemy. We are going to capture the town named Basra, where the Turks have retired to. The distance is reckoned to be 37 miles.

*20 November*. Time 9.0 p.m. We have been marching all day and night. It's the hardest march I've ever done. The men are exhausted and are falling asleep as we move along, and our feet are sore and tired. And we are hungry.

We are now camped about 3 miles from Basra, and we have orders to wash and shave, and clean our buttons, for tomorrow we have to enter Basra.

*21 November*. We are now in Basra, and our regiment occupies the late Turkish custom house, a big storehouse building on the shore of the river. When we arrived, we had to form up and present arms, as the Union Jack was run up on all the prominent buildings. The town is very much after the style of the towns in India, mostly mud houses. The population is composed of Arabs, Turks and Armenians, with several classes of Europeans, such as Americans, etc.

The Turks had set light to the custom houses when they retired, so before we could have any rest, we had to work hard putting fires out, and saving stores etc. We were so hungry that my chum Rusty Hellard and myself went and bought one rupee of Arab chappatties, and eight annas of dates, and we sat down and ate the lot, and they seemed beautiful.

They settled down to garrison the city, turning the local sheik's palace into a hospital, though 'palace' was hardly the best description: 'it's rather a shaky place, made of brick and mud, altogether a rotten place to put wounded and sick into'. There was little chance to rest after their efforts: 'we are doing guards, picquets and supply fatigues every day, and the work of unloading supplies is very hard'. Whenever they left their base, they had to be constantly wary:

*4 December.* One good point about Basra is that we can buy goods here, but we have to go out fully armed, and in parties of no less than six with a NCO. The goods are exceptionally dear though, but we pay, if not cheerfully. The town looks a hotbed of vice and fevers, so I shouldn't be surprised if we get some trouble later on. The troops are full of lice, and it's a laughable sight to see men hunting and cracking great big lice from their shirts, etc. Being near the river we can easily wash our clothes, so now the regiment is beginning to look like its old self, but there are many familiar faces gone.

*16 December.* A week has passed in which two men have died with fever, and a lot of Turks, who are knocking round here dressed as civilians, are sniping at our sentries every night. An order has been published on all buildings that the city is under martial law, and all persons with firearms are to hand them in before a certain date. Any person found with them, or caught in the act of firing at sentries after this date, will be in both cases treated as an enemy and will be hung in the market square.

Readers might notice a certain similarity between the conditions of 1914 and those which pertained ninety years later.

The tone of the conflict on the Mesopotamia front was set at this time. There would be advances and retreats (the British were only 40 kilometres from Baghdad in November 1915 but had to fall back), horrific episodes such as the Siege of Kut, which would end with thousands of British and Indian prisoners being taken on a long march to Turkey which few survived, while Baghdad was not finally taken until 1917.

Even as IEF 'D' was trying to pacify Basra, away to the west in Egypt, which had been under effective British control since the 1880s, preparations were in hand to mobilize an Egyptian Expeditionary Force, of which the prime purpose was to defend the Suez Canal against possible Turkish aggression. As part of this process a military intelligence headquarters was being established in Cairo with a view to searching out and supporting insurgent initiatives inside Turkish-held territory and generally advising the military high command. Among the members of this high-calibre 'think tank' were the distinguished archaeologist Leonard Woolley, the *Times* correspondent Philip Graves and two Members of Parliament who had formerly

served as attachés to the British Embassy in Constantinople, George
(later Lord) Lloyd and the Hon. Aubrey Herbert, a pre-war traveller
and adventurer of distinction. They were soon joined by a newly
appointed second lieutenant without regimental attachment named
T. E. Lawrence, sent there because of his knowledge of the Middle
East acquired during several years as an archaeologist in Syria. Lawrence's hour would come later; at this stage the member of this small
galaxy with the greatest allure and reputation was Herbert, who had
already proved himself to be one of the great characters of 1914. In
August, conscious that he would be refused enlistment because of his
extreme short-sightedness, he had bought himself the uniform of a
subaltern of the Irish Guards and slipped in among the officers of that
regiment at Southampton as they were about to embark for Le Havre.
Once he arrived in France there seemed no point in sending him
home, particularly since he was now among close friends who were
somewhat taken aback but delighted at his arrival. He had been
caught up in the fighting at Mons, had been badly wounded and had
even been reported as dead, but by now, fully recovered, was able to
assume what, given his knowledge of languages and of the Middle
East, was clearly a more suitable role for his talents. As events turned
out, he together with Lawrence would be sent to Mesopotamia in
early 1916 as part of an attempt to procure the release of British
troops caught up in the Siege of Kut. Blindfolded, the two officers
were taken through enemy lines to negotiate with the local Turkish
commander, but all they achieved in spite of the offer of a substantial
ransom was the liberation of a handful of sick and wounded. Having
already served at Gallipoli in 1915, Herbert would later publicize his
experiences in a hugely popular book entitled *Mons, Anzac and Kut*,
which did great things for British morale in the dark middle period of
the war.

\* \* \*

By December 1914, Admiral Graf von Spee's force had gone the way
of the *Emden*, but only after a dramatic success that had shaken the
British Admiralty and the nation. The Royal Navy's Western Atlantic
Squadron, under Admiral Sir Christopher Cradock, was instructed to
'be prepared to have to meet' the enemy and to 'search' for him. The
two squadrons met off Coronel on the Chilean coast on 1 November.

Cradock, controversially, interpreted his orders as requiring him to
attack; his awareness of the aggressive inclinations of the First Lord
of the Admiralty, Winston Churchill, must have seemed to leave him
no alternative. The Germans had the better ships, the better arma-
ment and the better position, for von Spee secured the inshore station
with the afterglow of the sunset silhouetting the British squadron
like so many targets at a fairground. Cradock's flagship, the *Good
Hope*, with two 9.2-inch guns, and the *Monmouth*, with only 6-inch
guns, were no match for von Spee's cruisers, the *Scharnhorst* and
the *Gneisenau* each with eight 8.2-inch guns. The *Good Hope* was
hit before she could open fire and sank within half an hour; the
*Monmouth* followed two hours later. The situation was summed up in
a letter written by H. W. G. Spencer, Chief Yeoman of Signals in the
armed merchant cruiser HMS *Otranto*, one of only two ships to avoid
the carnage: 'My God it was awful, on account of our helplessness
in the face of a vastly superior force.'

Within weeks, however, the Navy secured its revenge. Two of Britain's fastest and most prestigious ships, the battlecruisers *Invincible*
and *Inflexible*, under Vice-Admiral Sir Frederick Doveton Sturdee, were
sent to deal with von Spee's force. On 8 December the German admiral,
preening himself on his success and having been fêted by the Germans
at Valparaiso, approached the Falkland Islands intending to destroy
the docks and the wireless station at Port Stanley, only to find Sturdee
coaling in the harbour. Von Spee saw that his only hope lay in flight.

This time it was the German force that was overwhelmed. The
*Invincible* and the *Inflexible* took their time, taunting the fleeing
Germans by keeping them at the end of the range of the battlecruisers' 12-inch guns. One difference between the two actions was
that the Germans scored more hits than had been scored at Coronel,
though even so the British casualty list was minimal. The *Scharnhorst*
and the *Gneisenau* were sunk, as were two of von Spee's smaller ships,
the *Nürnberg* and the *Leipzig*. One cruiser, his fastest, the *Dresden*,
escaped, to carry the fight into 1915; she was caught and sunk in
March off the island of Juan Fernandez.

So many ships sunk meant so many men killed or maimed. A
naval clerk, Richard Steele, who was in HMS *Invincible* during the
Falkland Islands battle, witnessed the picking up of German survivors.
In a letter of 12 December he wrote:

As they're hauled on deck, they're taken below into the Wardroom ante room, or the Admiral's spare cabin. Here with knives we tear off their dripping clothing, then with towels try to start a little warmth in their ice-cold bodies. They are trembling, violently trembling, from the iciness of their immersion. Most of them need resuscitation. Some on coming to consciousness give the most terrible groans as if there was represented to their minds some very awful picture. What frightful sights they must have witnessed, some of them. Our shells did terrible damage, sometimes wiping out an entire gun's crew. One or two are horribly burned and some of their bodies are red where they have been peppered with lyddite. We have three surgeons on board and these do the best they can, relieving suffering frequently with morphia. I will draw a veil over the rest of this. I myself don't like to think of it. The human body is not beautiful in all circumstances! This is all I will say.

* * *

Another major theatre of operations in which the British were heavily involved in 1914 was Africa.

Germany held four colonies in the continent: Togoland, her small-est, bordered on the west by the British colony of the Gold Coast, now Ghana; the substantially larger Kamerun (known to the British as Cameroon, or the Cameroons), also bordered by Allied colonies, British-held Nigeria and French Equatorial Africa; German South-West Africa, now Namibia, with South Africa to the south and Bechuana-land, now Botswana, to the east, both British, while it shared its long northern frontier with Angola, which was Portuguese; and German East Africa, approximating to present-day Tanzania, also flanked by British and Portuguese territories.

Togoland was pocketed with amazing speed. While the French began moving on one side, the British moved on the other, and by 12 August two companies of the Gold Coast Regiment took possession of the colony's only port, Lome. But the prime target was the inland town of Kamina, where the Germans had built a powerful wireless station. The colony's garrison was minimal, consisting of 560 African recruits and eight Germans. Pushing northwards, British patrols made contact with German rearguards on or about 15 August, this being the first land action anywhere between Britain and Germany. There was harder fighting on 22 August, when in the confusion the British columns lost touch with each other in the bush and German machine-guns exacted a considerable toll, with 17 per cent casualties. But that was the end of the resistance, and on the night of 24–25 August the Germans destroyed the wireless station, which had been from the onset of hostilities a prime target of the Royal Navy in its operations against German commerce raiders. In the first three weeks of August it had handled 229 messages to other German colonies and to German shipping. This was a major Allied success in Africa, and achieved in the first month of the war.

The hero of the British initiative was the acting commanding officer of the Gold Coast Regiment, Captain, later Lieutenant Colonel, F. C. Bryant, who in an almost Nelsonian spirit went ahead without orders. Two brief cables, both addressed to Lord Kitchener, give the gist of the story: the first from the Gold Coast's Acting Governor, W. C. F. Robertson, the second from Bryant, who, in a further grand gesture, had promptly renamed the force he was leading.

The ACTING GOVERNOR TO THE SECRETARY OF STATE
(Received 5.15 a.m., 26th August, 1914)

TELEGRAM

25th AUGUST. Bryant telegraphs that wireless telegraph installation at Kamina has been destroyed by enemy and that they sent this afternoon flag of truce offering, if given all the honours of war, to capitulate and stipulating for specific terms. Bryant replied that they were not in a position to ask for terms and that they must surrender unconditionally.

He told them that we always respected private property and that there would be as little interference as possible with the trade of the country and the private interest of firms. He has advanced and has occupied the crossing at River Amu.

The German answer is expected to-night or early tomorrow morning.

ROBERTSON

LIEUTENANT-COLONEL BRYANT, COMMANDANT,
TOGOLAND FIELD FORCE, to the SECRETARY OF STATE
(Received 6.40 p.m., 26th August, 1914

TELEGRAM

AMUTSCHE, 26th August. I have the honour to inform you
that Togoland surrendered unconditionally to me to-day. I
occupy Kamina at 8 a.m. to-morrow.
        BRYANT

A third telegram, from Kitchener, though issued by his Cabinet
colleague, Lewis Harcourt, Secretary of State for the Colonies, offering
London's approval, and not forgetting the French contribution to the
outcome, completes the sequence:

The SECRETARY OF STATE TO THE GOVERNOR
(Sent 12.25 p.m., 27th August 1914)

TELEGRAM

FOLLOWING FOR BRYANT:—
        His Majesty's Government have received with much satis-
faction your telegraphic report of the successful conclusions of
the operations in Togoland, and desire you to express to the
Officer Commanding the French troops, and to all ranks, their
high appreciation of the gallant conduct of the allied forces. I
warmly congratulate you on the skill and dash with which the
operations have been carried out.
        HARCOURT

It is perhaps ironic that in the month when in France, in the Battle
of the Frontiers, 'dash' – or to quote its French equivalent *'guerre à
outrance'* – was found to be seriously wanting, it was being celebrated
in the context of the tiniest of sideshows in Africa.

Cameroon was to present far greater problems. Both the French
and the British took to arms on instinct, and after much prevarication
decided on an Anglo-French operation to take the colony's principal
port, Duala. It was to be conducted by Brigadier General C. M. Dobell,
commander of the 8,000-strong British West African Frontier Force
(known as the WAFF), based in Nigeria. While this major operation
was being prepared, local Allied forces mounted three independent
invasions. French colonial soldiers successfully seized frontier posts
in the north-east on 6 August, though a British thrust across the
northern frontier on 24 September was repulsed by better-trained
German units with heavy casualties. By 21 September a Senegalese
unit of 600 had established itself on the south-west coast.

The Allies' prime target, Duala, fell to the substantial Anglo-French force sent against it with naval support on 27–28 September, without serious resistance. A contemporary letter, held in the papers of Lieutenant M. C. Carr-Gomm (presumably written by him and sent to *The Times*, which printed it without attribution) offers a vivid description of the event, while also reminding the present-day reader of the assumption by so many participants in that war that their cause had God on its side:

> On the Friday and Saturday [25th and 26th] a British cruiser moved up the Cameroon river, lay about three miles off Duala, and comfortably bombarded the town, out of reach of the German forts. At the same time a landing of a small force of troops was attempted, but the enemy was in such force there that the landing was given up. The Germans had sunk at least 10 steamers in an absolutely unsuccessful attempt to block the channel. On Sunday the 27th, Duala disliked the cruiser's shells so much that they hoisted the white flag and surrendered the town. The Lord was with us in the most marvellous manner, as not only were the enemy unsuccessful in blocking the channel, but also not one of their floating mines did any damage to us. Our small patrol boats succeeded in blowing up about 12 of them by rifle fire, and we hear the enemy lost 11 men in the making of these mines. On the 28th General Dobell landed in Duala and took over the town.

This was far from the end of the campaign. It dragged on for months – even achieving, according to one officer's diary, its own brief Christmas Truce on 25 December, though unfortunately the officer in question, Major A. C. L. D. Lees, gave no further details. Basically neither Paris nor London had any desire to conquer the territory, but they did not know how to stop what they had begun. Eventually in March 1916 the colony was divided between Britain and France, after a conquest involving 18,000 British and French imperial troops. This was a campaign in which out of a death toll of 4,235 the majority were the victims of disease. Figures for the German side are not known.

German South-West Africa did not become a serious war zone until 1915, because the fighting in 1914 was within British South Africa itself, where the principal enemy were 'rebels' who had not become reconciled to the outcome of the Boer War and saw the

40. The first Territorial unit to be in action. Remnants of the London Scottish on 31 October after their heroic efforts in the defences of Messines. (Q 60737)

41. Lieutenant General Sir Douglas Haig (left) with General Sir Charles Monro, Brigadier General J. E. Gough VC (died of wounds, February 1915), and Brigadier General E. M. Perceval, October. (Q 54992)

42. A symbol of the Indian contribution to the First Battle of Ypres: wounded Indian soldiers in a French village, 31 October. (Q 533348)

43. One of thousands: funeral of a soldier of the 2nd Scots Guards, date unknown. (Q 57393)

44. Barriers erected at Folkestone against the possibility of invasion. (Miss Mary Coules, IWM Department of Documents)

45. Trenches being dug on the cliffs near Folkestone. (Miss Mary Coules, IWM Department of Documents)

46. Funeral of Postman Beale, killed at Scarborough during the raid of 16 December; escort provided by the town's postmen. (Q 53476)

47. Officers of the 2nd South Wales Borderers, Tientsin, north China; from the Major-General Williams collection. (HU 57522)

48. Battered wreck of the German light cruiser *Emden*, at the Cocos Islands. (SP 2067)

49. Mesopotamia: 'The Dorsetshire Regiment in the front line, ready for anything'; Private W. R. Bird was a member of this battalion. (Q 107187)

50. The end-game in German South-West Africa, early 1915; General Botha's victory address to the crowd at Windhoek. (Q 90475)

51. Entrenchment after First Ypres: 1st Cameronians settling into trenches at Houplines, on the Franco-Belgian border; subtitled by the photographer 'the back of our trenches, showing our bedrooms'. (Q 51530)

52. Entrenchment after First Ypres: 2nd Royal Scots Fusiliers in trenches south of Armentières. (Q 49104)

53. German trench, Flanders, winter 1914–15. (Q 63538)

54. German reservists at the front, decorating a tree for Christmas. (Bundesarchiv, Berlin)

55. Christmas Truce: a classic photograph showing two members of the London Rifle Brigade mingling with German soldiers; one of the best-known images of the truce, taken on Christmas Day at Ploegsteert, Belgium. (Q 70074)

56. Settling in: British trenches, spring 1915. (Q 48966)

57. Settling in: German trenches, spring 1915. (Q 51067)

Germans not as enemies but allies. This sideshow of a sideshow would become known as the Boer Revolt.

On 26 September Philip Kerr, a Cambridge-educated Englishman in his late twenties who was working in the Crown Mines outside Johannesburg, enlisted as a trooper in the Imperial Light Horse. The ILH, as Kerr usually names it in the detailed diary he kept of his subsequent adventures, was originally raised by loyal colonists in the Transvaal during the Boer War, in which it had performed well. As it had continued in existence after hostilities had ended, there was no problem in rapidly remobilizing it in August 1914. The ILH's four squadrons, 'A', 'B', 'C' and 'D', had begun their wartime training in Cape Town, and one of them, 'D', described by Kerr as 'more seasoned' than the others, had already been landed on the coast of German South-West Africa in the vicinity of the port of Lüderitz. Now the regiment was recruiting for a new 'E' squadron in Johannesburg. Kerr recorded: 'The ILH has been authorized to recruit 200 more men, and as this is the first call for volunteers pure and simple, you may imagine the competition is keen.' The scenes this appeal gave rise to are remarkably reminiscent of similar ones in the home country at the same period:

> Recruiting opened at 10 a.m. Our party arrived at 9.15 a.m. and found a crowd waiting. You had to pass in one at a time, and then wait in a pretty long queue before getting to the Recruiting Officer. The rate of admission was very slow, about one every ¼ hour. The reason for this being that having some 2,000 men applying, the authorities could pick and choose, so, consequently examined every candidate pretty thoroughly. The enthusiasm was very keen. I have never fought in a crowd more strenuously, in all my life, a coronation crowd was nothing to it. Recruiting was timed to stop at 1 p.m. so after waiting till 11.30, I saw no chance of getting in that day, consequently I left and went off to try and pull strings. I was lucky enough to catch Major Mullins VC, an old ILH officer whom I know pretty well. He promised he would do what he could for me and let me know.

The following day, thanks to a special pass given him by Major Mullins, Kerr was accepted. He went straight from the recruiting office to attempt the riding test:

This was not severe, but awkward, as one had to mount, carrying a rifle, which is a clumsy thing to handle when you are not used to it. Anyhow I scrambled through somehow, the Examining Officer, Captain Cornwall being very nice about it. I had now only to pass the doctor, so hurried off to him but arrived too late, so I arranged to come the next day. I already felt half a soldier, inasmuch as I had a Pass in and out of camp given to me under the name of Trooper P. W. Kerr.

Passed as fit by the doctor the following morning, Kerr began his career as a soldier, with the usual rituals such as inoculations and parades, plus, this being a cavalry unit, mounted drill and the vital matter of 'stable duty', or care of the horses, which would become increasingly important as the squadron moved into the veldt. He shortly acquired his own horse, which he named 'James' and which would effectively be his other half in the ensuing campaign. On 4 October they were inspected by their commander-in-chief, General J. C. Smuts, who expressed his approval, after which they were all given leave from 1 p.m. to midnight. On 5 October, en route for training at the Polo Ground, they rode through the town, making 'quite a sensation, as Johannesburg has not seen a great deal of the troops as yet'. On Saturday the 10th arrangements were being made for a special parade next day for the benefit of the public, when there was a sudden change of plan:

> We got back rather late for lunch. During lunch the orderly sergeant came round and told us that we were off to the front this afternoon, and to go and pack our kits at once. The news was received with whoops of joy.
> We did some pretty good work in the way of packing. We got the orders at 2.25 and were on the platform with our horses at 3.30. As is the way in the Army we did not actually get off until 10.30 p.m.

At a time when in Britain incessant rain was dousing the camps and dampening the ardour of Kitchener's volunteers, the overriding requirement in South Africa was for water. On 15 October Kerr noted:

> Various fatigues during the morning, later on I found a pool of water and had a wash, which was very refreshing. . . . We marched without a halt until 8.30 when we stopped for water, then marched again until

11.30 ... We pushed on at 2.0 a.m. and marched until dawn, when
we halted for ½ hour, and then on again until we reached water at
7.0 a.m.

There followed two short rides of three hours each with two brief
halts. Then

we started off again and rode until 11 p.m., when we halted again,
pretty dead beat, after being 24 hours in the saddle, with only 3 hours
sleep, snatched when we could. We were all half mad with thirst, and
there was a stampede for the water cart when we camped ... Brief
halts of two hours by no means imply two hours rest, as there is
usually very little accommodation at the water tanks, and it generally
takes at least an hour to water one's horse. Poor old James is doing
very well but he must be having a rotten time of it.

On 19 October, Kerr's birthday, they crossed the Orange River:
'Fortunately, it was not in flood. It was a fine sight to see the column
picking its way across.' There they caught up with 'A', 'B' and 'C'
Squadrons, who gave them a rousing welcome:

After some breakfast, and a feed for the horses, we took our
horses down to the river, and spent the day there loafing about under
the trees, and bathing. Mighty glad we were too to wallow in the
beautiful clear water, after our days of heat, dust and dirt. It was
absolute bliss to lie about in the shade, and hear the water rippling
by, never remember having enjoyed a birthday more.

The enemies they were searching for were rebel forces under a
number of dissident commanders, including General C. F. Beyers,
formerly the commandant-general of the South African defence forces
and a well-known Germanophile, and two district staff officers, J. C. G.
Kemp from the western Transvaal, and S. G. Maritz from the northern
Cape, adjacent to the German frontier, all of whom had come out in
opposition to the pro-British Smuts and his loyal associate, General
Louis Botha, who led the Union forces against the Revolt. This would
develop into an ugly little quarrel with few holds barred. Its uncom-
promising character became clear to Kerr on 23 November:

A spy was brought into camp today. He was carrying a letter from
Kemp to Maritz. They held a court martial on him, at which Botha

was present, and sentenced him to be shot at dawn. I am thankful
that I am not one of the firing party.

*Tuesday, Nov 24th.* We were woken by the volley, disposing of the
spy, at dawn.

Later that day they moved to a new position some eight to nine
miles off near a waterhole, where they encamped and took up
positions along the sand dunes for the night.

Up to this point they had had only a number of inconclusive
skirmishes with the rebels. The following day, 25 November, saw the
nearest the squadron came to a pitched battle, though it was more
like an old-style cavalry action of the high days of Empire than
anything happening at that time in Europe. Their mission was to
bring to book the by now self-styled General Kemp:

> We came back to the camp at dawn, and started off immediately
> in pursuit of Kemp. We kept to the road for about 8 or 9 miles, and
> then struck off across country. We soon sighted Kemp's lot in the
> distance, galloping like mad for the sand dunes. We immediately gave
> chase, and for a good many weary miles we pursued them, often
> sighting them on the skyline, but never seeming to get any closer. It
> was a fine sight to see the whole Regiment galloping across country,
> in line. We kept on like this for some time and gradually got round to
> their flank in the sand dunes. A few sniping shots came amongst us as
> we topped a ridge, so we changed our tactics, and kept along the
> valley. By now the enemy's shooting became more systematic, and
> bullets were flying round pretty freely, so we got under cover and
> dismounted, advancing gradually towards where the enemy's snipers
> appeared to be.
>
> By now we had quite lost touch with our main body, and were
> just three troops of E Squadron only. We gradually advanced and
> finally rushed the party who were sniping us. They proved to be an
> isolated lot of about 20, who had remained, to cover the retreat of
> the main body. They surrendered to us when we rushed them. We
> have suffered rather, Lt Froude who was in command of No 3 Troop
> has been killed, Whightman is killed and the Sgt Major so badly
> wounded that he cannot live. Devenish and Lt Bell are also slightly
> wounded. We have now been 24 hours without water, the horses
> must feel it dreadfully. I don't know quite where we are, and it is
> getting dark, so we must just hold on where we are until daylight.

*Thursday, Nov. 26.* No sign of any troops. We have sent a search party out to look for water. We have none, and all are pretty thirsty, especially the wounded. I had a spare bottle in my saddle, which has come in very handy for the wounded. Thank heaven our water party has returned, festooned with water bottles. A party of horsemen has just been sighted, which looks like our own people. We sent out a previous search party for water, during the night, who were captured by Kemp's men, who took the water bottles off them and let them go. The body of horsemen has proved to be a party of the Natal Light Horse, who tell us that the main body are encamped nearby. We are moving off there at once. We got there in about a ½ hour, and took the horses down to water. How they revelled in it.

Botha visited our camp this morning. Our casualties yesterday were 10 killed and 30 wounded. We, namely 1, 2, and 3 Troops of E Squadron captured 17 out of the 19 prisoners taken, so we are pretty pleased with ourselves. I must say that I was profoundly glad when the fighting stopped yesterday, bullets were flying all around us and it was most unpleasant. We shifted camp to a farm called 'Rooidam', where we buried our dead, 3 in number, Lt Froude, Sgt Major Grace, and Whightman. It is the first military funeral that I have seen and it was most impressive. All the more so for being out in the middle of the bare veldt. The whole Regiment fell in and followed behind the bodies. The firing party led off, then came the bodies, Lt Froude's charger, with boots reversed in the stirrups, being led immediately behind his body. The bodies were lowered into the graves and the chaplain read the burial service, after which the firing party who were drawn up on either side of the graves let off three volleys, and the Trumpeter Major sounded the 'Last Post'.

On returning to camp we got orders to march at once. The prospect appalls me, we are all dead beat and our horses more so, however it has to be done. We are in for an all night trek. I nearly rolled off my horse with sleep several times during the night.

They later heard that their role in the operation had won praise, but that there had been a significant failure elsewhere:

Whilst we were tackling the enemy in the sand dunes, Kemp and the main body made off towards GSWA [German South-West Africa]. Colonel Bouwer and his commando were lying in wait for him and practically got him rounded up. Then one part of Bouwer's forces

who were very advanced, in an important position, owing to bad
organization of ration supply or some such reason, got fed up and
came back to camp, thus letting Kemp through.

Fighting would continue in a similar desultory way for some time,
but the Boer Revolt had no realistic future and would soon end, if
somewhat untidily. Beyers drowned in the Vaal River on 8 December
while trying to evade government forces. Kemp was chased into
German territory where he linked up with Maritz. He attempted a
strike against the frontier town of Upington in January 1915, but it
failed and he was forced to capitulate. Maritz escaped into exile in
Spain and Portugal. Subsequently Union forces under Botha pursued
their prime war aim of overrunning German South-West Africa, forcing a surrender in July 1915.

Trooper Kerr was invalided back to Cape Town in March 1915. He
was offered a post on the staff of the Governor-General but declined,
having decided to exchange what he called 'the gymkhana war in
Africa' for the more important one in Europe. He returned to England
where he was commissioned into the Royal Field Artillery and served
for the rest of the war on the Western Front.

* * *

The longest-lasting of the four British campaigns in the continent
would be in German East Africa; indeed hostilities there continued, if
sporadically, throughout the war, and, if briefly, beyond.

As early as the middle of August 1914 it was decided by the India
Office in London that a seaborne attack should be made on the
colony's chief port, Tanga, and that, as in the case of the operation
against Mesopotamia, this should be carried out by an expeditionary
force mounted by the Indian Army. It would be named Indian
Expeditionary Force 'B'. A convoy of one light cruiser, HMS *Goliath*,
and twelve merchantmen was assigned to transport the force, which
finally sailed from Bombay on 16 October. There had been much
prevarication before the expedition was launched. In fact the Commander-in-Chief of the Indian Army and the Viceroy of India had
done their best to urge its cancellation, both being of the opinion
that 'it was a waste of good troops to embark on a side issue when
everything India could offer was so urgently needed in France and

elsewhere, especially as the fate of German E. Africa could obviously be settled by the main operations in Europe'.

The quotation is from a personal account by the officer who commanded the expeditionary force, Major General A. E. Aitken, aged fifty-three, who after a brief period in home regiments had been serving in India since 1882. Assigned to this mission from its inception, he was greatly relieved when it was shelved, being in entire agreement with the viewpoint of his superiors. He had travelled from Poona to Simla to receive his orders, only to make the return journey, a much happier man, a few days later. In early September, however, he received a wire stating that the expedition had been resuscitated and again offering him the command. Originally the scheme had envisaged that he should be assigned some of India's most highly trained units, but now the situation was less assuring:

> By this time all the best troops had been detailed or actually dispatched in some cases to France, Egypt and Persia, with the result that my force was now made up of a composite Brigade put together from whatever was left over, and included two Madras regiments of which it is sufficient to say that they are the worst troops in India, and, with the exception of the Pioneers and Sappers for purely technical work only, are never used on the frontier, as far as I am aware, and are certainly not trusted. It was openly said, repeatedly in my hearing, that evidently no serious fighting was anticipated, or these troops would not have been detailed.

The expedition arrived off the East African coast on 29 October. On the following day Aitken held a conference on board his 'transport', the P & O ship SS *Karmala*, with the Senior Naval Officer in the area, Captain Caulfield RN, based in HMS *Fox*, whose local knowledge and guidance were vital to the operation's success. Caulfield strongly endorsed the assumptions that had prevailed in India:

> Capt. Caulfield's information and general attitude on the whole question most clearly indicated a very strong opinion that there would be no great resistance on the part of the Germans, and that any show of force would be enough to break down any opposition there might be.

Leaving *Goliath* with the convoy, *Karmala* and *Fox* went into Mombasa, so that Aitken and Caulfield could consult with the

Governor of British East Africa and the local army commander, General Stewart. While they were there certain final measures were undertaken:

> We painted out the transport number of the *Karmala*, hoisted the red ensign instead of the blue, and did all we could to make our visit as inconspicuous as possible. It did not take long, however, to discover that our arrival was more or less public property, that the Germans had a very carefully and thoroughly arranged system of espionage. So there was little doubt that they knew all there was to be known in Mombasa.

Worse was to come. Aitken learned that on the outbreak of war the previous Senior Naval Officer on the station had agreed a local truce with the German authorities in Tanga, which Caulfield insisted he should observe until it was formally terminated. In other words the Germans were to be, in effect, informed in advance that their colony was about to be invaded.

The outcome was inevitable. When after numerous delays the attacking troops went in on 2 November the enemy was primed and ready, while predictions that there would be little or no resistance were proved to be seriously wrong:

> Far from Tanga not being held, or only lightly held, it was very strongly prepared for defence with a very adequate force to hold it. Every house had been prepared for defence with two, three, and even four tiers of fire and plenty of machine-guns. There was also a railway cutting just in front of the town which was completely enfiladed by machine-guns and rifle fire.
>
> In spite of all this I am absolutely certain that had the whole of my force consisted of reliable troops, or had the bad troops put up any semblance of a fight, we should have captured Tanga and been able to hold it. As it was, the fight ceased about 5.30 p.m. with our line completely held up about 500 yards outside Tanga, the units holding it being the only ones left out of my whole force with any fight left in them at all.

Aitken had hoped to rally his troops and go in again with the bayonet during the night. But even such battalions as had stayed with him were exhausted and suffering acutely from thirst, forcing him to withdraw another 500 yards to the vicinity of the port's German hospital, where water could be obtained. Returning to his head-quarters, he heard dismaying reports from his various commanders 'about the utterly demoralized rabble they had been dealing with all day since the fight began':

> They were all, without exception, emphatic about my not being able get the men to go in again as I wanted them to do, and that therefore my idea of a night attack was doomed to failure. I was faced with the immediate necessity of deciding what to do. I therefore issued orders to extricate the force next morning. I need not go into the details of that operation except to say that it was carried out successfully and unmolested by the Germans. Also, it was quite one of the best bits of staff work I have ever seen or am likely to see, and reflects the very greatest credit on my staff, naval and military, and on all those from on board ship who helped so splendidly to carry it through.

But campaigns are not won by evacuations, however expertly carried out. The disaster at Tanga was the unhappy overture to a campaign which dragged on for four years and of which the undoubted hero was the German General P. E. von Lettow-Vorbeck, who, like Müller of the *Emden*, would gain the great respect of his enemies as well as of his own side, and did not finally lay down his arms until a fortnight after the Armistice of 11 November 1918.

As for Aitken, his account of the operation as here quoted was not a memoir for his family or an article for a learned journal but, in effect, a heartfelt speech for the defence which he hoped might persuade a deeply sceptical War Office in London that, although the attack on Tanga had been an undoubted failure, this had largely been the consequence of circumstances beyond his control. His plea fell on deaf ears. At first demoted to the rank of colonel, he was ultimately allowed to resume the style of honorary brigadier general, but he was barred from any further active service. To all intents and purposes Tanga ended his military career.

Deliberately, news of the fiasco was suppressed throughout the war, not becoming known until many years later. This was a second misfortune, in that lessons learned at Tanga might have contributed to a better outcome when another landing on an alien shore was attempted just five months later in another war theatre. In the words of a recent historian of this campaign, 'Tanga was a warning that was to be ignored at great cost in men, money and material.' The horrors of Cape Hellas and Anzac Cove at Gallipoli might conceivably have been avoided if greater note had been taken of the Battle of Tanga, November 1914.

# CHAPTER THIRTEEN

# A STRANGE KIND OF CHRISTMAS

THE FIRST BATTLE OF YPRES had seen the last attempt by the Germans to outflank the Allies and return to open campaigning. The result of their failure was deadlock from the Channel coast to the Swiss border. Soon there would be a double line of trenches stretching, given diversions and indentations according to the terrain and the whims of local commanders, for some 450 miles. For the time being, too, there was a kind of ceasefire, or at least a reduction in mutual hostility, as if in acknowledgement that all concerned had been fought to a standstill and were just too weary to carry on. It was as though a sporting season had closed down for the winter, the last fixtures had been fought and a new season would open in the following spring. However, not everybody stayed where the fighting stopped. Between 15 and 22 November a major reorganization of the line took place. The French briefly took over the Ypres area – soon to enter British mythology as the 'Ypres Salient', and to be defined as either glorious or notorious, according to one's point of view – and by the evening of the 22nd the British were established on a front of 21 miles from St Eloi, just east of Kemmel Hill, to La Bassée, their sector including, or being close to, north to south, such places as Messines, Ploegsteert, Frelinghien, Armentières, Neuve-Chapelle and Givenchy. Their forces consisted of – again north to south – II Corps under General Sir Horace Smith-Dorrien, III Corps under Lieutenant General Sir William Pulteney, IV Corps under Lieutenant General Sir Henry Rawlinson, the Indian Corps under Lieutenant General Sir John Willcocks, and I Corps under General Sir Douglas Haig. For good measure it should be added that on 26 December the BEF would be formed into two Armies: the First Army under Haig, consisting of I Corps, IV Corps and the Indian Corps; the Second Army under Smith-Dorrien, consisting of II Corps and III Corps, with the addition of the newly arrived 27th Division. In short, they were shaking down for a long haul.

By now a number of units of the Territorial Force had joined their regular comrades in the field. The first to see action was the 14th Battalion, London Regiment, the London Scottish, which had been thrown into the Ypres battle near Messines on 31 October with no preparation and only the vaguest of orders. Having attacked 800 strong they were dismayed that their final muster found them some 350 short of their full complement. (One of their number who came through with a modest leg wound and lived not to fight but to act another day was the future Hollywood star Ronald Colman, while another who survived unscathed was the equally celebrated Basil Rathbone.) Their efforts had helped hold the line, but had not stopped Messines and its Ridge falling to the enemy, who would hold these gains for the next two and a half years. Whatever their gallantry or zeal, however, the 'Terriers' – long used to their dismissive label of 'Saturday Afternoon Soldiers' – knew they would not be easily accepted by the professionals and that they would have to work hard to win their spurs. Leslie Walkinton of the 16th Battalion, London Regiment, better known as the Queen's Westminster Rifles, would never forget an early encounter with members of a regular unit whom he and a handful of his comrades met when they were making an early visit to the front line:

> As they drew nearer we could hear them all talking and laughing unrestrainedly. Here and there a bold spirit was smoking a cigarette. 'Who are you?' a voice shouted as they reached the head of [our] little party. 'Queen's Westminsters,' said someone in front of me in a stage whisper. 'WHO are you?' said the voice as its owner marched past me. 'Queen's Westminsters, No 11 Platoon,' I replied as a real soldier (so at least I thought) should. 'Christ, they're the bloody territorials,' said the voice. 'Volun'bloody'teers,' said his pal, getting in the essential word with the facility which only comes after years of practice. 'Well, God help the silly b—s.' And so they passed . . .

* * *

Trenches had been dug regularly by all the armies involved since the first clashes in August. Only on the Aisne had they been lived in for more than a few days. Now there was a sea change. From now on the phrase constantly on people's lips was: 'The Trenches'. Until the logjam was finally broken in 1918 they would be the basic reality, and ever afterwards the defining concept, of the Western Front war.

The evidence is that, at first, most soldiers did not take kindly to them. There is little doubt that in the circumstances of the war's first winter they came as a shock and they felt like an aberration. This was not how things should be. Surely this new-style method of war was insupportable – it could not be allowed to continue. Such was the message coming strongly from the diary of a young Territorial, Private Mervyn Reeves of the Honourable Artillery Company (despite its name an infantry unit), writing just over a fortnight before the Christmas by which the war was meant to be over. A future successful officer but at this time an unhappy new arrival, he poured out his thoughts in his diary in a kind of stream of consciousness, in which the occasional good moment was swamped by the mass of bad ones:

> *Monday, December 7th 1914.* All day it has rained – I have lain down on my mackintosh sheet which is wet with my blanket over me which is also wet – my trousers, puttees and tunic are wet through so I have lain in a less wet pair of pants and a sweater – there are no opportunities of drying things so we take our chance of pneumonia etc. several people have got it this morning I think – we had some lovely hot soup at 4 p.m. and a post came in [but] I am still wet and very cold and I suppose my wet things will have to dry on me – we lost two men, I killed and I wounded, Corporal Fabian whom I know was one of those killed – This life is awful and I cannot think in this weather that the trench fighting can possibly continue long – no human beings can stand it – I heard today that just after we left the Royal Scots HQ two platoons of Germans came in and surrendered as they couldn't stand it any longer – the condition of the Royal Scots who were in the trenches next to us was more pitiful than our own – several of their men went off their heads from exposure and cold and wretchedness.

If conditions were bad in the trenches, they were also bad in the wagon lines, where men had to struggle with the constant moving and deploying of their guns and, equally vital, to take the best care they could of their horses. Trooper A. E. Brice, of the 1/1st Essex Yeomanry, 3rd Cavalry Division, wrote this terse but telling entry in his diary on 10 December:

Billeted in a farm. Stable guard. I am first relief – 5 p.m. to 7 p.m.,
11 p.m. to 1 a.m., and 5 a.m. to 7 a.m. Started to pour about 4 p.m.
Horses picketed out. Get what shelter I can from tree – miserable
job. Horses soon up to their knees in mud. It's an awful time for
boots – never dry and we have to sleep in them nearly always. One's
feet get perished. Took boots off on one relief and did get warm
sleep back of barn, my mare in shed – little better.

A wealth of valuable insights into the conditions of the war's first
winter are to be found in the diary of Brigadier General Frederick
Heyworth, who arrived in France with 7th Division on 14 October as
commander of 20th Brigade. This consisted of five battalions: 2nd
Border, 2nd and 6th Gordon Highlanders, 2nd Scots Guards, and 1st
Grenadier Guards. 20th Brigade was part of 7th Division, commanded
by Major General Thompson Capper, itself part of IV Corps. Heyworth's diary, covering the period 13 November to 14 August 1915, is a
written up daily in his copy of standard issue Army Book 152, is a
historical jewel; legible (not always the case in such documents),
lueid, laid back, but clearly carrying the authority of a highly professional soldier: and an experienced one, for he had served in the
Boer War. It also shows that a general at his level felt it his duty to be
close to his sector and close to his men: at 6 foot 4 he was a rather
too obvious target for enemy snipers – indeed he lost his life to one
when visiting front-line trenches in 1916. From the moment his
brigade entered the line – to the south of Armentières astride the
Sailly–Fromelles road – it was met by severe weather leading to
rapidly deteriorating, indeed high-risk, conditions, as is evident from
the following early entries:

*19 November.* Heavy shelling at 6.30 a.m, but some way off. Frost
again last night but not so hard as it was yesterday. It came on to
snow hard about 1 p.m. At 3 p.m. went out to see the 3rd line of
defence we are digging. Horrible day, snow just beginning to lie and
very wet under foot; am going into the trenches tonight.

*20 November.* Went into the trenches at 10 a.m. having had to crawl
down a very dirty ditch. Stayed there until 4 p.m.: a good deal of
sniping and a man of the Scots Guards was shot dead close to me, it
was not safe to show one's head for long over the parapet. Two
aeroplanes went over us one French and one German, the latter we

fired at but with no effect. We were going to make an attack on one
of the German trenches but the snow stopped it as it showed anyone
up so much, so we have postponed it.

Yet such attacks were made, if on a more modest scale. In fact, on
27 November Heyworth recorded what must be a very early example
of what would become standard fare in the following years, a trench
raid:

> The Scots Guards made a successful raid on the German trenches
> at 2 a.m. Lieutenant Sir E. Hulse, I Corporal and 8 men crawled out
> to the [enemy] trench, they were challenged in English by the German
> Sentries; they then rushed the trench and fired into a group of
> Germans sitting round a fire at the bottom. The Corporal had a rifle
> grenade which he also fired; they then got back to their own trench
> under heavy fire from the enemy with the loss of 2 men missing.

Heyworth's diary for December contains numerous entries suggesting that, far from improving with prolonged occupation, the state
of the trenches was if anything getting steadily worse. Hence this on
14 December:

> A lot of rain in the night again. Went into the trenches at 8.30 a.m.
> and found them in an awful mess. There were 2 men killed when I
> was in the trenches, I Gordon and I Border, both shot though the
> head. I rode this afternoon with Palmer and we visited the head-
> quarters of the Scots Guards, Border and 6 Gordons. We met the
> two companies of the 6 Gordons coming out of the trenches and I
> have never seen men in such a state of mud and so tired. I am afraid
> they will not be much good anyway at present. They are very young
> and this trench work completely beats them.

Despite such an unpromising situation, a two-brigade attack was
launched on 18 December, the 22nd Brigade to go over at 4 p.m., the
20th at 6 p.m. This was at the request of the French, who, being by
far the largest Allied force in the field, understandably felt they had
the right to dictate to the British and the Belgians in the matter of
strategy and tactics. They had an initiative planned for which they
required British support. Heyworth's diary for 19 December described
the outcome:

The affair of last night was not quite a success, but it was as good if not better than the other Brigade did. Lawford's Brigade attacked first and did not get up to the German trenches, they suffered heavily, 4 officers killed and several wounded and 300 rank and file killed and wounded. The Scots Guards got into the German trenches and killed a good many including an officer, but they got turned out by hand grenades which the Germans threw at them. They suffered pretty heavily.

Taylor (missing believed to be killed), Nugent missing: Saumarez – FitzIngram – Ottley (bad) Felix – Stacey (wounded and missing) [sic]. Loder led the attack and was the only one not hit; about 160 rank and file killed and wounded. The Borders had 1 officer killed and 4 wounded, Lamb very badly, nearly certain to lose his leg and also has a double fracture of one arm. The Borders did not get in and had about 60 casualties. Several of their wounded were left out and in the morning when they tried to crawl in the Germans shot at them, about 15 wounded had to stop in the trenches all day as they could not be got away before dawn. I stayed the night at the Gordons' Headquarters in the cellar but could not sleep as my feet were very wet and cold and I was always being rung up on the telephone. At 9.15 a.m. went into the trenches and found the communication trenches too filthy for words, liquid mud over my knees in some places. Came out of the trenches at 1.15 p.m. and then walked back to Headquarters. After a bath and shave found Allan and Jimmy and gave them tea and then went off to see Gen. Capper and tell him about last night's affair. Fearful night again, dark as pitch and raining.

Ironically, the French attack which these British efforts were meant to support was not launched. No ground was gained, little impact was made on the enemy and many young lives were lost to no purpose. No great battle was in progress as had been the case so often earlier in the year, yet the toll of casualties continued day after day.

* * *

What did the public back home make of this change to a radically different kind of warfare? How much did they know, and how were they informed? At least part of the answer is that Colonel

Ernest Swinton was still there, reporting, under his alias 'Eye-witness', with even greater vigour and frankness as the war became more horrific and more costly. His syndicated dispatch of 21 December, which would appear in numerous newspapers on Boxing Day, was anything but a pleasant Christmas present for the nation. This was his unflinching description of the forward area of the new-style British defence system in France and Flanders in mid-December 1914:

> Seamed with dug-outs, burrows, trenches, and excavations of every kind, and fitted [sic] with craters, it is bounded on the front by a long discontinuous irregular line fringed with barbed wire and broken by saps wriggling still more to the front. This is the Ultima Thule. Beyond, of width varying according to the nature of the fighting and of the ground, is neutral territory, the no-man's-land between the hostile forces. It is strewn with the dead of both sides, some lying, others caught and propped in the sagging wire, where they may have been for days, still others half buried in craters or destroyed parapets. When darkness falls, with infinite caution, an occasional patrol or solitary sniper may explore this gruesome area, crawling amongst the *débris* – possibly of many fights – over the dead bodies and the inequalities of the ground till some point of vantage is gained whence the enemy's position can be examined or a good shot obtained. On the other side of this zone of the unburied dead bristles a similar fringe of wire and a long succession of low mounds and parapets – the position of the enemy. And woe betide the man who in daylight puts up his head carelessly to take a long glance at it.

Long before Swinton's dispatch was sent to the printers, however, commercial companies back home had had to make up their minds as to how to approach the war's first Christmas. They reacted in a variety of ways. Thus a fashionable London firm of tailors, Messrs Thresher and Glenny, responding rapidly to the arrival of trench warfare, offered what they saw as appropriate dress for the changed conditions, with a particular eye for officers who might be at home for the festive season. Hence the following advertisement in the *Illustrated London News* of 19 December, complete with a sketch showing the item advertised as it might be worn:

By contrast, on the same page immediately below, there was an advertisement which seemed to make no acknowledgement that Britain was now a country in serious crisis: a handsomely printed panel, with seasonal holly-leaf surround, on behalf of the Great Western Railway, 'The Holiday Line', as it called itself:

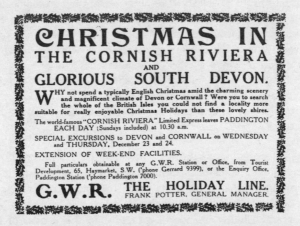

If nothing else, these two contrasting advertisements point up the inevitable dilemma faced by a country still trying to come to terms with the unfamiliar situation of being involved in what was rapidly becoming a total war. Meanwhile, even as such and similar advertisements were being read, letters informing families of the recent fatalities in Flanders would be arriving, along with Christmas cards and even presents, in the nation's post, while a vast flood of the same commodities would be making their way in the opposite direction.

* * *

The problem of how to cope with the war's first Christmas had been in the air internationally for some time. On 7 December the newly elected Pope, Benedict XV, had besought the belligerent powers 'in the name of the Divinity . . . to cease the clang of arms while Christendom celebrates the Feast of the World's Redemption'. There were, however, few takers for this apparently reasonable proposition. The fact that for the Orthodox Churches Christmas was on 7 January, not 25 December, added a serious complication to the possibility of any ceasefire on the Eastern Front, while further east the concept had no meaning at all in the case of Islamic Turkey (now engaged on the German side) or Japan (now fighting with the Allies). Germany accepted, but only on the understanding that the other powers involved would make a similar commitment, but for the Allies this bore all the hallmarks of gesture politics. Were not the Germans the aggressors? It was they, after all, who were holding territory not their own, the occupation of which even the briefest pause in hostilities would clearly help to prolong. One serving soldier who expressed himself vigorously on this subject was Lord Loch, now a senior staff officer, who wrote on 13 December, in one of his regular letters to his wife:

> What truth is there in the Pope proposing an armistice for Christmas? If true and accepted I don't think hostilities will be resumed – I don't think it ought to be accepted – We are out for war and this cannot be mixed up with 'Peace on Earth' 'good will towards men'. War is a brutal and loathsome business and the soonest way to end it is to make war with guns whole heart and soul regardless of cost and regardless of all the amenities of peacetime.

As it happened, the Pope acknowledged the failure of what he called 'our Christmas initiative' on that same date, 13 December; it had, he admitted, 'not been crowned with success'.

Loch's hard-line view would become one strong strand in the story of the 1914 Truce, but that episode would not have become the rich, complex tapestry it is now seen to be had not a very substantial number of participants and witnesses taken a different attitude.

Indeed, even as those in high places were discussing the Pope's and similar proposals – on 10 December a leading American senator, William S. Kenyon, proposed a twenty-day truce over Christmas which also received short shrift from the belligerent powers – at the front, in some areas at least, the troops in the trenches were beginning to make their own overtures. The very closeness of the two trench lines led to an inevitable curiosity as to what the enemy was like, and especially during the night hours there was much shouting and badinage, and even, in places, spontaneous entertainments, cheered on by both sides. A subaltern in the 1st Battalion, the Hampshire Regiment, Michael Holroyd, a graduate of Christ Church, Oxford, told his parents of one already legendary example in a letter written on 24 December:

> There is a beautiful story of – the Wessex, say – who had a fine singer among them, whom both sides delighted to honour: so the Germans just shouted 'Half time, Wessex', when desiring music, and everyone stopped firing. The songster climbed on to the parapet of the trench, and both sides joined in the chorus. If a senior officer of either side appeared, a signal was given and all hands lay doggo: then a fierce fusillade took place doing any amount of damage to the air twenty feet over the enemy's heads, and the senior officer went back delighted with his enemy's energy and zeal, not to say courage, in face of heavy fire. Then the concert recommenced.

Holroyd had only just arrived from England; indeed, he had barely reached the trenches before he found himself in a situation of which, as he put it, 'one excellent feature is the relations with the enemy'. (His battalion's trenches were on the eastern edge of 'Plugstreet' Wood, which had excited Second Lieutenant Tennyson's fury and had caused his serious fall just a few weeks earlier; it appears that there must have been some vigorous attempts at improving the chaotic conditions in the wood over the intervening weeks.) The 'Wessex' story formed part of a letter Holroyd wrote to his parents in which he described the start of the Christmas Truce, which had begun with another kind of inter-trench concert, this time not with just one voice, but with the full-throated mass singing of carols, the

Germans taking the lead and the British responding vigorously in kind:

> It is now for instance, Christmas Eve, and I've just been out with the doctor for an after-dinner stroll towards the enemy. We found the men in the intermediate lines singing loudly; not a shot from our own front or the Bavarians opposite. The moon looks down upon a slightly misty, pale blue landscape, and bending my ear to the ground I can hear a faint whisper of German song wafted on the breeze from their trenches half a mile away. I shall be greatly surprised if they or we fire a shot tomorrow; whatever Prussian warlords may do, Bavarian troops are pretty sure not to desecrate Christmas Day; and for ourselves, our 'general' idea is confined to the vague instructions not to fraternize with the enemy, but in case any of them get up with flags of truce or Christmas trees, to put a few shots well above their heads as a gentle warning that we're not open to any 'ruses', so beloved of the enemy-sportsmen-officers.
>
> You will of course remember, that all this is an interval of peace; it is not at all improbable that the enemy may seize the occasion to make a big general attack; if so, my next letter will give an account of some real war, and will no doubt be written in a far more serious frame of mind. Hitherto the Front appeals to me as a protracted and very enjoyable picnic, punctuated by the already unnoticed percussions of powerful pop-guns.

In a second letter, written on New Year's Eve, Holroyd was able to give a more measured account of the Truce, one which showed clearly that the Pope's efforts had made their mark among some at least of those serving in the line. He approached his subject circuitously, beginning with a wistful lament for the inevitable effect on family ties brought about by the arrival of the festive season in time of war:

> Your several letters written on Christmas Day have come in lately. Very sad, all the family separate like that. However, we don't so much mind so long as we can meet for next Christmas. And our Christmas out here was very remarkable. I don't mean the tinned turkey, crackers and preserved fruit with which we officers celebrated lunch and dinner. Nor do I mean the pork, turnips and baked potatoes and plum pudding which so delighted the men. No, I mean the peace on

earth that really happened, in spite of the Pope's failures. We and the Saxons (not as I thought Bavarians) who inhabit across the way had been in the habit of sniping at one another most of the time and they bagged at least one or two a day of ours, and we I daresay much the same. As Captain Palk [Holroyd's company commander] says, that's simply organized murder serving no purpose whatever so far as war's results are concerned. It simply couldn't go on on Christmas Day.

Sure enough, the carols of Christmas Eve were followed by friendly exchanges of greetings on Christmas morning. During the day both sides came out and fraternized in between the lines, buried stale corpses and reconnoitred the ground. All night again, no firing, and since then, not a shot has been fired across at us with intent to kill.

We usually keep well down, but the safety of working parties and others coming up to the lines is a great gain, and the few we or they could snipe hardly count. True, the strain on the enemy is relaxed but so is their discipline. I said just now, 'with intent to kill'. With what purpose? Why only last night they showed a red light and cried aloud 'Put your heads down'. Which we did and a ferocious fusillade came whizzing over our heads. After a space, fire ceased, a white light replaced the red one, and they shouted 'All right, Hampshires. Our officer's gone now.' Peace then resumed.

In effect, this was almost precisely his 'Wessex' story being relived in a Christmas context.

One matter raised by Holroyd's letter which was much discussed during the Truce and after was the apparent differing attitude on the enemy side of Prussian units as opposed to those from elsewhere in Germany:

> The Saxon Tommies of course loathe the war, realizing that the big bluff has failed and that Saxons have nothing to gain from a Prussian victory. This will have no effect during the war, since these tommies, unlike previous ones, have length with almost no breadth, and cannot hatch plots. But when they are back home and the war's over, that may start a better way of thinking. Dresden may yet be capital of Germany, and we'd be friendly enough then.

Saxon regiments were involved in another major fraternization further south, across the French border in the vicinity of Armentières, in which the participating British battalion was the Queen's Westminster Rifles. Reporting the episode in a letter of 29 December, Private Ernest Morley wrote of the people with whom they had celebrated Christmas: 'They were not Germans but a Saxon regiment the 107 and 179th.' The word 'Saxon' was vigorously scratched out presumably by the censor, but by leaving in the regimental numbers the message can be clearly interpreted: the 107 and 179 regiments were units of the XIX (Saxon) Corps.

Morley's engaging account of what he elsewhere in his letter described as 'a perfect scream' begins with an attempt by the British, not as was usually the case the Germans, to initiate Christmas celebrations, if not entirely in the spirit of peace and goodwill:

> We had decided to give the Germans a Christmas present of 3 carols and 3 rounds rapid. Accordingly as soon as night fell we started and the strains of 'While Shepherds Watched' (beautifully rendered by the choir) arose upon the air. We finished that and paused preparatory to giving the 2nd item on the programme. But lo! We heard answering strains from *their* lines. Also they started shouting across to us. Therefore we stopped any hostile operations and commenced to shout back. One of them shouted 'A Merry Christmas English. We're not shooting tonight.' We yelled back a similar message and from that time until we were relieved on Boxing morning at 4 a.m. not a shot was fired. After this shouting had gone on for some time they stuck up a light. Not to be outdone, so did we. Then up went another. So we shoved up another. Soon the two lines looked like an illuminated fete. Opposite me they had one lamp and nine candles in a row. And we had all the candles and lights we could muster stuck on our swords [i.e. bayonets] above the parapet. At 1200 [midnight] we sang 'God Save the King' and with the exception of the sentries turned in.
>
> Next morning, Christmas Day, they started getting out of the trenches and waving and some came over towards us. We went out and met them and had the curious pleasure of chatting with the men who had been doing their best to kill us, and we them.

Another account of a fraternization in which the Prussians were contrasted with the Saxons to the detriment of the former was written by Lieutenant Frederick Chandler, who had volunteered immediately after the start of hostilities and had been commissioned as a medical officer on 7 August. He was now at the front near Frelinghien with the 2nd Argyll and Sutherland Highlanders, next in line to the 2nd Royal Welch Fusiliers. In a letter written in the early hours of 1 January he described what he called the 'amazing thing' that occurred on Christmas Day:

> In the afternoon the Germans and our men shouted to each other and arranged an unofficial armistice – they got out of the trenches and met half-way and hobnobbed with each other, exchanged souvenirs and had drinks: they rolled a couple of barrels of beer over to the Welsh lines: and in one part 2 German officers came out with an orderly carrying glasses and two large bottles of Lager beer: they met one of our officers, shook hands, drank together and then decided they would have to call their men in: another officer – Stuart – had a box of good cigars given him: about 4 o'clock whistles blew and the men were called in but in our own lines and with the Germans opposite not a shot was fired the whole evening – everything was *perfectly* still and it was a bright frosty night – you can't imagine how delicious was that stillness and calm: for 2 months I have not had a quiet half hour and, oh, one does get sick of the crack crack of rifles. In other parts of the line they have no peace. They were Saxons opposite us, and they are good sorts I believe, they have no desire to be fighting the English. It is the beastly Prussians who have done all the harm.

One brief but engaging account of the Truce survives in a letter written by Sergeant J. Hancock, 1st Battalion, Royal Fusiliers, 6th Division, to a young girl of eight, Amy Griffiths, a pupil of St John's School in the Isle of Dogs, who had 'adopted' him as her front-line champion and had sent him gifts. Their correspondence had opened with a card from him dated 25 October, which read: 'Dear Missy, I thank you very much for your kindness in sending the socks to me. I received a pair, with your note in it, and am very grateful.' A letter of 25 November, this time thanking her for tobacco and cigarettes, suggests that the young Amy, like so many people back home, had been much influenced by Horatio Bottomley's vilification of the Germans, since Hancock wrote: 'I'm afraid you've given me rather a hard task in telling me to kill all the Germ-Huns, but I'll do my best for you, am afraid I can't manage the Kaiser as he won't come anywhere near me unfortunately, but I'll give him a look-up when we get to Berlin.' Adding a detail that would doubtless have interested Lieutenant Holroyd, he told her: 'The Germans serenade us in the evenings with their national songs, and we give them a cheer when they finish and we invite them over to our trenches, but they are too shy.' His next letter, however, was not about killing the 'Germ-Huns', but about sharing Christmas with them, though he clearly did not wish to make this sound too joyful an occasion. He wrote on 3 January 1915:

> I spent a rather interesting if not a happy Xmas, we made a truce with the enemy opposite us, they are only 60 yards away and exchanged cigarettes, papers, etc, a lot of them could speak English, they are Saxons, and object to be called Germans, they said they would be very glad when the war was finished, but they firmly believe they are going to win.

Perhaps again wishing to play down what had happened, he concluded: 'We are having very rainy weather – our trenches are rather like rivers, and are not at all pleasant to live in.'

An account by another soldier of Hancock's battalion, putting flesh on his brief narrative, was printed in an Isle of Man newspaper in early January 1915. Under the sub-headings ENEMIES SHAKE HANDS/AN IMPROMPTU FOOTBALL MATCH, the item read:

> A Douglas lady has received the following interesting letter from her brother, who is at present serving with the 1st Royal Fusiliers in the trenches:–
>
> 'I know you like to have news first-hand, so I am going to just let you know how we spent Christmas. Well, on Christmas Eve, the Germans stopped firing, and our chaps did the same. No firing was done that night, and on Xmas Day our chaps, ready for sport, went over to the Germans and shook hands with them. We exchanged beer and cigarettes for wine and cigars, and one of the Germans cut off all his buttons and gave them to one of our men in exchange for a pair of puttees. Then we took a football over, and we were just going to play them a match when along came one of their fussy officers, three parts drunk, and raised Cain. He went off shocking [sic], and ordered them back again; so we played ourselves, and they watched

and cheered. This is the truth, but as soon as 12 o'clock came, we
started to fight again. – Ted.'

There is perhaps a hint of toning down what happened for home
consumption in this letter too, in its claim of a return to fighting on
Christmas Day, so soon after what seems to have been a friendly, if
interrupted, meeting with the enemy; at the most there would probably have been a token flurry of rifle fire. The basic scenario, however,
rings true: the giving of gifts, the exchange of souvenirs; most significantly, the attempt, frustrated in this case, to arrange some kind of
football match. There were many such attempts up and down the line
that day, some successful, some not, some resulting in games played
with real footballs, though at least one was played with a tin can. At
several points there were actual matches with teams selected and
goals scored – *The Times* reported one such, without naming the
battalions involved, which the Germans won 3–2 – while other games
were just cheerful kickabouts in which anybody could join. A sharp
frost setting in on 24 December had hardened hitherto muddy
ground, making these attempts possible, while also providing an
appropriate seasonal backcloth – 'Christmas card weather' in a nice
description by one Tommy present. One thing that did not take place
was the showpiece 'England versus Germany' international football
match of popular imagination.

'In other parts of the line they have no peace,' Lieutenant Chandler
had stated, correctly, in his letter of 1 January. While some divisions
participated, often extensively, others took no part at all. In Haig's
I Corps, towards the southern end of the British sector, comprising
1st and 2nd Divisions, no units took part. In Smith-Dorrien's II Corps,
no units of 3rd Division, at the extreme north of the sector, took part;
but in his other division, the 5th, five infantry battalions participated,
one of which took over from a trucing battalion on the 29th. The
bulk of the fraternizing was in Sir William Pulteney's III Corps, where
the 4th and 6th Divisions took part, and in Sir Henry Rawlinson's IV
Corps, where numerous units of the 7th Division and some of 8th
Division took part. Remarkably, since Christmas was not a religious
festival for them, four units of the Indian Corps, including two front-
line battalions, also participated. Even within the trucing areas there
was no consistency; in the close-to-the-ground lateral world of the

trenches it was quite possible for a unit which had not relaxed its guard to go for some days without realizing that its neighbour had been celebrating the season with the enemy. Because of this some unfortunate fatalities occurred when men confident that a ceasefire had been agreed in a certain sector were caught in the sights of a zealous sniper not party to the plot.

In the non-trucing areas, business continued much as usual. One for whom there was no remission was Gunner Myatt, in 3rd Division, whose Christmas was anything but a joyous celebration. This, abbreviated, is his account of the period 22–26 December:

> *Dec 22nd.* Raining and sleet all night and all day and terrible cold. I feel proper fed up, bad with cold in the head. I pray for this to finish, bags of shrapnel over and around us today.
>
> *Dec 23rd.* Snowing all night, cold to the marrow, and a heavy bombardment going on all day. Hard at it, no advance on either side, only a heavy artillery duel in which we came off best. Towards evening it got heavy firing, the French are too mad. The flashes from their guns can be seen, they don't take enough cover and they draw the fire.
>
> *Dec 24th.* It is now Christmas Eve. In action not a very happy one either, a hot bombardment all night. We were firing at intervals all night, very cold, a bit of a frost going to snow again, hope to goodness it soon finishes, proper fed up.

If questions remain about the number and character of football games with enemies, Myatt was able to record a definite match – but with allies. His account of 25 December, generally a more cheerful one than any for quite some time, reads:

> Christmas Day. Not much firing all night but an hour's bombardment this morning, for a salute I suppose. We had a heavy frost all night which made the ground hard and better to get about. It came over very misty so we played the French batteries at a game of football, and beat them easy. A friendly game. We got a Christmas card from the King and Queen, a good souvenir, and also got tobacco, cigarettes and plum puddings from the [news]paper funds, but we had biscuits and bully beef for dinner, could have done with some fresh meat, never mind, roll on. Let's hope the next one ain't out here. Am

wondering what the dear ones are doing at home, we had a bit of a singsong in the evening. Nothing to drink.

So his diary continues, with some good days, others less so, but certainly with no awareness that anything quite out of the ordinary had occurred that Christmas only a few miles away along the line.

*  *  *

The diary of Brigadier General Heyworth, quoted earlier, presents an interesting case, in that it sheds light on the frequently asked question as to how senior officers reacted to the Truce. As it happened, he was in command of the Brigade which participated in one of the event's most moving episodes, a joint burial service between the trenches conducted by a Scottish chaplain and a German divinity student, and also produced its most famous chronicler, Sir Edward Hulse, leader of the trench raid already described, dated 27 November. Here is some of his evidence:

*24th December.* One of the Scots Guards Mercur by name went out last night and met some of the Germans who came out to meet him. He had a talk with them, and they said they hated the war and were told that Russia and France were both beat and it was only England keeping it going. When an officer came up they all stopped talking about their war and began about Christmas in the trenches and asked us not to snipe and they would not. They gave him some cigars and whisky. They also said they had 1 off[icer] and 20 killed in an attack of 18/19. On the left subsection Sergt. Reid Gordon Highlanders was out mending the parapet above the machine-gun, when he was shot through the thigh and had the bone broken. It was the only shot fired for about 2 hours.

*25th December.* We had Communion Service at 8 a.m. in a barn opposite my Headquarters and Abbot our parson came to breakfast afterwards. At 10 a.m. Heath my R.E. [Royal Engineers] officer came round and we went down to the trenches to see some work that had been done during the night. It [was] rather foggy and we could walk about in the open quite easily and the Germans are keeping their promise not to snipe. In my left subsection a German officer came out and was met by one of our officers. He wanted to arrange about burying our respected dead. When down at the trenches this morning

I could hear the Germans singing carols and very good voices they had. Have just heard from our trenches that we are out burying our dead: and that Taylor and Hanbury Tracey (Scots Guards) are dead and Askew (Border R). Some 70 to 80 Scots Guards have been buried. Nugent is wounded and a prisoner: I am afraid a very few prisoners were taken that night which means they are all dead, all those who are missing. I am afraid a lot of our men were killed by hand grenades, as some were blown to bits. Went down to the trenches at 4 p.m. just after General Rawly had been to see me, and met General Capper and we walked all down the Rue de Layes to find a solution to the flooding problem. General Capper thinks he has, but I have my doubts. The country is so flat there is not a fall of 2 feet anywhere. We were walking about everywhere as the Germans kept their promises about not sniping and so have we: I went over ground I would not have dared to under ordinary circumstances.

*26th December.* Bury and I went down to the trenches at 8.30 a.m. and got very wet in icy cold water getting in, but need not have done so as I found there was still a sort of armistice going on and the Germans were walking about their parapets, so we did the same and got a lot of useful work done which we could only have done otherwise under cover of darkness. Some of the Germans came half way across and gave our men tobacco. It really is an extraordinary war: shooting one day and afterwards shaking hands.

His diary continued in much the same way for several days. Thus on 29 December: 'The Germans were outside mending their parapets so we did and there was no sniping.' On 30th December: 'No sniping again and Germans and our men out working the parapets although there was quite heavy firing going on in front of the 8th Div. on our right.' On 31 December: 'Dined with the Gordon Highlanders and danced reels afterwards. The Germans fired at the incoming of the New Year, but up in the air, and we did the same.'

Remarkably or otherwise, the fact is that Brigadier General Heyworth took the truce in his stride, as did, in an important report on operations in his sector for the period 22–29 December, his divisional general, Major General Thompson Capper, who clearly saw the advantage of a time of relative calm for troops trying to improve their inadequate trenches – a courtesy, it should be noted, allowed to both sides:

Recently, I have purposely kept things rather quiet, as so much work has had to be done at close range from the enemy, that I could only carry it out by exercising a certain forbearance.

However, by 1 January it was clear Heyworth had had enough: 'Our artillery shelled the German trenches and did them a good deal of damage.' On the 3rd he reported an increase of hostility from the other side: 'Had lunch with Paynter [CO 2/Scots Guards]. After lunch we went down to the trenches and nearly got it from 5 German shells which fell about 10 yards from us. They were evidently shelling a working party which had just finished.' On the 6th: 'A lot of Germans showing and doing work on their parapet. I have ordered firing to start at 3 p.m. so that will stop all that'. On the 7th: 'We have started sniping again which makes the Germans keep under cover.'

So the 20th Brigade went back to war.

\* \* \*

There is a necessary codicil to this account of Christmas 1914. It would be some time before the news of the unusual festivities at the front reached the people of Britain, as it would do in a veritable spate of letters and newspaper reports, particularly in the first days of the New Year. Meanwhile, if there had been any truce intentional or otherwise over the skies of Britain it had now been broken. Records of air raids begin with a seaplane raid on Dover on 21 December with two bombs dropped; an aeroplane raid on Dover on 24 December with one bomb dropped; and a seaplane raid on Christmas Day in the area of the Thames estuary – more specifically, the plane flew over Sheerness towards London but was then chased away by three British aircraft – with two bombs dropped. There were no casualties. The British were swift to reply in kind. On Christmas Day the Navy mounted a raid with seven seaplanes on the north German seaport of Cuxhaven, ostensibly to bomb the Zeppelin sheds, though they found other targets as well. On the same day the Germans bombed Russian-held Warsaw. While the British press praised the Cuxhaven raid it treated the German feint towards London with scorn: 'If the much-vaunted air-raiding of England is to be no more formidable than the Christmas Day attempt on London, there is not much occasion for alarm.'

For countless officers and men that Christmas, however, there was little interest in happenings at the front, whether of a friendly or a hostile variety; rather their thoughts were of home and of the uncertain future. Lord Loch's seasonal thoughts from abroad must have been typical of many:

> Just one line on Christmas Day to wish you many happier Christmases than this. May we all be together next Xmas well, happy and peaceful is my constant prayer. You darling have far more to bear than any of us, and you bear all your trials so heroically that any but those who know you best would think you were well and happy. Oh darling, I do wish I could carry all your troubles for you but instead of that I only add to them. However, I hope our love for each other helps you as much as it does me. Whenever I am in the dumps I am always helped by the thought of you and how beloved you are to me. In fact without our love to strengthen us I feel as if I could not get on.

Six days later the year 1914 ended. One man for whom the next year would be a crucial one, for he would conclude it as British Commander-in-Chief, was Sir Douglas Haig. The general in the cocked hat who had caught the young Charles Carrington's eye at Aldershot back in June was well on his way to becoming Britain's most famous soldier of the First World War. His aide and confidant, Brigadier General John Charteris, as usual referring to his boss by his initials, wrote in his diary under the heading 'December 31/January 1, 1915':

> It is only 11 pm. I dined with D.H. and am just back. It was a very quiet dinner. Most of the talk was of what might happen in the New Year. No one likes to talk or even think of all the friends we might have lost in these last few months. Our speculation of the future led nowhere. D.H. summed it all up in a very telling phrase. 'We can hope, and we can wish, we cannot know. But what we must *do* is go forth to meet the future without fear.'

# Epilogue: Entering No Man's Land

It was a changed world that saw out the year 1914 and moved into what would become the second of five years to be dominated either wholly or in part by the so-called 'Great War'.

No previous wars, whether the Boer War or the colonial wars of the period 1880–1910, or, further back, the war with Napoleon, had had anything like the impact of the war that began in 1914.

The young able seaman at Antwerp who wrote, 'Englishmen at home read our papers over their eggs and bacon in the morning and probably say "how terrible" and forget about the war' was almost certainly wrong in his assumption. Even for those who had scarcely given a thought to issues beyond those affecting their own parish or region 'the war' soon became an ever-present reality. Newspapers were read voraciously as they had never been read in peacetime. The civilian diarist F. A. Robinson, who followed the war's progress avidly from August 1914 to November 1918, was dismayed when he heard that there would be no papers on Christmas Day: 'It creates an unpleasant feeling of apprehension to be cut off from the outside world even for a single day, and particularly in this case, when for months we have practically read nothing but the newspapers.'

Meanwhile, from the villages as well as the towns and cities young men en masse were leaving in their civilian clothes to come back sporting their uniform, readying themselves for the ordeal ahead. As the fighting intensified families became aware that the footsteps of the approaching postman might mean the arrival of an official envelope carrying the worst possible news. Telegrams were usually sent only in the case of the deaths of officers. For 'other ranks' the message from the War Office or the Admiralty expressing official regret that such and such a soldier had been killed in action or died of wounds almost always came with the letters, the postcards and the bills. Sometimes the envelopes had black borders, but generally there was no obvious indication that they were anything extraordinary. One Sussex butcher receiving a buff-coloured envelope put it to one side thinking it was a routine communication, to find when he eventually opened it that it contained a letter informing him of the death of his son.

Marching men under training, tramping past front doors or along the country lanes, sometimes in full voice – not always singing the cleanest of lyrics – were another reminder of the war, as were the countless tented camps appearing wherever a suitable area of terrain could be found, including deer parks and golf courses. From the war's first weeks Belgian refugees became a constant presence. By the end of the year 100,000 had been accommodated; by Michaelmas, Eton College had seven Belgian boys in residence, plus one Russian and one Serb. Scattered countrywide, they were a reminder that this was a war which included civilians as well as soldiers among its victims. Sometimes these two elements clashed, pathetically. Gordon Bartlett, a subaltern in the King's (Liverpool) Regiment, wrote to his father on 13 September from a hotel in Surbiton, Surrey: 'We have had 25 refugees in the hotel for a night. Poor folk we all feel very sorry for them. One little girl looked into the dining room and saw us in uniform. She cried out thinking we were German soldiers.'

If they were clearly Belgian, they were safe. If they could be taken for Germans or Austrians, or looked in any way European rather than British, they might be spies. 'Spymania' was rife. The animus against Prince Louis of Battenberg was not simply because he had been born a German; it fed on the widespread belief that he was a German spy. At one point in October it was rumoured that he had been imprisoned in the Tower of London, while another rumour had it that he had actually been shot. He made a joke of it, asking his friends, 'Didn't you know I was executed last week?' An actual spy who *was* executed in the Tower was Karl Hans Lody, a German reserve naval lieutenant who accepted the commission because of ill-health. Passing himself off as Charles A. Inglis, an American tourist, he was caught when his messages, sent via Stockholm, were intercepted by the Post Office. Court-martialled, he refused to say anything in his defence or plead for mercy, and at his own request was shot with his eyes unbandaged. In his own view, and that of some Britons who had met him, including Sir Basil Thomson of Scotland Yard, he was a patriot, but the British public had no such charity. F. A. Robinson commented: 'He no doubt thoroughly deserved his fate, and it is no time to show mercy to such miscreants.'

Lody himself uttered a text for the time: 'One smells a spy in every stranger.' The nation's obsession was shortly to be given a considerable boost by the publication of John Buchan's hugely successful novel *The Thirty-nine Steps*, written in 1914, in the nation's bookshops in 1915. In retrospect we see it as a rollicking yarn about the outwitting of a clutch of dastardly Germans. At the time it could seem a chilling, if also a thrilling, portent. Buchan went on to become arguably the most popular and prolific historian of the war, his Nelson's *History of the Great War*, written while hostilities were in progress, running to twenty-four volumes, this fact alone being strong proof of the war's grip on the public mind.

If spymania focused on the enemy within, fear of the enemy without had been given an immense surge before the year's end by the seaborne attacks on the east coast. Visitations from the air had only just begun, but although such raids as had been attempted had been met with derision a significant marker had been put down for the future. The first Zeppelin raid took place on 19–20 January 1915, the target being the already previously attacked Great Yarmouth; this time twenty-three bombs were dropped, and four people were killed and sixteen injured. In fact 1915 would see twenty Zeppelin raids, on places as far apart as Tyneside and Southend, Grimsby and Dover. London would suffer four attacks. There would be more, and much worse, to come.

If air power as a means of delivering terror was in its infancy in 1914, it was also becoming a serious instrument of warfare in, or over, the battlefield. Both these functions would develop remarkably as the war continued. Lieutenant W. R. Read, who began the war as a member of a Royal Flying Corps with sixty-three aircraft, ended it as a member of a Royal Air Force with 22,171 aircraft, while instead of 860 officers and men there were 291,175. Read himself, by 1918 a major in command of a bomber squadron, was only stopped by the cessation of hostilities from leading what would have been a morale-boosting RAF 'first', a bombing raid on Berlin.

Sea warfare would also be greatly changed because of the experience of 1914. 'Submarinitis' was almost a joke, if a bad one, in the early months of the war among the officers and men of the Grand

Fleet. Yet the time would come when German U-boats would seem to be on the verge of bringing Britain to her knees, her shipping losses in 1917 being such that Admiral Jellicoe, by this time First Sea Lord, came to believe that the war would be lost. The reintroduction of the concept of convoy, frequently used in the days of sail, played a key part in solving the problem. During this crisis the great ships contributed very little, spending most of their time 'swinging round the buoy' in Scapa Flow or the Moray Firth.

As for the war in the field, 1914 was a year that left a whole range of legacies.

One subject that has already been introduced is the matter of 'shell-shock'. The main reason why the military authorities bore down so heavily on those who failed in their duty or showed lack of moral fibre was that before 1914 the idea that involvement in war could have a destabilizing impact on soldiers' mental condition did not exist. There was courage, and there was cowardice, and not much in between. 'Shell-shock' was not part of the vocabulary of warfare. Yet it is important to add that its discovery, though it could have benign consequences and opened new vistas in terms of understanding the many territories of the human mind, was itself a two-edged sword. Thus the Australian medical historian, A. G. Butler, himself a doctor on the Western Front, asserted that 'the idea and the name of "shell-shock", though propounded in good faith as a helpful medical hypothesis, [became] through military and social exploitation and mass suggestion – a devastating menace'. His statement highlights the dilemma that arose the moment 'shell-shock' became part of the military equation: never better put than by an American general who stated in 1944: 'We don't want any damned psychiatrists making our boys sick.' The conflict between those seen as soft on trauma and those dismissive of it continues to this day.

What was so different about this war as compared with earlier ones? Why did it produce a reaction that seems not to have occurred, or was not recognized, during previous conflicts, many of them fought with the utmost ferocity? The answer would seem to be: industrialization. The machine had become more important than the man. That is why in this story the Battle of the Aisne is so crucial. In that month-long struggle in the valley of the Aisne a radically new style of warfare came into existence. It was here, as so many recognized, as the not always far-sighted Field Marshal Sir John French himself recognized, that the rules were changed. In stating that in the campaigns to come 'the spade will be as great a necessity as the rifle' (see page 140), the British Commander-in-Chief was not simplistically promoting the concept of the trench. He was saying that the guns now dominating the scene were so powerful that the only response was to get out of their way. In essence he was anticipating the fears that led to the massbuilding of air-raid shelters across the land in the late 1930s. Significantly, trenches at this stage were not carefully constructed emplacements out of a military textbook; they were, as many officers and men admitted (see pages 140–2), little more than rabbit-holes to hide in.

The disparity in artillery power between the two sides made it clear that this was no longer an equal duel. Out went military glory, in came the guns; it was as if the shape of things to come had already arrived. It would be many months before the soft caps worn in 1914 were replaced by the steel helmets – the so-called 'tin hats' – with which we are so familiar from the wartime newsreels and photographs; but the new headgear was inevitable, even if it took an unconscionably long time to become established. The poet–soldier Edmund Blunden saw the significance of the change and defined it thus: 'The dethronement of the soft cap clearly symbolized the change that was coming over the war, the induration from a personal crusade into a vast machine of violence.' Similarly, Siegfried Sassoon could remark on returning from leave that he was 'in the machine again'. From the enemy side there is the potent statement of Germany's most honoured Western Front soldier, Ernst Jünger, who wrote in his book *Copse 125*, 'The time will come when the single unprotected rifleman will be ground between the millstones of machinery ... It is a question no longer of launching men in mass, but machines.'

Thus, curious as it might seem, in regard to shell-shock, the areas of experience that gave the new mind-doctors a suitable point of departure were not recent wars, but, for example, railway accidents: the failures of the machine age, the dark side of the new industrialization. It was the previous century's and pre-war's horrific railroad collisions which – to quote an authority on 'traumatic neurosis' speaking in 1913 – 'created a lurid mental picture in the injured, and indirectly affected the general public in such a way as to prepare a fertile soil for nervous disturbance'. Badly maimed or severely shocked survivors dragged from the wreck of a crashed railway train were the best available comparison for those coping with men similarly affected who were sent back to base after breaking down in battle or under bombardment. By a curious twist, our own generation's disasters, on the airways and the motorways rather more than the railways (though they continue to have their rare but deeply disturbing moments of horror), can, in their turn, arguably assist our own awareness of the traumas of the trenches.

Another indication of the key role of industrialization is the statistic that in the Boer War, of the 22,000 British deaths 16,000 were the result of disease: in the First World War technology was the supreme killer. Above all artillery was the master of the battlefield. And (though it should not be forgotten that there were numerous quiet areas and numerous quiet times) between battles sporadic gun and sniper fire could produce the chilling conundrum that though nothing happened, men died.

Another legacy virtually unnoticed at the time was poison gas. In October 1914 at Neuve-Chapelle, an area that would shortly be taken over by the British, the Germans had tried the experiment of firing shrapnel shells in which small irritant gas canisters had been inserted. It had no effect on the French troops opposite, but this was the start of a long process that would in time raise the whole question of weapons of mass destruction in war. There was a more ambitious experiment on the Eastern Front in January 1915, but it too had no impact as the gas used (tear gas) froze in the cold weather. They did not try again on the Western Front until the following April, on the first day of the Second Battle of Ypres, when poison gas created panic, produced angry headlines and fouled not only the air of the Ypres Salient but the whole atmosphere of the conflict. This, plus the sinking of the *Lusitania* in May, would end much of the goodwill and camaraderie that had led to the Christmas Truce. It was following the introduction of poison gas that instances, if rare ones, of the killing of prisoners began to occur and at Christmas 1915 there was only a pale imitation of the fraternization of one year earlier.

A further key legacy of 1914 that must be mentioned, not only for its significance but also because it is so often overlooked even by serious students of the Western Front war, is that the year bequeathed to the Allies in France and Flanders the obligation to liberate territories that had passed into enemy hands. For the French, who had forfeited ten (of ninety) departments and much of their heavy industry, plus the most important city of northern France, Lille, this was a paramount task. Beyond the German trench lines were countless of their fellow countrymen desperately clamouring for release and their cry could not go unheard. That this was evident to the British at the time is clear from an eloquent letter by a British Cavalry officer, Captain E. W. S. Balfour, Adjutant of the 5th Dragoon Guards, who sensed the fury his Allies felt at the shaming loss of so much of their *mère patrie*, their mother country.

Writing to his family on 3 December he stated:

> To the French it is their own home and it makes them mad. We somehow fight on with no increased animosity. If we were ordered to retire again tomorrow, I don't believe we should lose morale. The French really are giving everything and it makes one wonder if people in England realize what the advance of an invading army over a country means.

The same was true of the Belgians, left with little more than a foothold in their homeland. By the fact of taking part, by sending her forces across the English Channel to join the French and Belgians in the field, the British automatically signed up to a contract which bound her to her Allies. This would mean that, for the rest of the war, the British would have to do all they could not just to help defeat the Germans in battle, but to assist in expelling them forcibly from territories not their own. They would not therefore, for example, following the disastrous opening of the Somme campaign in 1916, be able to put down their weapons, denounce the war as senseless and withdraw their forces (a concept seriously if absurdly promoted by some of the angriest critics of British generalship and competence). Apart from the matter of their own determination and pride, they had to continue fighting for the sake of their friends. No one criticizes the decision to launch the D-Day landings of June 1944, of which the prime aim was precisely the same as that of thirty years earlier: to liberate territories under the German heel. Essentially the task facing Britain at the end of 1914 was virtually identical with that facing her in 1940: to assist in the restoration of freedom and hope to a badly wounded continent. That task became hers from the moment the fighting ceased at the end of the First Battle of Ypres, leaving so much and so many in enemy hands.

The argument that the condition of the occupied territories was not as bad in the First World War as it was in the Second does not hold water. Admittedly, the ethos and aims of the Third Reich were far more sinister than those of Imperial Germany, but in both cases there was serious mistreatment of the local population. Some 100,000 Frenchmen and as many as 120,000 Belgians were sent to Germany for forced labour. French civilians of both sexes were deported from the cities of Lille, Roubaix and Tourcoing to other parts of German-occupied France. Belgium was effectively de-industrialized, with the Germans either transferring plant to the Fatherland or destroying it. Starvation was used as a weapon to force the Belgians to work for the invaders. As the French historian Annette Becker has observed: 'In occupied territory, war is total war.' Futility is a word much bandied about in relation to the 1914–18 war, but it was surely not futile to strive to release those kept captive in such destructive and demeaning circumstances.

* * *

Where did the events of 1914 leave Germany, with the aims with which her forces had first marched clearly unfulfilled, and her war plans, in spite of enormous efforts and massive losses, a conspicuous failure? This is how Captain Sir Morgan Crofton, 2nd Life Guards, 7th Cavalry Brigade, 3rd Cavalry Division, who arrived at the front in early November, assessed the situation in a diary entry he wrote on 8 December 1914. He was an unusual soldier in that he was also a military historian, one subject on which he had become an expert being the Battle of Waterloo. He accepted that Germany was striving to retain the territory she had occupied 'on the Bismarckian plan of *beati possidentes*' (meaning that what she had seized she intended to hold, on the principle that possession is nine-tenths of the law), but he saw her position overall as a negative one. Effectively, he believed, she had lost the plot, and therefore would lose the war:

It is quite clear now that Germany has been reduced to the strategic defensive.

The entire plan of campaign, of which time was a vital element, was shattered when the retreat to the Aisne began. In spite of immense efforts the initial failure has not only not been redeemed, but the German strategists, once their carefully elaborated scheme for crushing France was foiled, showed loss of military judgement and indecision. The master von Moltke [i.e the Moltke of 1870, not the failed one of 1914] would in this case have seen that it would have been easier to retire to the Rhine, and throw every available man into the Eastern theatre.

Instead of doing this, obsessed by the idea of reaching Calais, the German Staff expended the equivalent of more than five Army Corps, without any result except inflicting wholly disproportionate loss upon the Allies who are now stronger in numbers, positions and artillery than when the fighting in Flanders began.

The prestige of the German Army of 1870 has departed, never to return in this campaign. The economic pressure is becoming steadily more acute and after four months, the relative naval strength of Great Britain remains unimpaired.

But were the armies of the Allies, in particular the British Army, in a position to take advantage of this situation? How did it see itself after five months of war?

Some of the most thoughtful among Britain's surviving regular officers saw that the culling of the first divisions had been so extensive that it was inevitable that a new style of army would have to be brought into existence, which would have to be met not with suspicion or contempt, but be accepted, welcomed and given every support. Otherwise the cause would be lost. Captain E. W. S. Balfour of the 5th Dragoon Guards, quoted above, put the point forcibly in his letter of 3 December:

> There is not much left of the old Army and the new Campaign is going to be fought and won by a great half-trained National Army – where you've got to take what you can get and not laugh at people for being a certain class or making fools of themselves. But if the old Army is going to be worth its salt and remain the backbone of the show, it's got without jealousy and in humbleness to allow itself to be absorbed into a less efficient whole, and have amateurs put over them and see daily laughable mistakes and old lessons relearned in bitterness and go on helping without superior bearing.

Anyone who doesn't recognize the above is not either rising to the occasion or anything but a self-satisfied self-seeker. We've all got to simply sacrifice anything for an *esprit d'armée*. The end of the war will depend on it.

Change might be inevitable, but the time was not yet ripe to write off the divisions so heavily depleted by their valiant efforts in 1914. Look forward, yes, but also look back with pride. Hence this comment by the ever-eloquent intelligence officer, Captain Edgar Cox, writing on 18 January, 1915:

Kitchener says that his army, when it takes the field, in the spring, will be the finest in Europe. I daresay it will be but I do hope the splendid fellows who have been sacrificed ever since the first days at Mons in the struggle to keep the Germans off until we had time to train an army of decent size and build all the big guns, trench mortars and other equipment which the Germans had from the beginning, will not be forgotten. It makes me mad to remember how people at home used to sneer at the German menace and used to argue that the whole idea was fantastic as Germany would gain nothing by it, and hadn't Norman Angell proved that war was impossible. One felt the absurdity of it but did not realize that it would mean the loss of thousands of lives during the months it has taken to produce the men and material that the soldiers knew would be required.

Praise for the first divisions of 1914 from an NCO who was one of them might seem almost like self-congratulation, but this was not the aim of Lance Sergeant Frank Pusey. A gunner in the Royal Field Artillery, he felt that the real success had been achieved by those more closely and sacrificially involved than he had been in the heat and strain of action:

I think it is only right that I, as an artilleryman, should pay tribute to our wonderful Cavalry and Infantry, who by their heroic action, saved the Channel ports from capture. The loss of these would have altered the whole aspect of the War and would have resulted in the invasion of England. An 'Old Contemptible' who took part in the first Battle of Ypres can be justly proud of the fact.

Pusey's is an instructive case in that before 1915 was out this enthusiastic young soldier, who seems to bear the natural hallmark of a first-rate 'other rank', would move up in the social scale:

In June much to my surprise and complete satisfaction I was informed by my Commanding Officer that I had been recommended for a commission as a Second Lieutenant. A wonderful opportunity as I had less than seven years' service. With the growth of the new Army many Officers and NCOs were sent back to England and these included many promoted NCOs. I was commissioned in July and left in August with instructions to report to the War Office with orders as to my posting. I received notification to join the training depot at Weedon, Northamptonshire, where I soon settled down to my new appointment which was the training of men of the New Army and I found them excellent fellows. I was given a Batman/Groom – a London van driver named Harrison.

Yet, the survivors of the terrible culling of 1914 would hold to their own pride and their own codes. They were, in the rapidly expanding Army of the war's later years, a race apart, and they would express that in a number of ways, not least in the use of language – always a defining matter in areas where class and background played an important part. Let one small example suffice. On 1 January 1915 Captain Ralph Blewitt wrote in a letter to two of his lady friends in England: 'N.B. both of you. The best people don't talk of "shells" but "shell", one shell, two shell, thirty shell, etc.' 'Small point,' he added, but clearly in its way an important one. The world might have changed, but certain distinctions and differences had not. The use of a much-used term in an uninformed plural would clearly mark a man as being not 'one of us'.

* * *

How did those most closely engaged in the high strategy and the politics of the war react as 1914 ended and 1915 began?

Sir Horace Smith-Dorrien did not survive the year, being sent home in May. Nor did Sir John French survive as Commander-in-Chief. In December he was succeeded by Sir Douglas Haig, who would retain that position, if at times precariously, until the Armistice. Haig's views and attitudes are therefore the most significant in this context, and there was no doubt where he stood. Throughout the war Haig's thoughts would be solely concentrated on the Western Front. In March 1915 he stated, and never shifted from the affirmation: 'We cannot hope to win until we have defeated the German Army'; and this for him was not the German Army elsewhere in Europe, it was the German Army in France and Belgium.

Elsewhere, however, alternative strategies were stirring, not least in the minds of, among others, Winston Churchill, who on New Year's Day 1915 sent Prime Minister Asquith a memorandum which included the famous sentence: 'Are there not other alternatives than sending our men to chew barbed wire in Flanders?' No decisive result was likely to be achieved here, he asserted, although, as he added in a slightly bitter throwaway: 'no doubt several hundred thousand men will be spent to satisfy the military mind on the point'.

Another politician voicing similar views, if less dramatically expressed, was that of Arthur Balfour, founder in 1904 of the Committee of Imperial Defence and, although a Conservative, a regular member of Asquith's War Council (if best known for his Declaration of November 1917 regarding the founding of a Jewish state in Palestine). Responding to what became known as the 'Boxing Day Memorandum' on general policy from the Secretary to the War Council, Colonel Maurice Hankey, Balfour wrote on 2 January 1915:

> I agree, and I fear that everybody must agree, that the notion of driving the Germans back from the west of Belgium to the Rhine by successively assaulting and capturing one line of trenches after another seems a very hopeless affair; and unless some means can be found for breaking their line at some critical point, and threatening their communications, I am unable to see how the deadlock in the west is to be brought to any rapid or satisfactory conclusion . . . Put the matter . . . as we like, no dramatic *dénouement* of the present situation seems to be in sight.

The result of such conclusions, widely shared, was a whole range of ideas almost all of which began with good intentions and ended by being unacceptable or even absurd.

Pushing Churchill into some kind of immediate aggressive action was the newly appointed First Sea Lord, Admiral Sir John Arbuthnot ('Jacky') Fisher. A believer in the precept that 'moderation in war is imbecility', and a great admirer of Lord Nelson, Fisher had coined the verb 'to Copenhagen', out of veneration for Nelson's masterly strike against the Danish fleet, anchored off the Danish capital, in 1801. He was a man of outspoken opinions and forensic conversation. Indeed, in the last days before the war, after lunching 'tête à tête' with Churchill and having 'a momentous tête à tête' with Balfour, he 'got so violently hot from gesticulatory athletics' that on coming home late 'I got a bad chill and a severe attack of Pleurisy'. The quotations are from a letter written in August in which he had written, with angry underlinings: 'Had I been First Sea Lord I should have shot two British Admirals, (not à la Byng as I think a Court Martial is a tedious and dirty evasion of responsibility!)'; and in which he derided as 'Gobe-Mouches' – a term borrowed from the French meaning gullible imbeciles – those in the Navy

> who saw in every German Tramp(steamer) guns and powder and trained gunners who would sweep British Commerce off the sea. Not a German merchant ship is on any Ocean – and German Cruisers are fleeing for their lives and ought to be at the bottom of the sea but for two British Admirals who being Court Sycophants got employed – **D--n 'em**! (I suppose the hereditary 'snob' in Winston overcame him – a taint of Marlborough!)

Now he and Churchill were in harness, the latter's snobbery, in so far as it existed, had been forgotten, while into their energetic 'tête à tête' discussions Fisher was injecting some of his characteristically wild ideas. He had long harboured the notion of a direct joint-service pre-emptive strike against the German High Seas Fleet. (Indeed, he had held it for so long that the royal personage who reacted to it by saying, 'My God, Fisher, you must be mad,' was not George V, but Edward VII, who had died in 1910.) As a naval man through and through, to Fisher Britain's small professional Army was no more than a projectile to be fired at the enemy by the Royal Navy. His dream had been that the first stage of the inevitable Anglo-German war would include the headlong landing of an army, like a bolt from the blue, on Germany's northern coast. His belief was simply put: 'The coast of the enemy is Britain's frontier.' Now he raised his pet project again. For a short while Fisher and Churchill were so taken with the idea that they called into existence an armada of landing ships and warships for this express purpose, including three massive vessels with large guns and shallow draft, *Furious, Courageous* and *Glorious*, which were promptly nicknamed by the Navy *Spurious, Outrageous* and *Uproarious*. Perhaps not for the first time naval wit anticipated strategic reality: this was an idea that from the start was dead in the water.

Other ideas that surfaced at this time were: landing troops in Montenegro to add strength to the southern menace to Austria; a bid to persuade the Balkan States to make a combined attack on Turkey; and – the one seen to have the best prospects – an attempt to find an answer to what Balfour called 'the menacing question of Constantinople. Who is to own it? And what is to be the international position of the Bosphorus?'

The next name to appear in Balfour's litany of possibilities was that of 'the Dardanelles', the straits which gave access to the Bosporus and the Black Sea, and which would have to be secured by Allied naval forces if Constantinople were to be seriously threatened. By January 1915 Churchill was enthusiastically favouring the Dardanelles over the Baltic project and at first taking Fisher with him. But the consequence of this bold idea would be a skein of disasters. A fall-out between Fisher and Churchill would thrust the former out of office for good. The Navy's failure to force its way through the Dardanelles and into the Bosporus would lead to the ill-fated attempt to secure control of the region by invading the adjacent peninsula of Gallipoli. Much of 1915 and the first weeks of 1916 would be spent in discovering that this was a brutal and sacrificial campaign with no realistic future.

It ended in a humiliating, if expertly managed, evacuation and in the disgrace, if a temporary one, of its principal advocate, Churchill, who before the year was out was serving as a soldier on the Western Front. From 2 January to 3 May 1916 the former First Lord and future war leader took on the identity of Lieutenant Colonel W. L. S. Churchill, commanding officer of the 6th Battalion of the Royal Scots Fusiliers. Much of his time was spent at Ploegsteert, where Lieutenant the Hon. Lionel Tennyson had witnessed such horrific fighting in November 1914 and where Christmas had been cheerfully celebrated with the enemy just a few weeks later. It is perhaps fortunate for posterity that by 1916 Ploegsteert had acquired its long-lasting reputation of being a relatively quiet, 'cushy' sector.

So the focus came back to the land war – indeed, for those who called themselves 'Westerners' as opposed to pro-Gallipoli and other such far-flung schemes who became known as 'Easterners', it had never been away. Increasingly for the British their attention was on 'the trenches' – effectively the stadium in which so much of the war's fighting took place and which have become central to the folk memory of the war. Hindsight has demonized the trenches as labyrinths of horror, leaving later generations amazed that men could accept living in them without deserting en masse or going mad. It says much for the stoicism of the soldiers who manned them that what from today's vantage point seems insupportable and beyond endurance all too soon became the accepted norm. Initially rudimentary and basic, over time they were improved and added to and consolidated so that there came into being what one might fairly describe as a kind of 'trench world' – a special zone of its own, sophisticated, complex: and, of course, multiplied by two, with the Germans replicating on their side what the Allies were doing on theirs. In fact, even more so – because there was a crucial difference in the mindset of the Germans as opposed to the French and British. The Allies saw their trenches as temporary habitations only; they wanted to leave them as soon as possible and advance into the territory the enemy had occupied since 1914 and send them back to whence they had come. By contrast, the Germans were content to stay where they were unless forced to do otherwise, so therefore they aimed to build deep and well, defying the Allies to remove them. And this situation would continue for many long weary months, almost conveying the feeling that the war would go on for ever.

* * *

Meanwhile, the soldiers manning those trenches would be learning new martial skills, and, inevitably, a new vocabulary. Second Lieutenant Lionel Tennyson, as early as the stalemate on the Aisne, had noted the arrival of such concepts as the night patrol, the trench raid and the communication trench.

By the end of the year a new phrase was coming into use, which had been around for centuries in ordinary parlance, but, remarkably, had not been employed in a military context: 'No Man's Land'.

Researchers will look in vain for this phrase in early writings from the Western Front in 1914. It is not included in any of the contemporary descriptions of the Christmas Truce quoted in this book. Most accounts refer to soldiers meeting between the lines, or in the space between the trenches. A handful of witnesses do include the term, understandably, because it was just beginning to be accepted, though it had not become standard usage.

In fact its first known use in time of war has already been quoted in these pages, in the syndicated despatch by Colonel Ernest Swinton that appeared in *The Times* on Boxing Day, the keynote paragraph of which is included in the previous chapter. Offering a vivid description of the British sector of the Western Front as observed in the week before Christmas, the paragraph began as follows:

> Seamed with dug-outs, burrows, trenches, and excavations of every kind, and fitted [sic] with craters, it is bounded on the front by a long discontinuous irregular line fringed with barbed wire and broken by saps wriggling still more to the front. This is the Ultima Thule. Beyond, of width varying according to the nature of the fighting and of the ground, is *neutral territory, the no-man's-land between the hostile forces*. . . . [my italics]

Had it been a familiar concept, Swinton would surely not have needed to precede it by a deftly planted explanation. In fact, he had had the phrase ready and waiting since 1908, when he used it in a story called 'The Point of View' (one of his numerous military parables) in which he attempted to anticipate the kind of warfare that could well become the norm if there were a major conflict using the new deadly weapons of the burgeoning international arms industry. In it he included a vision of a future battlefield that would be seen in time as an uncanny prediction of the world of the Western Front from late 1914 onwards:

> As soon as the light faded altogether from the sky, the yellow flames of different conflagrations glowed more crimson, and the great white eyes of the searchlights shone forth, their wandering beams lighting up now this, now that horror. Here and there in that wilderness of dead bodies – *the dreadful 'No-Man's-Land' between the opposing lines* – deserted guns showed up singly or in groups, glistening in the full glare of the beam or silhouetted in black against a ray passing behind. . . .' [my italics]

His despatch of December 1914 was virtually a cut-and-paste from his story of six years earlier.

Should there be any question about this attribution, there is the modest affirmation of Swinton himself, who in a footnote to his book *Eyewitness*, published in 1933, stated: 'To the best of my knowledge this term, which became part of the English language during the war, was first used by myself in a story called *The Point of View*, to describe this neutral zone between two opposing trench-lines.'

Swinton's invention was soon sufficiently in the air for the British press to offer it to its readers as a new state-of-the-art coinage from the front. Thus on 5 January 1915 the *Daily Sketch* printed two contrasting photographs, one of British and the other of German trenches; the accompanying caption explained this, adding, 'The ground between them is known as No-Man's-Land.'

Subsequently the Germans and the French took over the phrase. In fact, the French followed Swinton's example almost exactly; having initially used the term *'la terre neutre'* – neutral ground – before long they switched to *'le nomansland'*. The Germans to begin with used the term *'Vorfeld'* – the ground in front – but later they too adopted the term, their version being *'Der Niemandsland'*. In both cases these were clearly straight lifts from the English original.

Looking back from almost a century later, it can be argued that 'No Man's Land' was more than just a new concept or catchphrase. The term can almost be seen as a metaphor for the whole conflict, which from the beginning of 1915 took the world into unknown regions from which it would never return, making it impossible for the beliefs and assumptions that pertained at the beginning of August 1914 ever to be re-established. The concept was not required during the first hectic weeks, nor did the first taste of siege warfare on the Aisne continue long enough for it to become necessary. Only with sustained entrenchment, with the beginning of what almost inevitably became an inhumane war of brutality and attrition, and with the shattering of so many of the illusions with which, on all sides, the war began, did its moment come.

No Man's Land was the territory the world entered as that amazing year 1914 drew to its end. We have been in No Man's Land ever since.

# Roll of Honour

Officers and men quoted or referred to in this book who lost their lives in the 1914–1918 war; ranks, names, date and cause of death, and place of burial or commemoration as in the records of the Commonwealth War Graves Commission.

**Lieutenant Rowland Auriol James Beech**, 16th (The Queen's) Lancers; died of wounds on 21 February 1915, aged 26; buried in Ypres Town Cemetery, Belgium.

**Sub Lieutenant Rupert Chawner Brooke**, Hood Battalion (Royal Naval Division); died from acute blood poisoning on 23 April 1915, aged 27; buried in an isolated grave on the island of Skyros, Greece.

**Captain (later Brigadier General) Edgar William Cox DSO**, Intelligence Corps; died from drowning on 26 August 1918, aged 36; buried in Etaples Military Cemetery, France.

**Second Lieutenant (later Captain) Geoffrey Boles Donaldson**, 7th Battalion, Royal Warwickshire Regiment; died of wounds on 19 July 1916; listed on the Ploegsteert Memorial, Belgium.

**Brigadier General Frederick James Heyworth CB DSO**, Officer Commanding 20th Brigade (7th Division), died of wounds on 8 May 1916; buried in Brandhoek Military Cemetery, Belgium.

**Lieutenant (later Captain) Sir Edward Hulse**, 2nd Battalion, Scots Guards, killed in action, 10 March 1915; buried in Rue David Cemetery, near Armentières, France.

**Private Theophilus Jones**, 18th Battalion, Durham Light Infantry; died on 16 December 1914, aged 27; buried in Hartlepool (Hart Road) New Cemetery, Hartlepool, County Durham.

**Second Lieutenant Geoffrey Archibald Loyd**, 2nd Battalion, Scots Guards; died of wounds on 13 November 1914, aged 24; buried in Poperinge Communal Cemetery, Belgium.

**Lieutenant Angus Macnaghten**, 1st Battalion, Black Watch; reported missing presumed killed on 29 October 1914, listed on the Ypres (Menin Gate) Memorial, Belgium.

**Captain W. G. Morritt**, 1st Battalion, East Surrey Regiment; died in captivity on 27 June 1917, aged 24; buried in Hamburg Cemetery, Germany.

**Captain the Honourable William Andrew Nugent**, 15th (The King's) Hussars, 2nd Divisional Cavalry; died of wounds on 29 May 1915; buried in Kensal Green (St Mary's) Roman Catholic Cemetery, London.

**Lieutenant Rowland Hely Owen**, 3rd Battalion, Duke of Wellington's (West Riding) Regiment; died of wounds on 18 April 1915, aged 22; listed on the Ypres (Menin Gate) Memorial, Belgium.

**Captain Charles James Paterson**, 1st Battalion, South Wales Borderers; died of wounds on 1 November 1914, aged 26; buried in Ypres Town Cemetery, Belgium.

**Second Lieutenant Reginald Herbert Secretan**, Hertfordshire Regiment; died of wounds on 31 July 1917, aged 22; listed on Ypres (Menin Gate) Memorial.

**Private Jesse Sheldon**, 7th Battalion, North Staffordshire Regiment; died on 29 October 1918, aged 38; buried in Stoke-on-Trent (Burslem) Cemetery, Staffordshire, on 11 November 1918.

**Second Lieutenant Robert Ernest Vernède**, 3rd Battalion and later 5th (attached 12th) Battalion, Rifle Brigade; died of wounds on 9 April 1917, aged 41; buried in Lebucquière Communal Cemetery Extension, France.

# Glossary and Definitions

*See also Historical Note, page xiii.*

Adjutant – usually a captain, staff officer to the commanding officer of a battalion, or equivalent

BEF – British Expeditionary Force

Blighty – England, home and beauty; Britain

C-in-C – Commander-in-Chief

CMG – Companion of the Order of St Michael and St George

CO – commanding officer, properly used for commanding officers of battalions or their equivalents; see also GOC and OC

DCM – Distinguished Conduct Medal

DSO – Distinguished Service Order

GHQ – general headquarters

GOC – general officer commanding (the commander of a brigade, division, corps or army)

IEF – Indian Army Expeditionary Force

Jack Johnson – German heavy shell, named after a famous black heavyweight boxer

MC – Military Cross

MM – Military Medal

MO – Medical Officer

NCO – non-commissioned officer

OC – officer commanding (properly used for officers commanding companies and platoons or their equivalent)

OR – other ranks: private soldiers and NCOs, as distinct from officers

RAMC – Royal Army Medical Corps

RE – Royal Engineers

register – to adjust artillery fire on to a target

RFA – Royal Field Artillery

RGA – Royal Garrison Artillery

RHA – Royal Horse Artillery

RSM – regimental sergeant major

SAA – small-arms ammunition

subaltern – general term for officers under the rank of captain

TF – Territorial Force: Britain's part-time home defence force, often known as 'Saturday Afternoon Soldiers'

VC – Victoria Cross

Yeomanry – a volunteer cavalry force originally mobilized during the wars of the French Revolution, by 1914 the cavalry element of the Territorial Force

## Ranks of an infantry battalion in ascending order

Other Ranks: Private, Lance Corporal, Corporal, Sergeant, Sergeant Major

Officers: Second Lieutenant (in command of a section), Lieutenant (in command of a platoon), Captain (in command of a company), Major (second-in-command), Lieutenant Colonel (commanding officer)

A Brigadier General was in command of a brigade (usually four battalions); a Major General was in command of a division (usually three brigades); a Lieutenant General was in charge of a Corps (two divisions in 1914, usually three divisions later); a General was in command of an Army. From 26 December 1914, First Army consisted of I Corps, IV Corps and the Indian Corps; Second Army consisted of II Corps, III Corps and a newly arrived division, the 27th. The rank of the officer in command of the whole expeditionary force was Field Marshal.

# Notes and References

For publication details of books referred to see the Bibliography. Participants or witnesses quoted whose collections are held in the Imperial War Museum's Department of Documents (abbreviated here as 'IWM Docs') are listed at the end of the entries for each chapter; for full details see the Index of Contributors.

## Prologue

*page*

xix     Wyndham Lewis quotation, *Blasting and Bombardiering*, page 1.

xx     A recent anthology: *Letters from Two World Wars*, edited by Ernest Sanger, 1993.

xxi–xxii     The Kaiser's 'contemptible' speech: for discussion as to its possible British origin, see Arthur Ponsonby, *Falsehood in Wartime*, pp. 84–7. It is perhaps noteworthy that the *Oxford Book of Modern Quotations* quotes from the speech not under the name of Kaiser Wilhelm but in its Anonymous section.

xxvi     Poem by Thomas Hardy 'Men Who March Away': significantly this poem provided the title for an important, much-reprinted anthology of First World War poetry published by Chatto and Windus in 1965.

IWM Docs: Major Herbert Trevor.

## Before the Fall

*page*

1     Material on Trooping the Colour, 1914: Dennis Judd, *The Life and Times of George V*, p. 92 and passim; Michael Gow, *Trooping the Colour*, pp. 46–7.

2     Comment on the Aldershot parade of 22 June 1914 by the Duke of Windsor, from *A King's Story, The Memoirs of H.R.H. The Duke of Windsor, K.G.*, p. 103; by Charles Carrington, from *Soldier from the Wars Returning*, pp. 53–4.

3  Kitchener material: Peter Simkins, *Kitchener's Army: The Raising of the New Armies, 1914–1916*, p. 35.

3  Churchill's description of Kiel Yachting Week: Winston S. Churchill, *The World Crisis*, Volume 1, *1911–1914*, p. 187.

5–6  Differing views on pre-war Britain: Osbert Sitwell, *Great Morning*, pp. 229–30; Barbara Tuchman, *The Proud Tower*, pp. xiii–xiv.

6–7  Evidence on popularity of pre-war anti-German literature in Britain: Michael Paterson, *Britain's Fear of German Imperial Rivalry, as reflected in popular literature and invasion scare novels, 1903–1914*; unpublished thesis, Birkbeck College, 1992.

7  Pro-war attitudes of General Friedrich von Bernhardi: Barbara Tuchman, *The Guns of August*, p. 22.

8–9  Quotations by A. E. Housman: from *A Shropshire Lad*, first published 1896.

## When the Lights Went Out

*page*

11–12  Examples of people remembering where they were when they heard of the assassination of Archduke Franz Ferdinand: R. J. W. Evans and Hartmut Pogge von Strandmann, *The Coming of the First World War*, pp. 41–2.

13  Reaction in London to the assassination: Keith Robbins, *Sir Edward Grey: A Biography of Lord Grey of Fallodon*, pp. 285–6.

15  Germany's decision to go for war in 1914: R. J. W. Evans and Hartmut Pogge von Strandmann, *The Coming of the First World War*, pp. 118–20. See also Peter Padfield, *The Great Naval Race: Anglo-German Naval Rivalry 1900–1914*, Preface to revised edition, 2004.

15–16  Countdown to war: John Terraine, *The First World War*, pp. 10–12; 'Chiffon de papier' quotation (normally translated as 'a scrap of paper'): Niall Ferguson, *The Pity of War*, pp. 182–3.

17  The changing reactions of the historian G. M. Trevelyan; pro-German letter in *The Times*, 1 August; comment by E. C. Powell on London on 3 August (from a memoir held by the IWM Department of Documents): all references from Niall Ferguson, *The Pity of War*, p. 176ff.

17  Quotations from the *Hampstead Record* and the *South London Observer*: from Adrian Gregory, 'British "War Enthusiasm" in 1914: A Reassessment', in *Historians and the Impact of 1914*.

17 German reservists, hurrying home to the Fatherland on 3 August: Malcolm Brown and Shirley Seaton, *Christmas Truce*, p. 4.

19 Comments by Asquith and Grey: from *Champion Redoubtable: The Diaries and Letters of Violet Bonham Carter 1914–1945*, p. 5.

19 Neville Chamberlain quotation: Niall Ferguson, *The Pity of War*, p. 165.

20 Extract from *The Autobiography of Margot Asquith*, Penguin Books edition, Volume II, pp. 144–5.

20 The Admiralty's war telegram to Royal Navy: Churchill, *The World Crisis*, Volume I, *1911–1914*, p. 229.

21 Sir Edward Grey statement; from *The Oxford Book of Modern Quotations*; comment by Captain J. L. Jack: *General Jack's Diary: The Trench Diary of Brigadier-General J. L. Jack DSO*, p. 22.

IWM Docs: Beatrice Kelsey, Miss M Coules, Revd James Mackay, E. L. Wright.

### Getting Back Home

IWM Docs: E. L. Wright, John Andrew Jellicoe, Beatrice Kelsey, William Armstrong, Mrs Ada Calwell, Dr Gault Calwell, Mrs Céline Williams, unnamed captain of SS *Tubal Cain*.

### The Shock of War

*page*

40 Intellectuals' response to war: Niall Ferguson, *The Pity of War*, p. 182; Norman Davies, *Europe: A History*, pp. 894–5.

40 H. G. Wells quotation: from William Purcell, *Woodbine Willie*, pp. 91–2.

40–1 War frenzy in St Petersburg: from *The Faber Book of Reportage*, edited by John Carey (Faber, 1987), pp. 448–50.

41–2 Paris scenes: *The Coming of the First World War*, pp. 137–8.

42 Joan of Arc cult: Hew Strachan, *The First World War*, Volume 1, *To Arms*, pp. 1118ff.

42 French priests' return from exile: *The Coming of the First World War*, p. 135.

42–3 Berlin scenes: Hew Strachan, *The First World War*, Volume 1, *To Arms*, p. 1120.

43 Germany as a modern, forward-looking power: ibid., pp. 1132–3.

43   Crowds in August 1914: Wyndham Lewis, *Blasting and Bombardiering*, p. 89.

44–5   The obsession with seizing enemy capitals: Barbara Tuchman, *The Guns of August*, p. 123; Osbert Sitwell, *Great Morning*, p. 297.

45   Quotation by Sir Douglas Haig re: war 'lasting many months, possibly years': letter to Lord Haldane, 4 August, quoted in John Terraine, *Douglas Haig: The Educated Soldier*, p. 70.

46   Harold Macmillan quotation: *The Winds of Change*, p. 59.

49   Queen Mary and the socks for troops campaign: James Pope-Hennessy, *Queen Mary*, pp. 490–1.

51   Sir Edward Elgar on his sympathy for horses in war: Jerrold Northrop Moore, *Edward Elgar, A Creative Life*, p. 670.

IWM Docs: Eva, Countess of Reading, Miss Mary Coules, F. A. Robinson, Lieutenant Arthur Maitland, H. C. Meysey-Thompson, Frederick Chandler, Douglas Laidlaw, Rifleman Graham Williams, Naval reservist Sydney Miller, Lieutenant Ralph Blewitt, Lieutenant Colonel G. T. G. Edwards, Captain Angus Macnaghten, Private Charles Rainbird, Lord Loch.

## Opening Gambits

*page*

57   Kitchener appointment as Secretary of State for War: Peter Simkins, op. cit., 34–5.

57–8   Violet Bonham Carter quotation: *Churchill as I Knew Him*, p. 316.

64–5   Eagerness for the British press and Churchill for dramatic victories: Roy Jenkins, *Churchill*, p. 246.

67–8   Haldane Army Reforms and British war plans: John Terraine, *The First World War*, pp. 17–18.

IWM Docs: Surgeon Captain Leonard Moncrieff RN, Lieutenant R. A. Trevor RN, Lieutenant Geoffrey Loyd, Gunner S. W. Crowsley, Lord Loch.

## From Mons to the Marne

*page*

75   Historians' surprise at Sir John French's behaviour on 23 August: see for example John Terraine, *Mons: The Retreat to Victory*, p. 81.

78   Walter Bloem, *The Retreat from Mons, 1914*, translated by G. C. Wynne (Peter Davies, 1930), pp. 53 and 75.

78    Extract from *Die Schlacht bei Mons* (The Battle of Mons), published by the German General Staff, 1919: quoted in the Official History, 1914, Volume I, p. 94.

83    Forest of Mormal: for description see Richard Holmes, *Riding the Retreat*, p. 151.

84    Description of the action at Landrecies: Official History, 1914, Volume I, pp. 134–5.

85    Unsoldierly behaviour at Le Cateau: diary of Sergeant Albert George, 120th Battery RFA, IWM Docs 66/113/1, quoted Malcolm Brown, *The Imperial War Museum Book of the Western Front* (first edition, pp. 14–15; revised edition, p. 16).

86    Sir John French's tribute to Smith-Dorrien re: Le Cateau: *General Jack's Diary*, p. 39.

86–8    Diary of Lieutenant W. R. Read RFC; quoted in Michael Moynihan, *People at War 1914–1918* (David and Charles, 1973), p. 19 and pp. 26–7.

88    Smith-Dorrien quotation re: situation after Le Cateau, *General Jack's Diary*, p. 40.

91–2    Sir Edward Spears on the action at Néry, *The Picnic Basket*, pp. 134–61.

96–8    Joffre versus Moltke, Marshal Joffre etc., *The Two Battles of the Marne*, p. 13.

98    Quotation on the BEF's fatigue at the end of the Retreat from Mons: Official History, 1914, Volume I, p. 283.

99    Execution of Private Highgate: Cathryn Corns and John Hughes-Wilson, *Blindfold and Alone*, pp. 107–12, 314.

IWM Docs: Private G. R. Juniper, Captain Arthur Acland, Captain C. J. Paterson, E. J. Cummings, Brigadier General Sir John Headlam, Lord Loch, Captain W. G. Morritt, Lieutenant G. A. Loyd, Lieutenant Roger West, Lieutenant William Synge, Lieutenant Rowland Beech, Gunner S. W. Crowsley, Lieutenant R. C. Blewitt, Lieutenant Colonel G. T. G. Edwards, Captain Edgar Cox. Additionally the Smith-Dorrien quotation from a contemporary letter on page 88 is from the Smith-Dorrien papers held in the Department of Documents.

## Business Not as Usual

*page*

101    A. J. P. Taylor quotation: *English History 1914–1945*, pp. 18 and 21.

*101*     Comment on motives for enlistment by Adrian Gregory: from his
          chapter on 'British "War Enthusiasm" in 1914: A Reassessment', in
          *Historians and the Impact of 1914*.

*102–3*   R. C. Sherriff quotation: from his chapter 'The English Public
          Schools at War' in *Promise of Greatness: The War of 1914–1918*,
          edited by George A. Panichas, pp. 136–7.

*103–4*   War career of Reginald Secretan: information from Mr Reggie Fair,
          Baldock, Hertfordshire. A pamphlet on his life and death included
          the tribute from his commanding officer: 'There was no braver
          boy in the whole Army'.

*104*     C. E. Montague quotation: from *Disenchantment*, p. 3.

*105*     Arthur Wadsworth story: Ralph N. Hudson, *The Bradford Pals*, p. 2.

*105*     Victor Sylvester: E. S. Turner, *Dear Old Blighty*, p. 34.
          The case of Private Jesse Sheldon: information from his grandson,
          Dr John Bourne, Director of the Centre for First World War
          Studies, University of Birmingham.

*109–10*  Animosity towards 'aliens' in the musical world: Jerrold Northrop
          Moore, *Edward Elgar: A Creative Life*, p. 670. It is perhaps
          noteworthy that Northrop Moore used as the title of his chapter
          on Elgar's war years A. E. Housman's famous phrase 'The Land of
          Lost Content'. See this book's chapter 1, pp. 8–9.

*110–11*  Material on Horatio Bottomley: Julian Symons, *Horatio Bottomley*;
          Alan Hyman, *The Rise and Fall of Horatio Bottomley*.

*112–13*  Address to troops of the Territorial Force by the Bishop of London:
          text from a contemporary pamphlet *A Call to Arms*, in the
          collection of A. G. Baker, IWM Docs 01/6/1.

*113–14*  Studdert Kennedy's reaction to the outbreak of hostitities: William
          Purcell, *Woodbine Willie*, p. 92ff.

*114*     Views on the problems facing chaplains at the front: Canon C. E.
          Cross, IWM Docs; quoted Malcolm Brown, *The Imperial War
          Museum Book of the First World War*, p. 246.

*114–15*  Variant reactions to the war of the Free Churches: Alan
          Turberfield, *John Scott Lidgett: Archbishop of Methodism?*, Chapter
          10.

*116–18*  Poem by R. E. Vernède: published in his posthumous collection,
          *War Poems and Other Verses*, Heinemann, 1917.

*118ff*   Material on Sport and War from recent academic writings: see
          Colin Veitch, ' "Play up! Play Up! And Win the War!" Football,
          the Nation and the First World War', *Journal of Contemporary
          History*, Vol. 20, No. 3, July 1985; J. A. Mangan, *Athleticism in the
          Victorian and Edwardian Public School*, Frank Cass, 2000; Tony

Collins, 'English Rugby Union and the First World War', *The Historical Journal*, 45, pp. 797–817, Cambridge University Press, 2002.

121   Heart of Midlothian Battalion, and quotation by Private George Blaney: Jack Alexander, *McCrea's Battalion: The Story of the 16th Royal Scots*.

120–1   Football match programmes, Leyton Orient and Tottenham Hotspur: R. W. A. Suddaby, private collection.

123–5   Controversy re: the sailing of the 1914 Shackleton expedition: Roland Huntford, *Shackleton*, Chapters XXX and LI.

125–6   Angels of Mons: *The Collected Arthur Machen*, edited by Christopher Palmer; Mark Valentine: *Arthur Machen*.

IWM Docs: Captain Edgar Cox, Geoffrey Donaldson, Alex Thompson, Bruce Seymour Bailey, Captain Eric Craig-Brown, Major A. N. Kennedy, Reg Bailey, Norton Hughes-Hallett, W. L. Green.

## Siege Warfare on the Aisne

*page*

127   Messages of Generals Foch and Franchet d'Esperey to their troops: Cyril Falls, *The First World War*, pp. 51–2.

127–8   General von Kluck referred to as 'One O'Clock': Tim Carew, *The Vanished Army*, p. 109.

130   Sir John French on Germany's determined stand on the Aisne: Richard Holmes, *The Little Field Marshal*, p. 240.

131   German VII Reserve Corps's rapid progress to the Aisne: John Terraine, *The First World War*, p. 371.

131–3   Colonel Swinton's comparison of the Aisne fighting to siege warfare: *Eyewitness*, pp. 61–2.

140   Sir John French's statement re: the spade and the rifle: Richard Holmes, *The Little Field Marshal*, p. 241.

145   'Disaster to the West Yorkshire': Official History, 1914, Volume 1, p. 445.

IWM Docs: Captain Arthur Acland, E. J. Cummings, Lord Loch, Second Lieutenant Lionel Tennyson, Major Henry Daniell, Gunner B. C. Myatt, Revd Frederick Smithwick, Second Lieutenant G. A. Loyd, Lieutenant Rowland Owen, Captain Arthur Maitland, Captain Angus Macnaghten, Private Charles Rainbird, Captain C. J. Paterson, Captain Eric Fairtlough, Brigadier General John Headlam, John McIlwain, Lieutenant Ralph Blewitt.

## The Bid to Save Antwerp

*page*

157    Historian quoted in first paragraph: Michael Glover, *A New Guide to the Battlefields of Northern France and the Low Countries*, p. 204.

16off    Churchill and Antwerp, Roy Jenkins, *Churchill*, pp. 248–51.

167–74    Sub Lieutenant Rupert Brooke, *The Letters of Rupert Brooke*, edited
*passim*    by Sir Geoffrey Keynes (Faber, 1948), pp. 623, 624–5.

170    Churchill's experiences at Antwerp: *World Crisis*, Volume I, pp. 347–8.

179    Letter of Sir Edward Grey to Mrs Churchill: Mary Soames, *Clementine Churchill*, p. 179.

IWM Docs: E. J. Cummings, Captain C. J. Paterson, Ordinary Seaman Ernest Myatt, Able Seaman Sydney Miller, Able Seaman Roy Ashenden.

## The First Battle of Ypres

*page*

180–1    Controversy re: Lord French of Ypres: see General V. M. Huguet, *Britain and the War*, translated by Captain H. Cotton Minchin (Cassell, 1928), p. 147n.

181    Comment on the defence of Ypres: C. R. M. F. Cruttwell, *A History of the Great War 1914–1918*, p. 105 (though it should be noted he is discussing the French and British only at this point).

181–2    The 7th Division at Lyndhurst and its arrival at Ypres, Tim Carew, *The Vanished Army*, p. 206.

182    German troops' first arrival at Ypres and the city's subsequent martyrdom: Rose E. B. Coombs, *Before Endeavours Fade* (Battle of Britain Prints International, 1976), p. 26.

182    8th Division's arrival, etc.: for concise information on the BEF's divisions, see Martin Middlebrook, *Your County Needs You*, passim.

182–3    Hew Strachan comment on Falkenhayn's new army: *The First World War*, Volume I, *To Arms*, p. 274.

184    Hooge Château shelled: Official History, 1914, Volume II, p. 324. Sir John French's appeal to General Foch for aid, stating that if he did not come, there would be 'nothing left for him but to go up and get killed with the British I Corps': John Terraine, *The Great War*, p. 42; the quotation is from Foch's *Memoirs*. See also Richard Holmes, *The Little Field Marshal*, p. 250.

185–8   Gheluvelt battle, 31 October: H. FitzM. Stacke, *The Worcestershire Regiment in the Great War*, pp. 32–5.

200   Account by Lieutenant Baines re: Oxfordshire and Buckinghamshire achievement at Nonne Boschen: Lt.-Col. R. B. Crosse DSO, *A Record of H.M. 52nd Light Infantry in 1914*, p. 85.

201   'They're shelling the bathroom': Official History, 1914, Volume II, p. 427, n2. Cartoon in *Punch*, Christmas edition, 1914; see illustration on p. 202.

204–5   Clifton College statistics and the fate of Captain A. E. J. Collins: Derek Winterbottom, *A Season's Fame*, Bristol Branch of the Historical Association, Bristol, The University, 1991.

206   Quotation by Captain Rudolph Binding on the German attack on Langemarck: from his memoir *A Fatalist at War*, dated 27 October. Wolfgang Schivelbusch on the significance of Langemarck: *The Culture of Defeat*, p. 63.

207   Verdict of the Official History on First Ypres: 1914, Volume II, p. 461.

207–8   Major 'Ma' Jeffreys on the fate of the 2nd Grenadier Guards: *'Fifteen Rounds a Minute'*, p. 158.

208–9   'Nervous and mental shock' among front-line troops: Ben Shephard, *A War of Nerves*, pp. 21–3.

IWM Docs: Lieutenant Ralph Blewitt, Captain Andrew Thorne, Captain H. C. Rees, Captain Eric Fairtlough, Second Lieutenant Lionel Tennyson, Captain Angus Macnaghten, Captain W. A. Nugent (G. A. Loyd Collection).


### Enemy at the Gates

*page*

210–11   Correspondence between Winston and Clementine Churchill: Mary Soames, *Clementine Churchill*, pp. 171–2.

215   Evidence re: Prince Albert and the Prince of Wales: Kirsty McLeod, *Battle Royal* (Constable, 1999), Chapter 2.

215, 217   Letters by Admiral Fisher and F. S. Oliver, *Letters from Two World Wars*, edited by Ernest Sanger, pp. 10 and 11.

218   Letter by Rupert Brooke re: invasion: original held in IWM Docs, collection Special Miscellaneous H.

219–20   Deteriorating conditions in British training camps from mid-October: chapter 'The Four Armies' by Peter Simpkins in *The Oxford History of the British Army*.

223–5   Account of attack on Hartlepool by Norman Collins (later
        Lieutenant, 1/5th Battalion, Seaforth Highlanders), dated
        26 November 1979, held with his wartime papers, IWM Docs
        66/104/1.
226–8   Evidence on naval defence of Hartlepool: IWM Docs Captain E. C.
        Brent Collection, p. 464.
230     Navy's failed attempt to exact revenge for the attacks on the
        British east coast: C. R. F. Cruttwell, *A History of the Great War,
        1914–1918*, p. 313; Hew Strachan, *The First World War*, Volume I,
        *To Arms*, pp. 428–31.

IWM Docs: Lieutenant Lionel Tennyson, Captain W. S. Scott, Lieutenant
R. A. Trevor, Norman Collins, Lieutenant Alan Ferrie, Mr I. Jordan Frazer,
Gunner Alan Sugden.


## Global War

page
232–4   Siege of Tsingtao and Japanese role in the war: Hew Strachan, *The
        First World War*, pp. 71–4.
234–6   Career and fate of the *Emden*: Cyril Falls, *The First World War*,
        p. 72; Hew Strachan, *The First World War*, Volume I, *To Arms*,
        pp. 479–80.
236–8   Campaign in Mesopotamia: Cyril Falls, op. cit., p. 72.
238–9   For the wartime career of Aubrey Herbert, see Margaret
        FitzHerbert, *The Man Who Was Greenmantle*, chapters 8–10.
239–41  Battles of Coronel and the Falkland Islands: Hew Strachan, *The
        First World War*, pp. 77–80; Malcolm Brown, *The Imperial War
        Museum Book of the First World War*, pp. 95–100.
241–4   The campaign in Togoland: Hew Strachan, *To Arms*, p. 508.
243–4   The campaign in Cameroon: Hew Strachan, *The First World War*,
        pp. 88–9, *To Arms*, p. 509ff.
244–50  The campaign in southern Africa: Hew Strachan, *To Arms*,
        pp. 543–69.
250–4   For the Tanga campaign, see Hew Strachan, *The First World War*,
        pp. 84–5; Ross Anderson, *The Battle of Tanga 1914*, passim.

IWM Docs: Captain Aubrey Williams, Private William Bird, Chief Yeoman
H. W. G. Spencer, Naval Clerk Richard Steele, Lieutenant Colonel F. C.
Bryant, Lieutenant M. C. Carr-Gomm, Trooper Philip Kerr, Major General
A. E. Aitken.

## A Strange Kind of Christmas

*page*

255 Formation of the Armies: *Military Operations, France and Belgium 1915*, Volume I, pp. 222–3.

256 Leslie Walkinton, *Twice in a Lifetime* (Samson Books, 1990), p. 30.

261 Swinton, 'Eyewitness' quotation: *Eye-witness's Narrative of the War*, pp. 166–7.

269–70 Isle of Man letter: courtesy of Manx National Heritage.

273–4 Comment by Major General Thompson Capper: quoted from Malcolm Brown and Shirley Seaton, *Christmas Truce*, p. 161. For background to this chapter see this book passim.

274 Air-raids, December 1914: H. G. Castle, *Fire over England*, Appendix of Raid Records 1914–1918; comment from *The Graphic*: quoted from *Christmas Truce*, p. 115.

275 Brigadier General Charteris on Haig's reaction to the end of 1914: *At G.H.Q.*, p. 67.

IWM Docs: Private R. M. E. Reeves, Trooper A. E. Grice, Brigadier General Reginald Heyworth, Lieutenant Michael Holroyd, Private Ernest Morley, Lieutenant Frederick Chandler, Sergeant J. Hancock, Gunner B. C. Myatt.

## Epilogue

*page*

276 'The young Able Seaman at Antwerp': Roy Ashenden, p. 169.

277 Refugee boys at Eton: Tim Card, *Eton Renewed* (John Murray, 1994), p. 14.

277–8 Spymania: suspicion cast on Prince Louis of Battenberg and apprehension and execution of Karl Hans Lody: E. S. Turner, *Dear Old Blighty*, pp. 61–3.

278 Zeppelin raids: H. G. Castle, *Fire over England* Appendix of Raid Records 1914–1918.

278 W. R. Read and the rise of the Royal Air Force: Michael Moynihan, *People at War 1914–1918*, Chapter 1: 'Cavalryman in the Flying Machines', pp. 19, 21.

279 Shell-shock as a two-edged sword: Ben Shephard, *A War of Nerves*, p. 408.

279–80 The consequences of industrialized war: Bill Rawling, *Surviving Trench Warfare*, p. 4.

281   Poison gas in October 1914 and January 1915: Stephen Pope and
      Elizabeth-Anne Wheal, *Macmillan Dictionary of the First World War.*
282   Captain Balfour's comment on the fury of the French at the loss of
      so much of their territory constitutes a powerful, if sadly rare,
      contemporary British appreciation of the trauma of countries
      suffering even partial occupation.
283   German exploitation of occupied territories: Gary Sheffield, *Forgotten
      Victory*, p. 50. The quotation by Annette Becker is from 'Life in an
      Occupied Zone: Lille, Roubaix, Tourcoing', in Hugh Cecil and Peter
      Liddle, *Facing Armageddon* (Leo Cooper, 1996), pp. 633–6, 640.
283–4 Comment by Captain Sir Morgan Crofton: *Massacre of the
      Innocents: The Crofton Diaries, Ypres 1914–1915.*
286–7 Haig quotation re: defeating the German army: quoted by John
      Terraine in his Preface to *Sir Douglas Haig's Despatches*, edited by
      Lieutenant Colonel J. H. Boraston (J. M. Dent, 1979), p. viii.
287   Churchill comment re: alternatives to chewing barbed wire in
      Flanders: Roy Jenkins, *Churchill*, p. 255.
287   Statement by Arthur Balfour, dated 2 January 1915: from Stephen
      Roskill, *Hankey: Man of Secrets*, p. 150.
288   Letter by Admiral Fisher: IWM Documents, Special Miscellaneous W9.
288–9 Fisher description: Jan Morris, 'Fisher's Face', in *The Great War:
      Perspectives on the First World War*, pp. 111–23.
291   Swinton's description of the Western Front, 21 December 1914:
      see reference to p. 261.
291   Swinton's story 'The Point of View' was published in *Blackwell's
      Magazine* in 1908, and in a collection of his stories entitled *The
      Green Curve* in 1909. An article by the present author on the
      subject of No Man's Land attributing the use of that phrase in a
      military context to Swinton was published in the *Military
      Historical Quarterly*, New York, in 1996 and republished in *The
      Great War: Perspectives on the First World War* in 2003.

IWM Docs: F. A. Robinson, Second Lieutenant Gordon Bartlett, Captain E.
W. S. Balfour, Captain Edgar Cox, Lance Sergeant, later Second Lieutenant
Frank Pusey, Captain Ralph Blewitt.

### Roll of Honour

*page*
294   Note that Private Jesse Shelken, who gave his age as 34 in 1914,
      was buried in accordance with his army age in 1918. There were
      many such cases.

# Bibliography

All books published in London unless otherwise stated.

Jack Alexander, *McCrea's Battalion: The Story of the 16th Royal Scots*,
    Edinburgh, Mainstream Publishing, 2003
Ross Anderson, *The Battle of Tanga 1914*, Stroud, Tempus Publishing, 2002
David Ascoli, *The Mons Star*, Harrap, 1981; Edinburgh, Birlinn, 2001
*The Autobiography of Margot Asquith*, Volume II, Thornton Butterworth,
    1922, Penguin Books, 1936
Correlli Barnett, *The Swordbearers: Studies in Supreme Command in the First
    World War*, Eyre and Spottiswoode, 1963
Rudolph Binding, translated by Ian F. D. Morrow, *A Fatalist at War*, Allen and
    Unwin, 1929
Walther Bloem, translated by G. C. Wynne, *The Advance from Mons, 1914*,
    Peter Davies, 1930
Violet Bonham Carter, *Winston Churchill as I Knew Him*, Eyre, Spottiswoode
    and Collins, 1965
Malcolm Brown, *The Imperial War Museum Book of the Western Front*, Pan
    Books, 2001
Malcolm Brown and Shirley Seaton, *Christmas Truce*, Leo Cooper/Secker and
    Warburg, 1984; revised edition, Papermac, 1994; Pan Books, 1999
Tim Carew, *The Vanished Army*, William Kimber, 1964
Charles Carrington, *Soldier from the Wars Returning*, Hutchinson, 1965;
    Arrow Books, 1970
*Champion Redoubtable: The Diaries and Letters of Violet Bonham Carter
    1914–1945*, edited by Mark Pottle, Weidenfeld and Nicholson, 1998
H. G. Castle, *Fire over England: The German Air Raids in World War I*, Leo
    Cooper/Secker and Warburg, 1982
Sir John Charteris, *At G.H.Q.*, Cassell, 1931
Winston S. Churchill, *The World Crisis*, Volume I, *1911–1914*, Thornton
    Butterworth, 1923
*The Collected Arthur Machen*, edited by Christopher Palmer, Duckworth,
    1988

*The Coming of the First World War*, edited by R. J. W. Evans and Harmut
    Pogge von Strandmann, Oxford, Oxford University Press,1988;
    Clarendon paperback edition, 1990

Cathryn Corns and John Hughes-Wilson, *Blindfold and Alone: British Military
    Executions in the Great War*, Cassell, 2001

Lieutenant Colonel R. B. Crosse DSO, *A Record of H.M. 52nd Light Infantry in
    1914*, Warwick, Spennel (printers), 1956

C. R. M. F. Cruttwell, *A History of the Great War, 1914–1918*, Oxford, Oxford
    University Press, 1934; 2nd edition, 1936; Paladin Books, 1982

Norman Davies, *Europe: A History*, Oxford, Oxford University Press, 1996

*The Faber Book of Reportage*, edited by John Carey, Faber, 1987

Cyril Falls, *The First World War*, Longman, 1960

Niall Ferguson, *The Pity of War*, Allen Lane, 1998

*'Fifteen Rounds a Minute': The Grenadiers at War, August to December 1914*,
    edited by J. M. Craster, Macmillan, 1976

Margaret FitzHerbert, *The Man Who Was Greenmantle*, John Murray, 1983

Michael Glover, *A New Guide to the Battlefields of Northern France and the
    Low Countries*, Michael Joseph, 1987

Michael Gow, *Trooping the Colour: A History of the Sovereign's Birthday
    Parade*, Souvenir Press, 1989

*The Great War: Perspectives on the First World War*, edited by Rob Cowley,
    New York, Random House, 2003

Ernest W. Hamilton (Lord Ernest Hamilton), *The First Seven Divisions*, Hurst
    and Blackett, 1916

*Historians and the Impact of 1914*, edited by Gail Braybon, Berghahn Books,
    2003

*History of the Great War Based on Official Documents* (British Official
    History):

— *Military Operations. France and Belgium, 1914, Volume I*: Macmillan,
    1925; Imperial War Museum/Battery Press, Nashville, Tennessee,
    1996

— *Military Operations. France and Belgium, 1914, Volume II*: Macmillan, 3rd
    revised edition 1933; Imperial War Museum/Battery Press, Nashville,
    Tennessee, 1995

Richard Holmes, *The Little Field Marshal: A Life of Sir John French*, Jonathan
    Cape, 1981; Weidenfeld and Nicolson, 2004

— *Riding the Retreat*, Jonathan Cape, 1995

Ralph N. Hudson, *The Bradford Pals*, Bradford, Bradford Libraries, 1993

Roland Huntford, *Shackleton*, Hodder and Stoughton, 1985; Cardinal, 1989

Alan Hyman, *The Rise and Fall of Horatio Bottomley*, Cassell, 1972

Samuel Hynes, *A War Imagined*, Bodley Head, 1990; Pimlico, 1992

*General Jack's Diary: The Trench Diary of Brigadier-General J. L. Jack DSO,*
    edited by John Terraine, Eyre and Spottiswoode, 1964; Cassell, 2000
Roy Jenkins, *Churchill,* Macmillan, 2001; Pan Books, 2002
Marshal Joffre, the Ex-Crown Prince of Germany, Marshal Foch, Marshal
    Ludendorff, *The Two Battles of the Marne,* Thornton Butterworth, 1927
Dennis Judd, *The Life and Times of George V,* Weidenfeld and Nicolson, 1973
*The Kaiser: New Research on Wilhelm II's Role in Imperial Germany,* edited by
    Annika Mombauer and Wilhelm Deist, Cambridge, Cambridge
    University Press, 2003
*A King's Story: The Memoirs of H.R.H. The Duke of Windsor, K.G.,* Cassell, 1951
*The Letters of Rupert Brooke,* edited by Sir Geoffrey Keynes, Faber, 1948
*Letters from Two World Wars,* edited by Ernest Sanger, Stroud, Alan Sutton, 1993
Wyndham Lewis, *Blasting and Bombardiering: Autobiography (1914–1926),*
    Eyre and Spottiswoode, 1937; Imperial War Museum, 1992
David Lomas, *Mons 1914,* Oxford, Osprey Publishing, 1997
Harold Macmillan, *The Winds of Change,* Macmillan, 1966
*Massacre of the Innocents: The Crofton Diaries, Ypres 1914–1915,* edited by
    Gavin Roynon, Stroud, Sutton Publishing, 2004
Martin Middlebrook, *Your Country Needs You,* Barnsley, Leo Cooper, 2000
C. E. Montague, *Disenchantment,* Chatto and Windus, 1922
Jerrold Northrop Moore, *Edward Elgar: A Creative Life,* Oxford, Oxford
    University Press, 1984
*The Oxford History of the British Army,* edited by David G. Chandler and Ian
    Beckett, Oxford, Oxford University Press, 2003
Peter Padfield, *The Great Naval Race: Anglo-German Naval Rivalry
    1900–1914,* Hart-Davis 1974; revised re-issue, Edinburgh, Birlinn,
    2004
*People at War 1914–1918,* edited by Michael Moynihan, Newton Abbott,
    David and Charles, 1973
Arthur Ponsonby (Lord Ponsonby), *Falsehood in Wartime,* Allen and
    Unwin, 1928
Stephen Pope and Elizabeth-Anne Wheal, *The Macmillan Dictionary of the
    First World War,* Macmillan, 1995
James Pope-Hennessy, *Queen Mary,* Allen and Unwin, 1959
*Promise of Greatness: The War of 1914–1918,* edited by George A. Panichas,
    Cassell, 1968
William Purcell, *Woodbine Willie,* Hodder and Stoughton, 1962
Bill Rawling, *Surviving Trench Warfare,* Toronto, University of Toronto Press,
    1992
Keith Robbins, *Sir Edward Grey: A Biography of Lord Grey of Fallodon,*
    Cassell, 1971

Stephen Roskill, *Hankey: Man of Secrets*, Volume I, Collins, 1970

Wolfgang Schivelbusch, *The Culture of Defeat*, Granta, 2003

Gary Sheffield, *Forgotten Victory*, Headline, 2001

Ben Shephard, *A War of Nerves*, Jonathan Cape, 2000

Peter Simkins, *Kitchener's Army: The Raising of the New Armies, 1914–1916*, Manchester, Manchester University Press, 1988

Osbert Sitwell, *Great Morning*, Macmillan, 1948

Mary Soames, *Clementine Churchill*, Cassell, 1979; Penguin Books, 1981

Major General Sir Edward Spears, *The Picnic Basket*, Secker & Warburg, 1967

H. FitzM. Stacke, *The Worcestershire Regiment in the Great War*, Kidderminster, G. T. Cheshire and Sons, 1928

Hew Strachan, *The First World War*, Volume I, *To Arms*, Oxford, Oxford University Press, 2001

— *The First World War*, Simon and Schuster, 2003

Major General Sir Ernest D. Swinton KBE CB DSO, *Eyewitness*, Hodder and Stoughton, 1932

— (anonymously), *Eyewitness's Narrative of the War: From the Marne to Neuve Chapelle, September, 1914–1915*, Edward Arnold, 1915

Julian Symons, *Horatio Bottomley*, Cresset Press, 1955

A. J. P. Taylor, *English History 1914–1945*, Oxford, Oxford University Press, 1965

John Terraine, *Douglas Haig: The Educated Soldier*, Hutchinson, 1983

— *The First World War*, Hutchinson, 1965; Papermac, 1984; Wordsworth, 1997

— *Mons: The Retreat to Victory*, Batsford, 1960

Barbara Tuchman, *The Guns of August*, New York, Macmillan, 1962

— *The Proud Tower*, New York, Macmillan, 1966

Alan Turberfield, *John Scott Lidgett: Archbishop of Methodism?*, Peterborough, Epworth Press, 2003

E. S. Turner, *Dear Old Blighty*, Michael Joseph, 1980

Mark Valentine, *Arthur Machen*, Bridgend, Seren, an imprint of Poetry Wales Press, 1995

Leslie Walkinton, *Twice in a Lifetime*, Samson Books, 1980

# Index of Contributors

This Index lists those whose writings, preserved in the Imperial War Museum's Department of Documents, are quoted in this book and gives due acknowledgement to those who have kindly allowed the publication of material in which they hold copyright. The names of such copyright holders, where known, appear in round brackets at the end of the entry with which they are associated. Every effort has been made to trace all copyright holders; the Museum and the publishers would be grateful for any information relating to those collections where no copyright holders are named. The reference numbers of the collections quoted are given in square brackets. Where the source is that of a published book, full details are to be found in the Bibliography. Other sources are listed as appropriate. Names of well-known personalities quoted are not given here; they can be found in the Bibliography and/or the General Index.

Ranks are given as they were at the time of the experience described, though later changes in rank or the subsequent award of military or other honours are also acknowledged where known. In the case of fatalities, the date, cause of death and place of burial or commemoration are included; these details also appear in the Roll of Honour on page 293–4.

Captain Arthur Nugent **Acland** (later Lieutenant General A. N. Floyer-Acland CB DSO MC DL), 1st Battalion, Duke of Cornwall's Light Infantry [IWM Documents ref: 03/29/1]    77, 128–9, 141–2

Major General (later Brigadier General) A. E. **Aitken**, GOC Indian Expeditionary Force, Tanga, East Africa [IWM Documents ref: 80/13/1] (Mrs Margaret Legg)    250–3

Able Seaman F. R. **Ashenden**, Royal Naval Division [IWM Documents ref: 86/86/1] (Mr Geoffrey Wilson)    165, 166, 169, 174, 276 (quoted anonymously)

Private R. J. 'Reg' **Bailey**, 7th Royal Berkshire Regiment [IWM Documents ref: Con Shelf & 92/36/1] (Mr Renzo Galeotti)    107–8

Lieutenant (later Lieutenant Colonel) C. S. **Baines**, 2nd Battalion, Oxfordshire and Buckinghamshire Light Infantry [Regimental history, though Colonel

## CIVILIANS

# Index

# MALCOLM BROWN

### The Imperial War Museum Book of

## The Somme

PAN BOOKS

The shadow of the Somme has lain across the twentieth century. For many it is the ultimate symbol of the folly and futility of war. Others see it as a hallmark of heroic endeavour and achievement.

This book offers a remarkably fresh perspective on the bitterly fought 1916 campaign; it also describes the later battles of the Somme in the Great War's final year, 1918. Using hitherto unpublished evidence from the archives of the Imperial War Museum, it tells its powerful and dramatic story through the letters and diaries of those who were there.

Distinguished military historian Malcolm Brown has woven the many and varied accounts by well over a hundred participants – mainly British, but with not a few Germans – into a rich tapestry of experience.

'Admirable . . . If you can buy only one book on the Somme,
it should be Malcolm Brown's powerful and scholarly account'
**Richard Holmes, *Times Educational Supplement***

# MALCOLM BROWN

## The Imperial War Museum Book of
## The Western Front

PAN BOOKS

The First World War was won and lost on the Western Front. Covering the whole war, from the noise of the guns of August 1914 to the sudden silence of the November 1918 Armistice, *The IWM Book of the Western Front* reveals what life was really like for the men and women involved. With first-hand accounts of off-duty entertainment, trench fatalism and going over the top, this is an extremely important contribution to the continuing debate on the First World War. Malcolm Brown has updated this edition, introducing new evidence on sex and homosexuality, executions, the treatment or mistreatment of prisoners and shell shock.

'An unrivalled and readable introduction to the years of Trench Warfare'
***Times Educational Supplement***

'A blockbuster . . . as near as anyone is likely to get to the authentic life of the trenches'
***Yorkshire Post***